The Impact of Globalization on Argentina and Chile

The Impact of Globalization on Argentina and Chile

Business Enterprises and Entrepreneurship

Edited by

Geoffrey Jones

Isidor Straus Professor, Harvard Business School, USA

Andrea Lluch

Professor and Researcher, CONICET, Argentina and Affiliated Researcher, David Rockefeller Center for Latin American Studies at Harvard University, USA

Edward Elgar
PUBLISHING

Cheltenham, UK • Northampton, MA, USA

Published by
Edward Elgar Publishing Limited
The Lypiatts
15 Lansdown Road
Cheltenham
Glos GL50 2JA
UK

Edward Elgar Publishing, Inc.
William Pratt House
9 Dewey Court
Northampton
Massachusetts 01060
USA

A catalogue record for this book
is available from the British Library

Library of Congress Control Number: 2015938628

This book is available electronically in the **Elgar**online
Business subject collection
DOI 10.4337/9781783473649

FSC www.fsc.org MIX Paper from responsible sources FSC® C013056

ISBN 978 1 78347 363 2 (cased)
ISBN 978 1 78347 364 9 (eBook)

Typeset by Servis Filmsetting Ltd, Stockport, Cheshire
Printed and bound in Great Britain by T.J. International Ltd, Padstow

Contents

Figures and tables

FIGURES

TABLES

Contributors

María Inés Barbero is Professor at Universidad de Buenos Aires and Universidad de San Andrés, and director of the Centro de Estudios de Historia y Desarrollo de Empresas in Argentina. She graduated from Universidad de Buenos Aires and Universidad Complutense de Madrid. In 2009 she was Alfred Chandler Visiting Scholar at Harvard Business School. Her current research is on the history of family firms, business groups and Latin American multinationals.

Marcelo Bucheli is Associate Professor of Business Administration at University of Illinois at Urbana-Champaign, in the United States. He received his Ph.D from Stanford University, and was the Harvard-Newcomen Fellow in Business History at Harvard Business School between 2004 and 2005. His publications include *Bananas and Business. The United Fruit Company in Colombia, 1899–2000* (New York, 2005), and he is currently researching the political economy of foreign direct investment in Latin America.

Gonzalo Islas is Professor at the Business School of the Universidad Adolfo Ibáñez in Chile. He has worked as a consultant for Chilean government institutions and the International Labor Office. He received his MA and Ph.D from University of California at Los Angeles. His research is focused on the history of corporate governance and business groups.

Geoffrey Jones is Isidor Straus Professor of Business History and Faculty Chair of the Business History Initiative at the Harvard Business School in the United States. He received his MA and Ph.D from the University of Cambridge, and holds honorary doctorates from Copenhagen Business School and the University of Helsinki. His recent books include *Beauty Imagined. A History of the Global Beauty Industry* (Oxford, 2010) and *Entrepreneurship and Multinationals. Global Business and the Making of the Modern World* (Northampton, MA, 2013).

Norma Silvana Lanciotti is Researcher at the National Council of Scientific and Technical Research of Argentina (CONICET) and Professor at Universidad Nacional de Rosario in Argentina. She received her Ph.D. from the Universidad Nacional de Rosario. She is the author of *De rentistas* *a empresarios. Inversión inmobiliaria y urbanización en la pampa argentina. Rosario, 1880–1914* (Buenos Aires, 2009).

Andrea Lluch is Researcher at the National Council of Scientific and Technical Research of Argentina (CONICET), Professor at National University of La Pampa in Argentina and Affiliated Researcher at the David Rockefeller Center for Latin American Studies at Harvard University. Between 2006 and 2009 she was the Harvard-Newcomen Fellow in Business History and a Research Fellow at the Harvard Business School. She received her Ph.D from the Universidad Nacional del Centro de Buenos Aires. She researches the history of direct foreign investment, family business and corporate networks in Latin America during the twentieth century.

Andrés López is Professor of Development Economics, University of Buenos Aires, in Argentina, and Director and Researcher at the Centro de Investigaciones para la Transformacion. He received his Ph.D from Buenos Aires University. He has been a consultant for many international organizations including ECLA and UNCTAD.

Rory M. Miller is Reader in International Business at University of Liverpool Management School, in England. He received his Ph.D from the University of Cambridge. He is currently the Joint Editor of the *Journal of Latin American Studies*. His research focuses on the historical impact of multinational enterprises in Latin America, specializing on British-owned companies after World War II.

Oscar Muñoz is Professor and Associated Researcher at Facultad Latinoamericana de Ciencias Sociales in Chile. He received his Ph.D from Yale University. He is a former president of Corporación de Estudios para Latinoamérica. He has served as coordinator of Public Policies Programs at the United Nations Development Programme and as an invited professor at Universidad de Chile. He has published extensively on the relationship between business, the state and economic development.

Javier Vidal Olivares is Professor of Economic and Business History at Alicante University in Spain. He received his Ph.D from Valencia University. He is author of *Alas de España. Iberia, Líneas Aéreas de España, 1940–2005. De aerolínea de bandera a trasnportista mundial* (Valencia, 2008).

Preface

This book considers the historical impact of globalization on the countries of Argentina and Chile. The two countries are neighbors in the Southern Cone of Latin America, but their histories have rarely been directly compared by business and economic historians. The book is designed to contribute both to the burgeoning business history literature on Latin America, and to the history of globalization generally.

This book emerged from the commitment of the business history group at the Harvard Business School to facilitate research and course development in business history beyond the United States and Europe. This led to conversations between Geoffrey Jones, the Isidor Straus Professor of Business History, and Andrea Lluch, the Harvard-Newcomen Fellow in Business History in 2006–07, about how the Harvard Business School could best support the growth of the subject in Latin America, especially Argentina where she was based, and neighboring Chile. Thanks to the support of Dean Jay Light, Lluch was appointed a Research Fellow at the School for two more years. During these years Lluch conducted over 20 oral history interviews with the most prominent business leaders in Argentina and Chile. This became the basis of Harvard Business School's Creating Emerging Markets program. A second outcome was a volume of essays published (in Spanish in 2011) as Geoffrey Jones and Andrea Lluch (eds), *El impacto histórico de la globalización en Argentina y Chile: Empresas y empresarios*.[1] This present book is a revised and updated version of this earlier work, extensively rewritten for the English-speaking market, and for researchers and students with little prior knowledge of the region.

The editors would like to thank the generous funding of the Division of Research and Faculty Development at the Harvard Business School and the David Rockefeller Center for Latin American Studies at Harvard University.

Boston, Massachusetts and Buenos Aires, February 2015

NOTE

1. Buenos Aires: Temas Grupo Editorial.

Introduction

Geoffrey Jones and Andrea Lluch

It is now commonplace that the contemporary era of globalization was preceded by a massive globalization wave which started in the second half of the nineteenth century and ultimately collapsed as a result of the World Wars and Great Depression of the twentieth century.[1] This book explores how these globalization waves impacted the countries of Argentina and Chile in the Southern Cone of Latin America. The story is stark and very relevant even for people with no knowledge of the region. In particular, the history of the two countries reveals the complex, asymmetrical and non-linear nature of globalization.

During the late nineteenth century both countries flourished as major export economies sending primary commodities to the West. In the case of Argentina, it was beef and wheat. Great riches were earned, modern industrialization began, and the country became one of the richest in the world. Chile boomed by supplying nitrates to the world economy, and even if they made the country less wealthy than Argentina, they still provided up to one half of government revenues.

The twentieth century was less kind to both countries. Chile encountered a huge fall in income following the collapse of nitrate prices in the Great Depression. The country shifted to an inward-looking economic policy and experienced one of the lowest rates of growth in the region for decades. It wasn't until the late twentieth century that it was reborn as a productive economy. Argentina suffered less of an immediate shock, but lost its earlier momentum. It then underwent a remarkable reversal of fortune and became a country associated with instability and stagnation. The star of the first global economy became a problem child of the contemporary global economy. The 'Argentina Paradox' as one recent study called it, continues to attract the attention of economists, historians and even business journals until the present day.[2]

This book explores the impact of globalization on Argentina and Chile through the lens of entrepreneurs and firms. It breaks new ground in many respects. The role of firms has not been central to much recent scholarship on the history of globalization. Yet business enterprises were enormously important actors in globalization as they shifted resources and innovatory capabilities across borders.[3] The business history literature has largely been focused on the developed West. This book also responds to recent calls for incorporating the experiences of Latin America, Africa and Asia into the central debates.[4] The moment is opportune as a vibrant literature, mostly in Spanish, has emerged on Latin America, especially Argentina, Chile, Colombia and Mexico.[5] It is apparent that firms in these countries resembled firms in the developed West in many respects, but they also developed distinctive capabilities as they encountered institutional voids and macroeconomic and political instability. As yet historiographies have been primarily national. This book offers a pioneering attempt to compare the business histories of Argentina and Chile.

The following chapters pursue three broad themes. The first theme explores the distinctive characteristics of business enterprise in the two countries. As in many emerging markets, family-owned business groups stand out as a dominant organizational form, both historically and in the contemporary period.[6] In Chapter 1, María Inés Barbero provides a pioneering assessment of the evolution of business groups in Argentina, exploring how their formation varied in different political and economic contexts. In Chapter 2, Gonzalo Islas also identifies the longevity and resilience of business groups in Chile, though also noting significant shifts in organizational structures over time. The core contribution of the chapter, however, is a pioneering examination of investor protection levels, stock ownership, and capital market development in three historical periods since 1854 which challenges core tenets of the law and finance literature. Before 1920, Islas shows that despite the lack of legal rights for minority investors, entrepreneurs used corporations as a mechanism to raise funds, which drove the development of a stock market in Chile. In contrast, in recent decades Chile has established high levels of protection for investors and creditors, but dispersed ownership companies remain as rare (or even rarer) in Chile now as they were in 1950.

In Chapter 3 on Chile's energy policies, Marcelo Bucheli identifies another dimension of the importance of business groups in the region. He focuses on the role played by business groups in nationalist energy policy-making and, particularly, in relations between host economics and multinational enterprises (MNEs). This chapter departs from most studies on oil nationalism in Latin America that have concentrated on host government relations with MNEs, largely neglecting the role played by local business elites and organizations. In the case of Chile, which lacked domestic oilfields, Bucheli shows that the state did not create a national, vertically integrated oil company, but it did support a private initiative to build Compañía de Petróleos de Chile, with which it then obliged MNEs to cooperate.

Bucheli's chapter also serves to introduce the second major theme in this book, which considers the impact of MNEs and the global economy. Although the role of foreign investment is a staple of Latin American business history, this book offers new evidence, perspectives and issues. In Chapter 4, Andrés López's analyses cycles of foreign direct investment (FDI) in Argentina since the late nineteenth century. He shows how strategies and impacts have changed in different economic contexts. He argues that MNE strategies in Argentina have primarily adapted to local conditions. This analysis also complements Barbero's chapter, as it explores the internationalization of local business groups and why Argentina has produced fewer so-called 'multilatina' companies than Chile, as well as Brazil and Mexico. The patchy internationalization of Argentine companies, he suggests, reflects the country's turbulent development path.

The following two chapters examine foreign MNEs in the region. In Chapter 5 Javier Vidal Olivares offers a longitudinal study of Spanish investment. The theme of non-linearity again emerges strongly. Spanish business and economic links with the Southern Cone flourished during the first global economy before the 1930s, and again during the second global economy from the 1980s, but were restricted in the intervening period. More recently too, the enthusiasm of Spanish MNEs for the region has waned in response to the Argentine economic crisis in 2001, the severe economic problems of the Spanish economy after 2008, and growing political risk, especially in Argentina. In Chapter 6, Rory M. Miller turns to the experience of British MNEs in Argentina and Chile. This chapter analyses the abilities and strategic role played by British companies' subsidiaries in Argentina and Chile from the late nineteenth century to the mid-twentieth century, and makes a major contribution by examining in detail local human resource management strategies and their impact on performance.

The third theme of the book deals with relations between business and the state. This is also a staple of the literature on long-term local economic development. In Chapter 7, Norma Silvana Lanciotti presents a new interpretation of state intervention in urban utilities in Argentina from the late nineteenth century to the middle decades of the twentieth century. She explores how the liberal era of light regulation before the interwar years created an asymmetric relationship between the state and utilities, hindering information transfer and collaboration between the State and utility companies, and contributing to the nationalization and extension of public ownership from the 1940s. In Chapter 8, Oscar Muñoz highlights the importance of public-private sector cooperation for economic development. He explores how public-private relations in Chile shifted from an informal and oligarchic nature during the first half of the twentieth century, to the more formal yet antagonistic ties that served as a backdrop to the Pinochet military coup in 1973, and finally entering a new stage during the early years of Chile's transition back to democracy as the private sector became more influential in public policymaking. The author examines in detail the building of a public-private consensus in this third era, as well as the limitations and challenges found in the process of forging ties between both sectors and organized labor.

The final chapter, written by the editors, examines the reversal of fortunes between Argentina and Chile during the second global economy and the impact on their business sectors. In Chile, policy continuities and institutional stability encouraged business to invest and grow. In Argentina, fluctuations in policy, macroeconomic instability and high inflation often encouraged a more short-term outlook. In both cases, the chapter emphasizes how contemporary globalization has offered new opportunities for economic growth, yet has also meant that peripheral economies were vulnerable to shocks far from their borders and beyond their control. Even in the successful case of Chile, as elsewhere, globalization was also accompanied by inequality of wealth and access. This trend raised fundamental questions about the future trajectory of global capitalism.

NOTES

1. Bordo, Taylor and Williamson (2003).
2. Taylor (2014); Campos, Karanasos and Tan (2014); *Briefing* (2014).
3. Jones (2005), (2013) and (2014).
4. Jones and Friedman (2011).
5. Barbero (2008); Dávila (2013).
6. Colpan, Hikino and Lincoln (2010).

REFERENCES

Barbero, María Inés (2008), 'Business history in Latin America: a historiographical perspective', *Business History Review*, **82**, 555–75.

Bordo, Michael D., Alan M. Taylor and Jeffrey G. Williamson (eds) (2003), *Globalization in Historical Perspective*, Chicago: University of Chicago Press.

Briefing (2014), 'Tragedy of Argentina: a century of decline', *The Economist*, 15 February.

Campos, Nauro F., Menelaos G. Karanasos, and Bin Tan (2014), 'From riches to rags, and back? Institutional change, financial development and economic growth in Argentina since the 1890s', IZA discussion paper no. 8654, November.

Colpan, Asli M., Takashi Hikino, and James R. Lincoln (eds) (2010), *The Oxford Handbook of Business Groups*, Oxford: Oxford University Press.

Dávila, Carlos (2013), 'The current state of business history in Latin America', *Australian Economic History Review*, **53**, 109–20.

Jones, Geoffrey (2005), *Multinationals and Global Capitalism*, Oxford: Oxford University Press.

Jones, Geoffrey (2013), *Entrepreneurship and Multinationals: Global Business and the Making of the Modern World*, Northampton, MA, USA and Cheltenham, UK: Edward Elgar.

Jones, Geoffrey (2014), 'Firms and global capitalism', in Larry Neal and Jeffrey G. Williamson (eds), *The Cambridge History of Capitalism, Vol. 2*, Cambridge: Cambridge University Press, pp. 169–200.

Jones, Geoffrey and Walter Friedman (2011), 'Time for debate', *Business History Review*, **85** (2), 1–8.

Taylor, Alan M. (2014), 'The Argentina paradox: microexplanations and macropuzzles', NBER working paper no. 19924, February 2014.

1. Business groups in nineteenth and twentieth century Argentina

María Inés Barbero

I. INTRODUCTION

From the mid-1800s to the early twenty-first century, the Argentine economy passed through several phases in terms of performance, economic structure and institutional framework. Argentina shifted from an open, deregulated economy (1870–1914) to one that was more closed and state-regulated (1914–75), and after a halting transition to greater liberalization (1976–90), the country plunged into a pro-market reform process in the 1990s that, in turn, came to an end with a major crisis in 2001.

Throughout these major political and economic shifts and crises, diversified business groups have remained the prevailing organizational pattern adopted by large local private companies in the country, as in many other late-developing countries in and outside of Latin America. Although they co-existed as business groups with stand-alone domestic firms, multinational enterprise (MNE) affiliates and state-owned enterprises, they have remained prominent and sometimes pre-eminent features of the Argentinian business landscape.

This chapter will explore the circumstances that led to the emergence and development of business groups in Argentina, identifying prevailing types at specific periods, and exploring the determinants of their predominant role among domestic private large firms. It draws upon new research conducted over recent decades, and offers case studies on several large business groups. As such, this chapter contributes to the comparative study of business groups in emerging countries, by offering empirical evidence that helps test existing hypotheses on why business groups exist, what their salient features are, and the types of capabilities that enable them to compete satisfactorily in several markets. A historical perspective provides a useful corrective to contemporary cross-sectional studies typically produced by economists and other social scientists by identifying changes over time.[1]

Discussion in this chapter has been divided into the following sections.

Section II provides definitions associated with the business group notion, and introduces the parameters to analyse and compare Argentine groups in the long term. Section III explores the emergence and development of a first generation of business groups during the booming export-based economy of 1870–1914. Section IV focuses on the interwar period, while Section V looks at the 1945–90 phase, with the creation and expansion of a second generation of groups, during both the peak of import-substitution industrialization and early attempts to introduce pro-market reforms. Section VI delves into the effects of the 1990s' pro-market reforms and the 2002 crisis on Argentine business groups. Finally, the concluding remarks in Section VII provide an overview of the evolution of Argentine business groups.

II. BUSINESS GROUPS AS AN ORGANIZATIONAL PATTERN

There is no universally accepted definition of a business group. There remain significant disagreements over the reasons behind the growth of business groups, as well as their impact on economic performance and on the societies in which they operate.[2] This chapter uses the definition of business groups provided by Khanna and Yafeh of business groups as sets of legally independent companies operating across (often unrelated) industries and bound together by persistent formal and informal ties.[3]

The chapter will focus on two issues. First, it will examine the types of settings where business groups emerged in Argentina, building on the insights of previous literature which has emphasized the role of market imperfections (primarily in capital and managerial resources markets),[4] institutional voids (information problems, inadequate regulation, inefficient judicial systems),[5] regulatory frameworks favorable to business group emergence that allowed or condoned agreements among companies,[6] and public policies that contributed to their emergence and growth.[7]

Second, the chapter will trace the most significant features of the business groups that emerged in Argentina in its history. The focus is on case studies of three groups dating back to Argentina's export-led growth stage (Bunge y Born, Tornquist, and Devoto) and on three other groups that emerged in the middle decades of the twentieth century, during the import substitution industrialization phase and early pro-market reforms (Techint, Arcor, and Pescarmona). In each case, we shall explore five parameters – group structure (integration and diversification levels, including their diversification into financial operations or not); ownership and control (family business or not, existence of holding companies);

competitive strategies and capabilities; the role of social networks in their emergence and dynamics; and, finally, their relations with the state.[8]

III. BUSINESS GROUPS IN ARGENTINA DURING THE EXPORT-LED BOOM, 1870–1913

Diversified business groups emerged in Argentina during the export-led expansion period between 1875 and 1913. This period was marked by high per capita gross domestic product (GDP) and high growth rates that placed the country among the world's wealthiest nations as result of its open, deregulated economy based on agricultural and livestock commodity exports. Argentina exhibited many typical traits of emerging economies, such as institutional voids, factor market imperfections, and high transaction costs, but in other areas – such as the development of business law, banking system, stock market, and credit reporting agencies – the country made substantial progress by early twentieth-century standards.[9] Argentina's educational system expanded considerably and achieved superior quality, though the supply of local professionals did not suffice to meet the growing demands for qualified labor.

The financial system also had big limitations. Credit access was still restricted for small and medium-sized industrial companies.[10] The domestic financial system was largely unregulated. There was no lender of last resort. The number of companies listed in the local stock exchange was limited as was the number of transactions. Many potential investors harbored qualms about corporate governance, transparency, and the protection of minority shareholder rights.[11] Domestic savings rose to international standards but varied with the country's economic condition and remained below the savings level of European nations and other countries of recent settlement.[12]

The fact that Argentina was so engaged in international trade, however, offset many of these shortcomings. Until World War I, it was one of the leading recipients of foreign investment – with funds coming mostly from the United Kingdom, but also from nations in Continental Europe, like France, Belgium, Germany and Italy. Argentina's high population growth rate (as a result of massive immigration), its rapidly expanding economy, and its gradual diversification provided numerous business opportunities that those with preferential access to funding could best leverage. These signs indicated that diversification incentives stemmed not only from market imperfections but also from ongoing market growth. It should be noted that investing in several sectors was a way to mitigate risk in an ever-changing environment that was highly vulnerable to external crises, as a result of Argentina's open economy. Additionally, with a growing domestic market that was still comparatively small (Argentina's population totaled 8 million in 1914), diversification seemed to be a virtual requirement for maintaining high investment levels.

In this setting, early diversified business groups emerged. In a pioneering work, Carlos Marichal identified five groups, outstanding 'not only for their mixed activities but primarily for their successful efforts to build diversified business empires, turning medium-sized trading (importing and/or exporting) firms into large companies with increasing involvement in financial and, later, industrial operations'.[13] Three of these groups – Tornquist, Bunge y Born, and Devoto – have been the subject of major published histories.[14] The chapter draws on these studies alongside more general works to show how business groups originated in Argentina during the export boom period.[15]

In the large company universe, business groups shared the market with foreign firms – which were mostly free-standing companies – as well as with domestic stand-alone companies and a few state-owned companies. A recent ranking of the largest firms in this period demonstrates that companies owned by business groups were among the largest firms in markets where they operated.[16] Some sectors, like roadroads, meat packing, and utilities, were dominated by foreign companies. In others, undiversified domestic large and medium-sized companies prevailed (for example, cigarette, wine, glass and shoe manufacturing, as well as leather processing).[17] It should be noted that, at this time, some of the largest companies were rural businesses that mainly belonged to Argentine families.

These three groups shared some general features that, taken together, outline a profile for business groups emerging at this point in time.[18] First, these groups were built by foreign businessmen (Ernesto Bunge and Jorge Born), immigrants (Antonio Devoto) or Argentine entrepreneurs of foreign origin with strong ties to their ancestors' communities (Ernesto Tornquist). This trait illustrates the significant role of immigration in the creation of Argentina's business community.

Second, these groups networked with European companies and businessmen, sharing family and friendship ties with them, as well as close business relationships. Bunge y Born relied on an organizational scheme with two headquarters – one in Buenos Aires and one in Antwerp – and operations in several international markets.[19] Tornquist was based in Buenos Aires but conducted a large share of its business with Belgian investors, mostly from Antwerp, and other European companies. Devoto was the most local business group, but it maintained strong ties with Italy through its international trade operations and its partnerships with Italian companies and businessmen. Thus, personal networks (based on family and friendship ties) and shared national identities played a central role in the birth and development of the three groups, as these features supported both the groups' interactions abroad and their partner and manager recruiting efforts in Argentina. The fact that group founders were foreigners, or of foreign descent, made it easier to forge ties with investors and businessmen in their respective communities – both inside and outside Argentina.

European partners viewed strategic management decision-makers at all three aforementioned groups as guaranteeing the reliability of the local ventures in which they engaged. The group leaders' personal reputations, as well as their contacts in local social and political circles, mitigated the uncertainty involved in doing business in new markets. Argentina's Bunge y Born group was part of a network of Bunge companies around the world, and communications among family members flowed constantly. As a result of his personal contacts, his talent, and his frequent trips to Europe, Ernesto Tornquist gained access to top-tier financial circles in Belgium, Germany, France, and Britain, turning into an intermediary between European investors and the Argentine market. In 1912, the Banco de Italia y Río de la Plata, in which the Devoto family and other Italian investors held an equity interest, became the sole intermediary for Italian immigrants' remittances transfer to Italy. The Devoto family's involvement in the Compañía Ítalo Argentina de Electricidad was used by its founders as proof of the new company's feasibility.[20] Ties to European nations then guaranteed these groups' preferential access to funding and information, as well as enhanced their ability to recruit new partners, managers, and technicians. For Bunge y Born and Tornquist, the founding families' former trading experience provided another highly valuable intangible asset.

Third, all of these groups featured broad investment diversification in trade, financing, farming and ranching, industrial, and other activities. In all three cases, they were involved in the ownership and management of banks and financial firms, had direct ties to European banks (even representing some of them in Argentina), and served as liaisons between European investors and Argentina's market. The Sociedad Ernesto Tornquist y Cía. was founded to export Argentine primary goods and to import textiles and machinery, but it started to diversify soon after its inception. The company not only acted as a trading firm but also as a financial institution, granting loans, discounting bills of exchange, and handling other operations. Revenues from trade and finance, partnerships with foreign investors, and access to local loans enabled the company to participate in numerous ventures.[21] By the onset of World War I, the group held interests in 34 companies, including financial, trading, industrial, farming and ranching, transportation, real estate, tourism, mining and fishing activities. Seven of these (mostly financial and land exploitation ventures) had been established in Antwerp, while the others were founded in Buenos Aires. Ernesto Tornquist y Cía. engaged in this diversification process primarily to enter several markets in pursuit of emerging business opportunities. Only in a few cases, like sugar production, did new investments represent a vertical integration strategy, since the group in this case owned cane growing lands, sugar mills, and a refinery. In other cases, there was a synergy between the group's financial and commercial operations and its other ventures. Otherwise, a clear synergy joined the group's financial and trading companies with its other businesses.

In the case of Bunge y Born, the early activities in South America included trade (since 1876, Ernesto Bunge had served as an agent for Antwerp-based Bunge & Co.), financial endeavors (the company participated in the creation of a bank with other European stockholders) and farming (they purchased land for cattle breeding). With the creation of Bunge y Born in 1884, international grain trading became the group's core business. By the early 1900s, Bunge y Born ranked among Argentina's top four exporting firms.[22] The company continued to diversify its investments in farming and finances, and it also ventured into industrial operations with flour milling and burlap bag manufacturing activities (burlap bags were used to pack grain for exports).[23] Most of these ventures involved European partners, led by Edward Bunge, the president of Bunge & Co. from Antwerp. In 1905, the group initiated its early internationalization process, crossing borders to other Latin American countries first, with an affiliate in Brazil (Sociedad Molinhos Santista) that manufactured flour.[24] While diversification drove this business group to engage in unrelated activities, such as trade, finance, and real estate, its industrial investments largely followed an integration rationale. Like Tornquist, Bunge y Born's other businesses complemented its financial investments.

Antonio Devoto arrived in Argentina in 1854 as an immigrant from Northern Italy. At first he was employed by a trading firm in Buenos Aires but, a few years later, he started his own retail business. In the 1860s, Devoto began to diversify his businesses, moving into imports and exports, partnering with his brothers to create Devoto y Cía., and also venturing into urban real estate. In the following decades, the Devotos invested in financial ventures, farming, manufacturing, extractive activities and electricity, pursuing a diversification strategy based on integration and synergies among financial and non-financial investments.[25] A key venture was Compañía General de Fósforos, a match manufacturing outfit that grew and increasingly integrated and diversified starting in the early twentieth century, and expanded into the chemical, textile, paper and publishing businesses.[26] The group's bank and insurance company provided services to its other ventures, further demonstrating the synergistic benefits to diversification.

Fourth, ownership of these groups remained largely in the hands of their founding families, supported by a small group of outside shareholders who had strong friendship and trust ties to the families. Family members, their closest partners and some professional managers – virtually all of whom were recruited in Europe – shared business management responsibilities.

From its inception to 1906, Ernesto Tornquist y Cía. was organized as a limited partnership. Ernesto Tornquist and some of his most trusted associates were responsible, as general partners, for the company's obligations and assumed leading management responsibilities. While at first, limited partners held a 75 percent interest, by 1906 their share had shrunk to 25 percent and Ernesto Tornquist had become the majority stockholder.[27] That year, the company became a corporation but one that the Tornquist family continued to control as its majority shareholder. Beginning in the 1880s, as the group diversified its investments, European and Argentine partners joined as minority shareholders in its new ventures. With regards to the group's structure and its management scheme, Ernesto Tornquist y Cía. served as a holding company, in charge of strategic planning and resource allocation. In this company, Ernesto Tornquist played a decisive role, supported by his partners and closest associates. After his death, one of his sons, Carlos, took over as president and served in that role for nearly 40 years. The group relied on a team of professional managers, largely German or Belgian, who were employed on the boards of several firms. For the most part, group companies maintained some measure of autonomy when it came to operating decisions.[28]

Bunge & Co. was owned by the European branch of the Bunge family, while Bunge y Born's ownership rested with four families – the Bunges, the Borns, the Hirschs, and the Osters – who shared the group's strategic management, sitting on the boards of companies located in several continents. Also involved in company management were minority shareholders and individuals who had married into these families. As the group expanded, its subsidiaries gained greater operating independence, but major decisions remained in the hands of owner families. Like in any family business, they could be volatile and dynamic. Antwerp served as the group's operating hub until 1927, when Edward Bunge died and the Latin American branch of the family took over. Since the 1920s, the Hirschs and Borns have grown stronger at Argentina's Bunge y Born.[29]

The Devoto group belonged to Antonio Devoto, his brothers and some Italian businessmen and professionals who, in addition to sharing the Devotos' ethnic and national identity, were close friends of the family.

Unlike Tornquist and Bunge y Born, the boundaries of this business group were less clear, since it lacked a vertical structure and instead consisted of a network of companies held together by loose ties, shared stockholders and interlocked directorates, and strong personal links between shareholders and managers. The center of the network was Banco de Italia y Río de la Plata (with the Devoto brothers and their partners at other ventures) and Devoto y Cía. (a company owned by Antonio Devoto and his siblings). Around these two core and strongly connected businesses, a number of other companies in a variety of sectors operated. Accordingly, group members revolved around Antonio Devoto. Some firms were solely owned by the Devoto brothers (Devoto y Cía., rural establishments and real estate outfits), while, in others, the Devotos held the controlling interest and engaged a small group of Italian businessmen and managers to work with them. In some ventures, like Banco de Italia y Río de la Plata, and Compañía Ítalo Argentina de Electricidad, they partnered with European investors and other Italian businessmen who had settled down in Argentina. The Devoto brothers, their partners and professional managers – mostly Italian – managed the group's companies. Intertwining stockholders and board members was a common practice in this group, as it was with the other two groups.[30]

Fifth, all business groups built and managed companies that largely proved competitive in their respective industries. The information available on the firms controlled by these groups revealed that they made significant investments in technology and management. While Argentina's food industry enjoyed comparative advantages, other domestic industries, like match manufacturing or steel, lacked any such benefits. In addition to investing in cutting-edge equipment, these firms hired mostly foreign professional technicians who served in more than one company at a time. They also acquired foreign patents both for product and process technologies, paying royalties or partnering with European companies.

Not all ventures initiated by business groups turned out to be profitable, even with world-class technologies and management. For example, Tornquist's Refinería Argentina, oversized for local market requirements, and Devoto's Frigorífico Argentino, unable to compete with British and American meat packers, both failed.[31] For most business groups, investment diversification provided a means to cross-subsidize, as businesses yielding more profits (like trade and real estate ventures) helped support less profitable ones.

Sixth, while group venture success rode largely on these business groups' competitive capability, political contacts and advantages provided by Argentina's institutional setting also bolstered their market position. In the agricultural export boom years, Argentina's economy remained open and deregulated, with foreign investment playing a decisive role in the absence of specific state policies intended to favor domestic companies, except in the sugar and wine industries. The lack of restrictions on foreign capital proved beneficial for the three groups discussed here, as a result of their close ties to investors abroad. The groups also benefited from the lack of a regulatory framework restraining conglomerates or business concentration. In grain trading, the absence of public programs – for instance, to build a silo network that would allow farmers to store their crops – provided large trading companies with significant opportunities to fill these voids. While Argentine tariffs were high by international standards, mostly as a result of taxes, this stage ending in World War I was characterized not only by a lack of industrial policies, but also by the growth of domestic industries and manufactured goods' imports at similar rates.[32] Business groups relied largely on their political contacts and on their leaders' standing in local society to lobby for policies that would contribute to their businesses.

IV. BUSINESS GROUPS, 1914–45

Like all other countries involved in the world market, Argentina was deeply shaken by the external shocks caused by World War I, the Great Depression and World War II. Amid a far more complex international situation, the economy became more closed than it had been in preceding decades, as evidenced by restricted foreign investment flows and dwindling immigration. Economic growth slowed, and manufacturing became the most dynamic productive sector, outperforming agribusiness. Although it was not until the early 1940s that industrial policies came into force, starting in 1930, the combination of the overall economic condition and state policies (exchange control, tariff raises) quickly caused locally produced goods to be substituted for imported manufactures.

No new business groups emerged in this new setting, but existing groups expanded.[33] While institutional voids and market imperfections remained,[34] some of the circumstances that had favored the emergence of these groups – primarily, their ability to work closely with European partners – disappeared and conditions that would promote the creation of new groups did not arise. In this period, the composition of large companies operating in Argentina changed gradually, as a result of new, large state-owned enterprises, the arrival of MNE affiliates, and the inception of some domestic private companies that expanded rapidly, seizing dominant positions in several industries (metal mechanics, steel, cement).[35] Business groups created before 1914 also grew during this period.[36]

The three groups analysed in the preceding section expanded their industrial investments intended to supply Argentina's domestic market and managed to maintain both their ownership structure and their rank among large local companies. Bunge y Born was the most active; its manufacturing operations gathered momentum in the 1930s when its core business, grain trading, took a severe hit from the falling international prices and volume of trade, in addition to greater state intervention that curtailed large trading companies' leeway. Accordingly, Bunge y Born diversified into food production, while entering new markets, like the textile and chemical industries (paints, synthetic fibers, industrial inputs).[37] The group's new investments were characterized by a higher degree of vertical integration and related diversification. For more technologically complex operations that strayed farther from its core capabilities, such as its ventures in the chemical industry, Bunge y Born built alliances with foreign firms like British-owned Imperial Chemical Industries and US-owned Dupont.[38] The group's industrial companies ranked among the largest players in their respective fields, remaining at the top until the late twentieth century, when the group eliminated them as part of a massive reorganization. During the interwar period, Bunge y Born also increased its operations in other South American countries, making new investments in Brazil (oils, textiles), Uruguay (oils, chemicals), and Peru (trade, financing, flour industry). Throughout this period, the group continued to be a part of Bunge's international business network, but the Argentine affiliate and its operations in South America increasingly took the spotlight after Edward Bunge died in Antwerp in 1927. New international market conditions created by the events of the 1930s and onset of World War II emphasized the autonomy of the group's South American branch, which grew increasingly focused on industrial operations, while Bunge's European companies suffered. Bunge y Born's controlling interest remained in the hands of its four founding families, with the Hirsch and the Born families taking on more central roles.[39]

The Tornquist group also adjusted to the new conditions. During the interwar period, it continued to diversify its investments, although it incorporated fewer companies during those years, largely because available outside funding dwindled and the group's financial businesses were severely compromised during the Great Depression. This forced the Tornquist group to reduce its investments, shrinking some operations and liquidating some assets.[40] It then focused on real estate and industrial operations. For some of its manufacturing ventures, it partnered with foreign companies that brought funding and know-how. For example, Luxembourg's Arbed group joined the Tornquist group to build TAMET, a steel company, and US-owned toothpaste and soap company Colgate Palmolive entered into a joint venture with Compañía de Productos Conen.[41] Between 1919 and 1928, ten new firms were created to operate in the industrial, agribusiness and service sectors, but the Tornquist group also liquidated some businesses, either because their lifecycle had come to an end (as was the case with *quebracho*, a tropical South American tree with very hard wood) or because they had proven unprofitable (as was the case of the group's investment in the petroleum industry).[42]

Ernesto Tornquist died in 1908, and, as noted earlier, his son Carlos served as chairman from 1913 to 1953, successfully retaining group leadership for the family's second generation. While the Tornquist group gradually lost dynamism after its founder's death, it did manage to keep its standing as a major local business group, with some of its companies dominating their respective markets. Following World War I, its role as an intermediary for investors based in Antwerp and other European cities declined, and the group grew increasingly dependent on its own ability to generate resources and to access credit or state support.

The Devoto group underwent significant changes after Antonio Devoto's demise in 1916, because his presence had been instrumental to the group's investor network, and because its businesses ceased to be immediately associated with his name. As a result of a consolidation and diversification process at one of its companies, Compañía General de Fósforos, the group reorganized itself under the Fabril o Fabril Financiera name,[43] with close ties to Banco de Italia y Río de la Plata and other companies in which Devoto had originally been involved.[44]

Compañía General de Fósforos (CGF) had been created in 1889, after the Devotos joined other sector businessmen who needed more capital. Its vertical integration process started early; by 1914, the company already owned printing workshops and a paper factory. During World War I it began to produce chemical supplies, and it moved into the cotton textile industry in the 1920s. CGF also crossed international borders early on, building a match factory and a printing workshop in Uruguay. In 1929, the group created a new holding company, Compañía General Fabril Financiera to control its paper, textile and printing ventures and to shed its original match manufacturing plant.[45]

Over the next 15 years, Grupo Fabril continued on its consolidation and diversification path, propelled by import substitution and sourcing difficulties caused by the Depression and World War II. Its investments included paper, chemical, textile, publishing, and industrial machinery ventures. The group also invested in real estate and other, unrelated businesses.[46] Grupo Fabril's ownership was shared by a large number of stockholders, while a team of professional managers oversaw its day-to-day operations; though Devoto family members and trusted friends were also involved as partners and managers. The group's ties to Banco de Italia y Río de la Plata, one of Argentina's strongest private banks, guaranteed its access to funding.

In short, the interwar period did not see the emergence of new diversified business groups. Rather, it fueled the expansion of existing ones. Strong external shocks battered the world economy, and Argentina's economy closed gradually in response, hindering the emergence of new groups linked to investors abroad. The state did not promote the creation of large, diversified domestic companies. At the same time, local and international conditions offered new opportunities for manufacturing operations as part of an import-substitution industrialization framework. The three groups studied here continued to diversify their investments, turning their focus to more industrial endeavors. Their trajectories grew further apart, as a result of tangible and intangible assets developed both before World War I and during the interwar period. Bunge y Born moved forward with its international expansion project, while Fabril zeroed in on the local market and industrial operations, and Tornquist became more diversified but lost some of its earlier dynamism.

V. BUSINESS GROUPS, 1945–90: INCUMBENTS AND NEWCOMERS

Encompassing the period of 1945–90 in a single section may spark some debate. Those objecting to this choice would mainly argue that, starting in the mid-1970s, economic conditions shifted both internationally, with the end of post-World War II prosperity, and domestically, as a result of policy changes that were a first attempt at openness and deregulation from 1976–81 after the March 1976 military coup. However, a look at the local setting reveals that this attempt was short-lived and limited. In the study of these business groups' development, these years demonstrate enough coherence to warrant their grouping in a single period – an approach supported as well by one outstanding Argentine historian.[47]

This period is far more complex and multifaceted than previous ones, though, and its traits prove harder to summarize. From the point of view of economic performance, a first period, spanning from 1945 through to 1974, was marked by rather remarkable growth, albeit at lower rates than international averages. A second period, from 1975 to 1990, was characterized by falling GDP per capita, declining, on average, at 1.3 percent per year.[48] Argentina faced periodical crises, with high inflation from the late 1940s to the hyperinflation peaks of 1989 and 1990. With regard to economic policies, the country alternated between populist, development,

Keynesian and liberal policies, with orthodox and heterodox stabilization programs. Constant changes in the rules of the game stemmed from severe underlying political and social conflicts, reflected by a succession of opposing civilian and military governments. Companies operated in a volatile setting that escalated in violence over the course of the 1970s.

Against this backdrop of institutional uncertainty and macroeconomic instability, however, some consistencies may be found. First, Argentina's economy maintained low openness levels, even during the second half of the 1970s, though it did become more open between 1977 and 1981.[49] Second, industrial support was the cornerstone of most economic policies enacted between 1943 and 1975, which translated into high tariffs, subsidies, beneficial credits, multiple exchange rates, and other policies. Starting in 1976, industrialization ceased to be a top priority of public policy, but most legacy promotion programs either remained in place or were expanded.

Apart from the public policies fostering industrialization, Argentina's pervasive economic instability and many of its institutional traits hindered the emergence, survival, and development of new companies. Despite the creation of a banking institution for industrial loans, Banco de Crédito Industrial in 1944, and its successor Banco Nacional de Desarrollo (BANADE) in 1969, access to funding continued to be limited for small and medium-sized manufacturing companies.[50] The capital markets remained weak and, for the most part, were deeply affected by local volatility and uncertainty. In the early 1990s, nearly all domestic large private companies in Argentina were still family-owned businesses.[51] In some ways, Argentina's institutional setting worsened during the post-World War II period, as a result of the country's political turmoil, its increased violence since the late 1960s, and its lack of an independent judiciary, professional congress or professional state bureaucracy, among other reasons.[52]

Until the late 1960s, there were no explicit state policies favoring the creation of new diversified business groups. During the Peronist years (1946–55), the government primarily supported state-owned large companies. Some existing business groups – notably Bunge y Born and Bemberg – were subject to hostility, while others benefited from industry-supporting policies. Most of the new groups that emerged in the second half of the twentieth century dated from the 1940s and 1950, but they did not begin as conglomerates but rather as medium-sized companies that later expanded, with gradual integration and/or diversification, becoming fully-fledged business groups in the 1970s.[53]

From the late 1950s through to the late 1960s, industrial policies particularly favored foreign companies. After this period, the state started to support large domestic companies, driving them to invest in basic industries (cellulose and paper paste, oil, aluminum, steel) and other operations (agribusiness, fishing, shipbuilding) by means of special sector programs and preferential access to BANADE loans and international funding with government support (mainly through the International Finance Corporation). A few years earlier, the first regional promotion program had been launched, offering tax benefits to companies settling down in provinces that needed a more dynamic economy – even if they were in mature industries, like the textile or food sectors. There is a substantive literature on the growth of Argentine business groups from the 1960s.[54]

These promotion policies for domestic companies initiated by a nationalist military government in 1970 were furthered by the 1973–76 Peronist administration and by the new military regime set up in 1976. This government, despite its pro-market orientation, completed most of the industry-specific projects already in place and launched new regional promotion programs.[55] These steps, combined with intense state involvement as a buyer (before and after 1976) and the withdrawal of foreign companies' affiliates in the 1970s (as a result of an international crisis and local economic changes), contributed to strengthening some existing business groups (Bunge y Born, Fabril/Celulosa, Alpargatas) as well as to the creation of new diversified groups (Techint, Fate/Aluar, Arcor, Bridas, Pérez Companc, Pescarmona, Roggio, SOCMA). By the early 1980s, corporate rankings showed the inception and rise of domestic business groups, although, due to Argentina's economic instability, they also demonstrated the demise or decline of others.[56]

These phenomena continued during the 1980s, when some groups were besieged by adverse macroeconomic conditions (for example, Celulosa) while others thrived and expanded (Arcor, Bridas, Pérez Companc, Pescarmona, Roggio, Bunge y Born, Alpargatas), favored by state policies, including private external debt nationalization and broadened regional promotion programs.[57] The most dynamic domestic business groups (Techint, Arcor, Pescarmona, Fate/Aluar) bolstered their competitive capabilities and turned to foreign markets with exports and direct investments. Diversification was also used as a strategy to mitigate risks. Table 1.1 lists the revenues and exports of the major diversified business groups created before 1990 and still active in 1995.[58]

It is apparent that by this time business groups were much more heterogeneous than in the past. The chapter will now turn to look at the development of the older business groups in this period before turning to the emergence of the new groups.

Table 1.1 Argentina's largest diversified business groups in 1995 by annual revenues (US$)[1]

Group	Year of inception	Number of companies	Annual revenues (US$ million)	Exports (US$ million)	Core businesses
Bunge y Born	1884	9	13,000.0	353.3	Food, trade
Techint	1947	61	4019.8	565.6	Steel, construction, telecom, engineering
SOCMA	1954	48	2741.9	373.5	Car manufacture, construction
Pérez Companc	1946	61	1467.0	277.4	Energy, telecom, agribusiness
Sociedad Comercial del Plata	1919	42	1200.0	29.4	Energy, telecom, services
Coto	1970	12	1034.0	121.2	Retailing, food
Arte Gráfico Argentino	1945	26	987.7	0	Printing and publishing
Sancor	1936	26	878.3	70.7	Dairy products
Arcor	1951	28	835.0	91.1	Food, agribusiness
Quinsa (Bemberg)	1895	25	753.0	4.1	Food and beverages
Roggio	1908	37	720.0	0	Construction, services
Industrias Metalúrgicas Pescarmona	1907	17	658.3	110	Construction, engineering, services
Acindar	1942	17	567.5	117.8	Steel, services
Fate/Aluar	1940	8	507.8	219.7	Aluminium, tires
Alpargatas	1884	21	417.7	111.8	Footwear, textiles, fishing
Fortabat	1926	n.a.	396.7	0	Cement, agribusiness, services
Laboratorios Bagó	1934	24	395.0	9.2	Pharmaceutical
Bridas	1928	6	352.9	109.7	Oil, fishing, services

Note:

1 This list does not include groups created after 1990.

Source: Based on Roberto Bisang, 'Los conglomerados económicos en la Argentina: orígenes y evolución reciente,' San Miguel: Universidad de General Sarmiento, Instituto de Industria, working paper no. 11 1998. This table does not include 12 groups (diversified or not) listed in Bisang's original ranking, with revenues below US$350 million; five groups with revenues exceeding that amount but weakly diversified in the late 1980s; three groups created after 1989; and YPF, which was a state-owned company until 1992 and was acquired by foreign investors in 1999.

A. The Incumbents

As noted earlier, Perón's presidential administration severely damaged Bunge y Born. In 1946, the nationalization of foreign trade left this group out of grain trading operations, and the group's investments in new industrial companies were limited in this period. To compensate, Bunge y Born increased its operations in Brazil and Peru. After the fall of Peronism, the group started new ventures, particularly in the chemical industry (partnering with German companies), and expanded the facilities of its other food, textile, and paint firms, diversifying and integrating its operations in those industries. In 1975, five Bunge y Born companies ranked among Argentina's largest privately-owned industrial firms, placing the group at the top of local business groups. Its investments in new product lines had materialized as a result of plant expansion and building as well as company acquisitions, using, in some cases, industry and regional promotion programs.[59]

An event that took place in 1974 clearly reveals how, regardless of state promotion programs, local instability and political violence negatively impacted business group operations. Brothers Jorge and Juan Born, sons of Bunge y Born's chairman, were kidnapped by Montoneros guerrilla members who demanded a hefty ransom (US$ 60 million) for their release.[60] The ransom was paid, and both hostages were freed, but, from then on, owner family members moved to Europe and Brazil, where group operations had been expanding since 1945, as noted earlier. While, for all legal intents and purposes, the group's management remained in Buenos Aires, its headquarters relocated to Sao Paulo.[61] After 1976, Bunge y Born restarted its investments in Argentina, broadening its diversification into oil and petrochemicals by exploiting state promotion mechanisms. In the 1980s, the group continued to top domestic business group rankings, but, by then, its operations in both Brazil and the United States had also gathered momentum.

When Carlos Menem took over as president in 1989, he invited Bunge y Born's senior managers to run the nation's Ministry of Economy. The group accepted the offer, but its short-lived administration proved unsatisfactory and created internal strife. In the 1990s, Bunge y Born sold its manufacturing companies in Argentina and focused its operations on agribusiness under the Bunge Argentina name (grain and fertilizer production, byproduct manufacturing for exports).[62] Finally, in 1999, the group's headquarters moved to the United States, though the company was formally incorporated in Bermuda as Bunge International.

The Tornquist Group continued to build new companies until the late 1960s, albeit at a slower pace than before 1929. During the Peronist administration, the group benefited from state loans and other industry-supporting policies. By the mid-1950s, Tornquist owned 17 companies, eight of them in manufacturing industries. In the 1960s, group investments turned to the financial sector, recapturing contacts abroad.[63] Carlos Tornquist's death in 1953 dealt a severe blow to the group. By then, the family's third generation was in the process of taking over the group's management, and related family rifts eventually led to the 1975 acquisition of Compañía Tornquist and its affiliates by a French business group associated with a local businessman.[64]

After the war, Grupo Fabril continued to grow, diversifying and integrating its operations. The group's relations with the Peronist administration proved uneasy as the government seized one of its companies, but, for the most part, its manufacturing firms benefited from expanded consumption and industry protection policies. By 1965, Grupo Fabril owned 19 companies that operated in the paper, textile, chemical, light machinery, and publishing industries. The group also held interests in nine other companies in other industries.[65] Celulosa S.A., an industry leader by this time (after merging with Papelera Argentina in 1965), received significant public loan support beginning in the early 1970s to develop large cellulose and paper pulp projects, and ranked second among Argentina's large private industrial companies in 1975.[66] The company, however, suffered greatly as a result of economic opening, and then as consequence of the 1980s crisis after that. Its high indebtedness combined with its ownership and management changes compounded its distress until, in 1991, Citibank purchased Celulosa S.A. for debt capitalization. The new owners closed obsolete facilities, sold off assets in associated companies (publishing house, print shop, and chemical plant) and concentrated on the paper industry, but the company failed to recover its earlier leadership.[67]

As for Banco de Italia y Río de la Plata, which had been managed since 1978 by a new controlling group, Argentina's Central Bank intervened in its affairs in 1985 and it was later sold to Banca Nazionale del Lavoro.[68]

B. Newcomers

Beginning in the mid-1960s, new companies emerged, laying the groundwork for future business groups. From the 1970s, these new groups started to rank among Argentina's top 100 industrial companies and continued to experience strong growth throughout the 1980s. As some of them increased both their revenues and the number of firms they controlled, they entered into new product markets and expanded to markets abroad. These new groups were far more multifarious than their predecessors. Most had originated in the 1940s and 1950s and had gradually turned into groups, starting in the 1960s.[69] While they had largely started off as industrial companies, several began operating in the transportation, construction, engineering, or trade businesses. Their size also varied, as did their diversification level: some groups diversified into many unrelated businesses and controlled a large number of controlled companies, while other groups pursued diversification into related industries and controlled fewer firms.[70]

Another significant difference between older and newer business groups was the latter's higher volatility and turnover. Traditional groups had managed to adjust to the transition from agribusiness exports to the import substitution era, and, while many of the new groups (most of the largest ones) continued to operate and expand amid the 1990s' pro-market reforms and the new opportunities brought about by privatization, a significant segment, consisting mostly of smaller business groups, were short-lived. Some went bankrupt or became clearly weaker in the 1980s, while others shrank or disappeared in the 1990s, as the result of purchase by foreign firms, or sale of some of their assets in pursuit of greater specialization. As will be seen in the next section, the 2001–02 downturn deeply affected groups that had outstanding performance over previous decades. Some of these groups were acquired by foreign companies in the 2000s, and others embarked on massive restructuring processes, selling parts of their firms. By the end of the new century's first decade, only nine of the 18 groups in Table 1.1 had continued to expand while also keeping their core businesses.

Recent case studies on three new groups, Techint, Arcor, and Pescarmona, which were founded before 1990, shed more light on the context leading to the creation of business groups, as well as on their characteristics and strategies.[71] Techint was founded in 1947 by Agostino Rocca, an Italian steel engineer with a noted track record as public manager in Italy since the 1920s.[72] When the war ended, Rocca founded an engineering firm (Techint) in Milan and immigrated to Argentina, where he resided until his death in 1978.[73] In 1947, he created a Techint affiliate in Buenos Aires, which became the company's headquarters. During the Peronist period, this firm carried out engineering projects in Argentina and other Latin American countries (Brazil, Peru, Uruguay, Chile, Mexico, El Salvador) with government contracts. At the same time, Rocca started developing industry ventures to supply his company's projects. In the late 1940s and early 1950s, he built a metallic construction company (Cometarsa), a roof tile and ceramic block manufacturing firm (LOSA) and a seamless steel tube manufacturing company (Siderca). In the 1960s, the group continued to integrate and diversify, adding a laminating company (Propulsora Siderúrgica), and in the 1970s the tube factory started to produce steel using the direct reduction system, completing its integration.

Beginning in the 1960s, Techint began to export seamless tubes – an operation that gathered momentum in the 1980s, as the company established sales offices abroad – and its international revenues accounted for an increasing share of its overall sales (75 percent at the end of the decade).[74] The company continued to expand over the next decade, with the acquisition of two formerly state-owned companies – SOMISA (steel) and SIAT (welded steel tubes). In the 1990s, Techint furthered its diversification plans, participating in additional privatizations (transportation, energy, telecommunications), but in the 2000s it withdrew from some of these companies, refocusing on steel operations, capital goods manufacturing and energy (oil and gas).[75] Also in the 1990s, Techint embarked on a production internationalization process that would gradually turn it into a global outfit, the largest Argentine multinational, with US$ 17406 billion in assets abroad by 2008.[76]

Beginning in the 1950s, Techint adopted a group structure, under the Organización Techint name, combining its engineering operations with industrial production to supply its construction projects (roads, bridges, oil and gas pipelines, power lines, oil drilling, port facilities, industrial compounds). This was primarily a process of value chain integration and related diversification, although the group also owned a financial company (Santa María, created in 1948 to support group operations) and ventures in other industries.[77] The lack of local suppliers and the desire to free the group from monopolistic vendors (state-owned SOMISA dominated local steel production) drove integration. The advantages of controlling several phases of production and supplying different markets, as well as Techint's ability to build new companies with multiple partners further propelled its integration. Until the 1990s, the group incorporated new companies by creating them, and, after that time, it largely acquired firms, both in Argentina and abroad. Group expansion efforts hinged on three pillars: first, the existence of an international network closely linking Techint Argentina and Techint Milano; second, the development of competitive capabilities through ongoing investments in production, management, and knowledge creation, and, third, Argentina's state support via protection, loans, and regional industrial promotion plans, in addition to government contracts and purchases.

With regard to the first of these expansion cornerstones, its international network, Techint resembles export-led Argentina groups, with its entrepreneurial engineer who settled down in Argentina, putting his vast steel knowledge and experience to work, supported by a large group of engineers and technicians who had worked with him back in Italy. Also, Techint's strong ties with Italy supported a collaboration strategy, with the Italian affiliate assuming a large share of technical responsibilities and its Argentine counterpart securing contracts, training engineers and technicians, and manufacturing industrial goods.[78] In time, the Italian site's role became less strategic, but it was instrumental at the outset. When Techint moved forward with its production globalization process, starting in the 1990s, it also began to operate as a networked company.[79]

To develop its competencies, Techint initially relied on Rocca's business acumen and his collaborators' expertise, while investing constantly in human capital and driving innovation.[80] Early internationalization in engineering paved the way for subsequent industrial internationalization – first through exports, and later, via direct investment, which enabled the acquisition of first-hand knowledge of other markets and spurred technical and managerial learning processes.[81]

Finally, Techint's relationship with the state proved instrumental both for its engineering operations as well as for its industrial companies. Government contracts, as early as 1947, largely supported the group's expansion, particularly in periods featuring heavy investments in public works. Techint's industrial companies benefited from a host of existing protection policies – tariffs, state loans, guarantees to secure loans abroad, state funding, steel industry promotion programs, state purchases, and the 1982 private external debt nationalization. At the same time, industrial policies in place since the 1940s increased the demand for goods produced by Techint to the mid-1970s. It should be noted that Techint's dealings with the state were not always cordial: some of its group projects (especially its plan to build an integrated steel plant in the 1960s) met strong resistance from Fabricaciones Militares, a state-owned company that monopolized pig iron production until the mid-1970s.[82] As Techint advanced its internationalization process though, it grew more independent of local conditions.[83]

Arcor was founded in 1951 as a small candy manufacturer in Córdoba, a province in central Argentina.[84] Its founders belonged to four families of Italian descent from neighboring towns in the so-called 'Pampa Gringa', an area where European immigrants had settled in the nineteenth century. The Pagani family has played a central role since the company's inception. Even as a startup, Arcor integrated its production to reduce transaction costs, neutralize glucose vendors' opportunistic behavior, offset the lack of local supply (machinery, electricity plant), and to control its value chain (cardboard, paper, printing, flexible packaging). It also integrated distribution operations early on and started to diversify its product line in order to broaden the assortment offered by its official distributors. As part of a strategy of related diversification, Arcor started manufacturing chocolates and candy bars, eventually moving into other foods and alcohol. It also invested in agribusiness and in other industries that were not closely related to its core competencies, like construction and hotels. Arcor furthered its backwards integration process to include dairy farms and sugar mills in the 1980s and 1990s. By the mid-1980s, Arcor owned 22 legally independent companies in Argentina, plus affiliates abroad.

In the 1960s, Arcor started exporting its products and its exports grew over the 1970s. By 1991, its sales abroad accounted for 13 percent of its revenues.[85] The company began to globalize its production in the mid-1970s, crossing national borders to Paraguay in 1976, Uruguay in 1980, Brazil in 1981, and Chile in 1989. This trend continued in the 1990s and 2000s (Peru, Mexico). Arcor emerged as a leading Argentine 'multilatina'. In 2008, it ranked second in total foreign assets, with US$ 491 million, although it lagged far behind Techint (with US$ 17.4 billion in total foreign assets).[86]

Arcor's expansion hinged on both the development of competitive advantages, and the use of all state-offered resources. To accomplish the former, the group invested heavily and constantly in production, distribution, and management, updating its equipment, developing new products, making sizable investments in research and development, and partnering with universities and MNEs for some projects.[87] It also built a distribution network that gradually broadened its coverage to include other Argentine regions, while also streamlining its organizational structure and management.

Arcor took advantage of several state protection and support mechanisms in place in Argentina at the time. First, Arcor benefited from the country's low economic openness, which enabled it to move into sectors where it had no experience or advantages. It also used state funding and guarantees to secure loans abroad and export refunds. Taking advantage of regional promotion programs, it pursued geographic decentralization by creating new firms, especially during the 1980s. Like most large companies, it benefited from the nationalization of private foreign debts in 1982. It should also be noted that Arcor was instrumental in the creation of Fundación Mediterránea in 1977, a local think-tank with great lobbying leverage. One of its members, Domingo Cavallo, served as president of the Central Bank of Argentina in 1982 and as Minister of Economy in the 1990s, driving the pro-market reforms enacted by President Menem's early administration.[88]

The Pescarmona Group (sometimes known as IMPSA)[89] grew from a metal workshop founded in 1907 in Mendoza, a midwestern Argentine province, to a producer of manufactured goods, primarily for the winemaking industry. It operated in this way until the early 1940s (though it was closed between 1931 and 1936), at which time it started to expand its operations, serving as a supplier for both private and public projects, fulfilling the needs of industrial plants and the army alike. In the 1970s, it began a process of strong growth, focusing on engineering projects, hydroelectric power plants, equipment for primary industries, ports, nuclear and hydroelectric plants, as well as factory construction. In the 1980s, the group began to expand internationally with engineering projects, hydroelectric power plants and port construction, partnering with foreign companies and operating in Latin America, the United States, and China. It continued its diversification and globalization process during the 1990s, and by 2008, IMPSA ranked third among Argentine Latin American multinationals based on its assets abroad, which were valued at US$ 300 million.[90]

Beginning in the 1970s, Pescarmona worked in two major and complementary sectors: engineering (project design and execution, hydroelectric power plant management) and equipment manufacturing for industries and other activities (ports, power plants). The group diversified further in the 1980s, moving into insurance, environmental services (waste collection and treatment), spare car parts, and transportation. Pescarmona has also owned a winery in Mendoza since 1920.[91] The group's diversification efforts serve several purposes: Its insurance company provides services to the group's companies, like its transportation business. Its environmental service outfit brings cash flow, while its winery is embedded in the family's and the province's cultural tradition. In the 1990s, Pescarmona moved into telecommunications, starting a company called IMPSAT that struggled with a heavy debt burden after the 2001–02 crisis and was eventually transferred to its creditors, who, in turn, sold it in 2006.

Like Techint and Arcor, IMPSA expanded as a result of the competitive capabilities it developed from within and its access to resources provided by the state, constantly intertwining both. Its growth in the 1940s and 1950s was closely tied to state demand, but, beginning in the 1960s, Pescarmona started to invest greater resources in innovation and in recruiting and training qualified personnel. Building on those capabilities, the group managed to enhance its role as a large public works' supplier in the second half of the 1970s. This boosted its know-how and competitiveness as a result of learning processes involved in operations with high quality requirements (especially for nuclear plant equipment) and joint projects with foreign companies (where the company acted as a minority partner). At the same time, IMPSA strengthened its engineering skill set, recruiting world-class professionals with expertise in different fields – many of whom participated in training programs abroad. Leaning on these newly acquired capabilities, IMPSA was able to compete in international markets beginning in the early 1980s when Argentina's public sector demand shrank. Generally speaking, since its inception the group benefited from protection policies for the winemaking industry enacted in the late nineteenth century, and from a number of tariff, public credit, and other government policies instituted in the 1940s and already described here. However, the group also experienced some tension with the local government in the 1970s and 1980s over public work project awards or continuation agreements.

These three groups started off as family businesses and remained so. Although some of the larger firms are listed on both Argentine and foreign stock exchanges, the founding families (Rocca, Pagani, Pescarmona) still retained control of their respective business groups as majority shareholders. In all of these groups, generational successions have been uneventful and led to sustained or greater growth. Both Techint and Arcor used ethnic/national identity to build cohesion within their groups, and the former also exploited this advantage when making international contacts. Techint started its operations with a combination of professional managers and family members in key positions, whereas Arcor and Pescarmona initially relied on family managers and then gradually hired professional managers. As they grew larger and more diversified, these three groups organized holding companies to control their companies.

While significant differences separate these business groups, they do share some traits. First, they have predominantly pursued a strategy of integration and diversification into related industries, founded on engineering and/or industrial operations, although they have all invested in ventures outside their core competencies as well. Two of these groups – Techint and Pescarmona – have ventured into the financial sector, while Arcor has not, but they have all enjoyed preferential access to credit. Second, group ownership rests firmly with the founding families, who also control and manage, with outside professionals, the holding companies that encompass other group companies. Third, all three groups combined their access to state resources with their developed competitive advantages to embark upon early expansion and internationalization projects that enabled them not just to survive, but to thrive, in spite of a difficult macroeconomic and institutional setting. Nonetheless, a remarkable difference sets Techint apart from Arcor and Pescarmona, bringing the former closer to the business groups that emerged during Argentina's export-led boom, because the latter two lacked a network spanning the Atlantic. These groups also differed in size, as Techint's total assets in 2008 were US$ 20.6 billion, while Arcor and IMPSA lagged behind with US$ 1.3 billion and US$ 919 million in assets, respectively.[92]

VI. ARGENTINE BUSINESS GROUPS FROM THE 1990s: FROM A COMPETITIVE TO AN ANTI-COMPETITIVE SHOCK

The institutional conditions that had favored the emergence and expansion of business groups from the mid-1940s changed dramatically in the early 1990s. During this decade, Argentina launched a swift process of market-oriented reforms that has been defined as 'competitive shock',[93] putting an end to a long period marked by a closed, regulated economy, with the state taking an active role to protect and subsidize domestic industrial companies, which promoted business groups' creation and expansion. To support the new rules of the game that primarily involved opening and deregulating Argentina's economy, as well as privatizing state-owned companies, the Argentine peso was pegged to the US dollar at a fixed one-to-one exchange rate.

These structural reforms radically changed the local market's competitive setting, as the world economy grew increasingly globalized, with intense dynamism for MNEs. The new institutional scenario provided expansion opportunities for the business groups that had managed to grow strong during the 1970s and 1980s, but it also brought new challenges, in addition to the much more competitive landscape. The new opportunities notably included the privatization of state-owned companies; economic stabilization and expansion in 1991–98, with growing domestic demand; the creation of the Mercado Común del Sur (MERCOSUR), a regional market bloc built by Argentina, Brazil, Uruguay, and Paraguay; access to external funding with favorable conditions; and the availability of foreign technologies via imports.[94]

In turn, local groups were forced to compete with multinationals, which flocked to Argentina, now lured by business opportunities and an institutional framework that favored foreign direct investment (FDI) by offering equal treatment to both domestic and foreign firms. Foreign investments in Argentina rose from less than US$ 6 billion in the 1980s to nearly US$ 80 billion in the 1990s, and the share of foreign companies ranking among Argentina's 500 largest firms climbed from 44 percent in 1993 to 64 percent in 2000.[95] The growing number of multinationals among the top 500 firms implied the retreat of state-owned companies and business groups from Argentina's corporate elite. Most state-owned companies were privatized between 1993 and 1996: by 2004, none ranked among Argentina's 100 top-selling companies.[96] Furthermore, the number of groups ranking among Argentina's 200 top-selling shrank from 60 to 39 in 1989–2003.[97] Over the first decade of the new millennium, MNEs continued to prevail among Argentina's largest firms, displacing not only business groups in general but also large stand-alone domestic companies.[98]

While business groups collectively lost their standing among Argentina's largest companies, their individual response to environmental changes differed, though the most dynamic and successful groups did share a strategic shift towards international growth. The 1990s' reforms allowed for globalization to be not only a means by which groups expanded abroad but also a tool they could use to support their domestic market positions.[99]

In general terms, the early 1990s brought increased diversification as a result of privatization, but, from then on, business groups tended to become more specialized, shedding their non-strategic assets.[100] Simultaneously, beginning in 1993, companies were sold to foreign owners, a process that gathered momentum after the 1995 Mexican crisis. Some groups sold businesses after realizing they would not survive direct competition with multinationals; some chose to change their investment focus, shifting towards agribusiness or energy, which leveraged Argentina's comparative advantages, while others were forced to sell to or partner with foreign companies as a result of funding difficulties.[101]

Argentina's macroeconomic conditions started to deteriorate in 1998, when the country began to show signs of a recession that came to a head in late 2001, with the most severe crisis the country had suffered since the mid-nineteenth century.[102] Stagnation, breaches of contracts, devaluation, and the unavailability of foreign loans wreaked havoc on companies. Groups focusing on the domestic market and/or those with debts in other currencies were the hardest hit. Between 1999 and 2006, out of the 18 groups listed in Table 1.1, four were sold to Brazilian companies (Quinsa, Acindar, Alpargatas, and Fortabat), and eight were critically distressed, forcing the sell-off of some of their firms (SOCMA, Pérez Companc, IMPSA, Roggio) or most of their stock (Sociedad Comercial del Plata), or forcing partnerships with foreign companies (Bridas, Mastellone) or debt restructuring (Sancor).[103]

In contrast, the groups that had expanded internationally were better able to navigate the crisis, even though their domestic businesses were hit hard. Techint, IMPSA, and Arcor provide three examples of successful performance during the 1990s and 2000s.

In the 1990s, Techint was one of the groups that took advantage of privatization to acquire state-owned steel companies (SOMISA and SIAT), while moving into other related and non-related businesses. At the same time, it began to globalize, becoming Argentina's largest MNE and Latin America's foremost player in the steel industry, as well as one of the world's leading steel producers.[104] Techint's investments abroad focused primarily on the acquisition of companies in Latin America, North America, Europe, and Asia. Its global expansion brought a need to reorganize the group in order to take better advantage of synergies among its companies and to boost efficiency. As a result, two new companies were created: Tenaris in 2002 and Ternium in 2005, both listed on the New York Stock Exchange.[105] Tenaris had tube manufacturing firms in Mexico, Italy, Venezuela, Brazil, Japan, Canada, the United States, and Romania; since 2004, the company has also operated a business unit in China. Ternium encompasses the group's flat steel manufacturing companies in Mexico, Argentina, Brazil, Colombia, the United States, and Guatemala. In 2012, Techint had an overall headcount of 59,196 full-time employees.[106]

IMPSA/Grupo Pescarmona began its international expansion in the 1980s with engineering projects, hydroelectric power plants, and ports, partnering with foreign companies and operating in Latin America, the United States, and China. Argentina's crisis in the 1980s and resulting cessation of public works projects pushed the group to expand abroad with the support of its IMPSA International affiliate created in Pennsylvania. By this time, IMPSA owned some businesses in Latin America and was starting to operate in the United States. In 1985, it opened a commercial office in Hong Kong, and in the late 1980s it began to distribute slowly its equipment and products in Asia, and it solidified its operations there the following decade with projects in Malaysia, Thailand, Taiwan, Indonesia, China, the Philippines, and Saudi Arabia, as well as branch openings in Kuala Lumpur, Manila, and Shanghai. In the 1990s, IMPSA also forged partnerships with Latin American, Asian, and European firms.[107] These international operations brought in addition access to funding, including the Development Bank of Brazil, where 77 percent of IMPSA's assets were located by 2012.[108] Beginning in the 1990s, Pescarmona Group began to diversify, turning towards telecom with the creation of IMPSAT, a US-based firm (associated with Morgan Stanley) and to cutting-edge technologies in Latin America. However, this company failed to meet its debt payments after the 2001–02 crisis and was taken over by its creditors.[109]

Arcor managed to successfully navigate Argentina's economic opening and deregulation in the 1990s. Rising to the challenges of pro-market reforms and the arrival of foreign MNEs, this group continued to expand, increasing its production capacity and acquiring several local firms, expanding its investments in management, marketing, and human resources training, and further globalizing. In the 1990s, Arcor's exports grew by 454 percent, accounting for 36 percent of its revenues by 2000.[110] At the same time, the group built new production units in Peru, Chile, and Brazil and commercial offices in the United States, Bolivia, Ecuador, Colombia, and Mexico.[111] Argentina's 2001 crisis presented a significant challenge to Arcor, whose domestic sales plummeted. In 2001–02, its Argentine revenues dropped by over 50 percent, while its revenues overseas grew from 35 percent to 60 percent of its overall sales.[112]

With the worst of the crisis behind it, Arcor strengthened its global operations. It made investments in Latin America with new marketing affiliates (Venezuela), enlarged and new production plants (in Chile and Mexico) and distribution centers, and acquired firms and made partnerships with both global (Danone) and regional (Mexico's Bimbo) firms. Arcor also increased its market share in North America via agreements with US firms (including contract manufacturing operations) and a new commercial affiliate in Canada. In 2002, it moved its international division to Barcelona in order to promote sales in Europe. The group also expanded operations in Africa and Asia, which, by 2014, accounted for 20 percent of its total exports.[113]

Arcor has remained Argentina's leading food manufacturer and the world's largest candy maker. In 2014, it exported products to over 120 countries across five continents, owned 39 industrial plants (29 in Argentina, 5 in Brazil, 3 in Chile, 1 in Mexico, and 1 in Peru), 13 commercial offices in the Americas, Europe, Africa, and Asia, 19 distribution centers in Latin America, and employed 20 000 employees around the world.

Business groups have not been able to return to the leading role they played before the 1990s. During the 1990s only a few new business groups were created, and those built in the 2000s largely came about through political connections. Meanwhile several former large groups gradually disappeared or shrank in size and scope.

VII. CONCLUDING REMARKS

A number of generalizations emerge from this study of the historical evolution of Argentine business groups. First, it is evident that business groups emerged in quite different historical contexts. In some of the literature, business groups have been associated with a specific type of political and economic context, especially a closed economy and public policies promoting domestic private companies.[114] This chapter has shown this view to be erroneous.

In the case of Argentina, some groups emerged during the era of an open and deregulated economy before 1914, and a number of these groups were still active in 1980. Other groups emerged during the closed economy and statist era between the 1960s and the 1980s. In the intervening era of 1914–60, characterized by an increasingly closed economy with greater state intervention, no new groups emerged. This finding contradicts the current literature on Argentina's business groups which has argued either that Peronism favored their emergence,[115] or that their prevalence in the local economy started in the early 1950s.[116] Finally, in the period after 1990, pro-market reforms followed by major economic crisis damaged many groups, although the most competitive were able to expand during this time through globalization.

Why were business groups created in the two specific periods of 1870–1914 and 1960–90? Institutional voids, imperfect markets and favorable regulatory frameworks were dominant features of both eras. The role of the state, though, differed greatly. The state was aloof in the first and actively engaged in the second. In the first stage, it was possible to build strong ties with foreign partners, using them to access several kinds of resources (funding, know-how, information, managers). This is relevant, as it paved the way for a specific type of business group, with links on both sides of the Atlantic, and with transnational traits that the existing literature has largely neglected. Techint displayed some of those traits starting in the 1940s.

During the period when the second generation of Argentine groups emerged, while supportive state policies supporting industries were in place from the 1940s to the mid-1970s, they were combined with periodic crises, high inflation rates and ongoing changes in the rules of the game and macroeconomic policy. This situation worsened after 1976, when institutional shifts became more intense and crises more severe. While the retreat of MNEs and a number of policy actions taken from 1976 to 1989 favored the position of business groups, political changes could benefit or harm them, depending on how new administrations perceived business groups. Chronic political instability hindered groups' relationships with public officials. Finally, as mentioned earlier, the violence of the 1970s affected some business groups directly. As a result, it is clear that not only the role of the state, but also that of political turmoil and institutional uncertainty, needs to be incorporated into explanations of business group longevity and performance. In Argentina, amid this instability, there were no consistent, pervasive policies intended to build national champions by an efficient state, endowed with a meritocratic bureaucracy, as was the case in other, more successful emerging economies such as South Korea.

Why did no business groups emerge between 1914 and the 1960s, despite continued institutional weaknesses? Part of the answer is that governments were at times more supportive of state-owned companies or MNEs. At other junctures, economic conditions promoted the emergence of small and medium-sized companies. In turn, first-generation groups continued to expand during the interwar period, seizing opportunities created by import substitution, and perhaps crowding out the emergence of new rivals.

The explanation for the weakening of business groups after 1990 is multi-causal. Structural reforms made the market much more competitive.

Both business groups and single product firms suffered. It was lack of competitiveness not the organizational structure which was the problem. Notably, more competitive groups such as Technit did well. Business groups were further hit by Argentina's 2001 crisis. It was the more internationalized and less indebted groups which survived. In addition, subsequent public policies proved largely unfavorable to groups, except for those close to political power.

A second broad set of generalizations relates to the organizational growth patterns. The three first-generation groups began with trade operations and diversified into finance, agribusiness, real estate, industry and other service industry ventures. Agribusiness investments stand out as a characteristic feature of this stage, reflecting the significant role for the primary sector in Argentina's economy. These three groups largely chose a path of diversification into unrelated industries, and all relied on their own banks or financial institutions to do so. Unrelated diversification and alliances with partners for specific ventures caused these groups to create legally separate companies instead of large outfits with many departments or divisions. Two of these groups (Bunge y Born and Tornquist) opted for a vertical organization, while the other (Devoto) preferred a more horizontal structure, though the networks connecting these groups to Europe were all horizontal in nature. As for their ownership and control patterns, these groups were family-owned (with one or more owner families); although owner families joined other partners in Argentina or overseas and hired professional managers early on.

These three groups gradually developed capabilities that enabled them to operate in multiple markets, and a sizable share of their companies boasted cutting-edge technologies and strong professional management teams. At the same time, Tornquist and Devoto combined productive investments with more speculative operations in, for instance, real estate. Social networks were important in building corporate capabilities, especially when these networks crossed national borders. Relations with the state did not play a decisive role in the creation and early growth of these groups, but these groups did build personal ties with particular officials.

It is evident that all three groups adjusted to economic changes after 1914, maintaining their leadership in several industries over a number of decades, and using the resources of an increasingly closed and regulated economy in which industrial endeavors proved the most successful. They relied on tangible and intangible assets created before World War I. After 1914, they leveraged their international networks of contacts to partner with foreign companies in several ventures – albeit to a much lesser extent than they had in earlier decades. These business groups also accessed new resources the state began to offer in the 1940s, and two of the groups – Bunge y Born and Fabril/Celulosa – took advantage of special programs launched in the late 1960s.

The three groups that emerged in the late nineteenth century eventually disappeared during the late twentieth century. Tornquist succumbed to family strife among third-generation family members. It collapsed in the mid-1970s. Devoto, later known as Grupo Fabril/Celulosa, failed to survive the harsh macroeconomic conditions of the 1980s. For Bunge y Born, the decision to sell the group's industrial companies in the 1990s was part of a globalization strategy, but as early as the 1970s, its businesses in Brazil and the United States were poised to take the lead, leaving Argentina behind.

Second-generation business groups also shared some features with older groups, though other characteristics set them apart. With regard to structure, these latter groups' diversification followed a different pattern, based more on a rationale of integration and related diversification, albeit with differences in each case. From their starting point in engineering (Techint) or manufacturing (Arcor, Pescarmona), and with investments in several operations that leveraged promotion programs or the strength of other partners, these groups began to create new, legally independent firms that remained under a common control and strategy. All three kept their core businesses in the industrial domain (Arcor) or the engineering and industrial realm (Techint and Pescarmona), regardless of their diversification efforts. The move into financial services was less widespread among these groups than it was with their first-generation counterparts. None of these three groups owned banks, although Techint had some financial investments and Pescarmona had an insurance company.

These three groups operated using a hierarchical organization, with holding companies and owner families in control, but family members and professional managers sharing managerial tasks. All three groups emerged in a closed economy, characterized by strong state intervention and active public policies to support industry, which gathered momentum in the late 1960s. While these three groups grew under the shelter of protection policies, promotional programs, public loans, and state contracts, their successful track records also reveal their ability to build competitive advantages. In addition to developing the skills required to approach public officials, these groups invested in product and process technologies, as well as in technical and managerial human resources, and innovated – to a lesser or greater extent – and forged alliances with companies abroad. Their early globalization – via exports, engineering projects or direct investments – was also noteworthy.

The big takeaway from this historical evidence is the need to move away from simplified views of the drivers of business group formation, and their organizational characteristics. There are plenty of similarities with groups in other emerging markets, but also differences. Unlike in some other cases, international networking and, more generally, globalization, was important for the emergence and growth of Argentine business groups. All such generalizations, however, need to note that there were significant changes over time in the various actors. For example, as elsewhere, there is a significant role for the state in this story, as all the business groups made use of government relationships of one kind or another, but Argentine government policies also emerge as less consistent and sometimes more damaging than elsewhere, forcing the business groups to deal with a setting riddled with volatility. Despite this, the business groups emerge as viable and broadly productive forms of business enterprise, some of them emerging as internationally competitive groups. While some groups did engaged at times in speculative businesses, rent-seeking strategies did not dominate most of their operations. It should be concluded that as a collective group, the groups were positive contributors to the development of Argentine industry.

NOTES

1. Jones and Khanna (2006).
2. The extensive literature can be approached in Guillén (2000); Granovetter (2005); Khanna and Yafeh (2007); Fruin (2008); Morck and Steier (2007); and Colpan, Hikino, and Lincoln (2010).
3. Khanna and Yafeh (2007): 331. This clarification is significant, as many authors who have studied Argentine business groups include nearly all large domestic private companies in this category. Other scholars have made a distinction between groups with related and unrelated diversification. See, for example, Carrera, Mesquita, Perkins, and Vassolo (2003); Fracchia, Mesquita, and Quiroga (2010).
4. Leff (1978).
5. Khanna and Palepu (1997).
6. Randall and Steier (2007).
7. Mork and Steier (2007); Guillén (2001); Schneider (2010).
8. These guidelines were chosen primarily on the basis of Khanna and Yafeh (2007); Morck and Steier (2007); Granovetter (1994); Granovetter (2005); Amsden and Hikino (1995); Guillén (2000) and (2001).
9. Guy (1982); Lluch (2008); Regalsky (1997); Nakamura and Zarazaga (2003).
10. Scarzanella (1983); Guy (1982). Fernando Rocchi argued that funding access was not restricted. See Rocchi (2006).
11. Nakamura and Zarazaga (2003); Paolera and Taylor (2001).
12. Taylor (2001).
13. Marichal (1974).
14. On Grupo Tornquist, see especially Gilbert (2001); Gilbert (2003); Gilbert (2004); Guy (1988); Jones and Lluch (2008); for Bunge y Born, see Green and Laurent (1988); Schvarzer (1989). On Devoto, see Barbero (1990); Barbero (2002); Barbero (2001); Scarzanella (2006). On Quilmes, see López (2001). For Alpargatas, see Gutiérrez and Korol (1998). On the general characteristics of business groups in this period, see also Marichal (1974).
15. Rocchi (2006). See also Lewis (1992) and Pineda (2009).

16. Dorfman (1970); Barbero and Lluch (2015).
17. Rocchi (2006).
18. While this chapter will focus on the three aforementioned groups, the Bemberg business group shared most of their features. See Barbero (2013).
19. From the early 1900s, the Bunges, of German descent, had established business companies in the Netherlands and Belgium.
20. Barbero (1990).
21. Gilbert (2001) and (2003).
22. Green and Laurent (1988).
23. It also acquired a tin packaging company.
24. Green and Laurent (1988).
25. Barbero (2003).
26. Barbero (2002).
27. Gilbert (2001); Jones and Lluch (2008).
28. Gilbert (2001).
29. Green and Laurent (1988).
30. Barbero (2003).
31. Guy (1988); Barbero (2003).
32. Díaz Alejandro (1975).
33. The interwar period also saw the fast integration and diversification of Alpargatas, the largest canvas footwear manufacturer from the late nineteenth century, which expanded into the textile industry. See Gutiérrez and Korol (1998).
34. Argentina's financial sector became more regulated after the creation of its Central Bank and a new banking law in 1935, but after 1929, the role of internal savings and local banks grew decisive. These banks were more fragile and conservative than their foreign counterparts, which limited the access to long-term credit. Many of them were severely hit by the Great Depression. Argentina's weak capital market was further weakened after 1929. See Nakamura and Zarazaga (2003).
35. Some companies created in this period later became diversified business groups. It is debatable whether SIAM, a metal manufacturer created a few years before the war that showed strong growth since the 1920s, was a business group or not, as it included several legally independent firms between 1950 and 1996.
36. It should be noted that, between 1920 and 1945, from the Great Depression through to World War II, a significant number of small and medium-sized companies emerged, particularly in the textiles and light mechanical industries.
37. Green and Laurent (1988); Schvarzer (1989).
38. Schvarzer (1989).
39. Hoste (2006).
40. Gilbert (2003).
41. Gilbert (2003); Phelps (1936).
42. Gilbert (2003).
43. Later this venture was also known as Celulosa (Azpiazu, Basualdo, and Khavisse (1986).
44. Barbero (2002).
45. Barbero (2002). A new paper manufacturing firm, La Papelera Argentina, was created after merging with two other companies.
46. Barbero (2002).
47. Tulio Halperín Donghi has characterized the 1945–89 period as 'Peronist Argentina' (Halperín Donghi (1994)).
48. Maddison (1997).
49. Between 1973 and 1975 Argentina's economy openness index stood at 16.6, and climbed to 20.4 in 1976–78, but dropped to 15.8 in 1978–81. See Berlinski (2003).
50. Rougier (2004).
51. Schvarzer (1995); Bisang (1996).
52. Spiller and Tommasi (2007); Berensztein and Spector (2004).

53. Such was the case of Techint, Fate/Aluar, Arcor, Bridas, Pérez Companc, Clarín, and SOCMA. Some of these business groups had been formed over earlier decades, but they had grown slowly (Sociedad Comercial del Plata, Roggio), and some even stopped operating for a while, like Pescarmona. Others had a more regional focus.
54. Acevedo, Basualdo, and Khavisse (1990); Azpiazu, Basualdo and Khavisse (1986); Bisang (1999); Bisang (1998); Carrera, Mesquita, Perkins, and Vassolo (2003); Fracchia, Mesquita, and Quiroga (2010); Schvarzer (1983) and (1995). See also Lluch, Salvaj, and Barbero (2014).
55. Schvarzer (1978) and (1993).
56. Schvarzer (1983).
57. Bisang (1999).
58. While this list may be biased by involvement in the 1990s' privatizations, it nearly matches the list of major groups active in the 1980s elaborated by Acevedo, Basualdo, and Khavisse (1990) and is compatible with the 1997 list in Carrera, Mesquita, Perkins, and Vassolo (2003).
59. Green and Laurent (1988); Schvarzer (1983) and (1989).
60. In 1979, Francisco Soldati, chairman of Sociedad Comercial del Plata, another expanding business group, was murdered by Montoneros guerrillas.
61. Green and Laurent (1988: 113) state that the group's headquarters were moved to Brazil.
62. See www.bungeargentina.com, accessed 18 November 2014.
63. Gilbert (2003).
64. Gilbert (2004).
65. Barbero (2002).
66. Schvarzer (1978).
67. Bisang (1999); Schvarzer (1993).
68. Quintela (2005).
69. Few companies created during or after the 1960s turned into business groups before 1990. See Fracchia, Mesquita, and Quiroga (2010).
70. The distinction between groups with related and unrelated diversification was made by Carrera, Mesquita, Perkins, and Vassolo (2003); the definition based on the number of controlled companies was made by Acevedo, Basualdo, and Khavisse (1990).
71. Pescarmona had to sell a telecom company it had founded in 1990.
72. Castro (2003), (2007), (2008) and (2013). On Agostino Rocca's life, see Offeddu (1984). See also Lussana (2005) and Artopoulos (2009), as well as Techint companies' websites.
73. Offeddu (1984).
74. Castro (2008).
75. Bisang (1996) and see www.techint.com, accessed 15 January 2014.
76. ProsperAr and Vale Columbia Center on Sustainable International Investment (2009).
77. Castro (2003): 131–2.
78. Castro (2007). Assumptions have been made about the role played by Italian investors in Techint's operations, but they have not been substantiated with evidence.
79. Artopoulos (2009).
80. Seijo (2008).
81. Castro (2007).
82. Rougier (2004); Offeddu (1984); Castro (2007).
83. Its two leading companies, Tenaris and Ternium, have been listed on the New York Stock Exchange since the 2000s.
84. This paragraph draws primarily on Kosacoff, Forteza, Barbero, Stengel, and Porta (2007), and more specifically from Barbero's chapter on the 1951–90 period. See also Barbero (2003) and Ramírez (2000) and www.arcor.com.ar, accessed 1 November 2014.
85. Kosacoff, Forteza, Barbero, Stengel, and Porta (2007): 215.
86. ProsperAr and Vale (2009).

87. Barbero (2003).
88. Ramírez (2000).
89. IMPSA is the group's leading company, specializing in engineering, power generation and equipment manufacturing. This section on Pescarmona draws primarily from Gutiérrez (2001) and (2003); Walter (1989): n. 8.
90. ProsperAr and Vale (2009).
91. Gutiérrez (2003).
92. ProsperAr and Vale (2009).
93. Fracchia (2002); Carrera, Mesquita, Perkins, and Vassolo (2003).
94. Bisang (1996).
95. See Chapter 4.
96. Barbero and Lluch (2015).
97. Castellani and Gaggero (2012).
98. See Chapter 9.
99. Kosacoff (1999).
100. Carrera, Mesquita, Perkins and Vassolo (2003).
101. Gaggero (2008).
102. See Chapter 9.
103. Bunge y Born had ceased to be a group by the 1990s after selling off its industrial companies to focus on its agribusiness core operations.
104. Goldstein and Toulan (2007).
105. Goldstein and Toulan (2007).
106. *Techint Group Brochure* (2012), accessed 15 January 2014 at www.techint.com.
107. Gutiérrez (2003); IMPSA (2006); Kosacoff (1978).
108. See www.impsa.com, accessed 17 January 2014.
109. López (2006).
110. Kosacoff, Forteza, Barbero, Stengel, and Porta (2007).
111. See www.arcor.com.ar, accessed 19 January 2014.
112. Ghemawat, Rukstad, and Illes (2009).
113. Kosacoff, Forteza, Barbero, Stengel, and Porta (2007).
114. For example, Guillen (2001).
115. Carrera, Mesquita, Perkins, and Vassolo (2003).
116. Lewis (1992).

REFERENCES

Acevedo, Manuel, Eduardo Basualdo, and Miguel Khavisse (1990), *¿Quién es quién? Los dueños del poder económico (Argentina, 1973–1987)*, Buenos Aires: Editora 12/Pensamiento Jurídico.

Alejandro, Carlos Díaz (1975), *Ensayos sobre la historia económica argentina*, Buenos Aires: Amorrortu.

Amsden, Alice and Takashi Hikino (1995), 'La industrialización tardía en perspectiva histórica', *Desarrollo Económico*, **35** (137), 3–34.

Artopoulos, Alejandro (2009), 'Sociedad del conocimiento en Argentina: el caso de una empresa-red: Tenaris', *REDES. Revista de Estudios Sociales de la Ciencia*, **15** (29), 241–6.

Azpiazu, Daniel, Eduardo Basualdo and Miguel Khavisse (1986), *El nuevo poder económico en la Argentina de los años 80*, Buenos Aires: Legása.

Barbero, María Inés (1990), 'Grupos empresarios, intercambio comercial e inversiones italianas en la Argentina. El casá de Pirelli (1910–1920)', *Estudios Migratorios Latinoamericanos*, **5** (15–16), 311–41.

Barbero, María Inés (2001), 'De la Compañía General de Fósforos al Grupo Fabril: origen y desarrollo de un grupo económico en la Argentina (1889–1965)', in V.V. A.A. (eds), *Problemas de investigación, ciencia y desarrollo*, San Miguel: Universidad Nacional de General Sarmiento, 327–59.
Barbero, María Inés (2002), 'Mercados, redes sociales y estrategias empresariales en los orígenes de los grupos económicos. De la Compañía General de Fósforos al Grupo Fabril. 1889–1929', *Estudios Migratorios Latinoamericanos*, **15** (44), 119–46.
Barbero, María Inés (2003), 'La formación de grupos económicos en la Argentina contemporánea. El caso Arcor (1951–1990)', in Mario Cerutti (coord.), *Empresas y grupos empresariales en América Latina, España y Portugal*. Monterrey: Universidad Autónoma de Nuevo León/Universidad de Alicante, 41–73.
Barbero, María Inés (2013), 'Business groups in Argentina during the export-led growth period (1870–1914)', in Gabriel Tortella and Gloria Quiroga (eds), *Entrepreneurship and Growth: A Comparative Historical Perspective*, Houndmills: Palgrave MacMillan, 69–90.
Barbero, María Inés and Andrea Lluch (2015), 'El capitalismo familiar en Argentina: modelos y dinámicas en el largo plazo', in Paloma Fernández Pérez and Andrea Lluch (eds), *Familias empresarias y grandes empresas familiares en América Latina y España: Una visión de largo plazo*, Bilbao: Fundación BBVA, 219–260.
Berensztein, Sergio and Horacio Spector (2003), 'Business, government, and law', in Gerardo della Paolera and Alan Taylor (eds), *A New Economic History of Argentina*, Cambridge: Cambridge University Press, 324–68.
Berlinski, Julio (2003), 'International trade and commercial policy', in Gerardo della Paolera and Alan Taylor (eds), *The New Economic History of Argentina*, Cambridge: Cambridge University Press, 2003, 204–6.
Bisang, Roberto (1996), 'Perfil tecno-productivo de los grupos económicos en la industria argentina', in Jorge Katz (ed.), *Estabilización macroeconómica, reforma estructural y comportamiento industrial*, Buenos Aires: CEPAL/Alianza, 391–3.
Bisang, Roberto (1998), 'Los conglomerados económicos en la Argentina: orígenes y evolución reciente', Working Paper No. 11, San Miguel: Universidad de General Sarmiento, Instituto de Industria.
Bisang, Roberto (1999), 'La estructura y dinámica de los conglomerados económicos en la Argentina', in Wilson Peres (ed.), *Grandes empresas y grupos industriales latinoamericanos*, México: Siglo XXI/CEPAL, 81–154.
Carrera, Alejandro, Luiz Mesquita, Guillermo Perkins, and Roberto Vassolo (2003), 'Business groups and their corporate strategies on the Argentine roller-coaster of competitive and anti-competitive shocks', *The Academy of Management Executive*, **17** (2), 32–44.
Castellani, Ana and Alejandro Gaggero (2012), 'La retirada heterogénea: estrategias y desempeños de los grupos económicos nacionales en Argentina de la década de 1990', *Apuntes*, **XXXIX** (70), 206.
Castro, Claudio (2003), 'De la industrialización tardía europea a la sustitución de importaciones latinoamericana: Agostino Rocca y los primeros años de la Organización Techint, 1946–1954', *Ciclos*, **XIII** (25–26), 119–144.
Castro, Claudio (2007), 'Un nuevo actor siderúrgico en la Argentina de postguerra: el grupo Techint', in Marcelo Rougier (dir.), *Políticas de promoción y estrategias empresariales en la industria argentina, 1950–1980*, Buenos Aires: Ediciones Cooperativas.

Castro, Claudio (2008), 'Una multinacional dirigida desde Buenos Aires. La internacionalización temprana de Techint, 1946–1976', in Guillermo Guajardo (coord.), *Innovación y empresa. Estudios históricos de México, España y América Latina*, México: UNAM/Fundación Gas Natural.
Castro, Claudio (2013), 'Desarrollo energético, cambio técnico y empresa. Origen y evolución de un conglomerado empresario con ventajas competitivas en la ingeniería y la siderurgia (1921–2001)', unpublished Ph.D. Thesis, Universidad Nacional de Córdoba.
Colpan, Asli M., Takashi Hikino, and James R. Lincoln (eds) (2010), *The Oxford Handbook of Business Groups*, Oxford: Oxford University Press.
della Paolera, Gerardo and Alan Taylor (2001), *Straining the Anchor: The Argentine Currency Board and the Search for Macroeconomic Stability, 1880–1935*, Chicago: The University of Chicago Press.
Devoto, Fernando (2006), *Historia de los italianos en la Argentina*, Buenos Aires: Biblos.
Dorfman, Adolfo (1970), *Historia de la industria argentina*, Buenos Aires: Solar-Hachette.
Fracchia, Eduardo (2002), 'Factores determinantes de la respuesta estratégica de los grupos económicos argentinos ante el shock competitivo de la década de 1990', unpublished Ph.D. Thesis, Universidad de Navarra.
Fracchia, Eduardo, Luiz Mesquita, and Juan Quiroga (2010), 'Business Groups in Argentina', in Asli M. Colpan, Takashi Hikino, and James R. Lincoln (eds), *The Oxford Handbook of Business Groups*, Oxford: Oxford University Press, 325–2.
Fruin, Mark (2008), 'Business groups and interfirm networks', in Geoffrey Jones and Jonathan Zeitlin (eds), *The Oxford Handbook of Business History*, Oxford: Oxford University Press, 244–67.
Gaggero, Alejandro (2008), '"Fui industrial durante muchos años . . ." Los grupos económicos nacionales y el proceso de extranjerización del empresariado argentino durante la década de los noventa', *Papeles de trabajo. Revista electrónica del Instituto de Altos Estudios Sociales de la Universidad Nacional de General San Martín*, **2** (3), 1–22.
Ghemawat, Pankaj, Jennifer Illes, and Michael Rukstad (2009), *Arcor: Global Strategy and Local Turbulence*, Harvard Business School Case No. 9–710–407, Boston: Harvard Business Publishing.
Gilbert, Jorge (2001), 'Empresario y empresa en la Argentina Moderna. El grupo Tornquist 1873–1930', unpublished M.A. Thesis, Universidad de San Andrés.
Gilbert, Jorge (2003), 'Entre la expansión y la crisis de la economía argentina. Ernesto Tornquist y Compañía', *Ciclos*, 25–26, 65–90.
Gilbert, Jorge (2004), 'Declinación y muerte de una empresa familiar. Ernesto Tornquist y Cía.', Buenos Aires: Mimeo.
Goldstein, Andrea and Omar Toulan (2007), 'Multilatinas go to China: Two case studies', in Robert Grosse and Luiz Mesquita (eds), *Can Latin American Firms Compete?*, Oxford: Oxford University Press.
Granovetter, Mark (1994), 'Business groups', in Neil Smelser and Richard Swedberg (eds), *The Handbook of Economic Sociology*, Princeton: Princeton University Press, 453–75.
Granovetter, Mark (2005), 'Business groups', in Neil Smelser and Richard Swedberg (eds), *The Handbook of Economic Sociology*, Princeton: Princeton University Press, 2nd edn, 429–50.

Green, Raúl and Catherine Laurent (1988), *El poder de Bunge y Born*, Buenos Aires: Legasa.
Guillén, Mauro (2000), 'Business groups in emerging economies: A resource-based view', *The Academy of Management Journal*, **43** (3), 362–80.
Guillén, Mauro (2001), *The Limits of Convergence, Globalization and Organizational Change in Argentina, South Korea and Spain*, Princeton: Princeton University Press.
Gutiérrez, Carlos (2001), 'I&D, Aprendizaje técnico-organizacional y posicionamiento comercial. La calificación internacional en tecnología hidroenergética de una firma metalúrgica argentina (1977–1997)', unpublished Thesis for the M.A. Program in Politics, Science and Technology Management at Buenos Aires: Centro de Estudios Avanzados, Universidad de Buenos Aires.
Gutiérrez, Carlos (2003), 'Atractivos y paradojas del éxito tecno industrial en la periferia: el caso de una empresa transnacional argentina en ingeniería', *Ciclos*, 25–26, 145–75.
Gutiérrez, Leandro and Juan Carlos Korol (1998), 'Historia de empresas y crecimiento industrial en la Argentina. El caso de la Fábrica Argentina de Alpargatas', *Desarrollo Económico*, **28** (111), 401–24.
Guy, Donna (1982), 'La industria argentina, 1870–1940. Legislación comercial, mercado de acciones y capitalización extranjera', *Desarrollo Económico*, **22** (87), 351–74.
Guy, Donna (1988), 'Refinería Argentina. 1888–1930: límites de la tecnología azucarera en una economía periférica', *Desarrollo Económico*, **28** (111), 353–73.
Halperín Donghi, Tulio (1994), *La larga agonía de la Argentina peronista*, Buenos Aires: Ariel.
Hoste, Stephane (2006), *Bunge in the Low Countries*, Rotterdam: Stad en Bedrifj.
IMPSA (2006), *IMPSA 100 años (1907–2007)*, Mendoza: IMPSA.
Jones, Geoffrey and Tarun Khanna (2006), 'Bringing history (back) into international business', *Journal of International Business Studies*, **37**, 453–68.
Jones, Geoffrey and Andrea Lluch (2008), *Ernesto Tornquist: Making a Fortune on the Pampas*, Boston, MA: Harvard Business School Case no.9–807–155.
Khanna, Tarun, and Krishna Palepu (1997), 'Why focused strategies may be wrong for emerging markets', *Harvard Business Review* (July-August), 3–10.
Khanna, Tarun, and Yishay Yafeh (2007), 'Business groups in emerging markets: Paragons or parasites?', *Journal of Economic Literature*, **XLV**, 331–72.
Kosacoff, Bernardo (1999), 'El caso argentino', in Daniel Chudnovsky, Bernardo Kosacoff and Andrés López, *Las multinacionales latinoamericanas. Sus estrategias en un mundo globalizado*, Buenos Aires: Fondo de Cultura Económica.
Kosacoff, Bernardo, Jorge Forteza, María Inés Barbero, Alejandro Stengel, and Fernando Porta (2007), *Globalizar desde Latinoamérica. El caso Arcor*, Buenos Aires: McGraw Hill.
Leff, Nathaniel (1978), 'Industrial organization and entrepreneurship in the developing countries: The economic groups', *Economic Development and Cultural Change*, **26** (4), 661–75.
Lewis, Paul (1992), *The Crisis of Argentine Capitalism*, Chapel Hill: The University of North Carolina Press.
Lluch, Andrea (2008), 'Las agencias de informes crediticios en la Argentina: una aproximación al funcionamiento de los mecanismos informativos en el mercado crediticio, 1892–c.1935', *Investigaciones de Historia Económica*, **12**, 111–40.

López, Andrés (2006), *Empresarios, instituciones y desarrollo económico: el caso argentino*, Buenos Aires: CEPAL.
López, Sergio (2001), 'Integración y especialización como estrategias empresariales. El caso de la Cervecería Quilmes (1890–1990)', unpublished Historical Research M.A. Thesis, Universidad de San Andrés.
Lussana, Carolina (ed.) (2005), *Techint 1945–1980. Origini e sviluppo di un'impresa internazionale*, Dalmine: Fondazione Dalmine.
Maddison, Angus (1997), *La economía mundial, Análisis y estadísticas*, Paris: OECD.
Marichal, Carlos (1974), *La gran burguesía comercial y financiera de Buenos Aires, 1860–1914: anatomía de cinco grupos*, Buenos Aires: Mimeo, 2–3.
Morck, Randall and Lloyd Steier (2007), 'The global history of corporate governance. An introduction', in Randall Morck (ed.) (2007), *A History of Corporate Governance around the World: Family Business Groups to Professional Managers*, Chicago: University of Chicago Press, 1–64.
Nakamura, Leonard and Carlos Zarazaga (2003), 'Banking and finance, 1900–1935', in Gerardo della Paolera and Alan Taylor (eds), *A New Economic History of Argentina*, Cambridge: Cambridge University Press, 295–323.
Offeddu, Luigi (1984), *La sfida dell'acciaio. Vita di Agostino Rocca*, Venezia: Marsilio.
Phelps, Dudley (1936), *Migration of Industry to South America*, New York: McGraw-Hill.
Pineda, Yovanna (2009), *Industrial Development in a Frontier Economy: The Industrialization of Argentina, 1890–1930*, Stanford: Stanford University Press.
ProsperAr and Vale Columbia Center on Sustainable International Investment (2009), *First Ranking of Argentine Multinationals Finds Diversified Successes in Internationalization*, accessed 8 November 2014 at http://ccsi.columbia.edu/files/2013/10/Argentina_2009_British.pdf.
Quintela, Roberto (2005), *Crisis bancarias y corrupción*, Buenos Aires: Dunken.
Ramírez, Hernán (2000), *La Fundación Mediterránea y de cómo construir poder. La génesis de un proyecto hegemónico*, Córdoba: Ferreyra.
Regalsky, Andrés (1997), 'Banking, trade and the rise of capitalism in Argentina', in Alice Teichova, Ginnette Kurgan-van Hentenryk and Dieter Ziegler (eds), *Banking, Trade and Industry: Europe, America and Asia from the Thirteenth to the Twentieth Century*, Cambridge: Cambridge University Press.
Rocchi, Fernando (2006), *Chimneys in the Desert: Industrialization in Argentina during the Export Boom Years, 1870–1930*, Stanford: Stanford University Press.
Rougier, Marcelo (2004), *Industria, finanzas e instituciones en la Argentina. La experiencia del Banco Nacional de Desarrollo. 1967–1976*, Bernal: Universidad Nacional de Quilmes.
Scarzanella, Eugenia (1983), *Italiani d'Argentina*, Venezia: Marsilio.
Schneider, Ben Ross (2010), 'Business groups and the state: The politics of expansion, restructuring, and collapse', in Asli M. Colpan, Takashi Hikino, and James R. Lincoln (eds), *The Oxford Handbook of Business Groups*, Oxford: Oxford University Press, 650–69.
Schvarzer, Jorge (1978), 'Estrategia industrial y grandes empresas. El caso argentino', *Desarrollo Económico*, **18** (71), 307–51.
Schvarzer, Jorge (1983), 'Cambios en el liderazgo industrial en el período de Martinez de Hoz', *Desarrollo Económico*, **23** (91), 395–422.

Schvarzer, Jorge (1989), *Bunge y Born: crecimiento y diversificación de un grupo económico*, Buenos Aires: Grupo Editor Latinoamericano.

Schvarzer, Jorge (1993), 'Expansión, maduración y perspectivas de las ramas básicas de procesos en la industria argentina. Una mirada ex post desde la economía política', *Desarrollo Económico*, **33** (131), 377–422.

Schvarzer, Jorge (1995), 'Grandes grupos económicos en la Argentina. Formas de propiedad y lógicas de expansión', in Pablo Bustos (ed.), *Más allá de la estabilidad*, Buenos Aires: Fundación Friedrich Ebert, 131–58.

Seijo, Gustavo (2008), 'La triple incertidumbre para la gestión de proyectos de innovación', *Boletín Informativo Techint*, **325**, 1–20.

Spiller, Pablo and Mariano Tommasi (2007), 'Political institutions, policy-making processes and policy outcomes in Argentina', in Ernesto Stein and Mariano Tommasi (eds), *Policymaking in Latin America. How Politics Shapes Policies*, Washington: Inter-American Development Bank/David Rockefeller Center for Latin American Studies, Harvard University, 69–110.

Taylor, Alan (2003), 'Capital accumulation', in Gerardo della Paolera and Alan Taylor (eds), *A New Economic History of Argentina*, Cambridge: Cambridge University Press, 170–96.

Walter, Jorge (1989), 'Modernisation sociale et innovation technologique: un dilemme de l'industrialisation argentine à la lumière d'un étude de cas', in *Cahiers de l'ORSTOM*, 8.

2. Corporate governance and ownership in Chile, 1854–2012

Gonzalo Islas

I. INTRODUCTION

The analysis of corporate governance practices and ownership schemes concerns both academics and public officials. The impact of these on financial development and economic growth has garnered increasing attention ever since the Asian financial crisis in the late 1990s and US corporate scandals in the early 2000s. Corporate governance issues have also been included in the debate over causes underlying the 2008 financial crisis.

Existing differences among corporate governance practices across different countries have also captured researchers' interest. A number of studies show that dispersed ownership – a common structure in the United States and the United Kingdom – is less frequent in the rest of the world where equity concentration prevails.[1] However, given that these studies are based on contemporary data, they fail to explain the origins of such differences. This has now encouraged a historical approach to the study of corporate governance.[2] This chapter contributes to this literature by providing a long-term perspective on the changes in ownership, corporate governance and their related legal frameworks in Chile since the mid-nineteenth century.

After declaring its independence from Spain and navigating uncertainty for a decade, Chile started to consolidate its institutions around 1830. Most companies were organized as simple or limited partnerships. There were no banks.[3] By 1850, Chile's economy saw the creation of its first railroads and financial institutions. This stimulated a need to raise funds from a larger number of investors. As a result, the first corporate law was enacted in 1854, and, thus, that is the date chosen for the beginning of this analysis.

The key argument in this chapter is that Chile's corporate governance history can be divided into three periods, following the pattern characterized by Rajan and Zingales as 'the great reversal'.[4] These authors revealed that global financial development was higher in 1913 than in 1980. They argued that this phenomenon resulted from the actions of incumbent stakeholders who opposed financial development as a means to curtail competition. It was only with a new openness to trade and increased competition from the 1970s that financial market development returned to its former levels. Applying this framework to Chile, the following analysis has been divided into three periods. In each period, the chapter will outline major trends in organizational decisions, investor protection, equity concentration, and capital market development.

The first period, between 1854 and 1920, featured laissez-faire and open trade policies, with scant governmental intervention and regulation.[5] While the law did not include rights for minority shareholders, Chilean businessmen or foreigners residing in Chile used corporations as a means to raise funds, expand their operations and launch new projects, which in turn led to the establishment of a stock market in Chile. This period featured the first examples of businessmen and family-owned businesses that diversified their operations into several industries creating business groups.

The second period, between 1920 and 1970, saw increased state intervention and protectionism. These trends were already evident before World War I, but the war and the Great Depression amplified them. There was a major impact on Chile's financial system and organization of its corporate sector. Figures 2.1 and 2.2 illustrate the fluctuating patterns of financial market development over the next century.

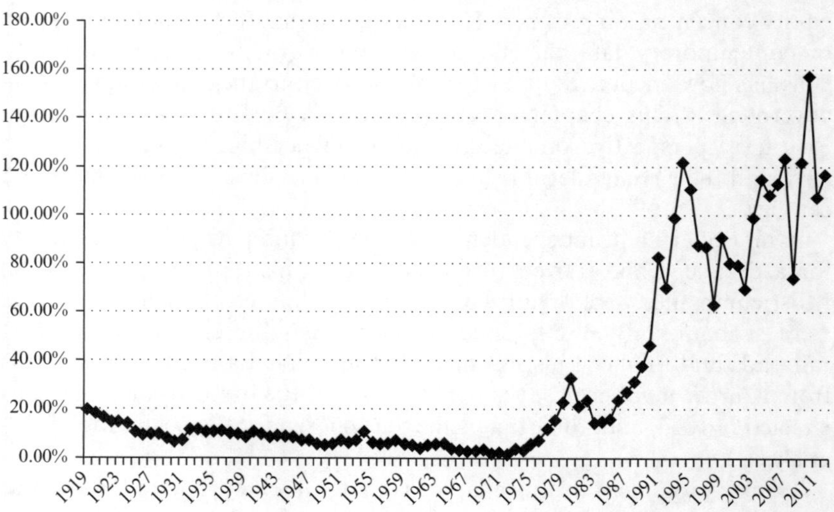

Figure 2.1 Market capitalization as a percentage of Chilean GDP, 1919–2012

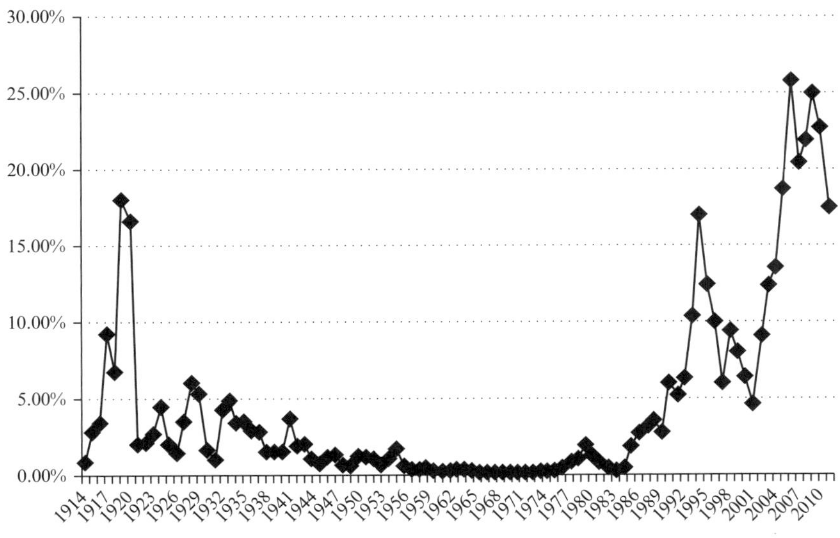

Figure 2.2 Stock market transactions as a percentage of Chilean GDP, 1914–2012

Figure 2.1, which shows market capitalization over gross domestic product (GDP) for 1919–2012, reveals the sharp decrease in the significance of the stock market in the economy between 1910 and 1970. Figure 2.2, which shows the evolution of transactions on the Santiago and Valparaíso Stock Exchanges over GDP, leads to a similar conclusion. Between 1920 and 1970, the volume of stock market transactions and total market capitalization dropped sharply. Companies rarely issued stock to raise funds and loans were mostly made by the state. Businessmen tended to support this institutional arrangement, and it was common for business associations to collaborate with the state on policy formulation, which enabled business groups to develop and consolidate.

A nationalization program launched by President Salvador Allende (1970–73) upset this balance between the state and business groups and marked the beginning of the third period. Allende's overthrow by the military coup of General Pinochet in 1973 was followed by trade and financial liberalization, as well as the privatization of state-owned companies. From a corporate governance standpoint, this new institutional arrangement featured a greater role for institutional investors and more protection for minority investors. There was increased stock market activity, more foreign investors and higher levels of financial development.

Despite the institutional shifts between periods, two significant patterns are evident. First, there has been concentrated equity ownership, which has increased over the years. The same pattern is seen in many developing countries. The second persistent theme is the dominant role of business groups. However, many studies use cross-sector data for a specific year or for relatively short periods of time, and so fail to illuminate how business groups emerged and how they change over time.[6] This chapter contributes to this literature through its longitudinal data and approach.

II. CORPORATE GOVERNANCE IN THE FIRST GLOBAL ECONOMY, 1850–1920

A. Business Organization before the Advent of Corporations

After the country's independence, trade and mining were among the leading economic sectors in Chile. Free trade regulations enacted after 1811[7] turned merchant houses, most of them of British origin, into primary agents in Chile's economy. These firms were mostly organized as collective partnerships (associated with some foreign company), and during this period, they expanded their operations from trade to include lending and, later, other industrial activities such as mills and foundries.[8]

Mining, especially nitrates, was the leading export.[9] This sector and its related activities created some of the greatest business fortunes of the time. Several noted entrepreneurs ventured into other industries after their success in mining, emerging as modern capitalist enterprises.[10] Political stability and port and railroad construction in the middle of the century stimulated a growth in corporate scale.[11] This is the moment when the first companies with shares began to appear in the seaport of Valparaíso, some with special permissions granted by the government, and others with an unclear legal status, as Chilean regulation did not explicitly acknowledge corporations.[12]

B. The Development of Corporations in the Nineteenth Century

After the Corporate Act was passed in 1854, the first companies to rely on this organizational format were the financial (banks and insurance companies) and transportation (railroad and shipping companies) sectors. The use of corporations (S.A., for its acronym in Spanish) spread slowly. By late 1859, only ten firms were legally incorporated in Chile.

Starting in 1865, the number of corporations began to climb, as did their paid-in capital, and this organizational format started booming in 1870 when large resources of silver ore were discovered in Caracoles, Bolivia.

Seventy-one mining (or mining-related) companies were incorporated between 1871 and 1873. Investor engagement also increased, with the average number of shareholders growing from 22.7 to 35.8 between 1871 and 1873. Equity investments, which had previously been restricted to a small minority, became available to a larger number of people. Subscriber lists for new companies included artisans, teachers and civil servants.[13]

The main causes of this boom were the development of Chile's banking system after the 1860 Banking Act which facilitated access to credit, and the promising reports coming from mining areas, which led to a stock bubble in 1872. This boom also brought the first stock and bond brokers to Santiago, the capital, and Valparaíso. These brokers engaged in real estate and farming operations as well.[14] Additionally, starting in 1871, newspapers in both cities began to publish financial asset prices. In this period, several attempts were made to build a formal securities market, but the collapse of the stock bubble and the ensuing economic crisis put an end to these efforts.[15]

Over the rest of the century, there were cycles of booms and busts caused by mining discoveries and international price fluctuations. Out of all the companies incorporated in Chile between 1854 and 1900, 224 (39 percent) were associated with mining. Stock issuance was one of the funding mechanisms which new mining companies used in this period. The mining companies operating in Chile, Peru and Bolivia sold their stock in Santiago and Valparaíso. In the late nineteenth century, mining companies accounted for 40 percent of Chile's overall stock market capitalization.[16]

Recent research suggests that in Europe concentrated equity ownership grew during the twentieth century.[17] Some studies have also suggested that equity ownership in Chile was also less concentrated before World War I.[18] Oppenheimer's study of The Santiago-Valparaiso Railroad Company and The Southern Railroad Company describes the composition of the stock of two highly capitalized corporations in the mid-nineteenth century.[19] Both companies were incorporated as limited liability corporations with a government investment. The railroad from Santiago to Valparaíso was incorporated in 1852 as a corporation with 85 shareholders; 82 of them owned a total of 435 shares, while the remaining three owned 1950 shares. The state held a 2000-share stake. The Southern Railroad, incorporated in 1855 with 121 shareholders, had a similar scheme. In other words, both companies had investors who were willing to hold minority stakes. These companies' shareholder lists for the period 1852–73 (both companies were finally acquired by the state in 1873) included interests held by merchant houses in Santiago and Valparaíso, as well as landowners from Chile's central valley, most of whom were Chilean.

Table 2.1 Ownership schemes in nineteenth century Chile

Industry	Number of companies	Average number of stockholders	Largest stockholder's share (%)	Minimum share for majority stockholder
Financial services	93	84.6	11.4	12.6
Mining	224	32.5	26.6	4.8
Manufacturing	68	34.4	28.4	5.6
Utilities	35	40	22.4	3.7
Transportation (railways and shipping)	35	40	22.4	3.7
Others	61	63	15.4	11.8

Source: Based on 'Boletín de las leyes y decretos del Gobierno.'

A larger company sample confirms the findings of dispersed shareholding in the nineteenth century. According to the 1854 Corporate Act, when companies submitted their by-laws, they were also expected to include a list of their shareholders and their respective number of shares. Using these lists (available in by-laws published in the *Official Gazette and the Law and Executive Order Bulletin*), it is possible to reconstruct companies' equity structures at the time of their incorporation. Table 2.1 shows statistical data on the ownership concentration of Chilean corporations in the nineteenth century.

When submitting their by-laws for government approval, the average corporation featured about 45 shareholders.[20] While this number may seem small by contemporary standards, it is similar to the average in other countries such as Germany during the same period.[21] On average, the largest stockholder owned 22.41 percent of all shares, and the average number of stockholders required to reach a majority was six.[22] Additionally, in this period it was common for shareholders to have a limited number of votes, which reduced the influence of stockholders with larger stakes in corporations.[23] Concentration levels were higher in mining and manufacturing companies and lower in the financial sector. As a result, it may be safe to conclude that in the nineteenth century Chile's market tended to display characteristics that leaned towards an Anglo-Saxon scheme, with minority investors and limited power for predominant shareholders.[24]

C. Diversification, Industrial Development and Early Protectionism, 1880–1920

For most of the nineteenth century, Chile's government adopted, either for political reasons or due to a lack of means to pursue more intrusive policies, a laissez-faire economic policy. Tariffs were relatively low, and the state did not get directly involved in business operations, except those associated with military supplies and railroads in the central and southern regions.

This situation started to change in the second half of the nineteenth century. Starting in 1877, there is evidence of governmental efforts to support Chile's manufacturing industry, either by set protective tariffs or by subsidies granted to new industries.[25] The manufacturers' association (Sociedad de Fomento Fabril, SOFOFA by its Spanish acronym), founded in 1893, also played a significant role. Manufacturing companies' share in Chile's overall market capitalization climbed from 1.5 percent in 1873 to 14 percent in the early twentieth century.

Chile's increased protectionism may also be attributed to a decline in local funding for mining operations. Chilean (or locally-based) investors and entrepreneurs were the key mining promoters until 1880, but by the turn of the century they had lost their standing. Copper mining companies were unable to overcome the depletion of higher quality ore copper, which provided a comparative advantage over their American competitors.[26] In nitrate operations, British investors seized control of offices added after the War of the Pacific (1879–83).

A third trend that explains the growth in protectionism involves the consolidation process in the Chilean industry, including, among others, beer, tobacco, sugar and match manufacturers. This consolidation enhanced the leverage of interests focusing on import substitution.

In his study on the origins and evolution of Chilean manufacturing, Kirsh analysed the ownership structure of major companies in 1920 and found that Chile's wealthiest families had expanded their business operations into several industries. Leading investors in the largest manufacturing companies (most associated with consumer goods and import substitution products) included families formerly associated with mining operations.[27] This suggests that, by the early twentieth century, the investments of the Chilean elite were increasingly shifting from operations focused on foreign markets (mining) to operations with a more domestic orientation (manufacturing industries).

The Cousiño family provides an example that illustrates this interest diversification and reorientation. Matías Cousiño began his business career in copper mining and milling. In 1852, he purchased coal fields to set up Compañía de Lota y Coronel, a company that would become Chile's foremost coal producer. His heirs expanded the company's business focus, building a glass factory and seeking vertical integration with shipping operations. In the late nineteenth century, Carlos Cousiño, Matías' grandson, further diversified the family business into beer manufacturing and cement production.

D. Law, Investor Protection and Chile's Capital Market Development

Chile's 1854 Corporate Act defined corporations as 'legal entities consisting of a common fund divided into shares, with limited liability stockholders'.[28] This regulation drew on European legislation, especially from the 1807 French Commercial Code and the 1829 Spanish Commercial Code. This law left most corporate governance issues to the purview of company by-laws, and there were no rules regarding investor protection. To start a corporation, founders requested a special authorization from the Ministry of Finance (a usual practice in Continental Europe at the time).[29] Typically, the government only made sure that the new corporation's by-laws abided by the law and did not question the company's internal organization and/or the rights it granted to stockholders. A special agent called the 'Commissary' was in charge of supervising the new corporation, but his role was viewed as temporary – in other words, there was no systematic surveillance. Chile's Commercial Code, sanctioned in 1865,[30] included the Corporate Act, which remained unchanged. Additional regulations were introduced in 1878 in reference to partially paid shares, and in 1887 Commissaries' tasks were modified. However, as in the 1854 law, supervision was still viewed as a resource to be used in extraordinary situations rather than as a systematic government role.

Contemporary literature argues that the existence of a legal framework to protect minority investors' interests is a necessary condition for the development of capital markets.[31] Clearly, Chile's Corporate Act did not meet this requirement. Nonetheless, in Chile the norms that every company's by-laws established, mitigated this lack of legal protection. An analysis of the clauses included in these by-laws reveals that most corporations' by-laws included provisions that favored minority investors, like their right to request extraordinary shareholders' meetings and to review accounts using audit committees. Chilean corporations' by-laws also required larger quorums for important strategic decisions and restricted the voting power of majority stockholders, through both maximum vote provisions and graduated voting scales.[32]

III. FINANCIAL MARKET REVERSAL AND THE BUSINESS STATE, 1920–70

The second period discussed in this chapter (1920–70), was characterized by growing state intervention and a shrinking role for private financial markets, especially the stock market, as sources of funding for the Chilean economy.

As noted previously, Rajan and Zingales identified this trend as a global phenomenon, pointing to protectionism and close relationships between elites and the state as important drivers. These elements were present in Chile. Trade barriers climbed between 1923 and 1973 although they had already been moving up previously. Several regulations restricted financial development, and the state took on a key role in resource allocation, both through state credit institutions' operations (later merged in the state bank) and Chile's Development Agency (Corporación de Fomento de la Producción, CORFO by its Spanish acronym) activities. The stock exchange virtually vanished as a source of funds for new (or existing) companies and stock exchange transaction volume dropped sharply.[33]

A. Protectionism, Financial Repression and the Business State

After the end of World War I there were growing challenges for the nitrate industry, which was both technologically backward and faced new competition from the artificial nitrates being produced by the European chemical industry. The Chilean government assumed a greater role in production and marketing. Tariffs were used not only as a protection mechanism, but also as a means to offset falling state revenues from this industry.

During this period, the government established a number of institutions to promote economic activities. As a result, Chile's public sector replaced private banks as the leading source of credit. By the late 1960s, the state bank and other public and semi-public agencies controlled over 70 percent of Chile's credit.[34] In an economy riddled with high inflation and restrictions on nominal interest rates, private banks also avoided long-term contracts, making state agencies the sole providers of long-term loans.

B. CORFO and the Entrepreneurial State

The next phase in the state's involvement in Chile's economy started with the founding of CORFO in 1939.[35] The law that created it intended for it 'to design a plan for national production development'. CORFO quickly became a central agent in the Chilean economy, lending to private sector borrowers, serving as an investment bank, engaging in research and development activities, and starting new, state-owned companies. Through CORFO, the state got systematically involved, for the first time, in the development of new companies, keeping its control over them and initiating the 'entrepreneurial state'.[36]

Between 1939 and 1943, CORFO invested in 53 companies (both start-ups and existing ones) that focused on manufacturing, mining, agriculture and energy. Measured as a percentage of equity, CORFO's stake averaged 46.8 percent, and, in 23 of these 53 companies, CORFO held a majority of the voting shares.[37]

Even though all of these companies were corporations, CORFO sometimes controlled 100 percent of their equity. CORFO created some companies as joint ventures with foreign investors, while with others CORFO transferred its shares to private investors once the companies proved profitable, and CORFO retained a minority interest. CORFO also promoted mergers among competing companies, increasing market concentration.

State intervention grew even stronger in the second half of the 1960s. A 1965 CORFO document states that 'the State deems it crucial to own the largest national companies'.[38] The government also acquired a majority stake in copper mining, which had been under foreign control since the turn of the century. In 1970, there were 68 companies partially or totally controlled by the state (either through direct ownership or through CORFO).[39]

At first, Chile's private sector disliked the state's involvement in companies' creation (and ownership) because it feared this engagement would curtail investment opportunities for private investors. Yet this initial suspicion soon gave way to support.[40] In a survey conducted in the late 1950s, 45 out of 46 executives viewed CORFO's role as 'positive' or 'very positive'.[41] Other surveys in the 1960s revealed similar opinions, showing overall support for the state's intervention in Chile's economy: 80 percent of trade union leaders supported the state's economic planning efforts, and 75 percent of them agreed with protective tariffs and subsidies.[42]

This shift in perception may be attributed to the private sector's newly acquired ability to influence public policy formulation, as a result of its inclusion on the boards at CORFO and other institutions, such as Chile's Central Bank, state-owned credit unions, as well as in official offices (both in the Executive Branch and in Congress). Business associations collaborated with the government to draft laws and served as cartel managers.[43] SOFOFA usually reviewed members' new investment plans to determine whether Chile's market would be able to absorb new production levels.[44]

The state's role in business before 1970 shows its involvement in company creation and funding, supported by policies that limited the entry of newcomers. Major business associations largely supported these protectionist and state intervention policies, and these associations became influential in local decision-making.

C. Business Groups, 1920–70

The first study on groups' structure and impact on Chile's economy came with Ricardo Lagos' study published in 1961. Lagos used the connections among directors to isolate business groups and identified 11 major groups – most of which revolved around banks.[45] After this book, business groups became more ubiquitous in academic and public policy discussions.[46] In 1966, the government submitted a bill to Congress to amend Chile's corporate law, including limitations on directors' service on multiple boards and other provisions intended to reduce business groups' influence.

Three hypotheses have been used to explain the origin and development of business groups in Chile's economy. The first one makes the case for market failure, concluding that business groups emerged and grew as mechanisms to overcome credit shortages and rationing in the 1950s.[47] A second hypothesis by Garretón and Cisternas argued that the 1960s marked the emergence of 'modern' groups.[48] While they recognize that since the nineteenth century some families controlled companies in a large number of industries, they also note that there were two significant changes in corporate governance in those years: (1) maximizing 'group' income became the foremost goal (rather than individual companies' profitability), and (2) operations were coordinated among companies belonging to one group. These authors suggest that these two features had been absent in previous decades.

The third hypothesis, which Schneider introduced, links the emergence and growth of business groups with state policies.[49] This author posits that different types of economic policies, regarding both industrial and macroeconomic issues, made a different impact on group creation and development. Based on this, it may be concluded that the 1920–70 period, characterized by high inflation, macroeconomic instability and protectionist policies, favored the development of this organizational form in particular.

As indicated in section II(C), several family conglomerates already displayed in business some group characteristics in the nineteenth century. The subsequent growth of such groups can be seen in the cases of Gibbs & Co., a business house, and Baburizza, a group based on family and ethnic relations.

Gibbs & Co. was the Chilean affiliate of Anthony Gibbs & Sons, a firm established in London in 1808 and in Chile in 1826. In the nineteenth century, it was the largest copper broker and held significant nitrate interests as well.[50] During the first half of the twentieth century, Gibbs & Co. held stakes in a large number of companies in several industries (nitrates, insurance, mills, winemaking, chemicals), and it was also a minority investor in companies where its Chilean affiliate's executives served as board members.[51] The firm's presence in Chile dwindled over the years and by the late 1960s its role was reduced to trade agent, with no significant investments in other companies.[52]

The second example was the group of companies which Pascual Barburizza and his associates controlled. Born in Croatia in 1875, Barburizza arrived in Chile in 1892 to work in the saltpeter provinces. He started trading cattle and later purchased nitrate lands. By 1920, he held substantial stakes in nitrate businesses, farming outfits and a commercial bank, sitting on the boards of 21 companies (and serving as chairman of five). A small group of executives, many of them of Croatian origin, served in administrative positions and on boards for several companies, which, in turn, coordinated their operations, with maximization of the group's overall value as their primary goal. Baburizza sold his stake in nitrate operations in 1928 and died in 1941, leaving no direct heirs.[53]

These examples show that, during the first half of the twentieth century, both family-owned and foreign companies acted as business groups, using individuals to coordinate decisions across several companies as a result of their involvement on multiple boards. The fact that it is possible to identify business groups back to a time preceding banking constraints and the state's increased role in resource allocation, raises questions for hypotheses that underscore such factors when explaining the existence of such groups. The existence during the early twentieth century of structures that resemble today's business groups is consistent with the survival of this organizational format during economic liberalization.

Questions remain as to how these business groups operated in that period. For instance, the relationship between business groups and the state still needs further study. The period of 1940–70 featured strong state intervention in resource allocation and active industrial policies. Did these policies especially favor business groups? Comparisons of performance between the companies within business groups and stand-alone firms remain largely unexplored. In addition, as will be shown below, there are some differences between these earlier business groups from the ones that would later play a relevant role in Chile's economy. The use of pyramidal schemes, common in Chile after 1973, was rare before 1960. Also, highly concentrated ownership in companies belonging to a group was less common than it is today. This difference may be attributed to a less active capital market in earlier decades, with lower competition for corporate control, allowing controlling stakes to be reduced without significant risk of takeover by other agents. Prior to 1960 there was scant competition for corporate control. The controlling groups in industrial companies seen in the early 1960s' data are similar to those Henry Kirsh found using data from the 1930s.[54] While the following section provides longitudinal data on stock ownership stakes from 1930 to 1950, further research is also needed to delve fully into this issue.

D. Capital Market, Ownership and Control in 1920–70

Capital market and corporate funding

While the number of companies listed grew from 1930 through to 1970, in practical terms only a few of these companies traded actively on a regular basis. In 1960, share turnover in Chile's 50 largest companies did not reach 5 percent. After 1980, share turnover was on average three times as high.[55]

As shown earlier in Table 2.1, corporations did not issue new stock to raise funds. Companies preferred instead to use their own funds (as dividends paid greater taxes, companies distributed earnings through shares) and loans (mostly with the state as agent). A study on Chilean companies' funding mechanisms shows that, from 1949 to 1960, stock issuance only accounted for 4.5 percent of overall funding.[56]

Ownership and control patterns

This section discusses the evolution of Chilean companies' ownership patterns in the period 1930–50. A large number of studies have analysed Chile's corporate ownership patterns from 1960 onwards, but few have looked at earlier periods. This present study uses a custom-built database that utilizes the shareholder lists published by every company, available at Santiago's National Library in Chile. Information from secondary sources complemented this data.[57] The ownership structure of publicly-traded companies has been calculated for 1930, 1943 and 1950 (the 50 largest companies with information available were chosen for each year.) The information collected accounts for a 62.8 percent average share of the market capitalization in that period.[58] Table 2.2 presents this data. Table 2.3 presents the data for the largest five shareholders (C5 index).

Table 2.4 shows the number of companies under foreign investors' control, those controlled by pyramid schemes, and companies that could be categorized as dispersed ownership firms in 1930, 1942 and 1950.[59] In those three benchmark years, foreign equity companies accounted for 25 percent of all companies included in the sample.[60]

Table 2.4 reveals that dispersed ownership companies were rare in Chile during this period. They were more common in the financial sector (particularly, two of the largest banks did not have a dominant

Table 2.2 Corporate ownership patterns in Chile, 1930–1950

	1930	1943	1950
Largest stockholder (%)	22	22.4	19.1
Five largest stockholders combined (%)	45	47	40
Herfindahl index	0.11	0.11	0.08
Number of companies	50	50	50
Share of market value (%)	64.5	71.1	52.7

Source: Author's research.

Table 2.3 Ownership patterns in Chile, 1930–1950: C5 index by industry

	1930		1943		1950	
Industry	Firms	Concentration (%)	Firms	Concentration (%)	Firms	Concentration (%)
Financial services	7	29	5	24.7	6	27.1
Natural resources	7	46	6	50.8	5	43.2
Mining	6	43.5	6	62.3	3	34.5
Manufacturing	12	52	13	40.4	12	43.1
Textile	3	46.2	4	36	6	31.8
Metallurgy	3	59	8	44.5	9	34.9
Utilities	7	33	3	15.4	3	35.8
Other	5	60	5	50.7	5	42.3

Source: Author's research.

shareholder), which explains why, despite their reduced number, these companies boasted a larger share of market capitalization. Pyramidal structures, which involve control over a greater number of companies with fewer resources than those needed to control each company in isolation through a chain of ownership relations, were also not widespread in Chile until 1950.[61] In each benchmark year, companies with a pyramidal ownership structure accounted for less than 15 percent of the companies included in the sample, and less than 10 percent of the overall market capitalization. Moreover, in most cases pyramidal control was the result of vertical integration rather than a drive for control diversification. For instance, Viña del Mar's sugar refinery was the majority stockholder in the city of Viña del Mar's port, and Compañía de Cervecerías Unidas was the majority shareholder in Cristalerías Chile – its largest bottle supplier.[62]

The absence of pyramidal structures is consistent with the 'lack of corporate competition' hypothesis. Indeed, because they faced no risk

Table 2.4 Ownership patterns in Chile, 1930–1950: pyramids, foreign control and dispersed ownership

	1930		1943		1950	
	Firms	Value share (%)	Firms	Value share (%)	Firms	Value share (%)
Pyramid scheme[1]	3	1	5	7	6	4
Foreign control	12	14	10	25	11	22
Dispersed ownership	5	22	6	19	7	26
Number of companies	50		50		50	

Note: 1. Pyramid scheme: companies controlled by another private company. Foreign control: companies whose majority stockholders are foreign banks or investors (holding at least 10 percent of shares). Dispersed ownership: companies where no single stockholder owns more than 10 percent of all shares.

Source: Author's research.

of takeover, business groups were able to maximize the number of companies they controlled without having to use their resources to secure a controlling stake in each and every company.

E. Laws and Capital Market in 1920–70

Between 1850 and 1920, Chile's legislation did not include any protection for minority shareholders or systematic oversight for corporations. In contrast, there was greater state control over corporations between 1920 and 1970. In 1920, the 'Corporate Regulations' were approved,[63] which mandated more detailed requirements for the contents of corporate by-laws.[64]

In 1928, a specialized regulatory agency was created.[65] In 1931 this merged with the insurance company regulatory agency to create Chile's Insurance, Corporation and Stock Exchange Commission.[66] It was mandated to oversee insurance companies' business, control stock market operations, and monitor corporations from their inception to their liquidation. This signaled a major change for the role of the state in supervising corporations compared to previously. The commission could review documents and request additional balance sheets or any other information it needed for oversight purposes. In addition, it reported to state credit institutions on the financial status of companies requesting loans. The commission was also entitled to join shareholders' meetings, convene special meetings and declare board agreements invalid if meetings failed to comply with the requirements of the law. It could also impose fines and serve as arbitrator in disputes involving shareholders and managers, which meant that the state had a platform to influence corporate decision-making. Most regulatory and supervisory institutions created in 1931 remained in force for the following 50 years with only minor amendments.

Board composition was a key issue in a bill on corporate governance introduced in 1966. The purpose of this reform was to remedy the alleged lack of representation of small investors. The new law intended to increase the commission's powers, expanding its role in the approval of new corporations, and raising fines. In addition, new rules were introduced for the selection of board members in order to reduce the number of interlocking boards. Right-wing political parties and business associations opposed the bill,[67] which Congress debated from 1966 to 1970, but finally approved in June 1970.[68] In addition to greater powers for the commission, the law imposed further restrictions on board members, and limited to three the number of boards on which individuals could serve. It also restricted cross-company stock ownership and set a mandatory dividend of at least 30 percent of earnings.

IV. CAPITAL MARKET AND CORPORATE GOVERNANCE IN 1970–2005

President Salvador Allende, elected in 1970, increased state involvement throughout the economy. The government seized control of a large number of private companies, either through acquisition (in the stock market or by direct negotiations with large shareholders) or by expropriation. By 1973, the state had nearly complete control of the banking sector and directly or indirectly controlled over 570 companies, including 71 out of the 100 corporations with the greatest market value as of December 1970. After a military coup ousted Allende on 11 September 1973, the generals who led the coup turned most companies over to private hands and implemented a number of pro-market reforms, including reducing and streamlining tariffs, removing price controls and lifting most restrictions on financial operations.[69]

A. Business Groups in Chile's Liberalization Period and the Role of Privatizations

The role of Chilean business groups after 1973 has attracted many studies.[70] It is useful to separate groups into three categories for the purpose of this analysis: (1) bank-based 'financial' groups; (2) groups focusing on exports, with interests in fixed asset-intensive operations, such as mining and forestry; and (3) import substitution-oriented groups.[71] The development of business groups, especially between 1973 and 1990, was closely linked to the privatization process that began after the coup. This process was divided into two stages: the first, spanning from 1973 to 1978, returned companies acquired or seized by state agencies to private owners, while, in the second round, utility companies and firms created by CORFO were privatized.

In the first round, the government returned companies that had been expropriated (325 firms) to their owners, and sold in installments through public auctions the companies that CORFO had acquired (207).[72] A comparison of major business groups in 1978 and 1970 reveals that the largest ones survived and regrouped after Allende's administration was overthrown. However, liberalization policies did not prove neutral for business groups. Chile's market opening policies had a negative impact on import-substituting groups, especially those in the textile and metal industries, and benefited those groups that focused on natural resource exports and had close ties to the financial sector. Swift privatization in a credit-restricted economy provided business groups that revolved around banks with significant advantages when it came to acquiring companies.[73] These groups continued to grow as a result of the intensive use of pyramidal structures and loans among associated companies.

The Vial and Cruzat-Larraín groups experienced the greatest expansion between 1973 and 1980. In 1970, these groups combined controlled ten public corporations that accounted for 6.2 percent of Chile's overall market capitalization. Ten years later, as Table 2.5 shows, they collectively controlled 33 public corporations, which accounted for 39.3 percent of Chile's stock market capitalization. Including private and limited liability companies, these two groups each controlled over 60 companies. Their scope was vast and included banks, mutual funds, insurance companies, operations involving natural resources, such as mining, forestry and fishing outfits, as well as consumer manufacturing and non-financial services.[74]

These two groups had high debt levels, a sizable portion of which was denominated in foreign currency. Loans to affiliated companies were also commonplace.[75] They also used resources raised through mutual fund operations to invest in associated companies' debt and stock. As a result, Chile's crisis and currency devaluation in June 1982 hit these groups particularly hard. The banks at the top of these pyramidal structures were on the verge of bankruptcy. In January 1983, the government rescued and seized control of eight financial institutions, including the banks at the apex of both the Vial and Cruzat-Larraín groups. As a result of this intervention, the state took over several companies that had been privatized in the second half of the 1970s, creating what was known locally as 'the strange area'.

Table 2.5 *Business groups in Chile: public corporations and their stock market value, 1980–2012*

Business group	1980		1990		2000		2012	
	Firms	Value share (%)	Firms	Value share (%)	Firms	Value share (%)	Firms	Value share (%)
Angelini	10	4.3	11	15.9	9	11.4	6	8.9
Matte	10	7.7	10	17.2	10	6.4	7	7.3
Luksic	8	1.3	8	3.2	11	5.4	7	7.1
Cruzat-Larraín	18	23.5	2	0.7	3	0.2	2	0.9
Vial	15	15.7	–	–	–	–	–	–
Enersis			4	11.2	9	14.1	5	10.9
Claro	5	4.7	5	5.0	7	2.6	6	0.7
CGE			2	3.3	6	4.4	8	1.6

Source: Based on information issued by Santiago's Stock Exchange and Chile's Securities and Insurance Commission.

A new privatization round started in 1984, when the government sold off such 'strange area' companies first, and then moved on to utilities. Nitrate and steel companies were privatized as well. This process paved the way for a number of changes in Chile's corporate sector.

The Chilean business groups that survived the crisis, which were mostly those that focused on exports and boasted low indebtedness, actually benefited from currency devaluation measures. The sale of 'strange area' companies in 1984–85 enabled them to expand, thus becoming the largest conglomerates in Chile's economy.

The two largest private banks were sold to small investors, which dispersed their ownership. This process was known as 'popular capitalism' and included tax benefits and credit facilities for stock buyers. The same method was used to sell some of the privatized utility companies.[76] Employees at these and other utility companies received incentives intended to help them purchase shares. In some cases, these buyers became the largest stockholder bloc in some companies.[77]

Additionally, this second privatization round brought new business groups to the scene. These groups did not involve families; rather, the executives of privatized firms built them and later expanded their operations to include other domestic industries and foreign markets. However, unlike earlier, family-owned groups (that tended to last longer), these new groups had a much faster lifecycle.

The organizational structure of business groups also changed. After the

1982 crisis, Chile's banking law was amended to curtail bank investments in shares of, and loans to, affiliated institutions, in addition to introducing loan diversification requirements.[78] As a result, Chilean banks ceased to hold a central position in business groups. Nonetheless, pyramidal structures remained in place, with investment companies replacing banks at the top.

As Table 2.5 indicates, while business groups have undergone changes in size (and while some have come and gone), they remained Chile's predominant organizational form, as elsewhere in Latin America.[79] In 2012, Chile's three largest family groups controlled 23.3 percent of its stock market capitalization.

Strategies and performance of business groups

How did business groups fare in the new economic landscape after Chile's liberalization? Economic theory would suggest that financial market liberalization and development should reduce the role of larger, more diversified groups, as their comparative advantages dwindle.[80] However, as discussed earlier, Chile's experience in the 1970s proves otherwise. In order to analyze Chilean business groups' response to liberalization policies, Table 2.6 calculates a diversification index using the Herfindhal index over paid capital and reserves in every industry.[81] To avoid double-counting issues, pyramid effects have been deleted, and calculations have excluded investment partnerships whose sole assets were shares in other companies. In every case, groups' overall shares are considered, including both direct and indirect investments.[82] Table 2.6 below shows the results of these calculations.

This table shows that the largest groups' (Vial and Cruzat-Larraín) had the highest diversification in 1980. All other groups consolidated after 1990, focusing their operations in one or two core industries. Additionally,

Table 2.6 Business groups' industry diversification, 1980–2012

	1980	1985	1990	1995	2000	2005	2012
Angelini	0.53	0.59	0.34	0.44	0.5	0.54	0.57
Matte	0.52	0.75	0.78	0.83	0.66	0.43	0.42
Luksic	0.30	0.35	0.29	0.25	0.37	0.33	0.31
Cruzat-Larraín	0.29	–	–	–	–	–	–
Vial	0.25	–	–	–	–	–	–
CGE	1	1	0.69	0.63	0.55	0.83	2.6

Source: Based on information issued by Santiago's Stock Exchange and Chile's Securities and Insurance Commission.

while it was common before 1990 for larger groups to hold minority stakes in many companies, these investments have shrunk, as groups have increased the size of their interests in the companies they control.[83] Furthermore, business groups have expanded overseas in the areas where they have more expertise. Some emerging groups have chosen to expand their core businesses overseas rather than diversifying their operations in Chile.[84]

It is informative to compare the performance of group-owned companies versus stand-alone businesses. Studies conducted in the 1970s showed that companies owned by business groups boasted greater operating margins and a higher return on equity.[85] However, recent studies, based on data from 1988 through 1996, reveal that belonging to a diversified group proves beneficial only if its diversification exceeds a certain limit – that is, only companies belonging to large, fully diversified groups see a positive impact on their results.[86]

Additionally, research suggests that the market consistently values more highly those companies that have close control over cash flows.[87] Similarly, the number of independent board members has a positive impact on companies' valuations.[88] One study has found that the impact of family ownership on results depends on its concentration: low family ownership concentration raises the value of a company, while the opposite is true in more concentrated companies.[89]

In conclusion then, starting in the 1990s, Chilean business groups have moved towards specialization, and globalized in areas where they enjoy comparative advantages, forgoing the formerly preferred domestic diversification strategy that large groups pursued before the debt crisis. Furthermore, studies of competitive performance show that competitive advantages drawn from group affiliation have dwindled. This fact is consistent with the hypothesis that posits that the value to companies of belonging to a business group tends to disappear when capital markets develop more fully.

B. Capital Market and Corporate Control, 1970–2012

The trend of falling stock market transaction volume and market capitalization that began in 1920 became more pronounced in 1970–73.[90] As shown in Figures 2.1 and 2.2, the impact of reforms introduced after 1973 on the stock market was clear, raising ratios of both equity transactions and stock market capitalization to GDP.

It should be noted that it was not until 1980 that the stock market capitalization to GDP ratio returned to its 1920 level. The reforms also had an impact on the composition of stock market value by industry.

Table 2.7 Ownership schemes in Chile, 1985–2012

	1985	1995	2005	2012
Largest stockholder (%)	40.9	43.4	52.9	44.2
Five largest stockholders combined (%)	65.1	68.2	79.1	69.9
Herfindahl index	0.27	0.27	0.26	0.29
Number of companies	51	65	74	95
Share of market value (%)	67.1	69.3	74.3	97.32

Source: Author's research.

Import-substituting sectors, like the textile and metal industries, took a back seat to companies that focused on natural resource exploitation. After the second round of privatization, utilities and energy companies took the lead in stock market values. In more recent years, retailing has joined the most dynamic market sectors, in terms of both the number of companies listed on the stock exchange in that sector and their market value.

As equity financing became an attractive funding source, companies turned to the stock market to raise funds, and the number of companies using initial public offerings (IPOs) to access resources and diversify their ownership base also grew. This increase in use of the stock market though did not go hand in hand with a change in ownership structure. Indeed, concentrated ownership continues to prevail in Chile's economy. Table 2.7 shows statistics for the largest 100 companies listed on the stock exchange for the benchmark years of 1985, 1995, 2005 and 2012.

The increases in ownership concentration compared to 1950 are quite clear. In fact, instead of dropping, ownership concentration seemed to have risen across all industries. This is confirmed by Table 2.8.

This increase came during a period when Chilean legislation reinforced the rights of minority investors. The persistence of high concentration in equity ownership, even during periods of liberalization and enhanced investor protection, is a phenomenon found in all of Latin America.[91]

Table 2.9 shows the number of foreign, pyramidal and dispersed ownership companies in 1985, 1995, 2005 and 2012 for the largest 100 corporations.[92]

This table reveals the significance of pyramid structures in Chilean corporate ownership. In December 2012, one-third of the 100 companies in the sample were part of a pyramidal structure, and this share has remained stable over the past ten years. When compared to the figures in Table 2.4, the increase in this type of organizational form is clear. Despite the strong

Table 2.8 Ownership schemes in Chile, 1985–2005: C5 index by industry

Industry	1985		1995		2005		2012	
	Firms	Concentration(%)	Firms	Concentration(%)	Firms	Concentration(%)	Firms	Concentration(%)
Financial services	11	55.8	10	66.4	11	81.4	12	78.2
Natural resources	8	60.9	5	75.5	7	77.6	8	73.1
Mining and metallurgy	8	57.7	7	61.4	6	74.8	5	63.8
Manufacturing	16	69.4	17	77.5	15	78.1	14	77.5
Investments	4	68.9	9	55.3	15	81.9		
Retail			2	50.5	5	59.2	6	69.2
Utilities	3	80.3	12	71.1	13	87.1	15	79.3
Other	2	69.7	2	73.9	5	74.8		

Source: Author's research.

Table 2.9 Ownership schemes in Chile, 1985–2012: pyramids, foreign control and dispersed ownership

	1985		1995		2005		2012	
	Firms	Value share (%)	Firms	Value share (%)	Firms	Value share (%)	Firms	Value share (%)
Pyramid scheme	28	30	39	57	39	47	34	47
Foreign control	10	10	13	13	36	36	24	29
Dispersed ownership	8	4	3	5	–	–	1	1
Number of companies	100		100		100		100	

Source: Author's research.

presence of pyramidal structures, it should be noted that most groups maintain cash flow rights over the limit required to keep control.[93]

It is also clear that dispersed ownership companies are even rarer in Chile's economy today than they were between 1930 and 1950. In December 2012, only one of the top 100 firms listed on the stock market could be characterized as a dispersed ownership company. This phenomenon may be attributed to higher concentration in the financial sector, where business groups and/or foreign investors seized banks sold during the 'popular capitalism' period. Foreign ownership in Chilean companies has also increased. Foreign investments have been particularly significant in utilities and financial services. In 2012, for 24 of the 100 largest public corporations, foreign investors controlled either directly or indirectly over 50 percent of all voting shares. At the same time, the engagement of foreign investors as minority shareholders has increased as a result of the use of American depositary receipts (ADRs).

C. Laws, Investor Protection and Pension Funds

Starting in 1973, a number of reforms introduced significant changes in Chile's economy. However, corporate laws did not change until 1980 when the Securities and Insurance Commission was created.[94] By law, its goal was to 'maintain public trust and guarantee market transparency'. This statement signaled a change from the objectives that the law, stressing direct oversight, assigned to the regulatory agency in 1931.

In 1981, Chile's Corporations Law was amended, and a new law was passed to regulate its stock market.[95] The new legislation assigned a greater supervisory role to the market, highlighting corporations' reporting duties (especially for those with securities on public offer). It also eliminated the requirement for government authorization for new corporations (which dated back to Chile's first Corporations Law, enacted in 1854). Stronger mechanisms were instituted to protect minority shareholders from expropriation, like increasing the quorum required for strategic decisions, incorporating exit rights and reducing the quorum required to convene special shareholders' meetings. These changes reflected a shift in the notion of supervision. Instead of direct government control over corporations, this new framework relied on the market as an oversight agent.

Another significant change hinged on the social security reform in 1980, which replaced the public pay-as-you-go pension system with individual capital accounts managed by private companies called pension fund managers (AFP, for its Spanish acronym).[96] The law declared that pension funds could not be actively involved in the management of the companies in which they were invested and that they had to vote for independent board members. This turned pension funds into stakeholders who had an interest in improving the standards to protect minority investors and also created incentives for companies to enhance their corporate governance practices in order to lure these investors.[97]

Le-Fort and Walker studied the link between economic shocks and changes in rules and regulation from 1967 to 1990. They argued that legal and regulatory changes in Chile followed a 'time-dependent' pattern, with most regulatory changes being introduced in the wake of economic crises. The Enersis public offering that Endesa Spain made in 1997 illustrates how sensitive Chilean legislation is to unexpected shocks or corporate scandals. This deal revealed that Chilean law did not include protection mechanisms for minority investors in public offerings, which fueled a debate over the use of share series and voting rights in corporations.[98] As a result, new regulations were introduced for public security offerings,[99] instituting the non-discrimination principle and safeguarding minority shareholders' rights in these events.

The law changed other corporate governance mechanisms as well, introducing an audit committee to consist mostly of independent board members that would supervise transactions among affiliated companies. A larger number of corporate officers were given fiduciary duties, and sanctions were increased. In 2009, as part of the legal reforms required to enable Chile to join the Organisation for Economic Co-operation and Development (OECD), new changes were made to the corporate law.[100]

V. CONCLUDING REMARKS

This chapter has provided a historical overview of major corporate governance trends in Chile. Following Rajan and Zingales, it identifies three distinct periods. The first period, from the mid-nineteenth century to 1920, was characterized by laissez-faire policies, with little government intervention. Despite the lack of legal rights for minority investors, entrepreneurs used corporations as a mechanism to raise funds in support of several operations, including mining, manufacturing and utilities, which in turn drove the development of a stock market in Chile.

Between 1920 and 1973, wars and the Great Depression severely shook Chile's economy. The impact of these external shocks on the institutional development of Chile's capital market was amplified because some groups already had enough power to influence and benefit from protectionist policies. This period featured increased state intervention, as the government created new companies, funded existing ones, promoted mergers and granted loans. Against this backdrop, capital markets played no significant role and the period between 1920 and 1973 saw a drop in stock market transactions and capitalization.

The economics literature posits that competitive pressures may force incumbents to stop supporting protectionism and financial repression, which in turn promotes market development. In Chile this process unfolded as a result of the political shock of the 1973 military coup. This event triggered a new set of economic policies. The key lesson learned from Chile's experience is that a swift privatization program, implemented without a large enough investor pool or a suitable institutional framework, may lead to corporate governance failings and extreme wealth concentration. In the 1970s, privatization enabled highly debt-dependent business groups to expand, but these groups eventually succumbed to massive financial distress during the early 1980s.

After this crisis, a new privatization program was launched. Based on Chile's past experience, efforts were made to diversify the ownership base and more stringent regulations were introduced in the banking system. In recent years, new measures have focused on enhancing transparency and protection for minority investors. As a result of several legal reforms, Chile now boasts high scores in legal protection for investors and creditors. Chilean companies have also leaned towards international standards, especially because some of the largest firms are listed in international markets.

Nonetheless, streamlined laws and regulations do not necessarily imply streamlined ownership structures. Dispersed ownership companies were still as rare (and even rarer) in Chile in 2012 as they were in 1950; pyramidal structures still control a sizable number of companies, and nearly all publicly listed companies in Chile have a single stockholder (either a family, a company or a foreign investor) with voting shares to choose most of the board. Similarly, as is the case in most Latin American countries, business groups continue to be the prevailing organizational form in the corporate sector. While the liberalization measures adopted after 1973 introduced significant institutional changes, the business group organizational form has proven to be resilient to such shifts, despite the fact that the process of creation and exit has become much faster in recent decades.

NOTES

1. La Porta (1999); Morck, Wolfenzon and Yeung (2005).
2. Morck and Steier (2005).
3. While there were several public and private initiatives to introduce banks, none proved successful, and loans were usually provided by merchant houses. See Cavieres (1988).
4. Rajan and Zingales (2003).
5. Except during wars, tariffs remained low as compared to the rest of Latin American countries. See Coatsworth and Williamson (2004).
6. Khanna and Yafeh (2007). These authors view 'groups' origin and creation' and their 'evolution and dynamics' as two topics largely neglected by current literature.
7. Rector (1985).
8. Cavieres (1988).
9. In terms of export volumes, agriculture competed with mining until the mid-nineteenth century, but the impact of farming on business activity and organization was minimal. See Bauer (1975).
10. Nazer (2000).
11. Ortega (2005).
12. After independence, Chile adopted the Bilbao Regulations, a 1737 Spanish compilation of laws, as the bulk of its commercial legislation. These Regulations only included simple and limited partnerships.
13. Research by the author on Law and Executive Order Bulletins (1854–77), as well as the Official Gazette (1878–1902).
14. Couyoumdjian, Millar and Tocornal (1992).
15. See corporate by-laws of 'Unión Comercial' (1872), *Boletín de Leyes y Decretos del Gobierno*, 941–4 and 'Asociación Comercial de Valparaíso' (1872), *Boletín de Leyes y Decretos del Gobierno*, 1073–7. Santiago's Stock Exchange was created in 1893, and the Valparaíso Broker Exchange was created in 1898.
16. All stock market capitalization figures in this section have been calculated by the author. For more on sources and methodologies, see Islas (2007).
17. Franks, Hannes and Mayer (2006). See also Aganin and Volpin (2003).
18. Cavieres (1984). This author studies the ownership structure of corporations incorporated in Valparaíso in 1861–80, revealing that a significant share may be categorized as having dispersed ownership. See also Ortega (2005), who includes subscriber lists for mining and manufacturing companies.
19. Oppenheimer (1982).
20. Chilean laws did not require a minimum number of shareholders for corporations.
21. Franks, Hannes and Mayer (2006) found that the number of shareholders in German corporations averaged 22.
22. This figure does not factor in voting rule effects. As voting scales and maximum voting limits were common at the time the actual required number was higher.

23. Islas (2007): 120–2.
24. This phenomenon was also present in other Latin American countries. See Musacchio (2009).
25. Palma (1985). See also Kirsch (1977).
26. Culver and Reinhart (1985) describe the causes underlying this decline. Copper mining did re-emerge in the early twentieth century, but under the control of American interests.
27. Kirsch (1977): 181–96.
28. Corporations Act (1 August 1854).
29. Even when the government authorization requirement was removed in most European countries (and in Latin America), Chile's government kept this attribute until 1980.
30. Commercial Code (23 November 1865).
31. La Porta and Shleifer (2008).
32. Islas (2007): 116–29.
33. Market transaction average values in 1960–69 amounted to only 12 percent of the 1920–29 transaction average.
34. Superintendencia de Bancos (n.d.).
35. Act 6.334 (29 April 1939).
36. Arriagada and Muñoz (1977).
37. Muñoz and Arriagada (1977): Appendix.
38. CORFO (1965).
39. Hachette and Luders (1992). This figure does not include companies where CORFO held a minority stake.
40. Muñoz (1977).
41. Lauterbach (1960).
42. Johnson (1967).
43. Cavarozzi (1975); Menges (1966).
44. Schneider (2004).
45. Lagos (1961).
46. Dahse (1984).
47. Lefort and Walker (2000a).
48. Garretón and Cisternas (1970).
49. Schneiderstate (2009). While, in this chapter, the author only mentions the Chilean case in passing, his overall analytical framework can be easily applied to it.
50. Gibbs & Co. operated as a limited corporation until 1948, when it became a corporation in Chile. According to its Articles of Incorporation, its London headquarters held a 91.4 percent share of its stock.
51. Rojas (1992).
52. Gibbs & Co. (1968), Annual Report.
53. Rojas (1990); Guzmán (1967).
54. Ratcliff and Zeitlin (1988).
55. Calculations made by the author, based on the Stock Exchange's annual reports. This lack of activity also affected brokers' business feasibility. Several brokers went bankrupt, and most had to reduce their headcount. See Tocornal (1994).
56. Instituto de Organización y Administración de Empresas (INSORA) (1962).
57. Garretón and Cisternas (1970); Kirsh (1977); Pacheco (1972); Ratliff and Zeitlin (1988).
58. Calculated as a simple average over 1930, 1943 and 1950. Table 2.2 provides more details on data composition and characteristics. For some companies, information for the previous or following year was used.
59. There is no consensus in the literature on how to operationalize the dispersed ownership notion. A 10 percent share is commonly used. In Chile, Zeitlin and Ratliff argue that, considering the ties among families, a high cut-off point may overestimate the number of dispersed ownership companies. For this research, I have characterized a dispersed ownership company as a firm where no shareholder holds more than a

10 percent stake. In turn, foreign companies are construed as having a foreign entity (either a firm, family or bank) as the largest stockholder, controlling more than 10 percent of its equity. In all cases, numbers are percentages are calculated on the basis of the total market capitalization for the 50-company sample.

60. This figure measures foreign equity in companies incorporated in Chile rather than the total number of foreign companies in Chile.
61. Almeida and Wolfenzon (2006).
62. Shareholders' lists of Compañía de Muelles, Población Vergara and Cristalerías Chile, in several years.
63. Decree 3,030 (22 December 1920) (publication date on the Official Gazette).
64. Rules were established to convene special meetings and to award rights to minority investors. These clauses were commonly included in corporate by-laws before Corporate Regulations were enacted.
65. Executive Decree No. 251 (20 May 1931).
66. Hereinafter 'the Commission'.
67. See *El Mercurio* editorials for 16 and 21 September 1966.
68. Law 17,308 (1 July 1970).
69. Silva (1996).
70. See Fazio (2005); Lefort and Walker (2000b); Abarca, Fuentes, Majluf and Rodríguez (1998); Sapelli (2002).
71. This classification is based on Silva (1996).
72. CORFO (1978).
73. As no foreign investors showed interest, access to credit became a significant advantage for groups based on financial institutions. Furthermore, using the stock of newly acquired companies as collateral for new acquisitions, these groups managed to quickly raise the number of companies under their control. See Hachette and Luders (1992).
74. See Dahse (1979) for a complete list.
75. Loans to associated companies accounted for over 40 percent of all placements at some banks owned by the largest groups. See de la Cuadra and Valdés (1990).
76. Valenzuela (1989).
77. Act 18,372 (12 December 1984).
78. Act 18,576 (27 November 1986).
79. Schneider (2008).
80. Khanna and Palepu (2000).
81. The following sectors have been included: retailing, construction, forestry and cellulose, mining, fishing, telecommunications, energy, light industries, heavy manufacturing industries, financial services, wines and others.
82. For example, in December 2005, the Matte family-owned business group held a direct 35.2 percent share of CMPC, as well as a 19.2 percent interest through PASUR (another public corporation where the Mattes held a 79.55 percent share). Therefore, the Matte family's overall share is calculated as: 35.2% + 19.2% x 79.55% = 50.03%.
83. This outcome is consistent with opinions shared by market analysts and group executives. See 'Estrategia', 11 May 2001, as well as Tarzijan and Rivera (2000).
84. The Matte group invested in forestry operations in Argentina, while the Luksic group invested in consumer products in Argentina and Peru. Emerging retail business groups such as Solari and Paulmann have expanded across South America as well.
85. González (1981).
86. Khanna and Palepu (2000).
87. Lefort and Walker (2005).
88. Lefort and Urzúa (2008).
89. Silva and Majluf (2008).
90. Most transactions between 1971 and 1973 were associated with the government's attempts to seize control of companies by having CORFO acquire shares. See Tocornal (1994).

91. Schneider (2008).
92. See Table 2.4 for definitions. In all cases, figures and percentages are calculated on the total market value of the 100 largest companies.
93. Lefort and Walker (2005). This phenomenon is consistent with international experiences. See Almeida and Wolfenzon (2006).
94. Executive Decree No. 3,538 (9 December 1980). It should be noted that some rules referring to board composition and directors' compensations introduced in 1970 were deleted or just ignored by the regulatory agency.
95. Law No. 18,045 and Law No. 18,046 (22 October 1981).
96. Executive Decree No. 3,500 (13 November 1980).
97. Gourevitch and Shinn (1999).
98. Agosín and Pasten (2003).
99. Law No. 19,705 (20 December 2000).
100. Law No. 20,382 (20 October 2009).

REFERENCES

Abarca, Nureya, Luis Fuentes, Nicolás Majluf and Darío Rodríguez (1998), 'Governance and ownership in Chilean economic groups', *ABANTE*, **1**, 111–39.

Aganin, Alexander and Paolo F. Volpin (2003), 'History of corporate ownership in Italy', Finance Working Paper 17, ECGI.

Agosín, Manuel and Ernesto Pasten (2003), 'Gobierno corporativo en Chile', Working paper 209, Banco Central de Chile.

Almeida, Héctor and Daniel Wolfenzon (2006), 'A theory of pyramidal ownership and family business groups', *Journal of Finance*, **61**, 2637–80.

Arriagada, Ana María and Oscar Muñoz (1977), 'Orígenes políticos y económicos del estado empresarial en Chile', *Estudios Cieplan*, **16**, 5–55.

Bauer, Arnold (1975), *Chilean Rural Society from the Spanish Conquest to 1930*, Cambridge: Cambridge University Press.

Cavarozzi, Marcelo (1975), 'The government and the industrial bourgeoisie in Chile 1938–1964', Ph.D. Dissertation, University of California.

Cavieres, Eduardo (1984), 'Estructura y funcionamiento de las sociedades comerciales de Valparaíso durante el siglo XIX (1820–1880)', *Cuadernos de Historia*, **4**, 61–86.

Cavieres, Eduardo (1988), *Comercio chileno y comerciantes ingleses 1820–1880: un ciclo de historia económica*, Valparaíso: Instituto de Historia, Universidad de Valparaíso.

Coatsworth, John and Jeffrey Williamson (2004), 'Always protectionist? Latin American tariffs from independence to great depression', *Journal of Latin American Studies*, **36**, 205–32.

CORFO (1965), *Instrumentos de política económica aplicados en el sector industrial*, Santiago de Chile: CORFO.

CORFO (1978), 'Privatización de Empresas y Activos 1973–1978', Santiago de Chile: CORFO, unpublished.

Couyoumdjian, Juan Ricardo, René Millar and Josefina Tocornal (1992), *Historia de la Bolsa de Comercio de Santiago 1893–1993*, Santiago de Chile: Bolsa de Comercio de Santiago.

Culver, William and Cornel Reinhart (1985), 'The decline of a mining region and mining policy: Chilean copper in the nineteenth century', in Thomas Greaves

and William Culver (eds), *Miners and Mining in the Americas*, Manchester: Manchester University Press, 68–81.
Dahse, Fernando (1979), *El mapa de la extrema riqueza*, Santiago de Chile: Aconcagua.
de la Cuadra, Sergio and Salvador Valdés (1990), 'Myths and facts about financial liberalization in Chile 1974–1982', Working Paper 128, Universidad Católica.
Fazio, Hugo (2005), *El mapa de la extrema riqueza al año 2005*, Santiago de Chile: LOM Ediciones.
Franks, Julián, Wagner Hannes and Colin Mayer (2006), 'The origins of the German corporation: finance, ownership and control', *Review of Finance*, **10** (4), 537–85.
Garretón, Oscar and Jaime Cisternas (1970), 'Algunas características del proceso de toma de decisiones en la gran empresa: la dinámica de la concentración', ODEPLAN, unpublished.
González, Jorge (1981), 'Evaluación social de la acción los grupos económicos en Chile', Escuela de Negocios de Valparaíso, unpublished.
Gourevitch, Peter and James Shinn (2005), *Political Power and Corporate Control*, Princeton: Princeton University Press.
Guzmán, Leonardo (1967), *Notas sobre la austera Vida de Don Pascual Baburizza S.: el carácter vigoroso de su raza, su acendrado patriotismo, su devoción al trabajo y su gratitud para Chile*, Santiago de Chile: Instituto Agrícola Baburizza.
Hachette, Dominique and Rolf Luders (1992), *La privatización en Chile*, Santiago de Chile: Centro Internacional para el Desarrollo Económico.
Iglesias, Augusto (1999), 'Pension reform and corporate governance: impact in Chile', *ABANTE*, **3**, 111–43.
INSORA (1962), *El financiamiento de la industria en Chile: análisis de fuentes y usos de fondos*, Santiago de Chile: INSORA.
Islas, Gonzalo (2007), 'Essays on corporate ownership and governance', Ph.D. Dissertation, University of California, 112–6.
Johnson, Dale (1967), 'Industrialization, social mobility and class formation in Chile', *Studies in Comparative International Development*, **3**, 127–51.
Khanna, Tarun and Krishna Palepu (2000), 'The future of business groups in emerging markets: long run evidence from Chile', *The Academy of Management Journal*, **43**, 268–85.
Khanna, Tarun and Yisnay Yafeh (2007), 'Business groups in emerging markets: paragons or parasites', *Journal of Economic Literature*, **55**, 331–72.
Kirsch, Henry (1977), *Industrial Development in a Traditional Society*, Gainesville: The University Presses of Florida.
Lagos, Ricardo (1961), *La concentración del poder económico en Chile*, Santiago de Chile: Editorial del Pacífico.
La Porta, Rafael, Florencio López de Silanes and Andrei Shleifer (1999), 'Corporate ownership around the world', *Journal of Finance*, **54**, 471–517.
La Porta, Rafael, Florencio López de Silanes and Andrei Shleifer (2008), 'Economic consequences of legal origins', *Journal of Economic Literature,* **46** (2), 285–332.
Lauterbach, Albert (1960), 'Las actitudes administrativas en Chile', unpublished.
Lefort, Fernando and Francisco Urzúa (2008), 'Board independence, firm performance and ownership concentration: evidence from Chile', *Journal of Business Research*, **61**, 615–22.
Lefort, Fernando and Eduardo Walker (2000a), 'The effects of economic and political shocks on corporate governance systems in Chile', *ABANTE*, **2** (2), 183–206.

Lefort, Fernando and Eduardo Walker (2000b), 'Ownership and capital structure of Chilean conglomerates: facts and hypothesis for governance', *ABANTE*, **3**, 3–27.

Lefort, Fernando and Eduardo Walker (2005), 'The effect of corporate governance practices on company market valuation and payout policy in Chile', Research Network Working paper n. R-5, IDB.

Majluf, Nicolás and Francisca Silva (2008), 'Does family ownership shape performance outcomes?', *Journal of Business Research,* **61**, 609–14.

Menges, Constantine (1966), 'Public policy and organized business in Chile: a preliminary analysis', *Journal of International Affairs*, **20**, 343–65.

Morck, Randall and Lloyd Steier (2005), 'The global history of corporate governance: an introduction', NBER Working Paper 11602.

Morck, Randall, Daniel Wolfenzon and Bernard Yeung (2005) 'Corporate governance, economic entrenchment and growth', *Journal of Economic Literature*, **43**, 657–722.

Muñoz, Oscar (1977), 'Industrialización y grupos de interés', *Apuntes Cieplan*, 7, 1–50.

Musacchio, Aldo (2009), *Experiments in Financial Democracy: Corporate Governance and Financial Development in Brazil, 1882–1950,* Cambridge: Cambridge University Press.

Nazer, Ricardo (2000), 'El surgimiento de una nueva elite empresarial en Chile: 1830–80', in Franco Bonelli and María Rosaria Stabili (eds), *Minoranze e culture imprenditoriali, Cile e Italia* XIX-XX, Rome: Carocci, pp. 68 and 71.

Oppenheimer, Robert (1982), 'National capital and national development: financing Chile's Central Valley railroads', *Business History Review* **56** (1), 54–75.

Ortega, Luis (2005), *Chile en ruta al Capitalismo. Cambio, euforia y depresión 1850–1880*, Santiago de Chile: LOM–DIBAM.

Pacheco, Luis (1972), 'La inversión extranjera y las corporaciones internacionales en el desarrollo industrial chileno', in Oscar Muñoz (ed.), *Proceso a la industrialización chilena*, Santiago de Chile: CEPLAN.

Palma, Gabriel (1985), 'External disequilibrium and internal industrialization: Chile 1914–1935', in Christopher Abel and Colin Lewis (eds), *Latin America: Economic Imperialism and the State*, London: Institute of Latin American Studies, 318–38.

Rajan, Raghuram and Luigi Zingales (2003), 'The great reversals: the politics of financial development in the 20th century', *Journal of Financial Economics*, **69**, 5–50.

Ratcliff, Richard and Maurice Zeitlin (1988), *Landlords and Capitalists: The Dominant Class of Chile*, Princeton: Princeton University Press.

Rector, John (1985), 'El impacto económico de la independencia de América Latina: el caso de Chile', *Historia,* **20**, 295–318.

Rojas, Gonzalo (1990), 'Los grupos económicos en Chile: una aproximación a su estudio, 1920–1940', M.A. Thesis, Universidad Católica de Chile.

Rojas, Gonzalo (1992), 'La casa comercial Gibbs y Co. y sus inversiones en Chile entre las décadas de 1920 y 1940', *Historia*, **26**, 259–95.

Sanfuentes, Andrés (1984), 'Los grupos económicos: control y políticas', *Estudios Cieplan*, **15**, 131–70.

Sapelli, Claudio (2002), 'Concentración y grupos económicos en Chile', *Estudios Públicos*, **88**, 67–95.

Schneider, Ben Ross (2004), *Business Politics and the State in Twentieth-Century Latin America*, Cambridge: Cambridge University Press.

Schneider, Ben Ross (2008), 'Economic liberalization and corporate governance: the resilience of business groups in Latin America', *Comparative Politics,* **40**, 379–97.

Schneider, Ben Ross (2009), 'A comparative political economy of diversified business groups, or how states organize big business', *Review of International Political Economy*, **16** (2), 178–201.

Silva, Eduardo (1996), *The State and Capital in Chile: Business Elites, Technocrats, and Market Economics*, Boulder: Westview Press.

Superintendencia de Bancos (n.d.), *Estadística Bancaria*, Santiago de Chile: State Department of Banks and Financial Institutions.

Tarzijan, Jorge and José Rivera (2000), 'Reasons for conglomeration: empirical analysis of management responses in Chile', *ABANTE*, **3** (2), 203–26.

Tocornal, Josefina (1994), *Mercado y corretaje de valores en Chile en la* época *del intervencionismo estatal: la Bolsa de Comercio de Santiago 1960–1975*, Chile: Universidad Católica de Chile.

Valenzuela, Mario (1989), 'Reprivatización y capitalismo popular en Chile', *Estudios Públicos*, **33**, 175–216.

3. Multinationals, business groups, and Chile's energy politics

Marcelo Bucheli[1]

This chapter studies the relationship between Chilean business groups, foreign oil multinationals, and Chile's energy politics between 1913 and 2005. The chapter employs Nathaniel Leff's definition of business groups as a 'multicompany firm which transacts in different markets . . . under a common administrative and financial control [where] participants are linked by relations of interpersonal trust, on the basis of similar personal, ethnic, commercial, background'.[2] Business groups have been crucial actors in the industrialization process of the major Latin American and Asian countries. They are characterized for having their roots in the family business, a diversified portfolio of investments in a wide variety of sectors (banking, manufacturing, and trade), and close relationship with policy makers.[3] In this chapter I show how business groups can become an important tool for industrializing net oil-importing countries aiming to increase domestic control of the oil industry, without expropriating foreign property. The Chilean state forced the multinationals to create a cartel with a domestic firm, and initially the foreign companies opposed this. In the long term, however, the multinational enterprises (MNEs) benefited from this arrangement because of the domestic firm's affiliation with the local business groups.

Having a well-connected firm in the cartel gave MNEs protection against hostile actions from the government, permitted them to have a partner with strong influence in the government, and gave legitimacy to the cartel (a kind of legitimacy hard to achieve if the cartel was solely in foreign hands). This arrangement collapsed when the local government abandoned its protectionist economic policy and industrial business groups lost their traditional political power.

The analysis proceeds in eight chronological stages based on the economic policies followed by the government. For each stage, the strategies followed by the Chilean state, the MNEs, and the domestic elite are discussed The two MNEs examined are the Standard Oil Company of New Jersey (hereafter Jersey) and Royal Dutch-Shell (hereafter Shell).

The local firm in the study is Compañia de Petróleos de Chile (COPEC). The historical literature on FDI (foreign direct investment) in Chile has overwhelmingly focused on the mining sector, which makes sense given the importance nitrate and copper exports have had in the Chilean economy, and the protagonism of Chile in these two goods in the global market.[4] Despite its economic importance, the energy sector in twentieth century Chile has been largely neglected by historians.[5] Besides the brief (23 pages) *Historia de la Energía en Chile* (1983), the book *El petróleo chileno* (1964), and the eight pages dedicated to the Chilean oil sector in George Philip's classic *Oil and Politics in Latin America* (1982), no other work has explored this issue.[6] Philip's study is the best quality work among the three and is largely based on documents from the British Foreign Office. This chapter uses the internal documents of Standard Oil of New Jersey (Jersey) collected by the US Department of Justice and gathered in the Petroleum Industry Anti-Trust Collection in the Baker Library at the Harvard Business School. By using these documents this chapter can analyze the strategy followed by the foreign corporations in their dealings with Chile. This chapter complements this source with declassified secret documents of the Central Intelligence Agency (CIA) on the government of Salvador Allende and its overthrow by General Augusto Pinochet.

I. BUSINESS GROUPS, MNEs, AND NATIONALISM

Business groups are an organization for collective action by the private sector. In his pioneering study on collective action, economist Mancur Olson defined two kinds of groups. The first were 'inclusive groups' which are those who benefit from a larger number of members, such as groups looking for lower taxes or higher tariffs. The second were 'exclusive groups' which are those who benefit from a small number of members, such as firms who associate to restrict output to increase prices. Olson predicts that collective action in smaller groups works better than in larger groups, because in the former each member is sensitive to other firms in the group and is aware that a hostile action against the group will be percieved and potentially punished by the group. Olson also predicts that in small groups the problem of 'free-riding' is minimized. Exclusive groups will work at their best when the members control 100 percent of the market. In his analysis, Olson considers the possibility of firms belonging to inclusive and exclusive groups at the same time.[7] In this chapter, the Chilean business groups would be inclusive groups, while the oil cartel would be an exclusive one. The MNEs benefited from the overall economic policy promoted by the inclusive business groups which promoted industrialization and protected national industrialists, while at the same time benefited from belonging to a cartel, which limited competition.

The Chilean oil cartel behavior after its creation followed the rationale predicted by Olson: after initially resenting the presence of the others, each member saw the other ones as collaborators rather than rivals. Olson, however, assumes that groups are created by the free initiative of its members, something that did not happen in the Chilean oil sector. In this case, the government gave no option to the MNEs different from joining a cartel with COPEC. My studies are partially consistent with those of Ben Ross Schneider, who challenged Olson with his study of Latin American business groups in the twentieth century. According to Schneider, Latin American business groups were either created as a reaction against pro-labor policies from the governments, or encouraged by the governments who needed a partner in the import substitution industrialization process.[8] Therefore, by including the actions of the state, Schneider found another element not considered by Olson for the creation of collective action groups. However, in the case of the Chilean oil sector, not only did the government encourage the cartel, it also sided with one of the members and forced the others to accept the arrangement. The benefits of reluctantly accepting a new member came in terms of legitimacy (another element neglected by Olson) and political influence.

In his studies on the relationship between economic policy, MNEs, and business groups in emerging economies, Mauro Guillén argues that import substitution industrialization policies reinforce business groups and lead MNEs to collaborate with them. 'In an import substitution environment', argues Guillén, 'multinational enterprises prefer to manufacture or distribute their products in collaboration with local entrepreneurs who know how to navigate through the treacherous conditions created by economic and political populism, including powerful labor unions, import competing interests, and idiosyncratic credit allocation practices . . . As long as [these policies] remain in place entrepreneurs and firms . . . will continue utilizing them to enter new industries in association with MNEs forming business groups in the process'.[9] My findings are consistent with this prediction, but it must be emphasized that in this case the MNEs collaborated with the domestic business groups only after they were forced to join forces with them.

The import substitution industrialization process that framed the development of the Chilean oil industry fits in Harry Johnson's definition of economic nationalism. For Johnson, '[economic] nationalism is a political sentiment that attaches value to having property in this broad sense owned by members of the national group. [As an economic program] nationalism seeks to extend the property owned by nationals'.[10] For Johnson, this can be done through expropriation or through public investment to support the private sector. Nationalist policies will focus on activities selected for their 'symbolic value' such as manufacturing and also those that create jobs for the middle class.[11]

II. THE STATE, THE WORKING CLASS, AND THE CHILEAN ELITE

There are several aspects that make Chile an exception within Latin America and that are relevant to this study. First, Chile began the twentieth century as one of the most developed countries in the continent, with a relatively high standard of living. This was possible due to high social spending from the government funded through taxation to the booming nitrate and copper exports controlled by foreign companies. Before the Depression, most Chilean exports were in the hands of American and British corporations operating in the copper sector. The mining sector paid insignificant taxes until 1925, when the Chilean government established income taxes. This permitted the government to develop social programs and public works, which significantly improved the country's infrastructure, and set the basis for some industrial development.[12] During the period 1920–72, Chile had the highest level of social spending as a percentage of the gross domestic product (GDP) in Latin America, focused on education, housing, and healthcare.[13] Between 1913 and 1929, Chile was fourth in literacy levels after Uruguay, Argentina, and Cuba, and fourth in GDP per-capita behind the same countries.[14] The high taxation income from the mining economy permitted the government to keep the high levels of social investment with little taxation of the local citizens or the private sector.[15] Despite taxation, mining attracted many companies and between 1913 and 1929, Chile was second in Latin America after Argentina in per-capita foreign investment.[16] Regarding oil consumption, the country was the second highest in South America after Argentina, with an annual consumption of around 800000 tons, making this country attractive for companies which acted as oil importers [17]

Despite the state industrializing efforts, by 1929 Chile still lagged behind other Latin American countries: while by 1929, industrial production was 22.8 percent of Argentina's GDP, 14.2 percent of Mexico's, and 14.2 percent of Brazil's, it represented just 7.9 percent of the Chilean GDP. Until 1929, the economy depended mostly on copper exports.[18]

The larger role of the state in the economy came parallel with a rise of the organized political left. With a large percentage of its population living in urban areas (40 percent by 1914) and 16 percent of the total workers employed in the manufacturing sector, Chile saw the rise of labor unionism early in the twentieth century. In 1909, the Chilean Workers Federation (FOCH, in its Spanish acronym) was created and the Socialist Party was established in 1912.[19] In 1920, President Arturo Alessandri won with strong left-wing support, and created a series of national institutions for the benefit of the working class. Chile went from having an average of nine strikes a year between 1890 and 1925, to 45 a year between 1925 and 1935.[20]

The rise of the left led the business community to organize itself as well. During the 1920s, several businessmen associated in sectoral associations, eventually grouped themselves under the umbrella Confederación de la Producción y Comercio (CPC) in 1933. These organizations emerged as a response to the rise of the left (membership in labor unions quadrupled between 1932 and 1940), but they eventually became partners of the government's development plans and their members directly participated in the government economic agencies giving the business groups strong influence in policy making.[21] By the late twentieth century, the Chilean business groups were among the largest and strongest in Latin America.[22]

In short, in the first decades of the twentieth century Chile consolidated itself as a protectionist country with a welfare state with a major role in the economy. The business communities organized themselves in associations in order to create a defensive bloc against labor demands and as a mechanism to influence the state without direct participation in politics. These social arrangements took place in the framework of political stability and good economic performance.

III. CHILE'S EARLY ATTEMPTS TO CONTROL OIL RESOURCES, 1908–28

The story of the oil sector in Chile before the 1930s is one of unrealistic hopes and constant frustrations. Since the late nineteenth century, several geologists claimed that Chilean Patagonia had untapped rich oil resources many local entrepreneurs tried to exploit. The first Chilean oil rush took place as early as 1899, when speculators acquired lands in Patagonia in the wake of rumors of rich oil deposits. Although not much was discovered, some locals created the Compañía de Petróleo del Pacífico in 1908. The big hopes that oil would be found in the country led some politicians in 1917 to propose legislation nationalizing the country's oil resources. The lack of success at discovering oil made the debate around nationalization drag on until 1926, when after realizing a modest interest by Shell and Jersey in acquiring lands in Southern Chile, President Emiliano Figueroa approved a law reserving all oil deposits to the state.[23] The British Chamber of Commerce criticized this law, arguing that it did not do Chile any good: it scared foreign investors away and the country did not even get the oil, because there simply was no oil.[24] Even though the country did not make any significant discovery of oil until 1946, the legislation remained in place.[25] Given this lack of crude sources, most political conflicts in the following decades revolved around refining, marketing, and distribution in Chile.

Figueroa's initiative reflected changing times in Chilean politics. Figueroa had been elected after the second administration of Arturo Alessandri (1920–25), who changed the Chilean constitution to decrease the power of the traditional landowning oligarchy in 1925. Elected with a social program oriented to the lower classes, Alessandri took power in the midst of an economic crisis generated by the post-World War I fall in nitrate exports. The Conservative Party and the landed oligarchy opposed Alessandri's government and overthrew him in 1924. Alessandri, however, came back to power soon after a counter-coup led by some followers in the army. This time the president lost no time writing a new constitution, which gave more power to the urban middle and working-class sectors, supported unionism, and gave the president leeway to enlarge the state and protect national industry, marking the beginning of the sustained expansion of the state in the following five decades.[26] Despite his alliance with the left, Alessandri also approached Chilean business groups, which he considered crucial actors in his import substitution industrialization projects. In his presidential message of 1924, he even praised the Sociedad de Fomento Fabril (National Manufacturers Association, or SOFOFA, in its Spanish acronym) and gradually started raising tariffs to protect national industry.[27]

Jersey and Shell started their operations in Chile before the political changes of the 1920s. Jersey arrived in Chile in 1913. It entered the country under the formal name Esso Standard Oil Company Chile and sold products as the West India Oil Company (WICO), a wholly-owned marketing company. The company opened storage facilities in 1921 and opened its first petrol station in Valparaíso that same year.[28] Shell arrived in 1919, opened storage facilities in Viña del Mar and imported different oil products, anticipating an ever-growing market given the increasing imports of cars.[29] From that moment until 1935, Shell and Jersey controlled close to 100 percent of the crude oil and products' imports and distribution in Chile.

The oil MNEs faced their first challenges in the early 1920s, when the Chilean coal miners confronted them. Coal miners had experienced gradual replacement of coal by oil in the nitrate mines in the Chilean

North: while in 1908, the mines used 663 327 tons of coal and 36 855 tons of oil, by 1914 the pattern had reversed with the nitrate mines consuming 488 802 tons of oil and 268 313 tons of coal.[30] Moreover, after a series of strikes in 1920, the coal mining sector faced a crisis that led it to unsuccessfully request higher tariffs on oil products' imports from the government.[31] In time, the nitrate mines of the north became the oil industry's largest consumers in Chile.[32]

IV. THE CHILEAN STATE ATTEMPTS TO END THE SHELL-ESSO CARTEL, 1929–32

The problems generated by the Great Depression generated the first threats by the Chilean state against Shell and Esso's absolute control over the Chilean oil market. The Depression increased government interventionism in the economy, unionization, and created further incentives for business groups to organize themselves. Chile was ruled by Carlos Ibáñez del Campo, who came to power in 1927 and ruled in an authoritarian style. Ibáñez took power when Chile enjoyed economic prosperity after the critical post-World War I years, which permitted the government to provide soft loans to the nascent industrial sector and heavily invest in infrastructure and social welfare. Agricultural production reached its historic peak in 1928 and US foreign investment had reached levels of $625 million in 1929, compared to just one million in 1900, with most of it coming during the reign of the Ibáñez government.[33]

The euphoric 1920s came to an abrupt end in 1929. No other country in the Western world suffered a worst crisis during the Depression than Chile.[34] In 1932, exports had fallen to less than 12 percent of their 1929 value. Imports had fallen to 20 percent and the government's budget shrank by 50 percent from 1929 to 1932. The mining sector – which represented 88.3 percent of total exports in 1929 was hit worse than all the other sectors in the economy: the value of copper and nitrate exports fell by 89 percent between 1927 and 1932, and mining production in general fell by 50 percent.[35] In the agrarian sector, the second most important sector of the economy, prices fell by 50 percent. Real wages fell by 40 percent between 1929 and 1932 and unemployment rose.[36] In the mining sector, employment decreased from 104 000 people to 42 000 during those four years.[37] The economic crisis also affected the petroleum sector badly. After having imported 27 578 673 tons of crude oil in 1930, Chile imported 13 143 910 tons in 1931.[38]

The crisis led to a confrontation between Ibáñez and foreign companies. He threatened the British-owned Chilean Electric Company with expropriation, unless the company provided him with a $2 million loan. He also tried to attract the British firm Antony Gibbs to invest in oil distribution in Chile in partnership with a Chilean state oil company, but Gibbs refused.[39] In February 1931, Ibáñez asked Congress for broader powers to counteract the economic crisis by having the government involved in oil exploration, for which Ibáñez had high hopes.[40] Ibáñez's lack of success in these two initiatives forced him to keep depending on Shell and Esso's imports.

The economic crisis created social unrest which the Ibáñez government tried to control through more repression. In July 1931, unable to control the wave of anti-government demonstrations, Ibáñez resigned and the country elected center-right Juan Esteban Montero who was committed to further import substitution industrialization.[41]

Montero inherited a country in deep economic and political crisis. Between 1 and 9 September 1931, in the middle of Montero's presidential campaign for the October elections (while serving at the same time as provisional president), he faced a naval mutiny. The mutineers demanded public and welfare spending to be financed by forced loans from the rich and land redistribution to poor peasants. The mutiny was defeated militarily and Montero blamed the Communists for being behind it. The left was immediately repressed, but the economic crisis eventually forced Montero to establish some price controls and reduce utility tariffs, an action that alienated the business community.[42]

Despite his strong anti-Communism views, Montero pragmatically approached the Soviet Union as a way to reduce Chile's dependence on Shell and Esso. In 1931, the Soviet Union offered to supply Chile with crude oil and also technical assistance to build a refinery in exchange for Chilean nitrates.[43] The center-right government was more willing to do business with a country with which it did not have any ideological affinity, but which was keen to buy nitrates nobody was interested in buying at any price.[44] In addition, this offer permitted the government to think seriously about the possibility of having a local oil company, something that encouraged several members of the House of Representatives to pass a bill permitting the establishment of an oil monopoly in which the concessionaire would pass 75 percent of the profits to the state. Although the proposal still needed to be approved by the Senate (it was not), it made the international press speculate that this would mean the expulsion of the MNEs.[45]

The MNEs strongly opposed the possibility of having Soviet oil imported to Chile. Shell and Esso quickly announced their refusal to process or handle any Soviet oil, something that was consistent with the general terms of the Achnacarry Agreement, the wide-ranging oil cartel agreed between the leading British and American oil companies in 1928.[46]

Unable to sign an agreement with the Soviets, the Chileans let this project gradually die.[47]

The Chilean government also considered the possibility of developing an alternative energy source by producing gasoline through hydrogenation of coal. Production of coal in Chile was significant and in the absence of domestic crude oil sources and Shell and Esso's control of oil imports, coal was a good alternative. In 1930, the government established that coal production would be coordinated by the government but ownership remained in private hands.[48] A letter from an Esso official writing from London to the New York headquarters strongly suggested that the company convince the Chilean government that the project was economically unfeasible. The sender added that if this attempt failed and the Chilean government proposed a monopoly, Esso should consider partnering with the government to create an oil refining and coal hydrogenation plant. The sender mentioned that he had already talked to 'our friends in Shell' and they agreed on proposing to the Chileans a plant for gasoline from coal which would use three-quarters of imported crude and one-quarter of hydrogenated coal. However, he insisted, the companies should emphasize the extremely high costs this would generate, and the advantages of the cheaper option of importing oil. Finally, only if the government really insisted on continuing with the project, the sender was of the opinion that the companies should propose that the Chilean government finance it and that the MNEs provide services and then distribute the gasoline through its own installations.[49] This project, however, never materialized in any form and the country remained dependent on imported oil.[50]

Some of Montero's policies to promote industrialization clashed with the interests of the MNEs. In 1932, Montero increased tariffs and devalued the currency in an effort to promote domestic production and discourage imports. In addition, the government reduced the supply of dollars and pounds to Shell and Esso, rationed gasoline, and controlled prices.[51] These actions were not accepted by the US and British embassies or Shell and Esso. For the MNEs, paying for the imported oil in dollars and selling it in devalued pesos was not a good deal, so in March 1932 they tried to compensate the devaluation by increasing the oil products' retail price. Scared of the social unrest this could generate, the government requested companies not increase prices, and the companies agreed to postpone the idea. Just a few weeks later, however, the companies announced again they were going to increase prices, this time with the political support of the US embassy. A series of negotiations followed in which the Chilean government almost pleaded with the companies not to raise the prices and requested American political support in the current crisis. In contrast with the American ambassador's position, the British ambassador warned Shell that increasing prices would generate social unrest and the Chilean government could respond by accusing the foreign companies of 'banditry'.[52] The companies increased the price of gasoline by 25 percent, sparking protests from bus and cab drivers.[53] Montero threatened the companies with expropriation if they did not decrease the prices, but the companies considered it a bluff and refused to comply. Losing this battle, Montero had no choice than to accept an agreement by which taxis and buses got cheaper gasoline than private cars.[54]

The lost battle against the companies led Montero to sign a new bill empowering the government. The bill, approved in May 1932, permitted the creation of a national state monopoly on imports, distribution, and sales and authorized the president to determine the starting date, something the MNEs immediately opposed.[55] Montero, however, did not put the law into effect because some important Chilean firms were highly dependent on the MNEs' distribution activities. The law, however, remained hanging over the foreign companies' heads, and was seen abroad as a legal tool that could be used to expell the MNEs.[56]

The internal politics of Chile soon created more uncertainties for the MNEs. In June 1932, Montero was a victim of a military coup led by Air Force Commander Marmaduque Grove, who declared Chile a Socialist Republic and announced the expropriation of foreign oil companies. This experiment (and sudden panic among foreign investors) was short-lived. A coup ended the Socialist Republic just a few days later, and the country went to elections again in 1932, re-electing former president Arturo Alessandri. The brief Grove Socialist Republic and the economic crisis did not go away without leaving a legacy. In the 1932 elections, the Socialist Party (with Grove running as its presidential candidate) finished second, with 16 percent of the votes, marking the beginning of an increasing influence of the left in Chilean politics.[57]

V. COPEC AND THE ENTRY OF THE BUSINESS GROUPS IN THE OIL INDUSTRY, 1932–36

With his return to power, Alessandri strengthened and consolidated the policies of protectionism, import substitution industrialization, and welfare spending. He also sought partnership with the business groups that had been created years before as a response against his own pro-labor policies. In 1933, shortly after his election he increased tariffs by 50 percent for all goods, and in 1934 he increased them again by 100 percent.[58] That same year, Alessandri attended the CPC inaugural convention.[59] He also devalued the currency (a protectionist mechanism maintained by subsequent presidents) and increased direct subsidies to local industry, something that had an immediate positive effect on industrial production. In fact, Chile was one of the Latin American countries that industrialized the most after the Depression.[60] In addition to restoring confidence in the private sector Alessandri reduced unemployment through deficit-financed public works.[61]

Alessandri made foreign companies feel safe. He permitted the oil companies to raise prices of gasoline, except for that used by public transportation buses, and announced that Chile was not going to consider buying Soviet oil again. The economic and political stability the country achieved by1933 made many believe that the threats of expropriation had disappeared. Explaining the nature of Chilean economic nationalism, the British commercial secretary in Chile reported that the Chilean government was not doing anything worse or better than what worldwide general trends showed, his only complaint being the legislation that forced foreign companies to employ Chileans for 85 percent of their workforce and to have the same percentage of total wages paid to Chileans.[62] This did not mean that political threats had dissappeared. In 1934, the government tried to give some exploration permits to foreign companies, but faced strong opposition in Congress by Socialists who succeeded in defeating the project.[63]

With the economic recovery, per capita income increased and demand for oil products with it. These created incentives for the Chilean business groups to show interest in the oil sector.

The Chilean business community, thriving under Alessandri's industrial protection, began its participation in oil in 1934. On 31 October 1934, a group of Chilean engineers led by Chile's future president, Pedro Aguirre Cerda, established COPEC. Other founding members included influential representatives of the Chilean economic and political establishment, like Roberto Wachholtz (senator and Minister of Finance), Francisco Bulnes (congressman and landowner), Jorge Marchant (industrialist), and Walter Müller.[64] At the time of COPEC's establishment, Müller was the president of SOFOFA and had previously worked as the director of the Santiago Gas Company.[65] Since its birth, then, COPEC was closely linked to the powerful Chilean business groups.

The founders of COPEC represented a new class of young engineers who emerged in the interwar decades, embraced Keynesian economics, and agreed that for Chile to achieve development it had to control imports through devaluation and engage in import substitution industrialization.[66] Most of them were members of business groups like SOFOFA, and had a strong interest in assuring cheap energy sources for industry. Many wrote articles emphasizing the need for a domestic control of energy sources, while at the same time opposing actions against foreign investors.[67] Before the creation of COPEC, Müller had openly supported the building of a refinery by Esso, arguing that local industrialists were not capable of doing this. Besides COPEC's founders, those arguing for a new energy policy included other influential members of the Chilean elite such as Reinaldo Harnecker, Fernando Palma Rogers, Hernán Edwards, José Luis Claro, and Darío Sánchez Vickers.[68]

After Alessandri, the Chilean business groups became an effective mechanism for the business community's collective action. Their role as consultative actors in the industrialization process with direct participation in the government's development agencies permitted the Chilean businessmen to use state resources for the benefit of their own business. A 'revolving door' between the private sector and the government was created in which some men went back and forth between government positions and high-ranking positions in the private sector.[69] Thus, it is not surprising that COPEC enjoyed full government support from the beginning in terms of a secure dollar exchange for imports at a favorable rate and political endorsement from the national government.[70]

Esso and Shell opposed COPEC from the beginning and tried to kill the Chilean company in a price war, but COPEC survived thanks to government protection. In 1935, Gustavo Ross, Alessandri's Minister of Finance, warned the MNEs that COPEC would receive complete government support in order to achieve a market share of at least 20 percent to avoid oil scarcities in the future.[71] At that point, the Chilean government could afford to keep subsidizing COPEC with the high income generated by the recovered copper industry.[72] The companies realized the political cost of trying to 'drive COPEC out of the market' through price wars and retreated from their goal of keeping their 100 percent market share.[73] A Jersey official also admitted privately that the creation of COPEC could be a result of the 'high handed methods of doing business then used by Jersey [Esso] and Shell'.[74]

Excited by growing state support, COPEC's leaders, Aguirre and Wachholtz suggested that President Alessandri declare an oil monopoly under COPEC, something Ross firmly opposed.[75] Ross went as far as proposing Shell and Esso lobby their governments to prevent the creation of the monopoly.[76] This was the beginning of a debate between Ross and Aguirre, in which the former believed that the country's long-term goals required foreign capital, while the latter believed that a truly nationalist policy had to avoid foreign participation.[77] Aguirre and Wachholtz resented Ross' intervention and started opposing his tenure as minister.[78]

The US government did not oppose the creation of COPEC, but mistrusted it. Some of COPEC's founders (particularly Müller) had good connections and business relationships with US corporations, but the US embassy did not trust COPEC's capabilities and warned American corporations not to do business with COPEC unless they were paid in full beforehand.[79] Similarly, the British embassy did not consider the creation of COPEC a hostile action against foreign companies, but also had little hope in this enterprise's success. The British commercial secretary in Santiago expressed an understanding of the government's desire to not depend completely on foreign corporations, but believed that the domestic market was not large enough for three companies to operate.[80]

Alessandri's approach to the business community was perceived as a shift to the right by part of his constituency. In 1936, the Socialists and the center-left Radical Party made a pact to create a new movement, the Popular Front. The Popular Front was an eclectic group whose members included the FOCH, left-wing intellectuals like Pablo Neruda, Vicente Huidobro, and Volodia Teitelboim, and nationalists from the Conservative Party. Former COPEC leader Aguirre became one of the new party leaders and was nominated for the presidential elections of 1938.[81]

VI. BUSINESS GROUPS, DEVELOPMENTALISM, AND THE CREATION AND GROWTH OF THE COPEC-SHELL-ESSO CARTEL, 1937–45

The mutual attacks between the MNEs and COPEC did not bear fruit to either side, so on 6 April 1937, under Ross' leadership COPEC, Esso and Shell agreed on dividing the market into thirds to avoid more price wars.[82] Making this kind of deal with foreign corporations went against Aguirre's ideas but it was during his tenure as COPEC president when the deal was approved. Aguirre did not represent the beliefs of all members of COPEC's board. While he and Wachholtz firmly believed in the benefits of a monopoly, Müller opposed the idea and defended partnership and cooperation with foreign capital. COPEC's board allied with Müller, leading to Wachholtz's resignation and Aguirre's approval of the deal.[83]

The cartelization decreased the MNEs' market share, but also ended their conflicts with the Chilean state and COPEC. In a group with only three members controlling 100 percent of the market, the chances of internal fights were minimal. Under the new agreement, foreign companies could not send profits home and were required to reinvest them in Chile.[84] Esso officials expressed that this was the only option available: 'While it cannot be definitely stated that Esso Chile could or could not have continued in business without having entered into the marketing agreement with COPEC in 1937, it obviously could not have continued marketing in Chile without suffering disastrous losses . . . It is a fact that had we not done so the monopoly would have been installed or we would have been driven out of the market'.[85]

The situation Esso and Shell faced in Chile was far from being unique. During the late 1930s, most European countries with a state-owned company proposed foreign corporations 'voluntary' cartel agreements with them.[86] Sharing the market on the Chilean government's terms was also consistent with the MNEs' latest agreements. Although the end of the Achnacarry Agreement was approaching, in 1937 Shell and Esso had set up a committee to study how they could complement each other in different markets.[87]

The most important consumers of Chile's small market were the mining companies. Copper companies are large consumers of diesel oil and most of the trade between the mining regions and the outside world took place through the port of Antofagasta.[88] Between 1932 and 1935, diesel imports through Antofagasta were disproportionately higher than in the rest of the country: 56 percent (1933), 36 percent (1934), 42 percent (1935). The imports of diesel were equivalent to around 10 percent of crude oil imports in tons.[89] The mining companies also consumed a large amount of the total oil imported to Chile. In 1933, the copper mines consumed oil equivalent to 17 percent of total oil imports, for the nitrate mines it was 15 percent, and in 1934, the figure for the copper mines was 24 percent.[90] These data suggest that for all the distributors, selling oil products to the profitable mining companies in a cartelized market could be attractive.

In 1938, Chile went to presidential elections with Aguirre running for the Popular Front, against his former rival in oil policy Gustavo Ross. In a competitive election, Aguirre won with 50.46 percent of the votes (with strong support among the urban working and middle class) against Ross with 49.53 percent.[91]

Shortly after winning the elections, Aguirre considered the nationalization of the whole Chilean oil industry. Aguirre appointed Wachholtz as his Finance Minister, who in January 1939 proposed the nationalization of oil to Congress and suggested to the foreign companies that they sell their properties voluntarily.[92] To consider the nationalization of the oil industry in 1939 – just one year after the Mexican expropriation – was a delicate issue. Despite the strong differences between Aguirre's government and the revolutionary government in Mexico, the US Department of State quickly drew parallels between the policies of both countries.[93] The companies rejected Wachholtz's proposal and responded by stating that they would be willing to sell their assets after their agreement with COPEC legally expired in 1942. Taking this reply as a challenge to the government, Wachholtz decided to pursue a plan to build a refinery, for which Chile applied for a

US loan. The American government, however, said that it was not going to provide any loan for the refinery if foreign property was expropriated. Under these circumstances, the plans for expropriation gradually died.[94]

In 1939, Aguirre strengthened the close relationship between the state and the business groups and the influence of the latter with the creation of the the semi-independent agency Corporación de Fomento (CORFO). CORFO's main role was to provide funding to the country's industrialization process. CORFO became so crucial to Chile's industrialization that between 1939 and 1954 its investments accounted for up to 30 percent of the country's total investment in machinery and equipment in a country witnessing rapid industrial growth: between 1940 and 1954, Chilean industrial production grew by 246 percent, American investments in the mining sector grew by 80 percent, and the urban population increased by 42 percent.[95]

CORFO's creation was enthusiastically supported by some other COPEC founders and members of the business and technocratic elite, such as Müller, Raúl Bertrand, and Vicente Izquierdo Phillips. Its first president was Harnecker, one of the leading voices of the pro-industrialization elite.[96] This business elite had direct participation in CORFO's decisions, something that gave the Chilean business groups enormous power in policy making. After 1939, most of the crucial economic decisions in Chile were not taken in the Senate but in CORFO's closed-door meetings.[97]

Aguirre died while he was still in power in 1941, but was succeeded by presidents who continued his economic nationalist plan of state planning, import substitution, industrialization and energy independence, keeping CORFO as a central institution, and pursuing economic development policies.[98]

In 1941, the Chilean government made a new attempt to debilitate the foreign corporations. In that year the government approached some Esso officials and told them that Chile was not interested in keeping Shell in the cartel. The government proposed that Esso divide Shell's quota and create a new cartel in which COPEC and Esso shared the market 50–50. Esso refused the proposal by saying, 'Shell, like ourselves, is an international oil company and positions differ in countries in which we both have operations'.[99] The government was in a weak position to try to make the foreign companies compete with each other. Moreover, 1941 was one of the hardest years for COPEC because of decreased oil imports generated by the war, so the company had no incentives to break the arrangement.[100]

During the 1940s, one of CORFO's main goals was to end Chile's dependence on foreign oil. Imports of oil and oil products had increased from 5.8 percent of total imports in 1925–29 to 10.9 percent in 1940–45.[101] In 1944, COPEC bought (at a loss) its first tanker to bring oil directly from

Peru.[102] Between 1941 and 1942, CORFO also financed oil explorations in the Chilean south, activities the government supported with a 1942 law which approved the participation of foreign companies in production (although only as subcontractors) – the Senate passed this law in 1944.[103] The US and British governments, however, discouraged their companies from joining anything under the Chilean terms. In 1945, CORFO found some oil so the Chileans enthusiastically continued with their oil projects in spite of the British and US opposition.[104] In the meantime, Esso's lawyers made clear to the government that the terms of the new legislation were not acceptable for them to risk capital in exploration or production.[105]

The American government opposed CORFO's ambitions of investing in oil exploration and production. After discovering oil in the Chilean south, CORFO applied for a loan from the US Export Import Bank (EXIM Bank) in order to develop a national oil company. Once the EXIM Bank received the application, John Suman (one of Esso's vice-presidents) sent a letter to Spruille Braden (at that time Assistant Secretary of American Republics Affairs at the US Department of State) strongly opposing the loan and arguing that private capital was available to do the job. Braden was the son of the founder of the Braden Copper Company of Chile. At the Department of State, some officials argued in favor of providing the loan believing it was better to allow the Chileans to create a state company, rather than support the US oil companies and face problems such as those they had already encountered in Bolivia and Mexico, where government expropriations of foreign oil companies occurred in 1937 and 1938 respectively. Braden, however, disagreed with this viewpoint and kept pressuring the EXIM Bank to not approve the loan. These discussions were leaked to the Associated Press and caused uproar in Chile. The American ambassador in Santiago himself requested that Braden reconsider his opposition, but Braden remained firm. In the end, Chile did not get the loan, so the country negotiated with two American corporations (Livermore Corporation and the Kellogg Pan-American Corporation) to provide capital and technical assistance for the creation of the national state company, but without ownership rights in this company. In this way, Chile managed to create its state-owned oil exploration company (the Empresa Nacional de Petróleo, ENAP) with mostly domestic resources.[106]

The COPEC-Esso-Shell cartel continued operating under strong criticism from different political groups. When the agreement expired on 1 January 1942, the foreign companies decided to allow a gradually higher participation of COPEC in the market as a way to decrease nationalist sensibilities. Under the new agreement COPEC's participation was to increase to 50 percent in the gasoline market and 33 percent in all the other products over the next ten years. With this agreement COPEC bought all the products from Shell and Esso in proportion to its previous participation in the market. What it had in excess could be sold in the market but in proportions equal to those it had before the agreement. The agreement also established that Esso and Shell's quotas could be changed at any time, but those of COPEC were to remain stable.[107]

The fate of the oil companies in Chile strongly depended on the fate of the mining sector, which consumed around a third of all the oil imports.[108] According to Stephen Randall the interest of the US government in the Chilean oil products marketing sector was not about the oil MNEs (who had much more profitable places in production and marketing all over the world), but about the US mining companies such as Kennecott or Anaconda. These companies needed a constant, smooth, and reliable flow of oil for their operations and the Chilean attempts to control marketing indirectly threatened the mining companies.[109] In 1944, an Esso official visited the nitrate mines in the north in order to inspect the situation of that industry. The mining firms informed him that they expected the demand for their products to decrease after World War II, forecasting the economic decay of that region and discouraging the company (Esso?) from fighting for better conditions in Chile.[110]

VII. CARTEL'S LEGITIMACY IN THE FACE OF ANTI-TRUST ACTIONS, 1945–58

The arrangement with COPEC gave the cartel a kind of legitimacy to defend itself against hostile government actions, one it would not have had if it had remained in the hands of foreign companies. In addition, the arrangement permitted the MNEs to do business with the government. As the 1951 deadline approached, Esso executives in New York wondered if it made sense to renew the cartel agreement with no significant changes and asked those working in Chile. The officials at the subsidiary responded that they believed the cartel could not be changed. Someone in the parent company disagreed, and sent a strong letter to the subsidiary saying, 'I think you can fully appreciate that any marketing arrangement, such as now exists in Chile, must be *strongly documented* [underlined in the original] to justify its existence, particularly when considering the fundamental policy of Esso to operate on a free competitive basis'.[111] The agreement, however, was eventually renewed without much change in 1952 for two more years (and later renewed again until the 1960s). Esso officials in Chile were clearly aware of the political benefits of the cartel.

The creation of ENAP gave the cartel more legitimacy. The use of oil as the main source of energy in Chile had increased from 22 percent in

1939 (coal represented 27 percent and wood 29 percent) to 30 percent in 1952 (coal decreasing to 25 percent and wood down to 20 percent).[112] New legislation permitted ENAP to contract foreigners for exploration and production (keeping restrictions on foreign ownership of oilfields), but Shell and Esso did not participate in these activities.[113] In 1950, the three companies, however, invested together in a new jointly-owned tanker, and in 1956 Esso, COPEC, and ENAP signed a deal for the construction of a pipeline.[114] The arrangement was not in danger even after the promulgation of the first Chilean anti-trust legislation in 1959 (the same year in which the Chilean government declared its support for a country's right to expropriate foreign property).[115] On the few occasions some challenged the legality of the cartel, the Anti-Trust Commission replied that as long as a Chilean company benefited from it, the government was not going to take any action against it. Thus, protecting COPEC was also meant to protect Shell and Esso.[116]

CORFO also infused COPEC with some capital by purchasing almost 15 percent of the shares. Contrary to what happened with ENAP and the general trend of a stronger participation of the Chilean state in the economy, COPEC always remained controlled by private shareholders. CORFO even financed the construction of an oil refinery in the city of Concón to refine ENAP, Shell, and Esso's oil.[117] ENAP's oil production, however, was always too small and the country continued depending on imported oil.[118]

VIII. SOCIAL CHANGES AND THREATS TO THE CARTEL, 1958–70

The cartel remained stable during the 1960s, but faced challenges by the end of the decade because of a new orientation in economic policy that focused on consumers rather than producers. Between 1958 and 1964, Chilean president Jorge Alessandri (son of former president Arturo Alessandri) tried to reverse the existing economic model by making the companies compete without state support. This attempt failed because the Chilean industrial class did not want to abandon its oligopolistic power and the president confronted an increasingly powerful and organized left.[119]

Chilean society was changing and this was reflected in its oil consumption patterns. In the 1950s, expenditure in petrol for automobiles, which highly affected the middle class, represented around a third of all expenditure in oil products, while expenditure in kerosene (used for heating and lighting by the lower class) represented around 10 percent of the total during this period. In 1964, Chile elected Christian Democrat Eduardo

Frei, whose main constituency was the middle class, who continued in protectionist tradition and increased welfare spending, and tried to encourage foreign investment, but criticized the pro-producer, anti-consumer bias of the existing economic model.[120]

COPEC faced difficulties during Frei's presidency. First, ENAP sold products to COPEC using the rising international oil prices, while at the same time the government did not allow COPEC to increase its sales prices.[121] In addition, Frei proposed a plan to nationalize gas distribution, which worried COPEC's directorship.[122] In the 1969–70 annual report, COPEC made a passionate defense of its role in Chilean society and economy by arguing that theirs was a nationalist project led by the private sector which was now challenged by different kind of nationalist ideas which advocated 'statization' of the oil sector.[123] Interestingly, in this defense COPEC does not mention its foreign cartel partners.

Frei's social programs did not bear the fruits the working class expected and by the end of his administration he faced an economic crisis that made his party unpopular among that class.[124] In 1970, Chile went to elections again and elected the Socialist candidate Salvador Allende.

IX. SALVADOR ALLENDE, SOCIALISM, AND NEW THREATS TO THE CARTEL, 1970–73

The literature on the conflicts between Allende and the foreign MNEs has overwhelmingly focused on the copper industry, while the crucial energy sector is barely mentioned. In fact, despite their participation in the conspiracy against Allende, the oil companies did not have their reputation tainted in the way the mining companies had. This can be explained by the relative smaller size of the oil MNEs in the Chilean economy in comparison to those in the mining sector, and the more open hostility of Anaconda and ITT against Allende. The Central Intelligence Agency (CIA) declassified documents which show that Shell, Esso, and COPEC were threatened by Allende's economic policy, and actively offered their support to the different forces opposing the government. During his brief but tumultuous administration, Allende faced fierce opposition from the Chilean upper classes, the foreign corporations, and the US government, whose interests converged to successfully conspire against the regime.[125] Among several policies, the business groups were affected by Allende when he decided to reduce SOFOFA's representation in CORFO, eliminating an important channel for the business groups to influence policy making.[126]

Allende knew that in order to have stronger state control of the economy, he needed to control the oil sector. Although the government claimed that it did not want complete expropriation of foreign property but a new kind of relationship with foreign corporations, in the oil sector it planned to have 100 percent state control of refined petroleum and 89.2 percent of state control in petroleum and coal derivates.[127]

Allende made the first step for state control of oil products distribution in March 1971, when he created the Empresa Nacional de Distribución (ENADI).[128] ENADI was one of several state agencies in charge of controlling distribution of goods with the goal of having price controls.[129] Given the short time Allende was in power and the challenges his administration faced, ENADI was never a serious threat to the cartel in terms of acquiring market share.

The CIA planned to sabotage Allende's government even before he won the elections, and so did part of the Chilean opposition. Going against venerated democratic tradition, many in the elite, the armed forces, and the US Department of State clearly believed that Allende should be prevented from taking power. Some in the Chilean opposition even planned terrorist attacks to provoke a military coup before Allende's inauguration.[130] The embassy, however, was planning economic warfare against Allende. '[During the first] six to nine months . . . Allende will be most vulnerable. If economic and administrative problems are sufficiently severe, [Allende's party the] Popular Unity could crumble', expressed US Ambassador to Chile Edward Korry, 20 days after the elections, but a month before inauguration.[131] Allende's triumph generated panic among private investors, something the embassy found useful for the economic sabotage.[132] During the same days, a representative of Esso, Shell, and COPEC contacted Korry, telling him that 'that the economic situation is bad, but it would be good if it got worse', and offered their cooperation with the embassy to damage the economy.[133]

Military conspirators also approached the oil companies. In October 1970, Major Ricardo Palma visited Esso's officials to inform them about the army's plans to oust Allende. Palma requested detailed information about the company's installations in order to protect them when the coup came, and about Esso's employees and contractors. Palma said that controlling gas stations and storage facilities would be crucial to the coup's success, so the oil companies had nothing to fear from the army.[134] Although the coup came three years later, this demonstrates the early collusion between the army and the oil companies regarding Allende.

COPEC's financial results for 1971 and 1972 were the worst in the company's history. The company blamed its huge losses on government price controls.[135] The year after, the company published in its annual report a document with which it proved that the government had intentionally tried to bankrupt it.[136] Given that the company had volunteered to sabotage the economy, it is hard to know the real roots of these poor financial results, but they were certainly useful in alarming the investment community.

Allende's opposition also used oil policies to oppose him. In February 1972, opposition senator Juan Hamilton proposed a constitutional amendment that would exempt the oil sector from being expropriated. Allende considered this proposal a provocation, so he did not take any action against oil corporations.[137]

The US and its Chilean allies succeeded in sabotaging the economy. By the second half of 1973, Chile faced rampant inflation and scarcity of basic goods, which also led to political chaos. On 11 September 1973, Allende was overthrown in a coup led by General Augusto Pinochet, and the dictator remained in power until 1989. During the coup, ENADI's stores were raided by the army because the company had access to material useful to manufacture explosives. ENADI's union boss was arrested and tortured, and the company was privatized in 1974.[138] By the end of Allende's government, the MNEs' positions in marketing remained unaltered.[139]

X. PINOCHET'S PRO-MARKET POLICIES AND THE END OF THE CHILEAN OIL CARTEL

Paradoxically, the cartel came to an end not because of Allende's socialist policies but because of Pinochet's free-market ones. Following Guillén's predictions, the end of an import substitution policy decreased the business groups' traditional power in economic policy making.[140] Breaking the long pre-Allende tradition, Pinochet did not ally with the business groups and purged representatives from business associations from the boards of CORFO, who were replaced by technocrats interested in reducing protectionist SOFOFA's power.[141] Even COPEC lost some independence when it was forced to accept a military official as a member of the board.[142]

Pinochet aggressively ended Chile's protectionist tradition and rapidly liberalized the economy.[143] By 1975, the first eight of Chile's ten largest companies had a state ownership of more than 50 percent, with ENAP as 100 percent government-owned. In the ranking of the top-100 companies in Chile, COPEC ranked tenth, and Esso and Shell ranked 25th and 42nd respectively.[144] That year, the government opened the exploration and exploitation sector to private capital, ending ENAP's monopolistic power.[145] By 1977, the government announced the gradual sale of its minority interests in COPEC, and in 1978 new legislation finally killed the COPEC-Shell-Esso cartel.[146] With this action, the Chilean government initiated a trend in the energy sector followed by other Latin American countries in the 1990s.[147]

The new legal environment also transformed COPEC's ownership. In 1982, Chile's richest man, Anacleto Angelini, purchased CORFO's participation in COPEC, acquiring 14 percent of the company's shares. Angelini kept buying COPEC stock, and in 1986 he controlled the company after attaining 42 percent of its shares.[148] This takeover occurred in the context of the 1982 economic crisis, marked by unprecedented street protests, during which Pinochet sought to reestablish links to business groups.[149]

Pinochet's deregulation altered the market shares of the previous cartel members. COPEC experienced a fall in its market share (from 51.6 percent in 1982 to 39.5 percent in 1991). Esso lost (from 28.1 percent in 1982 to 21 percent in 1991), while Shell gained (from 18.6 percent in 1982 to 22.3 percent in 1991) in market share.[150] Pinochet's deregulation sought to increase competition, but this did not happen in the oil marketing sector. By 2005, only one more company had significant participation besides the three former members of the cartel. This new presence was Argentina's YPF, which controlled 12.8 percent of the Chilean gasoline market, in comparison with COPEC's 40 percent, and Esso and Shell's respective 19.8 percent and 26.5 percent shares.[151] In spite of all the ENAP efforts, Chile entered the twenty-first century highly dependent on imported oil coming mainly from neighboring Argentina.[152]

XI. CONCLUDING REMARKS

This chapter has studied the long-term strategies of two MNE oil corporations and the state in the context of a late industrializing country with powerful business groups. It has been shown that the presence of these business groups determined the actions of both the government and the MNEs in Chile during the period between 1908 and 2005. The MNEs (Shell and Esso) controlled 100 percent of the Chilean oil products market between 1913 and 1937, and committed not to compete with each other as part of a global agreement by both firms. This absolute control of the Chilean market came to an end in 1937, when the Chilean state forced the MNEs to accept a local private company (COPEC) in their cartel.

COPEC reflected the changes experienced by Chilean society in the 1920s and 1930s; after World War I the government became gradually more protectionist in order to promote domestic industrialization. This process strengthened local corporations, which organized themselves in business groups to influence policy making and protect themselves from pro-labor policies. The MNEs initially opposed COPEC. In the long term, however, COPEC proved not to be a free rider in Olsonian terms, but rather an asset for the MNEs: as long as the import substitution industrialization process continued, the business groups became the government's main consultants in economic policy and even occupied influential positions in the government's development agencies. The 'revolving door' between the government economic agencies and the private sector was beneficial for the MNEs working together with COPEC.

During the 1940s and 1950s, this partnership even permitted the MNEs to do business with the government as sub-contractors. After more than three decades, however, the COPEC-Shell-Esso cartel faced different challenges from different types of governments. The first serious one came during the administration of President Salvador Allende (1970–73), who created a state-owned oil distribution company and planned a total nationalization of the oil industry. The cartel defended itself as a bloc, and the three companies actively conspired against the Allende government. The second challenge came during the first years of the Augusto Pinochet regime. Cartels did not fit in Pinochet's open market and free trade policies, so in 1978 the cartel was dismantled. After this, the companies had to compete in the open market.

The Chilean oil sector changed between the 1930s, when the business groups were used by the government for nationalist policies, and the 1970s, when the business groups joined the MNEs against nationalist policies that threatened their property rights. The cartel had its best relationship with the government during the times of unchallenged import substitution industrialization and participation of the business groups in economic policy. This shows us a situation in which the MNEs benefited from nationalist policies thanks to their membership of one of the cartel members to the business groups.

This study shows that the cartel was not created through the initiative of its members, even though it proved to be beneficial for them in the long term. The MNEs naturally did not want new members in their own cartel, so they had to be threatened and forced by the government. In the traditional analysis of Mancur Olson, the members of an exclusive group are aware of the benefits of creating the group and make the rational decision of forming the group on their own. However, this chapter shows that the role of the state was crucial. Paradoxically, in the long term this cartel was useful for the companies to defend themselves against the state. In addition, while the MNEs initially opposed COPEC's participation for considering that the Chilean company was going to be an Olsonian 'free rider', in the long term the MNEs were also 'free riders' in terms of protection against the state thanks to COPEC's involvement in the Chilean business groups. COPEC also benefited from the MNEs' political connections during the Allende administration, when the US embassy conspired against the government.

The oil MNEs' long-term strategy cannot be understood without considering the economic context that led to the creation of powerful business groups. Business groups remain predominant in the net oil-importing industrializing nations of the early twenty-first century. In a world economy with increasingly integrated markets, an institution like the business group (which rose under policies of protectionism between the 1930s and 1970s), will continue to influence the terms under which those nations acquire energy resources.

NOTES

1. This chapter draws heavily on Bucheli (2010).
2. Leff (1978): 663.
3. Granovetter (2005).
4. The most important works are Blakemore (1974); Mayo (1987); Monteón (1982); O'Brien (1982); Monteón (2003); O'Brien (1989).
5. Luis Ortega contributed with his studies on the coal industry, but focused on the nineteenth century. See Ortega (1982) and (1988).
6. Villalobos (1983); Vega (1964); Philip (1982).
7. Olson (1965): 37–43; Guillén (2000).
8. Schneider (2004): 10–14.
9. Guillén (2000): 367.
10. Johnson (1994): 237–8.
11. Johnson (1994): 238–9.
12. Reynolds (1965); Monteón (1998): 22–3.
13. Arellano (1985).
14. Cárdenas, Ocampo, and Thorp (2000): 26.
15. Meller (1990): 56.
16. Twomney (1998): 182–3.
17. Scott (1927): 45.
18. Mamalakis (1976): 31.
19. Arellano (1985): 26.
20. Meller (1990): 71.
21. Schneider (2004): 152–60.
22. Schneider (2004): 3–10.
23. Law 4109 of December 29, 1926.
24. Scott (1927): 35.
25. Wilkins (1974): 142–3.
26. Blakemore (1993): 73–79.
27. Kirsch (1977): 132–3.
28. Villalobos (1982): 22.
29. Automobile imports increased from 741 in 1924 to more than 5300 in 1928. See Murray (1930): 47. For information on the number and location of the storage and crude plants, see Mcleod (1923): 25.
30. Fernández (1981).
31. Guajardo (2007); Scott (1927): 29.
32. Federal Trade Commission (1952): 337.
33. Blakemore (1993): 82–3.
34. The League of Nations classified Chile as the hardest hit country during the Depression among countries with available data. See Pinto (1973): 168; Ffrench-Davis and Muñoz (1990).
35. Osorio (1990): 36.

36. Drake (1993): 93–4.
37. Osorio (1990): 37.
38. Pack (1934): 47.
39. Monteón (1998): 29–30, 36.
40. *New York Times* (1931a).
41. Drake (1993): 95–6.
42. Monteón (1998): 73–5.
43. The government also approved in that year a law that obliged foreign corporations to get government approval before building or establishing a refinery. See Burbach (1975): 108.
44. Philip (1982): 182–3.
45. *New York Times* (1931b).
46. Philip (1982): 183–4.
47. Philip (1982): 184.
48. Wenzel (1962).
49. Petroleum Industry Anti-Trust Collection (PIATC) (1931).
50. As late as 1936, there were still reports about the oil from the coal project, but there were still doubts of its economic feasibility. See Mitcheson (1936): 20.
51. *New York Times* (1932a); Monteón (1998): 76.
52. Philip (1982): 184–5.
53. *New York Times* (1932b).
54. Monteón (1998): 76.
55. *New York Times* (1932c).
56. *New York Times* (1932d); US Senate (1976): 82.
57. Drake (1993): 96.
58. Palma (1984): 79.
59. Schneider (2004): 155.
60. Burbach (1975): 32–3.
61. Mamalakis (1976): 90–1.
62. Pack (1934): 57–8.
63. Philip (1982): 187.
64. Ewen, Radcliff, and Zeitlin (1974).
65. The author would like to thank Guillermo Guajardo for Müller's biographical information.
66. Corbo and Meller (1978).
67. Ibáñez (2003): 86–95, 118–24; Burbach (1975): 60.
68. Burbach (1975): 26.
69. Schneider (2004): 154–6.
70. US Senate (1976): 328; Philip (1982): 187.
71. Philip (1982): 187.
72. Philip (1982): 4–5.
73. Philip (1982): 4.
74. Philip (1982): 3.
75. PIATC (1952): 5; *New York Times* (1936); Philip (1982): 187.
76. Monteón (1998): 150.
77. Fermandois (1997).
78. Ross did not have the same attitude towards other MNEs operating in other sectors. Regarding electricity he clashed with the British-owned Chilean Electric Light and Power Company. See Monteón (1998): 151–4.
79. Burbach (1975): 66.
80. Mitcheson (1936): 19–20.
81. Drake (1993): 102–5.
82. PIATC (1952): 5.
83. Burbach (1975): 67; Philip (1982): 188.
84. Knowlton, Larson and Popple (1971): 329.
85. PIATC (1952): 5.

86. Wilkins (1974): 235–7.
87. Howarth, Jonker, and Van Zanden (2007): 444.
88. Alvarado, Barrios, Jaques, and Maldonado (2002).
89. Author's calculations derived from *Anuario Estadístico 1933*, **7**, p. 3; *Anuario Estadístico 1934*, **7**, p. 4; *Anuario Estadístico 1935*, **7**, p. 3, Santiago de Chile: Imprenta Nacional.
90. Author's calculations derived by information from Chile: *Anuario Estadístico 1933*, **4**, p. 16; *Anuario Estadístico 1933*, **7**, p. 4; *Anuario Estadístico 1934*, **4**, p. 16; *Anuario Estadístico 1934*, **7**, p. 4. The *Anuarios* do not specify the percentage of diesel oil consumed by the mining sector.
91. Monteón (1998): 228–9; Drake (1993): 105.
92. Philip (1982): 188–9.
93. Monteón (1998): 262–3.
94. Monteón (1998): 263; Philip (1982): 188–9.
95. Douyon (1972): 87–89. The information on US investment in the mining sector covers the period 1940–60.
96. Ibáñez (2003): 96.
97. Schneider (2004): 155.
98. Loveman (1988): 199; Mamalakis (1976): 91–6.
99. PIATC (1952): 9–10.
100. COPEC, *Memoria 1941*, p. 4.
101. Pinto (1973): 176. The percentage of oil and oil products imports for the rest of the decade was between 4.5 and 7 percent.
102. COPEC, *Memoria 1944*: 4.
103. Philip (1982): 189.
104. Philip (1982): 189.
105. PIATC (n.d.): 17.
106. Burbach (1975): 108–10.
107. PIATC (1952): 5. In the final agreement, the division was Esso 41.77 percent, Shell 24.9 percent, COPEC 33.33 percent. See Federal Trade Commission (1952): 337.
108. Instituto de Economía de la Universidad (1956): 5; Federal Trade Commission (1952): 338.
109. Randall (2007): 75.
110. PIATC (n.d.): 21–2.
111. PIATC (1952): 7.
112. Instituto de Economía de la Universidad de Chile (1956): 163.
113. Odell (1964). A number of Chilean intellectuals considered foreign participation as a giving away Chilean oil to foreign corporations. See Baltra (1957).
114. COPEC contributed with 50 percent of the tanker's capital and Shell and Esso with 25 percent each. See COPEC, *Memoria 1950*, 5; COPEC, *Memoria 1956*, p. 5.
115. *New York Times* (1959).
116. Furnish (1971); COPEC, *Memoria 1961*, p 5.
117. COPEC, *Memoria 1954*, p. 4.
118. Douyon (1972): 267.
119. Stallings (1978): 77–88; Lundahl (1989): 16–20.
120. Lundahl (1989): 27–9.
121. COPEC, *Memoria 1967–68*, pp. 3–6; COPEC, *Memoria 1968–69*, pp. 8–9; COPEC, *Memoria 1969–70*, p. 4.
122. COPEC, *Memoria 1969–70*, p. 3.
123. COPEC, *Memoria, 1968–69*, pp. 1–4.
124. De Vylder (1976): 20–2; Lundahl (1989): 30–4.
125. Sigmund (1978): 48–84 and (1993); Uribe (1974); Vuskovic (1975): 79–121.
126. Schneider (2004): 163.
127. De Vylder (1976): 148; Ramos (1972): 1442–5.
128. Benavides, Cox, Garretón, Hola, Morales, and Portales (1978).
129. World Bank (1980): 197.

130. CIA Intelligence Telegram, 26 September 1970. CIA Chile Declassification Project Tranche III (1979–1991), United States Department of State, Washington (hereafter CIA Chile).
131. From Korry to Kissinger, 25 September 1970, CIA Chile.
132. From Korry to Kissinger and Johnson, 5 October 1970, CIA Chile.
133. From Korry to Kissinger, 25 September 1970, CIA Chile.
134. From Korry to Johnson, 5 October 1970, CIA Chile.
135. COPEC, *Memoria 1971–72*, pp. 1–3.
136. COPEC, *Memoria 1972–73*, pp. 1–2.
137. Rojas (1976): 103–4
138. Lira and Loveman (2000): 343; Cámara de Diputados (2004): 343.
139. Wall (1998): 391.
140. Guillén (2000): 367.
141. Schneider (2004): 164.
142. COPEC, *Memoria 1975*, p. 2.
143. Loveman (1988): 261–307.
144. *Chile Economic News* (1977a).
145. Ministerio de Minería (2007).
146. *Chile Economic News* (1977b); Fuentes, Paredes, and Vatter (1994): 2.
147. Campodónico (2007).
148. *El Mercurio* (2007). The Angelini group controlled 40 percent of Chilean exports between 1987 and 1989. See García (1989).
149. Schneider (2004): 165.
150. Fuentes, Paredes, and Vatter (1994): 21–5.
151. Balmaceda and Soruco (2005).
152. Stanganelli (2006): 275.

REFERENCES

Alvarado, S. , P. Maldonado, A. Barrios and I. Jaques (2002), 'Long term energy-related environmental issues of copper production', *Energy*, **2**, 183–96.

Arellano, José Pablo (1985), *Políticas sociales y desarrollo, Chile 1924–1984*, Santiago de Chile: CIEPLAN, 19–52.

Balmaceda, Felipe and Paula Soruco (2005), 'Asimetrías en la respuesta de los precios de la gasolina en Chile', Working Paper 217, Universidad de Chile, Facultad de Ciencias Físicas y Matemáticas, 6.

Baltra, Alberto (1957), *La desnacionalización del petróleo chileno*, Santiago de Chile: Nascimiento.

Benavides, Leopoldo, Cristián Cox, Manuel Garretón, Eugenia Hola, Eduardo Morales, and Diego Portales (1978), *Chile: cronología del período 1970–1973*, vol. 2, Santiago de Chile: Facultad Latinoamericana de Ciencias Sociales, 397.

Blakemore, Harold (1974), *British Nitrates and Chilean Politics: Balmaceda and North*, London: Athlone Press.

Blakemore, Harold (1993), 'Chile: From the War of the Pacific to 1930', in Leslie Bethell (ed.), *Chile Since Independence*, Cambridge: Cambridge University Press, 33–86.

Bucheli, Marcelo (2010), 'Multinational corporations, business groups, and economic nationalism: Standard Oil (New Jersey), Royal Dutch-Shell, and energy politics in Chile, 1913–2005', *Enterprise and Society*, **11** (2), 350–99.

Burbach, Roger (1975), 'The Chilean industrial bourgeoisie and foreign capital, 1920–1970', Ph.D. Diss., Indiana University.

Cámara de Diputados (2004), *Informe Comisión Privatizaciones*, Santiago de Chile: Cámara de Diputados.

Campodónico, Humberto (2007), *Gestión mixta y privada en la industria de hidrocarburos*, Santiago de Chile: CEPAL.

Cárdenas, Enrique, José Antonio Ocampo, and Rosemary Thorp (2000), *An Economic History of Twentieth Century Latin America*, New York: Macmillan.

Corbo, Vittorio and Patricio Meller (1978), 'Antecedentes empíricos de los sectores externo e industrial chilenos: 1950–1970', *Apuntes Cieplan*, **10**, 6–7.

CORFO (1977a), 'Chile's 100 Largest Companies', *Chile Economic News*, (March), 6–7.

CORFO (1977b), 'CORFO continues to sell its industry holdings', *Chile Economic News*, (August), 2–3.

De Vylder, Stefan (1976), *Allende's Chile: The Political Economy of the Rise and Fall of the Unidad Popular,* Cambridge: Cambridge University Press.

Douyon, Guy (1972), 'Chilean industrialization since CORFO', Ph.D. Diss., American University.

Drake, Paul (1993), 'Chile, 1930–1958', in Leslie Bethell (ed.), *Chile Since Independence*, Cambridge: Cambridge University Press, 87–128.

El Mercurio (2007), 'José Tomás Guzmán: Un Angelini visto muy de cerca', 2 September (online edition).

Ewen, Linda, Richard Radcliff, and Maurice Zeitlin (1974), '"New princes" for old? The large corporation and the capitalist class in Chile', *American Journal of Sociology*, **80**, 114–20.

Federal Trade Commission (1952), *The International Petroleum Cartel*, Washington: Government Printing Office.

Fermandois, Joaquín (1997), *Abismo y cimiento: Gustavo Ross y las relaciones entre Chile y Estados Unidos, 1932–1938*, Santiago de Chile: Ediciones Universidad Católica de Chile, p. 103.

Fernández, Manuel (1981), 'El enclave salitrero y la economía chilena, 1880–1914', *Nueva Historia*, **3**, 27.

Ffrench-Davis, Ricardo and Oscar Muñoz (1990), 'Desarrollo económico, inestabilidad y desequilibrios políticos en Chile, 1950–1989', *Colección Estudios CIEPLAN*, **28**, 127.

Fuentes, Rodrigo, Ricardo Paredes, and Jaime Vatter (1994), 'Desregulación y competencia en el mercado de la gasolina', *Estudios Públicos*, **56**, 1–29.

Furnish, Dale (1971), 'Chilean anti-trust law', *American Journal of Comparative Law*, **19** (3), 464–88.

García, Roberto (1989), 'Cambios industriales en Chile, 1973–1987', in Roberto García (ed.), *Economía y política durante el gobierno militar de Chile, 1973–1987*, Mexico City: Fondo de Cultura Económica.

Granovetter, Mark (2005), 'Business groups and social organization', in Neil Smelser and Richard Swedberg (eds), *The Handbook of Economic Sociology*, Princeton: Princeton University Press, 429–50.

Guajardo, Guillermo (2007), *Tecnología, estado y ferrocarriles en Chile, 1850–1950*, Madrid: Fundación de los Ferrocarriles Españoles, 25–6.

Guillén, Mauro (2000), 'Business groups in emerging economies: A resource-based view', *Academy of Management Journal*, **43** (3), 362–80.

Howarth, Stephen, Joost Jonker, and Jan Van Zanden (2007), *A History of Royal*

Dutch Shell. Volume I: From Challenger to Joint Industry Leader, Oxford: Oxford University Press.

Ibáñez, Adolfo (2003), *Herido en el ala: estado, oligarquías y subdesarrollo. Chile, 1924–1960*, Santiago de Chile: Biblioteca Americana.

Instituto de Economía de la Universidad de Chile (1956), *Desarrollo Económico de Chile, 1940–1956*, Santiago de Chile: Editorial Universitaria.

Johnson, Harry (1994), 'Economic nationalism in new states', in John Hutchinson and Anthony D. Smith (eds), *Nationalism*, Oxford: Oxford University Press, 236–40.

Kirsch, Henry (1977), *Industrial Development in a Traditional Society: The Conflict of Entrepreneurship and Modernization in Chile*, Gainsville: University of Florida Press.

Knowlton, Evelyn, Henrietta Larson and Charles Popple (1971), *New Horizons: History of Standard Oil Company (New Jersey), 1927–1950*, New York: Harper and Row.

Leff, Nathaniel (1978), 'Industrial organization and entrepreneurship in the developing countries: The economic groups', *Economic Development and Cultural Change* **26** (4), 661–75.

Loveman, Brian (1988), *Chile: The Legacy of Hispanic Capitalism*, Oxford: Oxford University Press.

Loveman, Brian and Elizabeth Lira (2000), *Las ardientes cenizas del olvido: vía chilena de reconciliación política, 1932–1944*, Santiago de Chile: Lom Ediciones.

Lundahl, Mats (1989), 'El camino a la dictadura: desarrollo político y económico en Chile, 1952–1973', in Roberto García (ed.), *Economía y política durante el gobierno militar en Chile, 1973–1987*, Mexico: Fondo de Cultura Económica, 16–20.

Mamalakis, Markos (1976), *The Growth and Structure of the Chilean Economy*, New Haven: Yale University Press.

Mayo, Jon (1987), *British Merchants and Chilean Development*, Boulder: Westview Press.

Mcleod, J.M. (1923), *Report on the Financial and Industrial Conditions in Chile*, London: Office of Overseas Trade.

Meller, Patricio (1990), 'Una perspectiva de largo plazo del desarrollo económico chileno, 1880–1990', in Patricio Meller and Magnus Blomström (eds), *Trayectorias divergentes: comparación de un siglo de desarrollo económico latinoamericano y escandinavo*, Santiago de Chile: CIEPLAN.

Ministerio de Minería (2007), *Licitación Internacional, Exploracion y explotacion de hidrocarburos, Cuenca de Magallanes*, Santiago de Chile: Ministerio de Minería, 8.

Mitcheson, John (1936), *Report on Economic and Commercial Conditions in Chile*, London: Office of Overseas Trade.

Monteón, Michael (1982), *Chile in the Nitrate Era: The Evolution of Economic Dependence, 1880–1930*, Madison: University of Wisconsin Press.

Monteón, Michael (1998), *Chile and the Great Depression: The Politics of Underdevelopment, 1927–1948*, Tempe: Arizona State University Press.

Monteón, Michael (2003), 'John T. North, the nitrate king, and Chile's lost future', *Latin American Perspectives*, **30**, 69–90.

Murray, Harvey (1930), *Economic Conditions in Chile*, London: HMSO.

New York Times (1931a), 'Chilean president asks for broad powers', 22 February, 47.

New York Times (1931b), 'Chilean advance oil monopoly bill', 31 October, 27.
New York Times (1932a), 'Gasoline rations decreed in Chile', 11 March, 8.
New York Times (1932b), 'Chile urged to use navy to import oil', 26 March, 24.
New York Times (1932c), 'Oil firms in Chile to fight monopoly', 27 March, 8.
New York Times (1932d), 'Gasoline monopoly authorized in Chile', 19 May, 30.
New York Times (1936), 'Chile debates oil decree', 26 November, 21.
New York Times (1959), 'Chile backs right of expropriation', 20 May, 4.
O'Brien, Thomas (1982), *The Nitrate Industry and Chile's Crucial Transition: 1870–1891*, New York: New York University Press.
O'Brien, Thomas (1989), '"Rich beyond the dreams of Avarice:" The Guggenheims in Chile', *Business History Review*, **63**, 122–159.
Odell, Peter (1964), 'Oil and state in Latin America', *International Affairs*, **40** (4), 659–73.
Olson, Mancur (1965), *The Logic of Collective Action: Public Goods and the Theory of Groups*, Cambridge, MA: Harvard University Press.
Ortega, Luis (1982), 'The first four decades of the Chilean coal mining industry, 1840–1879', *Journal of Latin American Studies*, **14**, 1–32.
Ortega, Luis (1988), *La industria del carbón en Chile, 1840–1880*, Santiago de Chile: Universidad de Santiago de Chile.
Osorio, Jaime (1990), *Raíces de la democracia en Chile*, México: UNAM.
Pack, Arthur J. (1934), *Economic Conditions in Chile*, London: Office of Overseas Trade.
Palma, Jose (1984), 'Chile 1914–1935', *Estudios CIEPLAN*, **12**, 61–88.
Philip, George (1982), *Oil and Politics in Latin America: Nationalist Movements and State Companies*, Cambridge: Cambridge University Press.
PIATC (1931), 'Illegible to clark', 20 March, Case 7, PIATC, Baker Library, Harvard Business School.
PIATC (1952), 'Division of markets: Chile', Case 5, PIATC, Baker Library, Harvard Business School.
PIATC (n.d.),'Report of Mr. E. E. Soubry on the trip which he made with Mr. G. H. Michler through Latin American countries, January-February 1944: Brazil, Argentina, Uruguay, Paraguay, Chile, Peru, Ecuador, Colombia', Case 6, PIATC, Baker Library, Harvard Business School.
Pinto, Aníbal (1973), *Chile, un caso de desarrollo frustrado*, Santiago de Chile: Editorial Universitaria.
Ramos, Sergio (1972), *Chile: ¿Una economía en transición?*, Santiago de Chile: CESO, Editorial Universitaria.
Randall, Stephen (2007), *Foreign Oil Policy Since World War I: For Profits and Security,* Montreal: McGill/Queens University Press.
Reynolds, Clark (1965), 'Development problems in an export economy: The case of Chile and copper', in Markos Mamalakis (ed.), *Essays on the Chilean Economy*, New Haven: Yale University Press, 207–32.
Rojas, Robinson (1976), *The Murder of Allende and the End of the Chilean Way to Socialism*, New York: Harper and Row.
Schneider, Ben Ross (2004), *Business Politics and the State in Twentieth Century Latin America*, Cambridge: Cambridge University Press.
Sigmund, Paul (1978), *The Overthrow of Allende and the Politics of Chile, 1964–1976,* Pittsburgh: University of Pittsburgh Press.
Sigmund, Paul (1993), *The United States and Democracy in Chile*, Baltimore: Johns Hopkins University Press.

Stallings, Barbara (1978), *Class Conflict and Economic Development in Chile, 1958–1973*, Stanford: Stanford University Press.
Stanganelli, Isabel (2006), *Las fuentes de energía en el Cono Sur*, Buenos Aires: Caviar Bleu.
Twomney, Michael (1998), 'Patterns of foreign investment in Latin America in the twentieth century', in Alan Taylor and John Coatsworth (eds), *Latin America and the World Economy Since 1800*, Cambridge, MA: Harvard University Press.
Uribe, Armando (1974), *El libro negro de la intervención norteamericana en Chile*, Mexico: Siglo XXI.
US Senate (1976), *American Petroleum Interests in Foreign Countries*, New York: Arno Press.
Scott, W.F. Vaughn (1927), *Report on the Industrial and Economic Situation in Chile*, London: Office of Overseas Trade.
Puga Vega, Mariano (1964), *El petróleo chileno,* Santiago de Chile: Andrés Bello.
Villalobos, Sergio (1983), *Historia de la Energía en Chile,* Santiago de Chile: Museo Histórico Nacional.
Vuskovic, Pedro (1975), *Acusación al Imperialismo*, Mexico: Fondo de Cultura Económica.
Wall, Bennett (1998), *Growth in a Changing Environment: A History of Standard Oil Company (New Jersey) Exxon Corporation, 1950–1975*, New York: McGraw-Hill.
Wenzel, Osvaldo (1962), 'Combustibles', in CORFO, *Geografía Económica de Chile*, Santiago de Chile: CORFO.
Wilkins, Mira (1974), 'Multinational oil companies in South America in the 1920s: Argentina, Bolivia, Brazil, Chile, Colombia, Ecuador, and Peru', *Business History Review*, **48**.
Wilkins, Mira (1974), *The Maturing of Multinational Enterprise: American Business Abroad from 1914 to 1970*, Cambridge, MA: Harvard University Press.
World Bank (1980), *Chile: An Economy in Transition*, Washington: World Bank.

4. Multinational enterprises in Argentina: from primary commodity exporter to the new liberal era

Andrés López

Foreign investment has been a crucial factor in the business and economic history of Argentina since the nineteenth century. Between 1880 and 1930, when economic growth was driven by agricultural exports, large foreign capital flows arrived in the country in pursuit of business opportunities in infrastructure (especially railroads), primary export processing (especially meat packing), and products and services associated with domestic market expansion (such as food, beverages, textiles, chemicals and cement). Later, during Argentina's import substitution industrialization (ISI) period from the late 1950s to the mid-1970s, MNEs played a key role as the country engaged in capital-intensive manufacturing development. Later, during the pro-market reforms of the 1990s, FDI again flowed in massively, shaping the new economic model that unfolded in that period.

There were times when foreign capital was viewed as a potentially negative factor for Argentina's development. Criticisms included their excessive influence in the domestic economy, which allegedly allowed monopolistic practices and blocked domestic technological development. Hence, at various moments governments nationalized foreign-owned companies and/or clashed with foreign investors. In addition, frequent crises and economic and political instability sometimes turned Argentina into an unattractive host economy.

At the same time, Argentinean firms have also invested abroad. In the era of agricultural exports, Argentine companies pioneered foreign investments in Latin America. Both during Argentina's ISI period, as well as during the 1980s and 1990s, Argentine companies continued to invest overseas. Nonetheless, this was a process riddled with discontinuities, as, with a few exceptions, these operations were carried out by different companies over time. As a result, this phenomenon did not become a decisive influence in Argentine economic growth as a whole, although it did prove relevant for the individual companies that invested abroad in the different stages of the country's development process.

This chapter will analyse Argentina's multinational cross-investment over time in the three different stages of the country's economic history. A final section concludes.

I. ARGENTINA'S AGRICULTURAL EXPORT-BASED MODEL

As the country's agricultural exports boomed between 1880 and 1930, Argentina ranked among the world's fastest growing countries,[1] with per-capita gross domestic product (GDP) levels equivalent to the most advanced economies.[2] Exports of wool and leather were followed by meat and grain. While it boasted undeniable natural advantages to pursue this export strategy, Argentina initially faced considerable domestic challenges, including an insufficient labor force and infrastructure, as well as political and institutional instability. Its lack of a stable legal framework for civil and commercial matters, which also led to a weak property rights, also handicapped its prospects to become a major exporter of agricultural commodities.[3]

By the late nineteenth century, many of these challenges had been overcome. On the one hand, the country's agricultural boundaries had expanded, and immigration policies facilitated the arrival of new workers. In addition, there was a significant drive to improve human capital following the 1884 Common Education Act, which rendered elementary education mandatory, free and secular. Infrastructure issues were tackled with foreign funding, not only through sizable loans, but also with numerous direct foreign investments in Argentina's commercial and transportation systems. Argentina also embarked on several endeavors to facilitate the growth of a capitalist economy, including establishing a national monetary system and organizing a functional judicial and legal framework. Argentina also achieved significant technological progress in its production processes, both in agriculture and cattle breeding, enabling the country's rapid growth as a world-class exporter. At the same time, it developed a modern manufacturing sector, with a large number of factories that used internationally competitive technologies in a range of consumer product industries including food and textiles, though this process proceeded more slowly when it came to capital and knowledge-intensive industries.

Both in export and domestic market-oriented industries, leading Argentine companies operated production plants featuring state-of-the-art technologies. It has been shown that a large share of Argentina's manufacturing

Table 4.1 Comparative foreign investment, 1913

	Per capita in 1900 US$		% capital stock[b]		% GDP	
	FI[a]	FDI[a]	FI[a]	FDI[a]	FI[a]	FDI[a]
Argentina	266	50	24	7	248	47
Australia	289	72	7	2	84	21
Brazil	62	18	17	7	270	81
Canada	375	73	28	10	161	27
Chile	119	52	n.a.	n.a.	205	90
Egypt	70	35	100	50	116	59
Indonesia	12	11	57	53	93	86
Mexico	92	43	43	26	186	87
Peru	40	15	n.a.	n.a.	119	46
South Africa	210	140	66	44	220	148

Notes:
a FI: Total foreign investment. FDI: Foreign direct investment except railroads.
b Data for Mexico is 1910, and 1914 for Australia, Canada and Egypt.

Source: Calculated by the author from Michael Twome,'Patterns of foreign investment in Latin America in the twentieth century', in J. H. Coatsworth and A.M. Taylor (eds.) *Latin America and the World Economy since 1800*, Cambridge: Harvard University Press, 1998.

production took place in modern facilities, with productivity levels comparable to international standards.[4] The technological standards in industrial plants underwent rapid improvement during these decades.[5]

Foreign investments grew rapidly in the Argentine economy at this time, as they did in other recently established nations like Australia, Canada and South Africa, as well as in many other Latin American and Asian countries (Table 4.1). In Argentina, Australia and Canada, the bulk of these investments were in railroads.

The impact of inward FDI, primarily American and British, was particularly great for the development of Argentina's transportation and service infrastructure, as well as for its meat-packing industry. These investments facilitated the introduction of modern production and labor management techniques into Argentina. The focus on commodity exports was typical of the emergent North-South divide in the global economy. However, while only 2 percent of both direct and portfolio foreign investments combined went to the manufacturing sector,[6] significant investments were made in industries such as food and beverages, cement, chemicals, pharmaceuticals, electrical supplies and car assembly, among others. These were market-seeking investments attracted by economic stability and domestic market growth. They were also encouraged by protective policies favoring some industries, even though Argentina's economy was largely 'open' in this period.[7] At the same time, the desire by American firms to undermine the domestic market dominance of British firms through imports also played a key role in investment decisions.

For the most part, foreign affiliates operated facilities that were notably larger than the average plants owned by local manufacturers. During the 1920s, FDI flows, particularly from the United States, brought about the introduction of more new products, as well as modern production and organization practices that renewed Argentina's industrial sector in the last years of the era of the agricultural export-led model.[8] This FDI-driven technological dissemination was fueled not only by industrial facilities, but also by commercial affiliates, as the marketers of foreign capital goods generally did not only focus on imports, but also provided services, produced spare parts, assembled and outsourced part manufacturing with local firms, encouraging the development of suppliers in the manufacturing sector.[9]

The positive impact of FDI on Argentina's agricultural export-led model was offset by cases of market power abuses and unfair business practices in industries like meat packing. This caused some animosity against foreign capital in several political, intellectual and social circles.

It should also be noted that foreigners prevailed in Argentina's industry because a large number of business ventures were founded by immigrants. In 1895, 84 percent of Argentine business owners had been born abroad, although by 1913 this share had dwindled to 65 percent.[10] Ties with interests overseas went beyond the direct engagement of foreign firms or businessmen in Argentine operations. The strong links between Argentine and European capital and labor markets provided local businesses with benefits that businessmen in other developing countries did not enjoy.[11]

Indeed, this phase in Argentine history saw the emergence of a group of business leaders who were part of the local social elite, and boasted vast knowledge of domestic markets, decision-making power, and access to both banks and public offices.[12] As several of these groups belonged to immigrant families, they usually relied on valuable contacts in Europe, especially to access funding. As a result, these groups enjoyed a privileged position to seize business opportunities which enabled them to build large business enterprises.

In the late nineteenth and early twentieth centuries, a number of these emergent business groups became the first companies from the non-Western world to engage in FDI.[13] The most striking examples included Bunge y Born (foodstuffs), Alpargatas (textiles), SIAM Di Tella (metal mechanics), Campomar (textiles), Águila (food) and Compañía General de Fósforos (diversified). Alpargatas even went as far as planning the deployment of factories in Spain and Italy, although these plans never materialized.[14] These internationalization processes were primarily driven by a response to domestic market saturation, and rested on the groups' greater efficiency as compared to their regional counterparts.[15]

II. THE ERA OF IMPORT SUBSTITUTION INDUSTRIALIZATION

During the era of ISI, Argentina gradually descended the rankings of international per capita income. However, this phase may be divided into two different periods. Argentina clearly lagged behind the world's most advanced nations in the first one, which lasted until 1957. In the following period, from 1958 until 1975, the gap with developed countries stopped increasing.[16] This era coincided with the beginning of the 'difficult' ISI phase, characterized by a move towards heavy industries, metal mechanics, chemistry, and electronics, while in the earlier period, Argentina had primarily focused on 'light' industrialization, concentrating on industries such as food and textiles.

Overall Argentina's performance was quite poor during the ISI era. As Table 4.2 shows, the country was among the poorest performing countries

Table 4.2 Annual growth of per capita GDP, labor productivity and exports, 1950–1973

	Per capita GDP*	Labor productivity**	Exports***
Japan	8.1	7.7	18.0
South Korea	5.8	4.1	24.0
Spain	5.8	6.4	11.9
Brazil	3.7	3.7	6.8
Mexico	3.2	4.0	6.5
Canada	2.7	2.9	9.9
All Latin America	2.5	n.a.	n.a.
United States	2.5	2.8	8.8
Argentina	2.1	2.4	4.5
Rank of Argentina	85 (out of 136)	39 (out of 42)	51 (out of 56)

Notes: (*) Measured in constant US dollars, based on the purchasing power parity (PPP) method. (**) Measured as GDP (in PPP constant dollars)-work hour ratio. (***) In current US dollars.

Source: Calculated by the author based on Angus Maddison, *Monitoring the World Economy 1820–1992*, Paris: OECD, Development Studies Centre, 1995, and idem, *The World Economy. A Millenial Perspective*, Paris: OECD, Development Studies Centre, 2001.

for which data is available for the growth of per capita GDP, labor productivity and exports. The latter is noteworthy as this was a period which saw fast growth in international trade.

This weak performance does not automatically support a view that ISI was a total disaster. On the contrary, several developments seem positive, particularly as regards learning processes and technological capability accumulation across a significant share of Argentina's industrial base. In addition, there was noteworthy social progress. However, Argentina's performance looked poor as many economies in this period grew rapidly and the country even under-performed the Latin American average, despite the fact that it seemed to be well-positioned to perform well in the post-war period.

Argentina's poor economic performance rested on a number of factors, including: (i) strong institutional volatility;[17] (ii) ongoing stop-and-go cycles that stemmed from the ISI model's underlying rationale and brought sharp relative price changes as a result of successive devaluation crises;[18] (iii) frequent economic policy shifts; (iv) relentless distributive clashes that became structural after 1945; and (v) an extremely closed economy in the post-war period that prevented Argentina from exploiting international trade advantages at a time of powerful expansion. This latter factor proved particularly damaging for local industrialization, as it increasingly stranded Argentinean firms in their small local market and sharply increased the costs of capital goods imports.[19]

Argentina's economy started to close after the 1930 crisis, as international conditions were increasingly unfavorable to serving the world market. During the 1930s, Argentinean governments opted for a 'pragmatic' approach, which involved adjusting local policies to external restrictions, but they failed to formulate a clear plan to drive industrialization.[20]

Changes started taking place in 1945, when Juan D. Perón took office as president, and his administration adopted a decidedly domestic market-oriented economic policy. As noted by Díaz Alejandro, this approach was closely associated with the wealth redistribution program fostered by Peronism, as with lagging productivity and delayed technological progress besieging most of Argentina's industrial base, high labor costs hindered the creation of a competitive manufacturing sector.

Subsequently, with the 'developmentalist' government that took office in 1958, the Argentine economy remained strongly closed, but industrial promotion mechanisms were instituted to promote investments on heavy and durable goods industries by means of generous tax and credit incentives. These were largely exploited by foreign MNEs.

It was only in the mid-1960s that Argentinean policies began to focus on expanding industrial exports, with new subsidies and other mechanisms.

As a result, industrial exports grew by the end of the ISI period. Tariff protection was also reduced, especially between 1967 and 1969, but still remained high.[21] Nevertheless, during the second period in Argentina's ISI phase, the local economy continued to be among the world's most closed economies.

In short, during its ISI phase, despite macroeconomic policy changes and institutional instability, Argentina maintained a pro-industrialization scheme based on domestic market protection, as well as fiscal and credit incentives. The local industry sector was a net borrower from the rest of the economy, at negative real interest rates throughout this period.[22] This policy regime created an environment that discouraged competition through innovation, quality and productivity, as it emphasized the supply of the domestic market rather than productive efficiency. Governmental 'pro-industrialization' policies failed to include incentives that promoted efficiency or facilitated productive and technological learning processes in businesses. Insofar as any learning occurred, it took place beyond the policy framework, and was the result of the accumulation of human skills and knowledge in industrial value chains.

Foreign Direct Investment during Argentina's Import Substitution Phase

During the 1930s, some investments, especially from the United States and Germany, continued to be made in Argentina, designed to serve the domestic market, and often replacing imports.[23] During the Peronist administration, however, there was a hostile attitude towards foreign firms.[24] German companies were nationalized after the end of World War II, creating the National Department of State Industries (or DINIE for its acronym in Spanish). The government also seized most of the utilities owned by foreign firms. FDI flows were affected by these measures. In 1940, American FDI in Argentina was 60 percent higher than in Brazil, while, in 1955, American FDI in Argentina only accounted for 40 percent of American FDI in Brazil.[25] By 1955, foreign capital accounted for only 5 percent of Argentina's overall capital, down from 48 percent at the turn of the century.[26]

Nonetheless, at the end of this period, the Peronist government decided to turn to foreign investments to fund Argentina's industrial accumulation process and develop the oil industry. This policy change translated into Act 14,222, the first law to systematically regulate foreign capital entry and operation. Under this law, agreements were signed with companies including Squibb, Mercedes Benz, California Petroleum and Kaiser, which led to the institutionalization of de facto trusts or market reserves and implied significant revenue transfers among sectors.[27]

Subsequently, President Frondizi's developmentalist administration (1958–62) gave a key role to foreign capital in its swift industrialization program. Act 14,780, introduced by Perón, which suppressed restrictions on earning transfers and capital repatriation, and Act 14,781, an industrial promotion law that granted tax and credit incentives, were introduced to attract foreign investments. In addition, oil operations were partially opened by means of exploration and exploitation contracts in some areas, under the supervision of the state-owned Yacimientos Petrolíferos Fiscales (YPF).

The steps taken by the developmentalist government proved successful, and FDI boomed. Between 1959 and 1962, a total of US$ 500 million of investments were approved, doubling all approvals granted in 1954–58 and in 1964–70. Of the investments approved in this period, 90 percent focused on chemical, petrochemical, oil by-products, automobiles and trucks, basic metals, electrical and non-electrical machinery industries.[28] The United States was the leading investor in Argentina, but significant investments were also made by British, German, French and Italian firms, among others.

During Onganía's military government (1966–69), a new wave of investments, primarily geared towards the acquisition of local businesses and the expansion of installed capacity, consolidated the leadership of MNEs in Argentina's industrial sector. As a result of these massive FDI flows, MNEs increased their share of local manufacturing production from 18.4 percent in 1955 to 24 percent in 1963 and to 28.2 percent in 1970 (see Table 4.3). As compared to local firms, MNE affiliates were characterized by (i) larger scale and higher productivity, imports and capital investment per employee levels and (ii) the use of technologies that were not cutting-edge but still seemed novel for the local market.

In this period, industrial FDI pursued protected domestic market supply strategies, based on stand-alone, multi-plant corporate schemes, following the market-seeking FDI rationale that hinged on tariff-jumping. Thus, the closed economy strategy that prevailed at the time proved useful for FDI goals. In general, MNE investments were funded with national savings and tended to create, after the positive impact of initial investments, a negative net exchange contribution, considering their low inclination to exports and their transfers – via dividends and royalties to headquarters.

While MNEs did not invest in Argentina explicitly to build a local technological infrastructure, many of them found that they had to make such investments in the light of idiosyncratic requirements of the Argentinean market. Their impact was significant, as MNEs created engineering departments and supplier development programs that led to knowledge accumulation and exchange among industrial producers during

Table 4.3 Comparative performance of domestic and MNE affiliates in Argentine manufacturing industry, 1955–1973

	Years	MNE affiliates	Domestic companies
Share of output	1955	18.4	81.6
	1963	24.0	76.0
	1970	28.2	71.8
Annual output growth rate	1955–1973	8.8	4.3
Average size (output or sales)			
All sites	1963	54.0	0.8
Sites with over 500 employees	1963	380.0	89.4
All private companies	1963	14.1	0.7
Labor productivity			
All sites	1963	0.8	0.4
Sites with over 500 employees	1963	0.8	0.5
Annual productivity growth rate	1955–1973	7.7	3.0

Source: Juan Sourrouille, Juan, Bernardo Kosacoff, and Juan Lucangeli, *Transnacionalización y política económica en la Argentina*, Buenos Aires: Centro Editor de América Latina and CET, 1985.

Argentina's ISI period. Although their research and development (R&D) investments were not high, these firms provided their labor force with training, exposing their personnel to their headquarters' technological and corporate culture and introducing tolerance and quality standards that became central to the industrial practices at that time. In some cases, MNE affiliates played a key role providing engineering service to other developing countries affiliates within their respective corporations. Still, MNE's technological efforts remained primarily adaptive, and their requests to science and technology institutes focused on measurement issues.[29]

This FDI-intensive industrialization process fueled greater manufacturing industry concentration, as measured in terms of larger business units' market shares. However, this concentration increase also reflected international trends at the time, and was a natural follow up of the SMEs-led manufacturing development process before 1955. Therefore, the emergence of more oligopolistic structures came as a result of a shift towards more capital-intensive sectors and a search for economies of scale to substantially improve Argentine industry's low productivity.[30]

The ISI-based industrialization process started to bear fruit at the end of this phase. Between 1964 and 1974, Argentina's industrial output grew at an accumulative annual rate of nearly 7 percent, while employment and productivity climbed 1.5 percent and 5 percent a year, respectively.[31] In turn, manufacturing exports grew from barely US$ 100 million in 1969 to US$ 900 million in 1974, when they accounted for 20–25 percent of overall Argentine exports. Total industrial exports (including agribusiness exports) totaled over US$ 2 billion.

Nonetheless, factories set up during this second ISI phase, even those owned by MNE affiliates, largely lagged far behind international scale and automation standards and were more vertically integrated than their counterparts in developed countries. It should be especially noted that these plants had been mostly planned for domestic market operations,[32] whose size did not allow for the economies of scale required to make an efficient use of the Fordist technologies that prevailed at this time.

In this context, where critical views on Argentina's development style and its resulting economic growth pace were common, rather hostile opinions and attitudes towards foreign capital started to emerge in intellectual, political and social circles. This sentiment was often associated, more or less directly, with anti-dependentist theories that were spreading fast in Argentina and other developing countries at the time, warning about the potentially negative role that MNEs could play in peripheral economic development processes, including issues such as blocking local technological activities, an undue use of patent systems, excessive earning transfers, and monopolistic practices. Thus, the representatives of small and medium-sized enterprises (SMEs) as well as nationalist intellectuals and politicians started to decry the negative outcomes of industry 'denationalization'. At the same time, even associations representing larger businesses, including the Argentine Industrial Union (UIA, for its Spanish acronym), began to feel wary of increasing MNE presence and lobbied for a more stringent regulatory framework.

After Onganía was ousted and a new military regime took over, foreign capital ceased to be viewed as the preferred means to facilitate industrialization. Two developments took place. First, Argentina's legislation became more restrictive both for investment authorizations and local affiliate operations.[33] Second, a 'silent bet' on (large) local capital was made, translating into public policies that favored domestic companies.[34] However, efforts to promote Argentina's local business community came at a difficult, volatile time in the nation's history. The return of the Peronist party to office in 1973 also brought a new shift to the state-business partnership game, as, at that time, the 'national bourgeoisie' of local SMEs was chosen as the preferred beneficiary of public polices, but this intended preference failed to materialize in a chaotic macroeconomic and political setting. Unlike many other late industrializing countries, Argentina did not pursue a sustained strategy to support 'national champions'.

Yet, even in this context, a dynamic set of local companies moved forward. As technological competences grew, they expanded their operations in Argentina's domestic market, exported their products to neighboring nations. They were able to sell their technologies to other Latin American countries, employing different modes including turnkey factory installation, licenses and support services.[35] In turn, a sizable number of domestic firms (nearly 100 of them) embarked on internationalization processes via FDI in neighboring countries.[36] In both cases, Argentine companies' intangible assets primarily included products and processes designed for and/or adjusted to regional production and consumption conditions.

FDI operations were mostly conducted by medium-sized, nationally owned firms and were based on their command of intermediate technologies. These investments focused on markets which were similar to Argentina, in terms of development or sometimes a little less developed where the production arrangements used in Argentina could be replicated and coordinated.[37] A significant share of these ventures took place in the metal mechanic industry as a result of its expansion in the domestic market. Most of the firms were family, stand-alone businesses, with little diversification in the local market and no ties with the financial system.[38] Their early development was supported by the ISI regulatory framework involving high protection, strong reliance on state lending, and promotion mechanisms, which enabled them to build their own technological acumen on product and process imitations, adapting them to local market conditions. As a result, these firms enjoyed advantages over local producers in the countries where they invested. Their technologies often proved more suitable for neighboring countries than the ones developed by MNEs in developed nations.

In some cases, outward FDI was driven by product characteristics that made it convenient for businesses to operate near markets because of costly freight charges or a need to provide post-sale and repair services. This was the case in food packaging and agricultural machinery. In a few cases, such as the oil industry, FDI focused on natural resource exploitation, while, in others, the key lay in a search for raw material supply control (ferroalloy production and the subsequent investment in Brazil to secure the supply of minerals, or an FDI made by a confectionary manufacturer in Costa Rica for guaranteeing chocolate supply). Some features of the ISI regulatory framework in Argentina and in neighboring countries also contributed to these moves, including trade restrictions, and fledgling regional integration projects.

III. FROM THE 'LOST DECADE' TO THE NEW LIBERAL ERA, 1976–2001

While this section deals with the 1976–2001 period as a whole, it is necessary to make a distinction between different sub-periods, both in terms of economic performance and policies as well as of institutional frameworks. Argentina's economic performance between 1976 and 1990 was a disaster: per capita GDP in 1990 was 23 percent lower than it had been in 1975. There was a drop in total factor productivity (TFP) of 23 percent, combined with low investment levels. In 1990, Argentina's capital stock was only 3 percent higher than in 1980.[39]

The second sub-period encompassed the so-called era of the convertibility program between 1991 and 2001, a stabilization program under which the Argentinean peso was managed by a currency board and convertible to US dollars. It had two different phases. The first one, featuring price stabilization and the adoption of pro-market measures, marked Argentina's return to the path of economic growth, interrupted only in 1995 (with the so-called 'Tequila effect' in the aftermath of Mexico's financial crisis). In 1991–98, Argentine per capita GDP grew at a 5.5 percent annual accumulative rate. In the second half of 1998, this growth process came to a stop, and Argentina succumbed to a long stagnation that ended with the end of convertibility in 2001, followed by its sovereign debt default and the virtual collapse of the financial system.

The period began with the military regime that seized power in 1976 adopting an adjustment policy intended to reduce inflation and improve the external accounts. While there was some early growth, the regime was unable to curb inflation to reasonable levels, and in 1979 a new economic program was launched based on the so-called 'balance of payment monetary approach' which intended to match domestic and international inflation rates by means of slowly devaluing the peso. At the same time, reform initiatives were also launched, including a trade liberalization policy that turned more intensive in 1978, as well as a modest privatization program. In 1977 a major financial reform was initiated, and starting in 1979, exchange controls were relaxed. The restrictions on foreign investment introduced earlier in the decade were also relaxed.

Argentina's greater economic openness was accompanied by currency appreciation. By 1980 the country had a high trade deficit, raising fears of devaluation reinforced by changing leadership in the military regime. Capital flight and a bank run followed. The policy response included a peso devaluation, and the government had to assume a large share of the private sector's indebtedness abroad. In 1982, the international debt crisis struck a new blow to Argentina's economy. There was a 7 percent drop in the GDP between 1980–82 after the Argentinean army invaded the Falkland Islands, a British colony claimed by Argentina as the Malvinas, only to be defeated and expelled.

After this crisis, domestic economic policies focused on achieving a positive trade balance in order to service annual debt service payments. The domestic economy was closed again, with new restrictions imposed on imports. During President Alfonsín's administration (1983–89), fiscal and external constraints consistently restrained economic policies, rendering them unable to mitigate inflation and to achieve sustainable growth. In 1989, Argentina's long-standing high inflation finally turned into hyper-inflation, unleashing an acute economic, social and political debacle that forced Alfonsín to resign. In 1989 alone, the nation's GDP fell by more than 6 percent.

The convertibility program launched in 1991 led to a sharp decline in inflation. It was introduced in the context of a wide and deep structural reforms program that had been slowly initiated in the late 1980s. New trade policies further reduced quantitative restrictions until they were all eliminated in early 1991. Simultaneously, tariffs were reduced in successive rounds, dropping from an average 30 percent in October 1988 to 18 percent in January 1991. At the same time, the Southern Common Market (MERCOSUR) was created, whereby Brazil, Argentina, Paraguay and Uruguay adopted an overall, automatic tariff waiving scheme that started off from a 50 percent minimal preference for trade transactions among members in 1991 to completely free trade among member states by 1994. In 1994, the four partnering nations were expected to streamline their international trade policies to build a customs union. This process was completed as scheduled, albeit 'imperfectly', insofar complete free intra-zone trade was never achieved, while the common external tariff adopted was full of national exceptions.

During President Menem's administration (1989–99), a new state reform law was sanctioned to oversee public asset transfers to the private sector. Argentina's massive privatization program began in 1989–90, with the sales of its telephone company, national airline, oil wells, media, railroads and highway maintenance, and later expanded to other areas, like electricity, natural gas and water services. Steel and petrochemical companies, like YPF, the state-owned oil company, were also sold to private bidders. Additionally, licenses were granted to exploit and explore mines as well as oil and gas fields, while domestic and international crude oil and fuel trade was deregulated.

FDI legislation, broadly liberalized since 1976, was amended in 1989 to repeal surviving restrictions. Equal treatment was afforded to both domestic and foreign capital, doing away with provisions requiring prior approval for inward FDI. From then on, Argentina imposed nearly no restrictions or differential rules for foreign companies' operations. The overall liberalization of FDI requirements, combined with an absence of tariffs for capital goods imports,[40] a deregulated technology transfer scheme and a new patent law in 1995 (based on commitments made for the World Trade Organization's (WTO) Agreement on Trade-Related Aspects of Intellectual Property Rights (TRIPS Agreement), provided the basis for the government's intended plan to modernize Argentina's economy and push firms to rise to the challenge of competing in a more deregulated, competitive environment.

In this liberalizing context, and as a result of the more attractive business opportunities offered by Argentina's domestic market, inward FDI flows went from below US$ 6 billion in the 1980s to nearly US$ 80 billion in the 1990s. After 1993 MNEs sharply increased their relative importance in the domestic economy. By 2009 over half the 500 largest firms had at least one-half of their capital held abroad.[41]

During the 1990s, the bulk of inward FDI flows came from outside Latin America, with developed countries, especially the United States and Europe, providing at least four-fifths of FDI flows. Also noteworthy was significant inward FDI from countries like Spain and Chile, mostly associated with privatizations that had not formerly ranked among major sources of FDI in Argentina. Service industries received over 40 percent of incoming investment flows during the 1990s mostly as a result of utility privatizations, but also on account of significant investments made in banks and retailing. The manufacturing sector received a lower share of FDI than it had garnered during Argentina's import substitution phase – barely 20 percent.[42] In the industrial sector, food and beverages, chemicals and transportation equipment (primarily cars) industries received a larger share of manufacturing FDI, as had happened during the ISI phase. Also outstanding was FDI in the oil (as a result of Spanish Repsol's acquisition of YPF, Argentina's state-owned oil company) and mining sectors – both formerly closed to foreign capital (35 percent of received FDI went to oil and mining). MNE's almost ignored 'labor-intensive' industries, and as a result Argentina practically hosted no FDI intended to produce goods for exports at low labor cost.

Inward FDI was primarily market-seeking investment, with a predominant focus on service industries, and was often associated with privatizations. However, there were also relevant resource-seeking flows targeting natural resources, as well as some efficiency-seeking strategies with a primarily regional scope, enabled by MERCOSUR's tariff barrier removal and allowing affiliates to specialize in product lines that could be regionally traded. Unilateral liberalization also paved the way for affiliates to complement their local offerings with imported goods and to replace domestic vendors with inputs, parts and capital goods imports. Nonetheless, few local affiliates aimed at pursuing corporate global efficiency strategies, as they remained focused on either their home market or at best the region.

The fact that most FDI arriving in Argentina in the 1990s came through the acquisition of existing companies,[43] combined with mergers and acquisitions among domestic companies, led to growing concerns about an increasingly concentrated economy, with its ensuing negative impact on well-being and efficiency. Until 1999, there were no effective controls or mechanisms in place to regulate mergers and acquisitions in Argentina. The government did not rely on any specific policies to encourage or discourage cross-border mergers and acquisitions over greenfield investments, while the 1970 Anti-trust Act (Number 22,262) did not feature any provisions for mergers, acquisitions or joint ventures. As a result, it was outdated and ineffective in the 1990s.[44]

A new local business player emerged in the 1990s – investment funds. In a setting characterized by relatively easy access to international funds, these entities captured resources in several markets primarily to acquire existing companies, turn them around and sell them, waging on short-term capital gains. These funds (Exxel, CEI, Citicorp Equity Investments – IRSA, MBA, among others) became significant players in the local economy in the 1990s. However, the largest one, Exxel, eventually divested the bulk of the companies it had managed to control (while other funds are still operating at present, and new funds have emerged since 2001). In any case, we believe the analysis of their behaviors and strategies hinges on gaining a better understanding of their businesses' financial issues rather than their productive or technological performance.[45]

During Argentina's last military regime (1976–83), despite a favorable legal framework for MNEs, new FDI inflows not only turned out to be relatively modest, but there were also many divestments. Between 1976–81, many MNEs, including General Motors, Citröen, Olivetti, John Deere, and Massey Ferguson, withdrew from the Argentine market or temporarily shut down. Two large foreign companies, Sudamtex and Tamet, were also taken over by domestic investors. Overall, the share of foreign equity in Argentina's industrial output dropped from 30.4 percent in 1973 to 26.8 percent in 1984.[46] Sourrouille et al. have argued that previous FDI had arrived in Argentina in previous decades and had conformed to the country's import substitution program and its tightly closed economy.[47] When these conditions changed, the business logic of the ventures had disappeared. However, MNEs were not convinced of the sustainability of the new macroeconomic and regulatory framework, and did not seek to develop new business models.

While MNEs remained cautious, a group of large, locally-owned and highly diversified conglomerates thrived under the industrial promotion laws still in force at the time, while they also seized the opportunities brought by both capital market openness and access to foreign lending.[48] At the same time, in the early 1980s, several ventures launched by Argentine companies abroad during the ISI phase had weakened considerably, leading to closures and exits. This loss of dynamism may be attributed to three key underlying factors. First, domestic economic and regulatory causes, mainly related to the early 1980s crisis, forced companies to pace their growth and cross-border expansion. Second, some of these experiences proved short-lived as a result of companies' lack of productive flexibility, their family management style, and their vulnerable technological and financial plans. Finally, economic crises and regulatory changes affected the economies where Argentinean firms had invested, either because of adjustment processes that hampered the respective domestic markets, or because (in the case of Brazil) Argentine companies' technological supremacy was quickly outdone by local producers.

Another group of local companies also chose to invest directly in neighboring countries. On average, these companies were somewhat larger than the firms that had engaged in FDI processes during Argentina's ISI phase. The industries involved also started to reflect the evolution of the Argentinean economy, as they were now led by food and beverages, oil, pharmaceutical and printing businesses, even though metal mechanic industry investments remained important.[49] Market saturation in Argentina's domestic market prompted these internationalization efforts, despite the fact that foreign investments largely accounted for a minor share of companies' accumulation processes. Argentina's overvalued currency also played a part in these moves, as it undermined industrial profitability.

During the 1980s, Argentina's industrial sector continued its structural transformation, consolidating some changes introduced during the military regime, such as increased local conglomerates presence and a shift from metal mechanic industries towards heavy industrial inputs (petrochemicals, steel, etc.) and some foodstuffs. Yet, the 1980s marked a consolidating period for local business groups, which continued to benefit from investment and export promotion schemes, including preferential energy and gas prices, as well as market reserves and better access to public purchases and contracts. These groups also undertook modest outward FDI. While it may be argued that macroeconomic instability did bring opportunities for highly profitable, short-term financial investments, they also hindered long-term planning, damaging the formulation of growth strategies that focused on the domestic market. As a result, these companies turned overseas to look for new investment opportunities.[50]

While business groups continued to seize new ground in Argentina's domestic economy, MNEs displayed a cautious investment behavior, first taking advantage of opportunities brought about by industrial promotion schemes and, later, exploiting the benefits of the debt capitalization program adopted in the late 1980s. Thus, a handful of large investment projects took off: possibly the largest one was Transax's Córdoba-based gearbox plant owned by Ford-Volkswagen. However, these projects did not suffice to make Argentina a more attractive host economy. MNE affiliates were largely confined to adaptive R&D which did little to enhance the level of technological innovation in the country.[51]

During the 1990s there was a reversal of the trend seen in the previous 15 years. MNEs expanded their investments in the country. In contrast, the business groups that had been growing steadily over past decades started to slow down, state-owned companies nearly disappeared and a considerable number of industrial SMEs left the market, either because they went bankrupt or were sold. These developments during the 1990s reversed the trend seen over the previous 15 years.

The new inward FDI wave unfolded in a different setting. There was a much lower need for adaptive technological efforts, while imported inputs weighed more heavily on production processes. At the same time, equipment renewal was made easier, rendering unnecessary local plant engineering efforts to extend machinery lifecycles as had been required before. In addition, MNE affiliates moved closer to completely imitating the product mixes seen in their home economies, as industrial organization models grew 'global' and online operations connecting affiliates to the rest of their corporations became commonplace. Thus, R&D and process engineering departments could be eliminated or reduced when subsidiaries joined worldwide integrated production systems and R&D and engineering tasks were streamlined at headquarters. In short, product technology and process gaps closed – albeit partially – and local innovative efforts lost significance.[52]

Despite such local and international changes, industrial MNE affiliates continued to primarily cater to Argentina's domestic market, as they had done during the ISI phase. However, this does not mean that MNEs did not embrace significant operating changes, pursuing more 'open' production and trade strategies than their local counterparts (with intra-company trade weighing notably), often amidst the above-mentioned efficiency-seeking strategies enabled by trade liberalization and MERCOSUR integration.[53]

A. The Impact of FDI in Argentina in the 1990s

There was considerable negative comment on the impact of inward FDI on Argentina during the 1990s. However, more recent research has demonstrated that such criticism was exaggerated. While it is true that the macroeconomic impact of FDI on the growth of GDP was not great, this new research has shown that the microeconomic and social impact of FDI was stronger, albeit with both positive and negative outcomes. The key takeaways from this new research can be summarized as follows.[54]

(1) MNE affiliates were more productive and traded more than local firms, both in terms of absolute values and as a percentage of sales.
(2) When foreign firms acquired local businesses, R&D spending at acquired firms did not change much, but these companies became more likely to introduce new products and/or processes.
(3) There were no negative or positive FDI spillovers upon local firms, except for (a) local firms with high absorption capabilities,[55] which benefited from MNEs operating in their respective industries, and (b) MNE local suppliers became more likely to launch new products or processes. In light of this, it may be argued that domestic firms need to enhance their technological assets in order to become MNE suppliers.
(4) As opposed to frequent assumptions, there was no evidence to support that Argentine employment either rose or fell whenever foreign investors acquired a domestic firm. The same goes for salaries. Yet, business acquisitions did have an impact on employment composition, increasing the share of qualified jobs over total labor.
(5) FDI had a positive impact on skilled workers' salaries and contributed to enlarging the gap between qualified and non-skilled workers' incomes.

In short, these findings indicate that foreign investors have transferred inputs (such as organizational and production technologies) to acquired firms, making it possible for the latter to launch new products, increase their labor productivity and their trade operations abroad, without having to raise their R&D spending, as MNE affiliates can access the technologies available in their corporations. Spillovers from these processes onto local firms have been limited and heterogeneous, depending primarily on local firms' capabilities and possibilities to partner with foreign affiliates. In turn, FDI flows do not seem to have caused unemployment, though they may have contributed to greater income disparity. However, the impact of FDI on inequality is likely to have paled into insignifance as compared to other factors, including trade liberalization, unequal access to education, or unemployment.[56]

B. Business Groups' Internationalization in the 1990s

The strategies and performances of domestic business groups during the 1990s proved uneven in a setting where, as a group, they tended to lose some of the clout they boasted in earlier decades. To illustrate this retreat, suffice to say that, considering the 24 largest business groups listed in Bisang[57] as representing this group in the early 1990s, and comparing their sales with those of the largest 1000 local firms in 1992 and 2001, their share dropped from 18 percent to 11 percent in that period. Furthermore, several surviving groups had to partner with foreign companies – in some cases, yielding the controlling stake (Bridas, Acindar, Alpargatas) or move their headquarters to other countries (Bunge y Born). It should also be noted that by 2005, two of the groups that were left standing after the 1990s, Bemberg and Loma Negra, no longer belonged to local owners, while Pescarmona's and Pérez Companc's revenues had shrunk considerably as a result of key asset sales (the telephone company IMPSAT and its entire energy business, respectively).

Indeed, the declining fortunes of Argentine conglomerates compounded by the remarkable progress made by MNE affiliates in the local economy, sparked concerns in business, intellectual and political circles. In the late 1990s, demands grew for the reconstruction of Argentina's 'national bourgeoisie', reversing the multinationalization process or, at least, creating the necessary conditions to safeguard surviving local companies. Nothing came of these concerns during the 1990s.

During the 1990s, while the reduction of state industrial promotion schemes, subsidized loans and contracts reduced opportunities for local firms, it also brought new business prospects through the privatization programs, in addition to those created by the stabilization process itself and renewed growth. Reforms also forced the business groups to confront international competition by undermining their ability to grow exclusively in their local market.[58]

Nonetheless, a few of these business groups engaged in more 'proactive' strategies. Companies like Techint, Arcor,[59] Pérez Companc, SOCMA, Bagó, Urquia, Pescarmona, and Aluar strengthened their positions in their local market, often refocusing on their core businesses and increasing their operations abroad, not only through exports but also with FDI.[60] Many of them underwent generational changes, management professionalization processes, enhancing their marketing and logistics operations while moving towards modern holding schemes –separating production from corporate activities.[61] They also reverted to their vertical integration schemes in non-strategic areas, while venturing into new areas with privatizations and moving forward in their respective value chains towards greater value-added businesses, where they would compete not on prices but on product differentiation. Yet, even in these cases, groups needed to rethink their core businesses when their growth in pre-existing areas proved difficult (notably, Pérez Companc switched from energy to food), and some of their attempts to diversify into more dynamic businesses ended in failure (IMPSAT, Pescarmona's telecom company, was sold a few years ago as a result of financial distress).

Several conglomerates moved towards an FDI-based internationalization processes. In a 1999 study, Kosacoff studied the impact of these processes on a set of groups whose sales abroad accounted for 20 percent of their overall revenues in 1997, with assets overseas adding up to 21 percent of their total assets, and 35 percent of their employees working abroad. These data illustrate how relevant their internationalization process had become (more so than in earlier years).[62] In most cases, these endeavors came as part of each group's evolution – at one time or another, Argentina's reduced domestic market size led these companies to turn to exports, which gradually weighed more heavily in their operations over time. FDI-based internationalization normally came as a later step. The search for raw materials or 'strategic assets' – for example, better access to funding or specialized human resources – also contributed to drive these groups' internationalization processes.

The reforms of the 1990s turned FDI into a means not only to expand across national borders, but also to support groups' positioning in the domestic market. There was a new ethos of 'acquire or be acquired', prompted by the need to increase the size of the company in order to be able to survive in the changed context. As they embarked on internationalization ventures, some groups also reduced excessive diversification in order to capture economies of scale in their respective core businesses. In turn, internationalization processes reinforced organizational learning and human capital investment. FDI-based internationalization also required enhanced financial management capabilities, not least in order to access international capital markets, though this remained challenging for local firms.[63]

Arcor and Techint provide the most compelling examples of FDI-based internationalization. The latter started its internationalization process in the 1990s, with its seamless tube business. It acquired companies in Mexico, Italy, Brazil, Venezuela, Japan, Canada and Romania, emerging as the world's largest maker and exporter of seamless tubes for oil industry applications.[64] As part of this process, the group created a holding called

Tenaris to encompass all its affiliates, whilst maintaining its corporate decision-making in Argentina. The group substantially improved its image in developed markets as a result of significant quality improvements and the creation of modern customer service systems. It also invested further in in-house technological innovation in three large research centers, the largest one based in Argentina.[65] Techint's global expansion was driven by learning, investment and technological knowledge accumulation processes which had already been developed in earlier decades. While this process was certainly supported by the state, it was also the result of the decisions taken by corporate executives which led to the creation of distinctive capabilities in the Argentine economy of the time.[66]

Arcor also provides an illustrative example. This company was founded in Argentina's hinterlands, and initially catered to unchallenging markets that held no interest for Western candy and food manufacturers. Gradually, it expanded its operations, incorporating new product lines and starting an ambitious forward- and backward-integration investment program even in the challenging conditions of the 1980s. Later, unlike its counterparts at Bagley, Terrabusi and other companies in the same industry, Arcor's controlling stockholder group chose to retain company ownership, and embarked on an expansion process based on exports and FDI. Arcor ventured into regional markets, and later, to Asia and elsewhere, becoming the world's leading candy manufacturer and thirteenth largest confectionary maker. Like Techint, Arcor's internationalization process required organizational changes, more professional management, and investment in enhanced product differentiation and competitiveness.[67]

In contrast to these successful cases, of the 11 conglomerates that had relied on FDI to take their operations across national borders included in the 1999 study, three were acquired by foreign firms. These were Bemberg (acquired by Ambev), IMPSAT (at which financial investors seized control and sold it to a global telecom firm) and YPF (which was acquired by Repsol).[68] However, in 2012 the Argentinean government nationalized YPF. Meanwhile, another group, Pérez Companc, withdrew from the business where its internationalization process had advanced the most. Brazil's Petrobras acquired its energy businesses, while the group turned to foodstuffs. SOCMA also abandoned a large share of its business operations in Brazil. This suggests that the environment created by the reforms of the 1990s, set against the context of an international economy where competition has become more globalized than in the past, was more challenging for domestic companies than in previous decades.

IV. CONCLUDING REMARKS

MNEs have been key players in Argentina's economic development over the past century and a half, even though their strategies have changed both with shifting policy regimes and the broader changes in global capitalism as a whole. In a long-term perspective, their economic influence has been increasing steadily, reaching in 2015 a level that is both unparalleled in Argentine history and extremely high by global standards, despite the resurgence of nationalizations after the end of the convertibility plan.

The impact of foreign-owned firms has not always been seen as positive. At various times, critics have questioned the role of MNEs. These sentiments were strong in the late ISI phase, when politicians and planners tried to curtail MNE operations and to promote locally-owned firms. At other points, as during the 1976–83 military regime, MNEs opted to avoid Argentina because of economic and political risk.

It is challenging to make a definitive judgment regarding the impact of FDI impact on Argentine development. At some points in Argentina's history, MNEs were the agents chosen by governments to implement key investments designed by policy makers. This was the case of railroads and meat packing plants in the agricultural export-led economy, heavy industry and durable consumer goods during the ISI phase and utilities in the 1990s. In this regard, it is difficult to disentangle the impact of FDI from that of government policies.

Regardless of this caveat, this chapter has shown that MNEs generally had higher productivity levels and employed more advanced technologies than local firms, and they were probably more focused on international trade. Spillovers on local businesses have been more sporadic, especially so in the era of liberal policies and overvalued currency in the 1990s. More generally, MNEs in Argentina have failed to develop an export-oriented model similar to the one seen in Singapore, among other countries, and they have largely adjusted to the local setting, rather than becoming a transformation driver for domestic productive and technological structures.

A full analysis of the impact of foreign MNEs on Argentina would need to address the counterfactual question of what would Argentina's economic development have been like if local companies had been the agents chosen to pursue the above-mentioned policy goals at different points of time in the country's history? This raises the question whether local entrepreneurship could have stepped up to the challenge in the absence of foreign firms. The widespread skepticism that they could not points to the decisive role played by MNEs in Argentina's economy being partly attributable to the poor image of local businessmen.[69] This in turn raises the issue whether this was a perception or reality. It is striking that local companies, primarily organized as business groups, embarked on FDI at every stage in Argentina's economic development. However, this phenomenon was also characterized by discontinuity. The companies that followed that path were typically unable to sustain their internationalization processes, and in some cases were acquired by MNEs or failed. Indeed, as of 2015, Argentina is the home economy of only a modest number of 'multi-Latina' companies compared to not only Brazil or Mexico, but even Chile. The existence of so few 'national champions' must be seen as largely a result of Argentina's unstable economic development path. It also suggests that as a last resort and probably because of the local economic context, locally owned firms would have been challenged to match the performance of foreign MNEs in the domestic economy.[70]

NOTES

1. Some estimates indicate that between 1875 and 1912, Argentina's per capita GDP rose at a 3.9 percent annual rate. This was a high rate considering that during that period population grew at nearly 3.5 percent per year. Between 1912 and 1927, per capita GDP dropped slightly, at a −0.3 percent yearly rate, as a result of the sharp fall in trade as a consequence of World War I, which was not entirely offset by later growth (in 1919–27, Argentina's per-capita GDP grew at a 3.4 percent annual rate). See Cortés Conde (1997).
2. Angus Maddison's estimates show that, among the world's top 56 countries with GDP data dating back to 1870, Argentina ranked 17th in 1870 and climbed to the 11th position by 1929.
3. See Oszlak (1997).
4. Bercovich and Katz (1993).
5. Katz and Kosacoff (1989).
6. Kosacoff, Lucángeli and Sourrouille (1985).
7. Hora (2000).
8. Villanueva (1972).
9. Barbero (2003).
10. Kosacoff, Lucángeli and Sourrouille (1985).
11. Díaz Alejandro (1975).
12. Schvarzer (1996).
13. Katz and Kosacoff (1989); Barbero and Rocchi (2002).
14. Gutiérrez and Korol (1988).
15. Bisang, Fuchs and Kosacoff (1992).
16. See also Gerchunoff and Llach (2003).
17. For a discussion on long-term Argentine institutional issues, see Spiller and Tommasi (2000).
18. On one hand, there was a competitive sector, agriculture, which was the main source of foreign exchange and supplied key wage goods. On the other hand, the manufacturing sector produced almost exclusively for the domestic market and was protected by high tariffs. This sector relied on imported inputs and capital goods. Hence, its growth depended on the foreign currency generated by agricultural exports. See Braun and Joy (1968).
19. See Gerchunoff and Llach (2003); Taylor (2003).

20. Díaz Alejandro (1975).
21. In 1959, the average tariff stood at 151 percent, which was higher than the highest tariff applied in Europe and the rest of Latin America at the time. See Berlinski (2003).
22. Kosacoff and Ramos (2005).
23. Schvarzer (1996).
24. Several regulations discouraged foreign investors, including stringent provisions regarding profit transfers and fund repatriation. Additionally, the Constitution's Article 40 stated that utilities and natural resources (except agricultural land) belonged to the Argentine nation. See CEPAL (2001).
25. Díaz Alejandro (1975).
26. CEPAL (2001).
27. Katz and Kosacoff (1989).
28. Kosacoff, Lucángeli and Sourrouille (1985).
29. Katz (1999).
30. The need to foster an industrial concentration process in order to increase microeconomic efficiency was recognized even in official statements (for instance, CONADE's 1970–74 National Development Plan).
31. Rates estimated on the basis of data drawn from Barbero and Rocchi (2003).
32. Even industrial promotion schemes followed the same rationale, as illustrated by Bahía Blanca's Petrochemical Hub project in the late 1960s, whose plant scales were calculated on the basis of domestic demand growth forecasts.
33. In 1971, a new legal framework for foreign investments was instituted, setting the rules for new investment approval as well as for earning transfer and capital repatriation. In addition, this framework favored investments that featured partnerships with local investors. In 1973, this legislation was replaced by a law that required investments to be filed for registration and to await approval. Capital repatriation would not be possible until five years after approval or for amounts exceeding 20 percent a year. Top percentages were also set for earning transfers. At the same time, telecom companies' access to industrial promotion regimes was restricted at this time.
34. Schvarzer (1996).
35. Ablin and Katz (1978).
36. Katz and Kosacoff (1983).
37. Katz and Kosacoff (1983).
38. Kosacoff (1999).
39. Kweitel and Maia (2003).
40. Capital goods imports in the 1990s were 4.5 times higher than those in the previous decade.
41. See Chapter 9.
42. By 1980, the industrial sector held 62 percent of FDI stock in Argentina. See UNCTAD (1994).
43. Chudnovsky and López (2001).
44. In 1997, Argentina's Congress started discussing a new anti-trust bill, but it was only in 1999 that a modern anti-trust law was approved. The transfer of YPF's entire stock to Spain's Repsol in the early months of 1999 (YPF had gone public in 1993) rushed the approval process.
45. It should be noted that the practice of indebting-acquired companies was meant to deduce interests from income tax payments. See Naishtat and Maas (2000).
46. Azpiazu (1992).
47. Kosacoff, Lucángeli and Sourrouille (1985).
48. Bisang (1996).
49. Katz and Kosacoff (1989).
50. Bisang, Fuchs and Kosacoff (1992).
51. Bezchinsky and Kosacoff (1993).
52. Cimoli and Katz (2003).
53. Chudnovsky and López (2001).

54. The remainder of this section is based on Chudnovsky, López and Orlicki (2007).
55. Absorption capabilities are measured in terms of firms' human capital availability and their expenditures on different training and innovation activities.
56. For a discussion on this topic, see Gasparini, Marchionni and Sosa Escudero (2001).
57. Bisang (1996): 38–82.
58. Kosacoff (1999).
59. For an analysis of this conglomerate's background, see Kosacoff, Forteza, Barbero, Stengel, and Porta (2001).
60. See Kosacoff (1999).
61. Bisang (1996).
62. By mid-1998, sample companies owned 63 companies overseas, with 46 of them operating in production and marketing industries and the remaining 17 serving as commercial affiliates (this survey only considered the most economically significant investments). Neighboring countries were the primary destinations for FDI, but some investments were also found in the North American Free Trade Agreement (NAFTA) region, Europe and Asia. Techint was, and continues to be, the leading firm in this regard.
63. Kosacoff (1999).
64. This group has also expanded internationally with its flat steel business, first with the acquisition of Venezuela's largest steel manufacturer in the 1990s, and in 2005 with the acquisition of a Mexican steel manufacturer.
65. López and Ramos (2010).
66. Artopoulos (2004).
67. Kosacoff, Forteza, Barbero, Stengel, and Porta (2001).
68. Loma Negra, recently sold to Camargo Correa, a Brazilian company, is not included in this list as it did not embark on an internationalization process in the 1990s.
69. For a discussion on this topic, see López (2006).
70. López (2006).

REFERENCES

Ablin, Edward and Jorge Katz (1978), *De la industria incipiente a la exportación de tecnología: la experiencia argentina en la venta internacional de plantas industriales y obras de ingeniería*', working essay No. 14, Buenos Aires: Programa BID/CEPAL.

Artopoulos, Alejandro (2004), 'Nueva economía en Argentina. El caso de una empresa red: TENARIS', presented at the Interdisciplinary Seminar of the Information Society chaired by Professor Manuel Castells at Universitat Oberta de Catalunya.

Azpiazu, Daniel (1992), 'Las empresas transnacionales en una economía en transición: la experiencia argentina en los años ochenta', paper presented at the Simposio de Alto Nivel sobre la Contribución de las Empresas Transnacionales al Crecimiento y el Desarrollo de América Latina y el Caribe Santiago, 5–7 October, Santiago, Chile.

Barbero, María Inés (2003), 'Impacto de la inversión extranjera directa en la industria argentina en la década de 1920. Estrategias empresariales y sus efectos sobre el sector productivo local', Anais do V Congresso Brasileiro de História Econômica e 6ª Conferência Internacional de História de Empresas.

Barbero, María Inés and Fernando Rocchi (2002), 'La industria (1914–1945)', in Academia Nacional de Historia, *Nueva Historia de la Nación Argentina,* t. IX, Buenos Aires: Planeta, 61–83.

Bercovich, Néstor and Jorge Katz (1993), 'National systems of innovation supporting technical advance in industry: the case of Argentina', in Richard Nelson (ed.), *National Innovation Systems. A Comparative Analysis,* New York: Oxford University Press, 451–75.

Berlinski, Julio (2003), 'International trade and commercial policy', in Gerardo della Paolera and Alan Taylor (eds), *A New Economic History of Argentina,* Cambridge: Cambridge University Press, 197–232.

Bezchinsky, Gabriel and Bernardo Kosacoff (1993), 'De la sustitución de importaciones a la globalización. Las empresas transnacionales en la industria argentina', in Bernardo Kosacoff, et al., *El desafío de la competitividad,* Buenos Aires: Alianza.

Bisang, Roberto (1996), 'Perfil tecno-productivo de los grupos económicos en la industria argentina', in Jorge Katz (ed.), *Estabilización macroeconómica, reforma estructural y comportamiento industrial. Estructura y funcionamiento del sector manufacturero latinoamericano en los años 90,* Santiago de Chile: CEPAL/IDRC-Alianza.

Bisang, Roberto, Mariana Fuchs and Bernardo Kosacoff (1992), 'Internacionalización de empresas industriales argentinas', *Desarrollo Económico,* **32** (127), 323–56.

Braun, Oscar and Leonard Joy (1968), 'A model of economic stagnation: a case study of the Argentine economy', *The Economic Journal,* **78** (312), 868–87.

CEPAL (2001), *'La inversión extranjera en América Latina y el Caribe' en Informe 2001*, Santiago de Chile: CEPAL.

Chudnovsky, Daniel and Andrés López (2001), *La transnacionalización de la economía argentina,* Buenos Aires: Eudeba.

Cimoli, Mario and Jorge Katz (2003), 'Structural reforms, technological gaps and economic development: a Latin American perspective', *Industrial and Corporate Change*, **12** (2), 387–411.

Cortés Conde, Roberto (1997), *La economía Argentina en el largo plazo*, Buenos Aires: Sudamericana-Universidad de San Andrés.

Díaz Alejandro, Carlos (1975), *Ensayos sobre la historia económica argentina,* Buenos Aires: Amorrortu.

Gasparini, Leonardo, Mariana Marchionni and Walter Sosa Escudero (2001), *La distribución del ingreso en la Argentina. Perspectivas y efectos sobre el bienestar,* Buenos Aires: Fundación Arcor.

Gerchunoff, Pablo and Lucas Llach (2003), 'Ved en trono a la noble Igualdad. Crecimiento, equidad y política económica en la Argentina, 1880–2003', Working Paper 003, Fundación PENT.

Gutiérrez, Leandro and Juan Carlos Korol (1988), 'Historia de empresas y crecimiento industrial en la Argentina. El caso de la Fábrica Argentina de Alpargatas', *Desarrollo Económico,* **28** (111), 401–24.

Hora, Roy (2000), 'Terratenientes, empresarios industriales y crecimiento industrial en la Argentina: los estancieros y el debate sobre el proteccionismo (1890–1914)', *Desarrollo Económico,* **40** (159), 465–92.

Katz, Jorge (1999), *Reformas estructurales y comportamiento tecnológico: reflexiones en torno a la naturaleza y fuentes del cambio tecnológico en América Latina en los años noventa,* Santiago de Chile: CEPAL, Serie Reformas Económicas, No. 13.

Katz, Jorge and Bernardo Kosacoff (1983), 'MNEs from Argentina', in Sanjaya

Lall (ed.), *The New MNEs: The Spread of Third World Enterprises,* London: Wiley, 137–219.

Katz, Jorge and Bernardo Kosacoff (1989), *El proceso de industrialización en la Argentina: evolución, retroceso y prospectiva,* Buenos Aires: CEAL.

Kosacoff, Bernardo, Jorge Forteza, María Inés Barbero, Alejandro Stengel and Fernando Porta (2001), *Globalizar desde Latinoamérica. El caso Arcor,* Bogotá: McGraw Hill.

Kosacoff, Bernardo (1999), 'El caso argentino' in Daniel Chudnovsky, Bernardo Kosacoff and Andrés López, *Las multinacionales latinoamericanas. Sus estrategias en un mundo globalizado,* Buenos Aires: Fondo de Cultura Económica, 65–164.

Kosacoff, Bernardo, Jorge Lucángeli and Juan Sourrouille (1985), *Transnacionalización y política económica en la Argentina,* Buenos Aires: CEAL-CET.

Kosacoff, Bernardo and Adrian Medina Ramos (2005), 'Cambio estructural y comportamientos microeconómicos en la industria argentina', *Boletín Informativo Techint*, **318**.

Kweitel, Mercedes and José Luis Maia (2003), 'Argentina: sustainable output growth after the collapse', National Department of Macroeconomic Policies, Argentina's Ministry of Economy and Production, accessed 8 September 2003 at http://www.mecon.gov.ar.

López, Andrés (2006), *Empresarios, instituciones y desarrollo económico: el caso argentino.* Buenos Aires: CEPAL.

López, Andrés and Daniela Ramos (eds) (2010), *La exportación de servicios en América Latina: los casos de Argentina, Brasil y M*éxico. Montevideo: Serie Red Mercosur No. 17.

Naishtat, Silvia and Pablo Maas (2000), *El cazador. La historia secreta de los negocios de Juan Navarro y el Grupo Exxel*, Buenos Aires: Planeta.

Oszlak, Oscar (1997), *La formación del Estado argentino. Orden, progreso y organización nacional,* Buenos Aires: Planeta.

Schvarzer, Jorge (1996), *La industria que supimos conseguir. Una historia político-social de la industria argentina*, Buenos Aires: Planeta.

Spiller, and Mariano Tommasi (2000), *Los determinantes institucionales del desarrollo argentino: una aproximación desde la nueva economía institucional*, Buenos Aires: CEDI, Document 33.

Taylor, Alan (2003), 'Capital accumulation', in Gerardo della Paolera and Alan Taylor (eds), *A New Economic History of Argentina,* Cambridge: Cambridge University Press, 170–96.

UNCTAD (1994), *World Investment Report: Multinational Corporations, Employment and the Workplace*, New York, Geneva: UNCTAD.

Villanueva, Javier (1972), 'El origen de la industrialización argentina', *Desarrollo Económico*, **12** (47), 451–76.

5. Spanish business in Argentina and Chile since 1880

Javier Vidal Olivares

The growth of Spanish business in the Southern Cone of Latin America began in the late nineteenth century. It was initially driven by massive Spanish emigration to Argentina, and to a lesser extent, Chile and Uruguay.[1] Simultaneously, Spanish exports boomed, and to attract foreign direct investment (FDI) a number of institutions, especially the Chambers of Commerce, were created.[2] Between the 1920s and the outbreak of the Spanish Civil War in 1936, there was extensive Spanish business operations in this region. Between the end of the Spanish Civil War in 1939 and the early 1960s, Spain's closed economy and the economic policies of the Franco regime thwarted outward FDI, and curtailed the presence of Spanish companies in the region.

Spain's liberalization, beginning in the early 1960s and culminating in the transition to democracy and accession to the European Union (EU) in 1986, led to a revival in Spanish multinational enterprise (MNE) investment in the region. Starting in 1980, Spanish FDI in Argentina and Chile, as well as Uruguay, grew spectacularly.[3] Spanish investment was driven by large companies that focused on banking and finance, energy, telecommunications and transportation, sanitation, and utilities.[4] Spain became the leading investor in Argentina, and the second largest investor in Chile, during the 1990s and early 2000s.[5] However, Spanish MNE investment lost its momentum again as a result of both policy shifts in Latin America, especially Argentina, and a major economic crisis in Spain after 2008.

The first section of this chapter describes how the Spanish investment network developed in this region as a result of emigration, individual entrepreneurship and business relations. The changes brought about by World War I paved the way later for a qualitative shift in company ownership and in Spanish capital in the region, particularly in Argentina, the country that had garnered the most interest among Spanish business leaders and companies. The second section discusses the gradual increase in Spanish FDI after Spain's economic opening in 1960. The following section focuses on the massive flow of Spanish capital into Latin America after 1986. A final section concludes.

I. EMIGRATION AND SPANISH BUSINESS IN THE SOUTHERN CONE, 1880–1920

Spanish emigrants began flocking to Latin America in the 1880s. The strong expansion of the economies of Argentina and Chile, as well as that of Uruguay, was a major attraction. Also at this time, Southern Europe faced a severe agrarian crisis that drove many Europeans to view transoceanic emigration as an alternative to dire economic conditions. Italians and Spaniards crossed the Atlantic to seek their fortunes.

The Spanish first settled in Buenos Aires and later, moved to the hinterland as Argentina's frontier of settlement advanced. The port of Buenos Aires boasted the largest concentration of Spaniards in Latin America in the colonial period. After Argentine independence in 1818, relations between Spain and Argentina were frozen, hampering migration. This scenario changed drastically in the last third of the nineteenth century, due to Argentina's expanding economy just as Southern Europe entered a crisis. Diplomatic relations between Spain and Argentina improved, which provided further support of migration.

Amid these new conditions, with a massive flow of Spaniards arriving in Argentina, Buenos Aires strengthened its position as the center of the Spanish settlement, enhancing its role as trade intermediary between the country and foreign nations. Spanish merchants increased their presence and identity, reinforcing their interests and business operations with imports from Spain. They exported farming products and food, as well as to a lesser extent, manufactured products, mostly textiles. They primarily imported oils and wine, with some diversification between 1900 and World War I.

According to the research of Alejandro Fernández, close ties between Spain and Argentina were forged between 1900 and 1913.[6] As Spanish investors withdrew from Caribbean markets after Spain's trade collapsed there after the American occupation of Cuba and Puerto Rico in 1898, Spanish exporting companies focused on the River Plate area.[7] This new phase coincided with a drastic drop in Spanish wine imports, and the growth of imports of olive oil, saffron, paprika, sherry and woolen products. The volume of Spanish imports in Argentina grew at 10 percent per annum before 1914, and continued throughout the war, taking advantage of the absence of the major economic powers engaged in the conflict.[8]

During the first third of the twentieth century, the most important business association representing Spanish interests in Argentina was created. Founded in 1888, the Spanish Chamber of Commerce in Buenos Aires played, from its inception, a key role.[9] Largely consisting of merchants and importers at first, its membership grew and expanded to include all industries, from graphic arts and pharmaceuticals to banking. Both the chamber's operations and its lobbying capabilities were further expanded when Spaniards created additional chambers in provincial cities, like Rosario in Santa Fe Province.[10]

The chambers used the mechanisms of organized business groups to conduct their institutional operations, serving as liaisons between product importers and distributors, in addition to arbitrating trade conflicts, safeguarding brands and patents, launching promotion and advertising campaigns for Spanish products and merchandise, building platforms to lobby for tariff and custom duty reductions before governments making trade policy, and finally, providing local contacts for Spanish businessmen and investors.[11] The intermediation efforts of the chambers focused on lowering transaction costs and on facilitating interactions between Spanish investors, merchants and exporters and the Argentine market. Also noteworthy were these business associations' efforts to train immigrant labor for recruitment by Spanish business owners.[12] In support of these ends, Buenos Aires' Spanish Chamber of Commerce steadily grew and consolidated its operations, turning into a powerful platform for Spanish business interests in Argentina during the first third of the twentieth century.[13]

Both the institutional efforts of the Spanish chambers and World War I bolstered trade between the two economies. However, after the war environmental changes and the swift recovery of the major industrial powers slowed Spanish-Argentine trade from the early 1920s. Spain, which ranked fifth in Argentine imports in 1916, had dropped to the ninth spot by 1924.[14] The growth of tariff barriers in Argentina prompted the growth of Spanish FDI to the country.

II. SPANISH INVESTMENT IN ARGENTINA AND CHILE, 1920–36

The star of Spanish direct investments in Argentina was CHADE (Compañía Hispanoamericana de Electricidad). CHADE grew out of CATE (Compañía Transatlántica Alemana de Electricidad), the company that had first supplied electricity to Buenos Aires in 1898. In the wake of World War I, its controlling stockholder, Deutsch Ueberseeische Elektricitäts Gesellchaft, entered a financial crisis, hit by the closure and sale of its companies in Chile under British pressure. To avoid similar problems in Argentina, CATE sold part of its stake to Spanish businessmen in a joint transaction, with a majority of the equity held by the Belgian group SOFINA (Société Financière des Transports et d'Entreprises).[15] The conditions that the Allies imposed on Germany after World War I forced German businesses to reorganize their management structures in their companies abroad. Typically, they turned to third countries and investors for help. The original company forged new partnerships with Spanish investors who agreed to invest funds into the new company. The network of contacts between CHADE's new leading investors and Argentina's economic, financial and institutional circles contributed to this agreement and allowed the Germans to rely on the 'Spanish solution' as a way to dodge the legal restrictions that the Allies imposed.[16]

According to initial estimates, in May 1921, the Spanish share of this investment amounted to 22 percent of the company's 120-million peseta startup capital,[17] which increased over the decade with successive capital contributions (in 1924, 1926, and 1928) to reach a total of 260 million pesetas. During this time, the business grew by acquiring new companies and collaborating with other firms, both in Argentina and abroad. By 1926, CHADE had become a holding company with diversified investments in electricity in South and Central America, and in Europe, including Germany, Belgium, Spain, and France.[18]

Starting in the 1910s, the company concentrated its investments in Buenos Aires City and Province, foregoing those it had made in other areas of Argentina, such as in Mendoza, and in other Southern Cone economies. It sold companies and businesses in Chile and Uruguay in order to focus on the growing Argentine capital city.[19] At the end of the decade, the company enlarged its board to welcome new European financial partners, who supported the acquisition of companies such as Bernal's Compañía de Fábricas de Gas, the Compañía de Electricidad de la Provincia de Buenos Aires, and a stake at the Primitiva Gas Company of Buenos Aires Ltd. These were electricity and gas production and distribution companies based in the counties of Buenos Aires Province.

CHADE navigated the economic crisis of the early 1930s. In 1931, its board deemed its earnings as 'satisfactory' and maintained its asset acquisition policy, continuing to focus on Buenos Aires Province's electrical sector, and purchasing energy plants that supplied two railroad companies. The restriction on capital outflows that Argentina's government imposed in 1932–33 prevented the company from furthering its business enhancement policy in electricity and gas distribution in Buenos Aires and its surrounding province.

CHADE maintained its affiliation with the Belgian SOFINA, which had supported the company financially and technologically throughout the

1920s. It also maintained its significant stake, acquired in January 1923, in the Société Internationale d'Energie Hidroelectrique de Bruselas (SIDRO), a parent company that controlled electrical production and distribution companies in Spain and Mexico.[20] CHADE maintained its investments even during the first half of the 1930s and its ties to international companies, with a strong Spanish capital investment until after World War II. In 1936, as a result of the Spanish Civil War, CHADE became the Compañía Argentina de Electricidad (Argentine Electricity Company).

During the 1920s, Spanish investments also grew in other sectors of the Argentine economy, albeit to a lower extent than they did in CHADE. In publishing and graphic arts, Spanish publishers started opening branches in Buenos Aires.[21] Given the counterfeiting, copyright infringement, unfavorable tax treatment, and distribution penalty issues plaguing Southern Cone markets and other Latin American countries, publishing houses sought to build local presences in these markets, although with some difficulties. As María Fernández Moya has explained, there were no agreements among Spanish publishers to formulate a common strategy for book exports before the early 1930s, and the Spanish government had little interest in supporting the industry.[22] CIAP (Compañía Iberoamericana de Publicaciones), Sopena, Calpe and Sáenz Calleja were among the publishing houses which opened offices in Argentina during the 1920s.

Founded in 1925 by a group of editors who had specialized in assorted small circulation publications before 1914, CIAP grew to a considerable size, supported by financiers such as Ignacio and Alfredo Bauer, the representatives of the Rothschild bank in Madrid. It integrated its production and distribution processes. The company saw and used the Latin American market as a means to achieve volume growth, and sought to replace the existing incumbents including publishing houses based in France (Garnier, Bouret), Germany (Editora Internacional de Berlín), Britain and the United States, all of whom published books in Spanish for the Latin American market.[23] In 1927, CIAP acquired several publishing and printing shops, expanding by means of a wholly-owned network of bookstores in Chile, Uruguay, Ecuador, and especially, Mexico and Argentina. In Mexico, it installed a warehouse for the Cuban publisher Cultural SA, which CIAP acquired, and launched a readership loyalty program based on purchase commitment discounts. CIAP's ambitious expansion unfolded at the same time as other Spanish publishing houses, like Gustavo Gili and Mundo Latin, who embarked on similar efforts to exploit the synergies between Spanish-reading markets.[24] The company went bankrupt in 1931, mostly due to poor financial management. The acquisition of CIAP by its competitors allowed them to take advantage of its assets, including an extensive catalogue and a large list of authors, and from its market position.[25]

Spanish investments, driven by renewed emigration in the 1920s and early 1930s, also found their way into industries such as chemicals, textiles and agribusiness.[26] The creation of Spain's Banco Exterior in 1929 did not fully mitigate funding scarcity issues that most business groups in Spain, and mainly in Argentina and other Southern Cone countries, pointed out.[27] While it was important for international trade operations, this bank did not prove as effective for financial and direct investments in Latin American markets. In Argentina, the Banco Español del Río de la Plata, which the resident Spanish community founded, focused its attention on deposits and transfers, largely neglecting export funding, because it catered to the needs of Spanish merchants operating through Buenos Aires' Spanish Chamber of Commerce.[28]

The structure of Spanish-Argentine trade relationships, based on migration flows, began to weaken in the early 1920s. The attempt to preserve the operations of traditional importers and exporters based in Buenos Aires, supported by an official Spanish policy based on 'practical Spanish-Americanism', began to crumble, gradually losing its advantages.[29] As a result, in the second half of the 1920s, direct investments emerged as a mechanism to overcome protectionist barriers both in Spain and Argentina. The membership of Buenos Aires' Spanish Chamber of Commerce, the largest and most powerful agency for Spanish interests in Argentina, started to reflect these changes, incorporating businessmen who worked in manufacturing sectors that were not as closely related to traditional commercial professions. The number of Spanish-based members also began to grow. The chamber's by-laws had been changed in 1923 to allow Spaniards residing in Spain to join as members.[30] There was growing interest in the Argentine economy as a market which offered opportunities beyond the traditional export trades, and the changes going on in the country included further market integration and investments from MNEs.[31]

In October 1929, the proceedings of the Second National Spanish Overseas Trade Congress showed a unanimous desire for more FDI in Latin America, indicating a consensus that the previous reliance on trade should be replaced.[32] However, the 1930 financial crisis and the outbreak of the Spanish Civil War in 1936 thwarted this desire for FDI in sectors other than agriculture.

During these decades Spanish investment in Chile was much less, although not insignificant. During the first three decades of the twentieth century Spanish business played a significant role in the former country, particularly in Valparaíso and Santiago. These two cities hosted most of the

Spanish community's commercial and industrial operations, which thrived in the 1920s and 1930s in areas such as banking, insurance, saltpeter mines, mining, forestry, as well as the textile, food and tobacco industries.[33]

III. THE ERA OF STAGNATION, 1939–70

After the end of the Civil War in 1939, Spain's economy remained virtually stagnant and isolated from international markets until the mid-1950s. In the second half of the 1950s, Spain initiated a transition that ended with its economic opening as a result of the so-called Stabilization Plan, approved in the summer of 1959. This process hinged on a new exchange policy, foreign trade and capital investment liberalization, and a set of initiatives intended to reduce controls, state intervention and administrative bureaucracy. These measures were geared towards better positioning the Spanish economy within a European context marked by rapid recovery from World War II growth compared with Spain's stagnation.

Spain's gradual economic recovery saw a new business leadership emerge in the late 1950s and early 1960s, as the Spanish domestic economy and its exports grew. While Spain was primarily a recipient of FDI, Spanish companies started to venture abroad cautiously. Overall FDI by Spanish firms remained modest. As late as 1980, the stock of Spanish outward FDI was only $1.9 billion, representing less than 1 percent of the country's gross domestic product (GDP). This compared with Italy's $7 billion and France's $24 billion at that date.[34] Table 5.1 shows the sectorial distribution of this modest amount of outward FDI.

By the 1960s, Latin America was attracting more Spanish FDI than Europe. The growing preference for investment in Latin America seen in

Table 5.1 Regional distribution of Spanish FDI flows, 1963–1978 (percent)

Region	1963–1969	1970–1978
Europe	42.8	30.4
Latin America	46.7	47.2
United States	2.0	4.9
Africa	7.5	8.3
Asia	0.4	4.7

Source: Juan José Durán and María Paloma Sánchez (1981), *La internacionalización de la empresa española. Inversiones españolas en el exterior*, Ministerio de Economía y Comercio: Madrid, pp. 168–71.

the final decades of Franco's rule grew stronger during Spain's transition to democracy and membership of the EU.

IV. SPANISH FOREIGN DIRECT INVESTMENT IN ARGENTINA AND CHILE SINCE THE 1980s

Although the Mexican debt crisis in 1982 caused a temporary downturn in Spanish FDI outflows to Latin America, the Spanish corporate sector began to explore global investment opportunities after Spain joined the EU in 1986. FDI into Latin America increased sharply. During the 1990s, Spanish FDI accumulated flows to Latin America amounted to €80 billion, representing nearly one-half of the total EU FDI flows to the region of €161.7 billion. US FDI flows to Latin America during that decade were $97 billion (€144 billion).[35] Between 1993 and 2001, the region accounted for 56 percent of total Spanish outward FDI amounting to €160,000 million. Total outward Spanish FDI flows reached €423,000 million over the subsequent period of 2002–13, but following Argentina's 2001 economic crisis, Spanish firms shifted their attention to Europe and the United States. As a result Latin America only represented 17 percent of total Spanish FDI flows.[36] Nevertheless Spain remained a substantial investor in Latin America. Between 2007 and 2012, 9 percent of the FDI flows received by Latin America came from Spain, second only to the United States which represented 22 percent of the total.

Table 5.2 shows the industrial distribution of Spanish FDI flows both worldwide and in Latin America between 1993 and 2006.

Table 5.2 Industrial distribution of accumulated Spanish FDI flows 1993–2006

	Latin America	World
FDI flows (in million €)	110,904	331,935
Electricity, gas and water (%)	12	6
Oil and natural gas (%)	14	5
Transportation and communications (%)	29	28
Banking and other financial services (%)	22	24
Construction (%)	2	2
Industry (%)	15	16
Other sectors (%)	6	19

Source: J.J. Durán (2008), 'Geografía de la empresa multinacional española', *Boletín de Estudios Económicos*, ***63***, 193, 40.

Table 5.2 shows that Spanish FDI in the region was especially focused on utilities and energy, with substantial investment also in financial services. This reflected in part the unusual importance of a cluster of Spanish companies which were either recently privatized or had grown large in their sheltered domestic market. These firms engaged in rapid MNE investment. In communications, the firm was Telefónica and its mobile telephone brand, Movistar;[37] in electricity, gas and water distribution, Endesa, Iberdrola, Gas Natural, and Aguas de Barcelona; in financial services, Banco Santander,[38] BBVA, and Mapfre;[39] and in crude oil and energy, Repsol.[40] These companies often invested in multiple countries in the region.

After 1990, many small and medium-sized Spanish companies, often family owned, also invested in Latin America, typically in fewer countries than their larger counterparts. In tourism, for example, companies such as Sol Meliá,[41] Barceló, and Riu have focused on countries with perceived high growth potential, including, Mexico, Dominican Republic, Cuba and Costa Rica, and they have also ventured into hotels in Argentina, Brazil, Chile and Uruguay. Spanish companies have also ventured into sectors such as logistics, security, agribusiness, food and fishing. Less restrictive regulations in this period allowed smaller companies with limited funding to enter these sectors They were supported by a Spanish public agency, ICEX (Spain Trade and Investment) which was charged with facilitating the globalization of Spanish firms, as well as by a revitalized Spanish Chamber of Commerce network in the region, which supplied support services, consultation support and commercial ties with local businesses. The growth of Spanish FDI reflected new regional policies that opened markets and privatized firms.[42] In the Southern Cone, the two economies that displayed the greatest transformation and dynamism were Argentina and Chile, followed to a lesser extent by Uruguay.

Spanish FDI in Chile remained modest before the 1990s, but it began growing stronger following the Friendship and Cooperation Treaty between the two countries in 1990. During the 1990s, Spain climbed to second place in the ranking of inward investors in Chile after the United States. By the end of the decade, Spain had become the leading investor in the country, a position it retained until 2009.[43]

In 1991 Telefónica's investment in Chile became a pivotal moment which paved the way for the arrival of other Spanish-owned companies. Newcomers spanned virtually all sectors, with banking and pension funds leading Spanish investment. Before 2000, Spanish investments were highly concentrated, with 12 companies accounting for 90 percent of Spanish FDI in Chile. These firms mainly acquired local companies, mostly in services. There were only three major greenfield investments, all in construction.[44] Nearly 80 percent of Spanish investment came from four companies: BBVA, Santander, Enersis,[45] and Telefónica.

However, it was Argentina which attracted the bulk of Spanish FDI during the 1990s. Argentina was a more familiar, both culturally and socially, country for Spanish business. Investments began to increase with the more liberal economic policies adopted during the Menem administration after 1989.[46] Between 1989 and 1993, Spanish companies acquired many companies, sharing their ownership with local partners and financial institutions, largely American banks with sizable shares of Argentina's sovereign debt that earlier governments had issued. This was the result of regulatory conditions established to sell state-owned business assets. The experience accumulated in this process enabled Spanish companies to later acquire full ownership, either in market transactions or through direct negotiations with former partners. In this process, Spanish banks funded acquisition deals, with the largest banks, Santander and BBVA, also purchasing local banks. While Spanish companies largely sought to enter Argentina's economy to access the domestic market, some companies ventured into this market in an effort to secure resources and greater business group efficiency.[47]

Spanish FDI in Argentina peaked in 1999, when Repsol acquired Argentina's state-owned oil company, YPF. From the turn of the twenty-first century, however, Spanish FDI flows to Argentina fell away, first as a result of the 2001 crisis, and then because of continued instability, exchange controls and restrictions on remittances. Overall Argentina attractiveness and importance as a host economy for MNEs declined. By 2013, it was only receiving one-half of the flows of FDI that Chile received.[48] While the stock of FDI was equal to 77 percent of the GDP of Chile in that year, it was only 23 percent of that of Argentina.

Chile continued to attract Spanish investors, especially in sectors such as construction, finance, services and electricity. By 2013, Spain accounted for 13 percent, the largest share, of FDI flows into the country. The United States was in second place with 10.5 percent. In contrast, Spanish FDI in Argentina shrank, especially after the nationalization of the 51 percent stake in YPF held by Repsol. In 2012, there was hardly any new Spanish FDI in the country; the Netherlands was the largest investor with 24 percent, followed by the United States with 16 percent, Canada with 15 percent and Chile with 10 percent.[49] However, overall, and largely thanks to the heavy investments seen in the 1990s, Argentina was the second biggest host for Spanish FDI in Latin America between 1993 and 2013, accounting for some 21.5 percent of the total. Brazil was in first place, with 32 percent, Mexico third with 21 percent and Chile fourth, with 9.8 percent.[50]

V. CONCLUDING REMARKS

This chapter has highlighted the lack of linearity in the historical business and economic relationship between Spain, Chile and Argentina. In particular, it has shown how two periods of closeness were separated by an era of relative isolation during the middle decades of the twentieth century.

The first phase started with the large flow of Spanish emigrants who began flocking to this sub-region in 1880 and continued until 1936. Institutional arrangements facilitated this investment. Chambers of commerce were effective mechanisms which provided connections that enabled Spanish companies to globalize, either by greenfield investment in new markets or by acquiring stakes in domestic businesses. Especially in the 1920s, the Spanish government was also instrumental in encouraging business relations across Latin America, by supporting existing chambers, bolstering the role of embassies' commercial attachés, and sometimes setting up new chamber organizations. Advertising campaigns in Latin American media and conferences on trade and business held in Spain further supported Spanish-Latin American economic ties. The results of these efforts became evident in the 1930s, when emergent industries, like cinematography and broadcasting, received new Spanish investments, while more traditional businesses, such as electricity, represented by CHADE and publishing, consolidated further. However, the Spanish Civil War and early years of Franco's regime resulted in the virtual end of Spain's investment in the region.

The beginning of Spain's economic liberalization in the early 1960s rekindled the country's re-entry into world markets. An economic crisis in the 1970s and Spain's transition to democracy slowed this process, but it regained momentum in 1986, when Spain joined the EU. As Spain privatized businesses and modernized its business system, Spanish FDI grew through both greenfield investment and mergers and acquisitions. The transformation of the Spanish corporate system coincided from the 1980s with a major policy shift in Latin America as governments reduced tariff barriers and privatized public sectors. In this new era, Spanish MNEs made large market-seeking investments in Argentina and Chile, especially in services including utilities and finance. They also invested heavily in oil and gas resources. It was noteworthy too that many small- and medium-sized enterprises, often family owned, invested in industries including machinery and tool manufacture, automotive parts, food, wine making, chemicals and pharmaceuticals, in addition to services such as tourism.

Spain, which was only a peripheral economy in Europe in the 1960s, had become by 2000 a major international investor, boasting the largest FDI flows into Latin America. Spanish firms acquired major stakes in both the Argentinean and Chilean business sectors. Subsequently, the severe problems of the Spanish economy after 2008 and growing political risk, especially in Argentina, saw many Spanish companies retreat to other locations, although Spanish business remained a significant investor in the region in the second decade of the twenty-first century.

NOTES

1. Sánchez Alonso (2006); Yáñez (2006).
2. Vidal Olivares (2011a).
3. Durán (2005a); Toral (2005); Béjar (2008): 319–38; Toral (2011).
4. Durán (2005b); Guillén (2005).
5. Chudnovsky (2001); Chudnovsky and López.
6. Fernández (2004).
7. In 1899, the Spanish Consulate in Montevideo asked Uruguay's Spanish Chamber of Commerce for its collaboration 'to survey Spanish merchants in order to encourage the trade with Spain in order to substitute part of the markets lost in Cuba and Puerto Rico' (letter written by José Calatayud, Spanish Consul, to Domingo Martí Torres, chamber chairman, on 12 July 1899), *Boletín de la Cámara de Comercio Española de Montevideo.*
8. Fernández (2000).
9. Vidal Olivares (2011b).
10. Lanciotti (2006).
11. Boswell (1980); Benneth (1998).
12. This was a regular practice among chambers from other countries, like Great Britain or Germany, as businessmen jointly provided training courses for workers delivered by the chambers, see Gospel and Foreman (2006). In 1918, the Spanish Chamber of Commerce in Mexico approved the creation of an elementary school that started operating in the early 1920s, see (1919) *Acción Económica. Revista Mensual Hispano-Mexicana*, **II** (8), 10.
13. Other immigrant communities in Argentina, like Italians, did the same. See Choate (2007).
14. (1926), 'La importación española en la República Argentina. Su proceso decreciente. Su relación con las otras procedencias', *Cámara de Comercio Española en la República Argentina. Memoria del Ejercicio 1924–1925*, Buenos Aires: Cámara de Comercio Española, 14.
15. On CHADE, see Dalla Corte (2005) and (2006).
16. The Instituto de Economía Americana (IDEA) was created in 1901. It became a powerful group that gathered Spanish investors, especially in Catalonia, and developed an excellent network of agents that reported on developments in Latin America, especially in Argentina. See Dalla Corte (2006).
17. Pabón (1969).
18. Compañía Hispano Americana de Electricidad, SA (1928).
19. In 1928, the company Luz y Fuerza, which provided electricity to Mendoza City and its tramway company, was sold. In 1926, CHADE's Montevideo Electrical Tramway Company, *La Transatlántica*, was acquired by the Uruguayan State.
20. La Barcelona Traction Light & Power Ltd and the controlling stake in Mexico Tramways, which, in turn, owned the Mexican Light & Power Co. Ltd.
21. (1925), 'El libro español en la Argentina', in *Memoria de la Cámara Oficial Española de Comercio en la República Argentina*, 1924–1925, Buenos Aires: Cámara Oficial Española de Comercio en la República Argentina, pp. 86–98.

22. Fernández Moya (2009) and (2011); Martínez Rus (2002) and (2008).
23. (1925), 'El libro español en la Argentina', in *Memoria de la Cámara Oficial Española de Comercio en la República Argentina*, 1924–1925, Buenos Aires: Cámara Oficial Española de Comercio en la República Argentina, pp. 85–96.
24. These efforts would continue in the 1930s and early 1940s with the creation of Editorial Sudamericana. On Uruguay, see Jacob (2011): 262–3.
25. López-Morell and Molina (2012).
26. In the textile industries, efforts were made to marshal investments to the wool sector through the creation of the Textile Exporting Union, which remained an export consortium, in 1924–29. See Fernández (2004): 226–34.
27. The bank was unanimously welcomed by participants of the Second National Spanish Overseas Trade Congress, held in Seville in October 1929. See National Ministry of Economy, II Congreso Nacional del Comercio Español en Ultramar, Conclusiones, Madrid, December 1929, 28–30.
28. On the Banco Español del Río de la Plata, see Regalsky (1995).
29. This notion has been referred to by Fernández (2006), to link traditional trade relations, based on foreign trade, to migration flow behavior and the policy upheld by Spanish importers in Argentina. These interests were defended before Spanish authorities by means of adequate policies to safeguard their interests.
30. (1924), *Memoria de la Cámara Oficial Española de Comercio en 1923*, Buenos Aires: Cámara Oficial Española de Comercio en la República Argentina, pp. 83–92.
31. Lluch and Fernández (2008); Lluch (2007); Barbero (2004).
32. These included utility contract bids, as claimed by Spanish merchants in Rosario, 2° Congreso Nacional del Comercio Español en Ultramar. 1929. Ponencia de la Cámara Oficial Española de Comercio, Industria y navegación en Rosario de Santa Fe, 47.
33. In the 1920s, the largest foreign community in business in Valparaíso was the Spanish community. See Navarro Azcue and Estrada Turre (2005).
34. Dunning and Lundan (2008).
35. Chislett (2003): 20.
36. Adán (2014); Durán (2008).
37. Gallardo (2005).
38. Guillén and Tschoegl (2008).
39. On Mapfre, see Caruana, García Ruíz and Tortella (2009).
40. Tortella (2008).
41. Vidal Olivares (2008a). For Iberia's investments in Latin American airlines, see Vidal Olivares (2008b).
42. Vidal (2001).
43. Medina Giacomozzi and González Pascual (2008).
44. Giacomozzi and González Pascual (2008): 195.
45. Enersis was a Chilean company that Endesa acquired and turned into the parent company of a holding with investments in several Latin American countries: Argentina (CDS, Costanera CBA, El Chocón, Edenor, Edesur); Brazil (Cerj, Coelce, Cachoeira Dourada); Peru (Edegel, Edelnor); Colombia (Betania, Emgesa, Codensa). See Mochón and Rambla (1999).
46. Schvarzer (2006).
47. Chudnovsky and López (1997): 25.
48. Economic Commission for Latin America and the Caribbean (2014).
49. Comisión Económica para América Latina y el Caribe (CEPAL) (2012); Alberola and López (2013); Santander (n.d.).
50. Adán (2014): 163, 163.

REFERENCES

Adán, Antonio (2014), 'Historia reciente de las inversiones Españolas en América', *Regional and Sectoral Economic Studies*, **14** (2).

Alberola, Enrique and Esther López (2013), 'La evolución de la inversión directa Española en América Latina', Dirección General Adjunta de Asuntos Internacionales, *Boletín Económico*, June, 61–9.

Barbero, María Inés (2004), 'Impacto de la inversión directa en la industria argentina en la década de 1920: estrategias empresariales y sus efectos sobre el sector productivo local', *Estudos do Século XX*, **4**, 201–22.

Béjar, Ramón Casilda (ed.) (2008), *La gran apuesta. Globalización y multinacionales españolas en América Latina. Análisis de los protagonistas*, Barcelona: Granica.

Bennett, Robert (1998), 'Business associations and their potential to contribute to economic development: re-exploring an interface between the state and market', *Environment and Planning,* **30** (8), 1367–87.

Boswell, Jonathan S. and John H. Dunning (1980), 'Social cooperation in economic systems. A business history approach', *Review of Social Economy*, **38** (2), 155–77.

Caruana, Leonardo, José Luis García Ruíz and Gabriel Tortella (2009), *MAPFRE 193320082008: de mutua a multinacional*, Madrid: Mapfre.

CEPAL (2012), *La inversión extranjera directa en América Latina y el Caribe,* Santiago de Chile: CEPAL.

Chislett, William (2003), *La inversión directa española en América Latina. Retos y oportunidades*, Madrid: Instituto El Cano.

Choate, Mark (2007), 'Sending states' transnational interventions in politics, culture, and economics: the historical example of Italy', *International Migration Review*, **41** (3), 728–68.

Chudnovsky, Daniel (ed.) (2001), *El boom de inversión extranjera directa en el MERCOSUR*, Buenos Aires: Siglo XXI.

Chudnovsky, Daniel and Andrés López (1997), 'Las estrategias de las empresas transnacionales en Argentina y Brasil: ¿qué hay de nuevo en la década de 1990?', Working Paper 23, Fundación Cenit, 25.

Chudnovsky, Daniel and Andrés López (2007), 'Inversión extranjera directa y desarrollo: La experiencia del MERCOSUR', *Revista de la CEPAL*, **92**.

Compañía Hispano Americana de Electricidad, SA (1928), *Memoria que el Consejo de Administración somete a la aprobación de la Junta General Ordinaria de Accionistas convocada para el día 31 de mayo de 1927*, Barcelona: Tipografía Emporium, 8.

Dalla Corte, Gabriela (2005), *Casa de América de Barcelona (1911–1947*), Madrid: Lid.

Dalla Corte, Gabriela (2006), 'Empresas, instituciones y red social: la Compañía Hispanoamericana de Electricidad entre Buenos Aires y Barcelona', *Revista de Indias*, **LXVI** (237), 519–44.

Dunning, John H. and Sarianna M. Lundan (2008), *Multinational Enterprises and the Global Economy*, Cheltenham, UK: Edward Elgar, 24.

Durán, Juan José (2005a), 'Spanish direct investment in Latin America, 1960–2002', in Felix E. Martín and Pablo Toral (eds), *Latin America's Quest for Globalization: The Role of Spanish Firms*, Aldershot: Ashgate, 1–57.

Durán, Juan José (2005b), *La empresa multinacional española. Estrategias y ventajas competitivas*, Madrid: Minerva.

Durán, Juan José (2008), 'Geografía de la empresa multinacional española', *Boletín de Estudios económicos*, **63** (193), 17–44.

Economic Commission for Latin America and the Caribbean (2014), Tables. Inward and Outward Foreign Direct Investment Flows in Latin America, 24 October, accessed 18 April 2015 at http://www.cepal.org/sites/default/files/pr/files/tabla_ingresosied_eng_actualizacion.pdf.

Fernández, Alejandro (2000), 'La inmigración española en la Argentina y el comercio bilateral', *Amérique Latine, Histoire & Memoire*, **1**, accessed 18 April 2015 at http://alhim.revues.org/index57.html.

Fernández, Alejandro (2004), *Un mercado étnico en el Plata: emigración y exportaciones españolas a la Argentina, 1880–1935*, Madrid: CSIC.

Fernández,Alejandro (2006), 'Los grupos mercantiles españoles de Buenos Aires y el "hispanoamericanismo práctico"', in Alicia Bernasconi and Carina Frid (eds), *De Europa a las Américas. Dirigentes y liderazgos (1880–1960)*, Buenos Aires: Biblos, 199–223.

Fernández Moya, María (2009), 'Multinacionales del castellano. La internacionalización del sector editorial español, 1898–2008', *Revista de Historia Industrial*, **40** (2), 29–44.

Fernández Moya, María (2011), 'La promesa del gran mercado del libro. Un siglo de editoriales españolas en Argentina', *Revista de Historia de la Economia y de la Empresa*, **5**, 205–40.

Gallardo, Fernando (2005), 'Spanish telecoms in Latin America: Telefónica', in Felix E. Martín and Pablo Toral (eds), *Latin America's Quest for Globalization. The Role of Spanish Firms*, Aldershot: Ashgate, 186–204.

Gospel, Howard and Jim Foreman (2006), 'Inter-firm training co-ordination in Britain', *British Journal of Industrial Relations*, **44** (2), 191–214.

Guillén, Mauro (2005), *The Rise of Spanish Multinationals: European Business in the Global Economy*, Cambridge: Cambridge University Press.

Guillén, Mauro and Adrian Tschoegl (2008), *Building a Global Bank: The Transformation of Banco Santander*, Princeton: Princeton University Press.

Jacob, Raúl (2011), *Aquellos otros inversores*, Montevideo: Arpoador.

Lanciotti, Norma (2006), 'Tras el liderazgo del sector inmobiliario. Recursos sociales y estrategias económicas de los empresarios españoles en Rosario (1875–1925)', in Alicia Bernasconi and Carina Frid (eds), *De Europa a las Américas. Dirigentes y liderazgos (1880–1960)*, Buenos Aires: Biblos, 179–97.

Lluch, Andrea (2007), 'Crédito e información. Una aproximación a la evolución histórica de las agencias de reporte crediticio en la Argentina. 1892–1940', in Jorge Schvarzer, Teresita Gómez and Marcelo Rougier (eds), *La empresa ayer y hoy. Nuevas investigaciones y debates*, Buenos Aires: UBA, Facultad de Ciencias Económicas. Centro de Estudios de la Situación y Perspectivas de la Argentina, 335–74.

Lluch, Andrea and Alejandro Fernández (2008), 'Comercio y redes de comercialización mayoristas y minoristas en la Argentina de comienzos del siglo XX', in Susana Bandieri, Graciela Blanco and Mónica Blanco (eds), *Las escalas de la historia comparada, Tomo II: Empresas y empresarios. La cuestión regional*, Buenos Aires: Miño y Dávila, 57–88.

López-Morell, Miguel and Abril Molina (2012), 'La Compañía Iberoamericana de Publicaciones, primera gran corporación editorial en castellano', *Revista de Historia Industrial*, **49** (2), 111–45.

Martínez Rus, Ana (2002), 'La industria editorial española ante los mercados americanos del libro, 1892–1936', *Hispania,* **62** (212), 1021–58.
Martínez Rus, Ana (2008), 'Exportando cultura: las estrategias trasatlánticas de los editores españoles, 1892–1936', *Revista de la Historia de la Economía y de la Empresa*, **2**, 183–204.
Medina Giacomozzi, Alex and Julián González Pascual (2008), 'Caracterización de la inversión directa de empresas españolas en empresas chilenas' *Análisis Económico,* **XXIII** (52), 185–99.
Mochón, Francisco and Alfredo Rambla (1999), *La creación de valor y las grandes empresas españolas*, Barcelona: Ariel.
Navarro Azcue, Concepción and Baldomero Estrada Turre (2005), 'Migración y redes de poder en América: el caso de los industriales españoles en Valparaíso (Chile) 1860–1930', *Revista Complutense de Historia de América,* **31**, 115–46.
Regalsky, Andrés (1995), 'La evolución de la banca privada nacional en Argentina (1880–1914). Una introducción a su estudio', in Pedro Tedde and Carlos Marichal (eds), *La formación de los bancos centrales en España y América latina (siglos XIX y XX*), vol. II, Madrid: Banco de España, 35–59.
Sánchez Alonso, Blanca (2006), 'Labor and inmigration', in Victor Bulmer-Thomas, John H. Coatsworth and Roberto Cortes Cortés (eds), *The Cambridge Econonic History of Latin America, Vol. II The Long Twentieth Century*, Cambridge: Cambridge Univesity Press, 377–426.
Santander (n.d.), 'Chile: Foreign investment' and 'Argentina: Foreign investment', accessed 18 April 2015 at https://en.santandertrade.com/establish-overseas/chile/foreign-investment and https://en.santandertrade.com/establish-overseas/argentina/foreign-investment.
Schvarzer, Jorge (2006), 'Inversiones españolas en la Argentina. Una relación nueva, estrecha y sugerente', Working Paper 16, Centro de Estudios de la Situación y Perspectiva Argentina, Facultad de Ciencias Económicas, Universidad de Buenos Aires.
Toral, Pablo (2005), 'The advantage of Spanish firms in Latin America, 1990–2002', in Felix E. Martín and Pablo Toral (eds), *Latin America's Quest for Globalization: The Role of Spanish Firms*, Aldershot: Ashgate, 31–57.
Toral, Pablo (2011), *Multinational Enterprises in Latin America since the 1990s*, New York: Palgrave Macmillan.
Tortella, Gabriel (2008), 'Del monopolio al libre mercado en las empresas petroleras españolas. Campsa y Repsol', in Guillermo Guajardo (coord.), *Innovación y empresa. Estudios históricos de México, España y América Latina*, México: UNAM-Centro de Investigaciones Interdisciplinarias en Ciencias y Humanidades-Fundación Gas Natural, 67–96.
Vidal, Gregorio (2001), *Privatizaciones, fusiones y adquisiciones. Las grandes empresas en América Latina*, Barcelona: Anthropos, UAM, UNAM.
Vidal Olivares, Javier (2008a), 'Empresas multinacionales españolas: los casos de Iberia y el grupo hotelero Sol-Meliá, 1956–2004', in Guillermo Guajardo (ed.), *Innovación y empresa. Estudios históricos de México, España y América Latina*, México: UNAM-Centro de Investigaciones Interdisciplinarias en Ciencias y Humanidades-Fundación Gas Natural, 133–70.
Vidal Olivares, Javier (2008b), *Las Alas de España. Iberia Líneas Aéreas. De aerolínea de bandera a transportista mundial (1940–2005),* Valencia: Publicaciones de la Universidad de Valencia, 231–43.

Vidal Olivares, Javier (2011a), 'Entre la mediación y la organización empresarial: las Cámaras españolas de Comercio en América Latina', *Revista de Historia de la Economía y de la Empresa*, **5**, 241–64.

Vidal Olivares, Javier (2011b), 'Sirviendo a las empresas en el mercado internacional: las Cámaras de Comercio españolas de comercio en Argentina y México (1888–1936)', *Revista de Historia de la Economía y de la Empresa*, **V**, 241–60.

Yáñez, César (2006), 'La emigración española a la Argentina en la época de las grandes migraciones', in Alicia Alted Vigil, Alumeda Asenjo, Maria José Aguilar, *De la España que emigra a la España que acoge*, Madrid: Fundación Caja Duero y Fundación Largo Caballero, 81–97.

6. Staffing and management in British MNEs in Argentina and Chile, 1930–1970[1]

Rory M. Miller

I. INTRODUCTION

Business history in Latin America has undergone a remarkable expansion.[2] The retreat of the political Left and the declining influence of dependency theory in universities and research institutes, coupled with a shift in economic policy to favour the private sector, helped to open up research on domestic business groups and their inter-relationships with foreign firms and the state, the dominant actor in most Latin American economies in the mid-twentieth century.[3] At the same time the study of foreign business moved away from the issues of power that dominated the research agenda in the period when the imperialism and dependency paradigms were dominant. In part this has meant a reversion to traditional business history approaches in the form of company histories emphasising strategy. However, at the same time new areas of study have opened up, such as the cultural contrasts and conflicts between foreign bosses and Latin American workers, or the role of foreign business in changing patterns of consumption in Latin America. This growth in research both on domestic and foreign firms has meant that Latin America has been of interest both to those compiling collections of essays on international business history and to the international journals that specialise in the subject.[4]

Despite these advances, the state of business history in Latin America is, in the eyes of those at its leading edge, some way behind other areas of the world.[5] Much of the work remains empirically based, devoid of conceptual and theoretical insights and, at the same time, largely unable to contribute to the development of the subject more broadly. It is noticeable, for example, that the *Oxford Handbook of Business History*, published in 2008 and written almost entirely by North American and Western European authors, includes virtually no references to Latin America, even in chapters where Latin American specialists might have something distinctive to contribute, for example on business groups, business-labour relations, and business-state relations.[6] While this may, in part, be due to linguistic limitations, it also reflects the failure of Latin American(ist)s to contribute to broader debates.

Commentators in Latin America have made several suggestions about concepts and theories that might help to inform historians working in individual countries. Historians have considered, for example, the use of the insights of the business historian Alfred Chandler on the strategy and structure of firms, although María Inés Barbero has argued that the Chandlerian paradigm, with its concentration on the large single-industry firms allegedly typical of the United States, has less relevance for Latin America.[7] Carlos Marichal has suggested utilising approaches from New Institutional Economics.[8] The growing literature on 'varieties of capitalism' offers another possibility. Ben Ross Schneider, in delineating a distinctive Latin American variety of 'hierarchical market capitalism', laments the underdevelopment of business history in the region, and hence constraints on understanding the evolution, strengths, and shortcomings of Latin American capitalism.[9] Those working on foreign business in Latin America might take up the implicit challenge of Geoffrey Jones and Tarun Khanna and consider the development of MNEs in the light of concepts and debates from the international business literature.[10]

In light of the significance, first of free-standing companies, and then of multinational firms, in twentieth-century Latin America, this is worth considering. International business has become a multidisciplinary field, moving away from the economists' studies, which characterised its early stages and concentrated on the reasons for the existence, growth, and location of multinational firms, to encompass a range of different problems faced by companies operating overseas: strategy and structure (which echo Chandler's central concerns), business-state relations, cultural issues and conflicts, marketing, logistics, staffing, labour relations, the financial and legal aspects of operating overseas, and risk. There is thus considerable scope for applying insights from this literature to historical issues, although it is dependent on the availability of international firms' archives. As Peter Buckley has written, 'International business theory can illuminate the seemingly disparate strategies of firms in given historical circumstances'.[11] This chapter considers the strategic role and competence of British firms' subsidiaries in Argentina and Chile in the mid-twentieth century, the policies followed to recruit and develop executives, and the consequences for British business in the region in the light of literature on the organisation and control of subsidiaries and international human resources management.

II. THE TRANSITION IN BRITISH INVESTMENT IN ARGENTINA AND CHILE

In 1914, Argentina accounted for approximately 40 per cent of Britain's investments in Latin America, Chile for about 7 per cent.[12] Irving Stone and later historians have shown that much of this took the form of direct investments. In the late nineteenth century, the normal channels for such investment were free-standing companies which possessed a small headquarters in London and operations in just one overseas country. Such apparently independent firms were often effectively controlled by merchant houses and other investment groups, especially in smaller economies like Chile where the nitrate firms were grouped into clusters managed by merchant houses.[13] However, the larger companies, such as the banks and railroads in Argentina and Chile, were largely autonomous of other interests. After World War I, the total scale of British investments did not change significantly and few new free-standing companies were formed. Many of the nitrate firms in Chile ceased operations in the late 1920s, undermining the trading houses which had developed and controlled them. Nevertheless, there were new British investments in Argentina and Chile throughout the interwar period and after 1945, and this involved a transition away from the dominance of the free-standing companies such that the complexion of British interests, by the 1950s, was rather different from that which prevailed before 1914. What were the significant changes?

First, there was some divestment in the traditionally important areas of railroads and urban utilities. In 1928, Pearson sold Whitehall Electrical Investments in Chile to the American and Foreign Power Corporation (AFPC). In Argentina, ITT bought the United River Plate Telephone Company early in 1929, and soon afterwards AFPC purchased the Atlas Trust's electricity interests.[14] While the Argentine railroads, despite rumours of possible sale, remained in British hands until nationalisation in 1948, after 1930 competition with road transport and exchange rate depreciation undermined their dominance and their profits. The Antofagasta and Bolivia Railroad Company in Chile was an exception to the general decline in the railroad business: it retained its British ownership, its autonomy, and its dividends, sustained by long-distance mineral traffic, until the 1980s.[15] Second, the separate British commercial banks were consolidated into the Bank of London and South America (BOLSA), which was affiliated to Lloyds Bank. BOLSA was formed in 1923 with the merger of the London and River Plate Bank, which had interests in both Argentina and Chile, and the London and Brazilian Bank. The remaining independent British bank in the region, the Anglo-South American Bank, which had commenced operations in Chile in 1889 and expanded into Argentina through acquisition in 1900, ran into difficulties in 1931 due to its heavy exposure to the nitrate industry and was eventually acquired by BOLSA in 1936, completing the consolidation.[16] Third, the merchant houses on the West Coast of Latin America had to adjust to the volatility of commodity markets and changes in their host economies. Graham Rowe, one of the four major firms which had interests in both Chile and Peru, was liquidated in 1931. The other long-standing trading houses, Antony Gibbs & Sons, Balfour Williamson, and Duncan Fox, all of which remained independent until the 1960s, already had a series of investments in agriculture, agro-industrial enterprises, and mineral resources. From the 1930s, Gibbs and Duncan Fox, especially, were investing in nascent manufacturing industries, a process which Graham Rowe had pioneered. By the late 1930s, all these firms had in effect become investment groups involved in external trade, internal distribution, and directly managed and portfolio investments in their host economies, especially in Chile.[17] Fourth, British manufacturing companies began to establish subsidiaries, first in Argentina (and Brazil) and later in smaller economies such as Chile, a development that is missed in data based on investment flows through the London Stock Exchange, with the consequence that historians have hardly noticed it. An incomplete Foreign Office survey in 1935 counted 18 subsidiaries of British manufacturing firms in Argentina, yet overlooked those of J. & P. Coats, Glaxo, and Reckitt & Sons; there was an additional expansion, including firms like Pilkington and Beecham, between then and the outbreak of war, further investment in the late 1940s, and the appearance of new enterprises and expansion of old plants after the fall of the Perón administration in 1955.[18] The last of these phases of growth in Argentina also coincided with the investment of consumer goods firms like Unilever in Chile. Overall, it could be argued, there was a transition in forms of British investment from free-standing companies to multinational firms and investment groups operating in several Latin American countries. The manufacturing companies were beginning to operate across the world. How did they organise and staff their subsidiaries in South America?

III. ORGANISATION AND STAFFING IN INTERNATIONAL BUSINESS

Apart from the resource-seeking firms in sectors like mining and oil which, with the exception of Royal Dutch-Shell (hereafter Shell), were dominated by US corporations after World War I, most international firms were seeking markets in Latin America. Their entry was, at least in part, stimulated by a variety of measures in the 1930s when exchange controls, import quotas and licences, and deliberate attempts to foment manufacturing were added to the high levels of protection that already characterised Latin American countries, a policy package that became known as Import Substitution Industrialisation (ISI).[19] This meant that the MNEs' subsidiaries in Latin America were largely unable to export to neighboring countries. They became focused on the expanding, if occasionally problematic, markets of their host economies. These subsidiaries were, for the most part, managed in isolation from those of the same firm in neighboring countries, and they reported directly to boards located in Britain. In the context of the literature on typologies of international business, such enterprises were 'multidomestic' or 'polycentric' market-seeking firms. This had implications for both their management and their staffing.[20]

Not all the subsidiaries and branches in Latin America were of equal weight. In the case of the merchant houses/investment groups operating on the West Coast, many of which also had branches in Peru and Bolivia, Chile was always the most significant centre of profits and losses. However, for the manufacturing firms, many of which arrived much later, Chile was rarely more than a marginal market. Investing there might be in the expectation of reasonable returns from small-scale operations within a highly protected market, or else to forestall the establishment of a global competitor.[21] In contrast, the wealth of Argentina in the early twentieth century meant that for British manufacturing firms it was often one of the earliest places where they established factories outside Western Europe, the United States, and the Dominions. Almost every major British manufacturing firm with overseas investments had at least a sales office and often a factory there by 1970. In 1942, the British Chamber of Commerce in Argentina listed 46 British industrial firms with subsidiaries in Argentina, and in 1973 it listed 68.[22] For BOLSA, which was, in contrast, a regionally based multinational rather than a global one, Argentina and Brazil were, for commercial and historical reasons, the two markets where it had concentrated its resources. Argentina remained central to BOLSA's strategy, especially when confidence returned after the fall of Perón's administration in 1955: one sign of its commitment was the opening of an impressive new headquarters in Buenos Aires in 1966. While Chile did not contribute to BOLSA's turnover in the same way as Argentina and Brazil, it remained one of the bank's major countries of activity, and BOLSA's acquisition of the Balfour Williamson trading group in 1960 enhanced its importance.[23]

The effective organisation and management of subsidiaries of differing strategic significance to the firm has attracted much attention from international business theorists. One of the best known models, developed by Christopher Bartlett and Sumantra Ghoshal, is summarised in Figure 6.1.

Bartlett and Ghoshal related a firm's chances of success to the competence

		Strategic importance	
		High	Low
Local managerial competence	High	Strategic leader	Contributor
	Low	Black hole	Implementer

Source: Christopher A. Bartlett and Sumantra Ghoshal (1989), *Managing Across Borders: The Transnational Solution*, Cambridge, MA: Harvard Business School.

Figure 6.1 Bartlett and Ghoshal model

of its managers in particular subsidiaries. It required high-calibre management in important markets. These could become 'strategic leaders' within the firm where new products and techniques could be fully developed and tested. In smaller countries a multinational might have excellent local managers whom it could not utilise fully, given the scale of the national market. Nonetheless, such subsidiaries could become significant 'contributors', taking the lead in developing products and techniques that the company could introduce on a wider scale, even though they might not add much to turnover in the original market. 'Implementer' subsidiaries had the role simply of acting on decisions transmitted from above in markets of relatively low significance to the firm's success. The real problems lay in the so-called 'black holes', countries that were strategically important to the multinational, but where its management was incapable of taking initiatives that could drive the firm forward either in the local market or globally: here, unless it resolved its management problems, the firm would at best stagnate, and the function of the subsidiary might become one of little more than acting as a 'listening post'.

This model has implications for the management of British MNEs in Argentina and Chile. In the case of global manufacturing firms one would probably expect their subsidiaries in these countries to play an 'implementer' role, working under the direction of the British board but undertaking little in the way of fresh initiatives, even in Argentina. The 'strategic leader' subsidiaries of such firms would potentially be those in North America and Western Europe. However, the management in these subsidiaries might be sufficiently competent and entrepreneurial to go beyond implementing a strategy laid down from above, developing products or techniques that could be transferred to other countries, and in effect moving towards a 'contributor' role. The case of the regionally based multinational firms, such as BOLSA and the trading houses, was rather different. A highly competent management in Buenos Aires was vital to BOLSA's long-term future, given the resources invested there and the difficulties of disengagement. The same considerations applied to the trading houses in Chile. However frequently directors and senior executives visited their subsidiaries, something that varied considerably from one firm to another, local managers often had to take operational decisions without reference to Britain, and a successful strategy could not simply be formulated in London and implemented in Argentina or Chile without considerable consultation, mutual understanding, and consideration for the abilities of the management.

These points raise the issue of how managers were recruited, developed, and controlled, in particular the role played by London in assigning expatriate managers to subsidiaries and the interaction between expatriates and locally recruited managers.[24] By the end of the twentieth century, international business specialists would expect that in multi-domestic firms the need for subsidiaries to be responsive to local markets would require the employment of managers from the host economy (host country nationals or HCNs) as opposed to expatriates (parent company nationals or PCNs).[25] In the case of British manufacturing companies in Argentina and Chile, this is certainly now the norm. However, at the time that most of the industrial subsidiaries started production, as well as the banks and trading houses well into the 1960s, it was not: the great majority of the senior management in almost every major British firm in Argentina and Chile around 1960 had English surnames. So why did British firms in Argentina and Chile fill senior management roles with expatriates in the mid-twentieth century, when and how did they make the transition to locally recruited managers, and what effects did this have on the continuity and success of the firms? Was this simply an ethnocentric strategy based on assumptions of superiority and trustworthiness, or was it a more deliberate attempt to drive business and exert effective control and coordination?

The literature on the staffing of subsidiaries has developed considerably since the early 1990s, although the seminal paper dates from 1977 when Anders Edström and Jay Galbraith outlined three reasons for an international firm to use expatriate managers in its subsidiaries: first, in order to fill positions when qualified local managers were not available; second, to develop management capabilities through executives gaining international experience prior to moving into strategic positions either in key subsidiaries in developed economies or at the firm's headquarters; third, for reasons of control and coordination.[26] Here they argued that socialising managers into the firm and transferring them among countries created informal networks through which the firm could control its subsidiaries. The assumption of many scholars has been that employing expatriates is expensive and such assignments often fail because of the expatriate's inability to accommodate himself to the local business and cultural environment; Edström and Galbraith were suggesting positive benefits for the firm that could offset the costs and risks. However, later researchers found other reasons to question the use of expatriates in firms operating overseas. Stewart Black and Hal Gregersen, in particular, argued that expatriates might cease to act in the interests of the parent firm, either by becoming 'free agents' and working for their own personal interests, or by 'going native' and acting in the interests of the subsidiary rather than the firm as a whole.[27]

In a series of articles based on extensive questionnaires and desk research, Anne-Wil Harzing tested the arguments of Edström and Galbraith. Several of her conclusions are relevant to the experience of British firms in Argentina and Chile in the middle of the century.[28] First, she found significant differences among home countries in terms of the number of expatriates that were used in overseas assignments and the reasons why they were sent. British and US firms were less likely to use expatriates than their German and Japanese counterparts. In part she ascribed this to the different institutional structures of national business systems, but also to the greater trust that German and Japanese firms had in their own nationals, and hence the extent to which they could control subsidiaries. British and US companies tended to be less risk-averse and hence used expatriates to fill positions where local managers were not available, rather than to ensure control.[29] Second, host countries were different. International firms were more likely to use expatriates in countries where there was greater political risk. They employed a much higher proportion of expatriates in senior positions in Latin America than in any other part of the world, except for Africa and the Middle East. While risk was an important factor, Harzing explained this also in terms of the lower availability of local management talent and greater cultural distance.[30] 'Subsidiaries in Latin American countries', she commented, 'attached a higher importance to [the position-filling] function than subsidiaries in other regions'.[31] Third, industries differed. Not very surprisingly, the more sophisticated the technology being used, the more likely it would be that firms would employ expatriates overseas. However, financial services firms also used a high proportion of expatriates; Harzing ascribes this to the need for control.[32] Fourth, there were differences in terms of functional areas: local managers tended to reach senior positions first in human resource management and marketing, while financial functions remained in the hands of expatriates for longest.[33] This was especially marked in the case of British firms: Harzing comments tellingly that 'British MNCs are the only ones in which the financial director in subsidiaries is more likely to be a PCN than is the managing director', and she explains this in terms of British companies' obsession with short-term financial results.[34] Finally, the age of subsidiaries and the mode of market entry also played a role. Position-filling was more important in large greenfield subsidiaries where local managers with the requisite skills would be unavailable when the firm started production.[35] It should be noted that Harzing's questionnaires, however, were designed to survey the situation in the light of Edström's and Galbraith's propositions and subsequent German literature; she did not ask senior executives directly about the motives for using expatriates, but rather ascribed them in the light of the results.

This international business literature therefore suggests several hypotheses about the development of staffing and control mechanisms in British firms in Argentina and Chile during the ISI era from the Depression to the 1970s. First, given the strategic importance of its subsidiaries to the firms' overall performance, one should expect BOLSA and the merchant houses to put a high value on recruiting and retaining the best managers; the alternative would be to drop into the 'black hole' suggested by Bartlett and Ghoshal. At the same time one would also expect BOLSA to maintain expatriates in senior and middle positions for longer because of the perceived need for trust and control that Harzing found characterised firms in financial services. Edström and Galbraith also saw the need for control as a strong reason for employing expatriates but they expected this to be achieved through the circulation of staff and hence informal mechanisms of socialisation. In theory BOLSA could have used local recruits to fill executive roles in its subsidiaries, like the national banks, and found other means of 'socialising' them into the firm, but it preferred to employ expatriates despite the expense. For the merchant houses in Chile, however, there was a tension between the need to use expatriates for reasons of trust and control, especially given the political and economic risks, and employing locally recruited managers, who might be better connected with the market and Chilean political and business networks. For them, the quality of management was the priority. If they could not attract a sufficient number of good managers in Britain, they would need to apply themselves to recruiting in the local environment, and training and socialising Chilean managers into the firms. Second, since these markets had relatively low strategic importance for the manufacturing MNEs, one should expect them to use expatriates extensively in the initial stages of investment in order to fill positions, but then to move rapidly towards using local recruits. It would be likely that HCMs would first fill senior positions in areas like personnel, sales, and marketing, with the finance director's and the local chairman's role following later, again because of the perceived need for trust and control. These firms might use expatriates for any of the three reasons outlined by Edström and Galbraith. The problems for them would be to socialise locally recruited managers into the corporate culture, give them opportunities to learn from other subsidiaries, and retain the best despite limited openings for advancement in their home country. If they did not achieve this the subsidiary would probably never be more than an 'implementer', and the more entrepreneurial managers might begin to follow their own interests.

IV. DATA AND SOURCES

Clearly not all the British firms, many of which no longer exist, can be surveyed in the style of international business research. While historians can use interviews and oral history, they are normally dependent on patchy documentary evidence surviving in corporate archives, to which access may be difficult. In this particular case the accidental survival of archives has left us with some extremely rich documentation about several firms involved in Argentina and Chile, but there are also some significant gaps in the archival record.[36]

The principal archives used here are those of BOLSA, particularly board and executive committee minutes and supporting papers; Antony Gibbs & Sons, which possesses a particularly rich and complete set of correspondence between London and Chile; and various manufacturing firms, of which Unilever and Glaxo (including its acquisitions in the Wellcome Foundation) have the most extensive and informative archives.[37] The research also makes some use of the archives of Reckitt & Colman, where material becomes sparser after the mid-1950s, J. & P. Coats, the thread manufacturers, the British steel companies that operated in Argentina and Chile, and a series of interviews with senior and retired executives, which were especially useful for reconstructing the history of ICI in Argentina. The archives of ICI itself, like those of British American Tobacco (BAT), Pilkington, and Beecham, all of which had important operations in Argentina dating from before World War II, remain unavailable for research, and the same is true of other firms that invested after 1945 such as Lucas, Thornycroft, British Motor Corporation, Yardley, and Wiggins Teape.[38]

V. THE HISTORICAL CONTEXT OF STAFFING IN BRITISH FIRMS

Much of the international business literature assumes that large multinational firms possess an unlimited supply of competent and ambitious managers prepared to work abroad in order to enhance their career development and promotion prospects. By the 1980s, for example, Unilever stressed the need for international experience and mobility for its top executives.[39] Such policies have been helped by the growth of international air travel, which has enabled firms to send managers abroad for short trouble-shooting assignments, or to gain experience through a senior management role in a subsidiary lasting two or three years. Even when Edström and Galbraith were writing in the 1970s, they regarded this as the norm for an expatriate assignment.[40]

It was rather different before World War II. British firms operating in South America usually recruited young men to work overseas on renewable three-year contracts. The expectation was that if the first contract proved successful for both parties the manager would probably spend the bulk of his career overseas in the same place. The contract, which included a commitment to paid home leave when the contract ended, provided the parent company with a significant means of control. During their first contract young men, especially in the major port cities and capitals, would be socialised both into the firm and into the British community, which supplemented the company's means of control by imposing informal constraints on their behaviour.[41] Senior executives from Britain would visit South America from time to time, which offered them an opportunity to evaluate the state of the business and assess the potential of the staff, but the regularity of such visits varied considerably from one company to another. The firm clearly faced the threat that full and accurate information, whether regarding the state of the business and risks it was facing in South America or strategic developments in the parent firm, would not be transmitted from one side of the Atlantic to the other. In addition, resident managers might 'go native', become 'free agents', produce work of poor quality, or otherwise escape from corporate control without the British parent detecting this, especially if senior executives visited only infrequently.

This system of renewable long-term contracts still prevailed when the manufacturing companies arrived between the wars. While it had commenced with the merchant houses, the banks, and free-standing companies like the railroads in the nineteenth century, the firms like Unilever and Reckitts that invested in Argentina before 1930 adopted similar arrangements for expatriate staff. However, while the supply of potential managers available for South America remained intact before 1939, it declined thereafter. After the war Britain returned to full employment, so men coming out of the forces or leaving school had less incentive to seek their future overseas. At the same time many British manufacturing firms were rapidly expanding their foreign direct investments, setting up additional requirements for management recruits. By 1954, the board of the Wellcome Foundation identified a shortage of suitable candidates for management as a possible constraint on expansion, noting that there was 'a grave shortage of first-class men on the scientific and commercial sides'.[42] Moreover, compared with emigration to the white Dominions, where the culture and the language at least appeared familiar, taking up a contract in South America probably seemed much less attractive. The image of the Peróns was hardly one that would encourage men to emigrate to Argentina. And even for those sympathetic to moving to South America, Brazil, where many British firms were also investing in the 1950s, might seem more attractive.

British firms operating in Argentina and Chile, especially the manufacturing companies, began to face a shortage of potential recruits at the very time that they were increasing the scale of their activities and expanding into new markets. Filling technical posts presented particular problems. The British university system was small and elitist, so there was an insufficient supply of suitably qualified graduates; university systems in Latin America, with their emphasis on the professions of law and medicine, also offered little that could compensate. In 1961, the Buenos Aires manager of Glaxo reported that he was unable to recruit two Argentine chemists for training in Britain, as the chairman had suggested. There were only ten organic chemists in the whole country due to the lack of demand for such skills before the growth of the petrochemicals and paint industries; the only one due to graduate that year was being fought over by Shell and Esso.[43] In 1964, during an especially rapid period of expansion, the shortage of management talent seemed as much a constraint for Unilever as it had for Wellcome ten years earlier. The firm's Special Committee (its executive committee) explicitly warned 'the Overseas Committee to have in mind in considering any further development overseas the growing pressure on the Concern's management resources and the cost of maintaining expatriate management in countries overseas'.[44] The dissatisfaction of many of the management recruits sent to South America exacerbated the situation. BOLSA in 1951 noted the 'existing shortage of junior executives and the alarming number of resignations in the past twelve months of trainees and of those just completing their training period', while the senior partners of Antony Gibbs & Sons, ten years later, expressed their concern about 'the alarming exodus of young Englishmen from G. & Co's staff'.[45]

There was, however, one element that might alleviate the shortage of expatriates for the firms which, for reasons of control, trust, and cultural affinity, were unwilling to reduce the 'British' element in their South American subsidiaries: the British communities that were the result of the emigration of large numbers of British contract staff in the late nineteenth and early twentieth centuries to work in the banks and free-standing firms like the railroads. The community in Argentina was the largest outside the Empire and the United States. While it is difficult to calculate its size accurately, since everyone born in Argentina automatically became an Argentine citizen, the British embassy in the 1930s estimated it at just under 40000 people. At the same time Chile, with an estimated British community of just under 5000, ranked third in South America (that in Brazil was slightly larger).[46]

Before 1914 the British firms operating in South America seem to have discriminated against children of British parentage born there, preferring to send out contract staff recruited in the United Kingdom.[47] In 1905, for example, Sir Archibald Williamson, the senior partner of Balfour Williamson, wrote: 'My father [who had established the firm] never had any confidence in young Fellows brought up in Chile and he always said that on no account would he ever make a partner of any one who was brought up there, even of English parentage. Get your clerks out from home as a rule'.[48] Three years later he wrote to one of his partners in Chile in much the same vein: 'We do not wish these natives or semi-natives to occupy important positions in our offices. They nearly all turn out unsatisfactorily in the end. Borrowman is one of the few exceptions . . . Unfortunately he has shown a tendency to employ semi-Chileans which we do not approve of'.[49] However, by the end of World War II the British communities in Argentina and Chile were much more firmly established, with schools such as St George's, St Andrew's, and St Alban's in Buenos Aires or The Grange in Santiago, which educated boys in the British system, sent several to British universities, and were used by senior managers of British firms in South America themselves for their children.[50]

With new managerial talent in short supply in Britain, recruiting from these communities offered British firms the possibility of retaining the subsidiary's national character, although it also created potential problems in terms of parity between local recruits and incoming contract staff. However, use of 'Anglo' staff alone could not solve the difficulties of recruitment. Michael Lubbock, the BOLSA director responsible for personnel issues, remarked in 1952 on 'the great competition for Anglo-Argentines, and indeed for the best-quality nationals' in Buenos Aires.[51] Like the British companies, expanding US firms offered good employment opportunities for those who were bilingual. Demand was such that the best qualified Anglo-Argentine graduates almost had a choice of the firm for which they wished to work. However, like their independent school counterparts at home, the British schools in South America did not turn out students qualified to fill the gaps that emerged as more technologically advanced firms arrived, especially when a new wave of investment occurred after the fall of Perón. Apart from those who went to British universities, the route for others was to start as 'office boys', learn on the job, and then, perhaps, obtain a management position. Firms offered little structured training that might improve the quality of management; if any individual wished to pursue further qualifications they normally paid for it themselves.[52]

Shortages of expatriates who wished to go to South America, a supply of Anglo-Argentines and Anglo-Chileans that was variously qualified yet insufficient to meet demand, and a continuing reluctance to employ the local talent that might have been available thus created serious difficulties for British firms after World War II. All those that operated in Argentina and Chile had to meet these challenges, but their responses were different, and this had consequences both for the firms as a whole and for the managers whom they employed.

VI. THE TRADITIONAL EMPLOYERS: THE BANKS AND MERCHANT HOUSES

In 1955–56, the Bank of England sent one of its senior staff, G.J. MacGillivray, on a six-month visit to evaluate Britain's business interests in Latin America. In his report he paid particular attention to BOLSA, complaining that its London headquarters followed conservative and unimaginative policies, that it was less flexible than local and other foreign banks in the region, that the directors and London staff possessed little overseas experience, and that the managers in Latin America were of poor quality and lacked the drive and the contacts to attract business.[53] As Geoffrey Jones has written, BOLSA 'needed an entrepreneurial figure who could take a strategic view of what was happening and perceive opportunities to do something about it'.[54] The bank had struggled to come to terms with the changed environment for foreign business in Latin America since the war. Its published financial data showed fairly flat net profits since 1946, below those of the war years. The level of deposits it controlled had scarcely recovered from the accounts it had lost when the Argentine, Brazilian and Uruguayan governments nationalized British railroad and utility firms in the late 1940s.[55] Change in strategy came with the transfer of Sir George Bolton from the Bank of England to become BOLSA's executive chairman in 1957. Under his direction the bank took a deliberate decision to rebuild its position in its traditional markets and to diversify internationally. As Bolton explained to the Chancellor of the Exchequer in 1961, he had developed a ten-year strategy, with the encouragement of the Bank of England, 'to help improve the position of British banking and the battered British image in Latin America . . . Briefly we proposed to develop an international banking organisation incorporating a merchant bank and an investment instrument capable of raising capital in any financial centre, and to use our unique and comprehensive information service to bring British industry and Latin American needs together'.[56]

Such a programme required not only appropriate strategic direction from London, but high-quality staff in South America, capable not simply of implementing orders but building up business on their own initiative. Using the Bartlett/Ghoshal typology of subsidiary capabilities and roles Argentina should have been acting as a 'strategic leader', for the alternative was for it to become a 'black hole', given its importance to the bank's revenues. The country management had to implement a succession of initiatives, including the construction of a new headquarters, the development of an insurance business and an investment bank (the Compañía Financiera de Londres), a joint venture with English Electric to form an information technology company, and a major investment in motor manufacturing through loans to SIAM di Tella. While the volatility of the Argentine economy in the 1960s and problems with its partners may have contributed to the disappointing outcome of many of these enterprises, the quality of management was also an issue. A report on the Financiera in 1964 commented that the staff were 'quiet and well behaved', but had little experience of investment banking.[57] This was hardly a recipe for entrepreneurial initiative and accurate risk assessment. An internal report ascribed the crisis of the joint venture with English Electric in 1968 to poor management and possible fraud.[58]

Staffing had, in fact, been a central concern for BOLSA for over a decade. As early as 1949, Michael Lubbock, an executive director, forecast that the bank would face problems in staffing senior positions over the next 30 years and needed to increase its recruitment of potential executives. However, he lamented, among headmasters and university appointments committees 'there [was] still a tendency to regard banking, at least for the outstanding or more adventurous young men, as the last choice'.[59] Two years later the Bank's Establishments Committee noted that possible trainees from British clearing banks were no longer coming forward, and that 'large British industrial and commercial firms' offered better prospects and salaries.[60] As noted already, it was losing many recruits after only a few months. By 1954, it estimated that only half the executive trainees recruited since 1946 remained.[61] In a wide-ranging review of the bank's future the following year, Sir Francis Glyn, another director, reported that staffing was in crisis; recruitment for overseas work was becoming more difficult each year, and consequently the bank was making poor appointments.[62] But BOLSA was still working on the assumption that its senior executive management should be expatriated. Doing business in the volatile, inflationary, and nationalistic environments that characterised Argentina and Chile from World War II to the mid-1970s, was far from straightforward. It required high-calibre management with the capacity to develop networks, think strategically, assess risk, and act quickly. Poor-quality expatriates with little initial experience of the countries where they were working would not suffice.

The bank clearly fell short in all phases of its staffing processes. Recruitment procedures for potential executives appeared haphazard. Ron Weir, later an economic historian at York University, tells of his experience:

> [In 1969] I had made a provisional commitment to join the Bank of London and South America. This was after a mildly unusual interview which consisted of three opening questions: 'Did I play golf?', 'Did I play tennis?' and 'Did I intend to get married in the next six months?' to which the answers were 'not any more', 'yes', and 'possibly but unlikely' – in that order. These were followed by a fascinating discussion of the pleasures of home grown tobacco . . . Like much else in British industry, selection processes were quite relaxed and certainly less rigorous than in the universities.[63]

From what we know of training in the bank, in the days before there was any real academic expertise in management or on Latin America in British universities, it was equally haphazard.[64] The level of salaries that BOLSA offered was also a problem. 'Naturally we can never hope to pay as much as industrial firms, such as Shell or Lever', an internal minute read in 1951, 'but at the same time we cannot remain as far behind them as we have been in the past'.[65] Lubbock estimated in 1952 that BOLSA was paying 10–20 per cent less than other British firms and making annual rather than quarterly adjustments, despite rising inflation, and Bolton also commented, shortly after taking over as chairman, that BOLSA managers were less well treated than their counterparts in other banks.[66] A further problem in retaining good staff was the top-down control exercised from London; the bank clearly regarded its senior executives in Latin America simply as implementers rather than partners in the strategic direction of the bank, who might develop new lines of business on their own initiative. Avoiding the loss of good senior staff was one reason for the granting of more autonomy to the River Plate management in 1966.[67] Over the longer term the bank was still suffering from the legacy of the 1930s, when BOLSA's own serious problems, the emergency acquisition of the Anglo-South American Bank, the subsequent rationalisation of its branch network, and caution about further expansion had forced it to reduce recruitment drastically, with the result that it lacked the experienced middle management that Argentina and Chile required in the post-war years.[68]

There is a certain path dependence here, the expectation that expatriate staff should continue to take charge, that recruits from the British communities in South America were the next best thing, and that local initiative should be restricted, that appears to apply also to other long established British companies in Argentina and Chile.[69] In conditions of full employment in the United Kingdom and a problematic environment in South America, this was a recipe for long-term problems. The one British-owned railroad remaining in Chile also continued to rely heavily on expatriates, even though Chilean managers and engineers successfully operated the state railroads system further south. As late as 1971, during the Allende administration, the company's 23 senior staff in Chile mainly comprised expatriates paid in sterling. When the Chilean Central Bank prohibited this, the majority left and Chilean staff replaced them, contrary to the firm's previous assumptions that it needed to employ expatriates because the best Chilean railroad managers would not work in the north.[70]

Documentation about staffing in the merchant houses survives from only one, Antony Gibbs & Sons, but this was the most prominent and it is in line with evidence from other trading houses in South America, such as Wilson Sons & Co. in Brazil. In some respects their experience appears similar to BOLSA's: a continued preference for British recruits, especially at the executive level, and problems in recruiting and retaining staff, largely due to poor salaries. However, in contrast to BOLSA, the Gibbs management in London showed only sporadic interest in policy and hence it suffered a 'free agent' problem.

The firm continued to insist that the chairman in Chile should always be British. Although this was later diluted in 1961, to there 'always be[ing] at least one English educated Englishman on the Board of Gibbs & Co., Chile', even in the mid-1960s men were still being recommended for appointment with the explicit intention of maintaining 'the British element on the Board' in Santiago.[71] Gibbs did recruit extensively from the British schools in South America: a list of actual and potential directors in 1947 contained 11 British executives and 10 Anglo-Chileans, the majority of them educated at St George's in Buenos Aires or The Grange in Santiago.[72] However, with one exception, the board in Santiago comprised either British expatriates or Anglo-Chileans into the mid-1960s.

Like BOLSA, Gibbs suffered enormous problems with retention.[73] In 1965, a London director commented that 'there is a horrible suspicion here that we keep losing these young Englishmen who go out to Chile because they don't get paid enough', and in the inflationary conditions of the 1960s they continually found their salaries and allowances slipping behind those of British firms.[74] A subsequent attempt to recruit two new British staff, one a Cambridge graduate in Spanish, and the other one with extensive selling experience in Uruguay, foundered on the question of contract length, leave, and salaries.[75] Staff training and development were minimal, recruits being expected to learn on the job, and with directors visiting from London only occasionally, the problems of management recruitment and development simply festered. This also created agency problems, as an internal report in 1961 brutally remarked:

> The overall impression with which one leaves Chile is that Gibbs & Co. is slowly dying. It appears to lack direction and drive. There seems to be a complete absence of ideas for developing business. The policy of the firm, if the word policy can be used, appears to be to allow the directors and departments to develop their own business and their own interests. There seems to be no thought given to the future management of the company.[76]

Despite its importance to the firm overall, the Gibbs management in Chile fits neatly into the Bartlett/Ghoshal characterisation of a 'black hole'. Very few of the expatriates sent out since 1945 had remained, and many local directors had, in effect, become free agents, working simply in their own interests. Was Gibbs unique among trading houses? Evidence from interviews suggests not. One former executive of Balfour Williamson and Inchcape, with long experience in Chile and Colombia, commented that the senior management of the trading companies in the 1960s had been trained informally, lacked entrepreneurial vision, and had little experience of modern management accounting techniques. Another remarked that his family's firm, Weir Scott, aimed simply at standing still.[77]

The problems of firms like BOLSA and Gibbs reflect their longevity, their dependence on a particular region of the world, and their inability to adjust to a situation where good expatriate recruits were no longer plentiful and senior management was unable to adjust their attitudes sufficiently quickly. This undermined any attempts from London to implement new strategies, for, as BOLSA discovered, the lack of recruitment in the 1930s meant that the senior and middle ranking executives in the subsidiaries lacked the capacity for effective 'change management'.

VII. THE NEW EMPLOYERS: THE MANUFACTURING COMPANIES

The growing manufacturing companies had less to lose, except for their competitive position in a particular market, if management could do little more than implement directives from above. Yet despite the difficult economic environment, few major British manufacturing firms actually withdrew from Argentina in this period. They appeared to have made the transition to locally recruited executives more quickly than BOLSA or Gibbs, taking advantage of the supply of potential recruits from the British communities. In practice, a combination of greater interest from visiting directors and entrepreneurship on the part of local executives meant that these subsidiaries could, on occasion, become 'contributors' to the firm overall rather than mere 'implementers'. Two examples will suffice. First, the sales management system that Unilever developed in Argentina in the 1930s consistently attracted praise from visiting senior executives, who recommended that it should also be implemented in Brazil. Managers from Unilever's Brazilian subsidiary were sent to Buenos Aires for specific training into the 1950s.[78] Second, an Anglo-Argentine accountant initially recruited by ICI/Duperial as an office boy in Buenos Aires in the early 1950s developed an inflation accounting system which the firm adopted for other inflationary countries in 1968.[79]

MNEs like Shell, Unilever, BAT, and ICI, which had been present in Argentina, were, in BOLSA's view, the leaders in paying good salaries to expatriates, as noted above. However, they were also limiting their use of expatriates in senior positions locally. According to David Montgomery, who worked as general manager for Shell in Chile in the 1950s and then elsewhere in Latin America, all his successors in small markets were Latin American nationals.[80] While there is no direct evidence of Shell's staffing strategy for Argentina, elsewhere in South America Shell was moving towards recruiting local managers and employing them at quite senior levels. BOLSA remarked on Shell doing this in Brazil in 1954. It was also happening in Venezuela, as a British minister noted in 1951: 'The Shell Group are fully conscious of the need to forestall nationalisation by developing . . . the human side of the industry. This means progressive Venezuelisation or the introduction of more and more nationals into more and more responsible positions with no limit except ability'.[81]

However, it was not just a response to economic nationalism that lay behind such changes. For market-seeking MNEs, locally recruited managers potentially had better understanding and knowledge of the local environment, as well as political and social networks that might help the firm's business. Also, the cost of employing expatriates was rising, salaries and allowances were difficult to adjust in inflationary circumstances, governments were imposing nationality requirements on a company's payroll, and at the same time the supply of qualified local managers, although still limited, was increasing. Manufacturing companies might continue to exhibit some preference for British expatriates: the Glaxo board agreed in 1961 that it would normally have two British members on the board of every major subsidiary. However, during the same meeting the board also agreed that it should actively encourage local recruitment and training and remove salary differentials between expatriates and locally recruited executives, although expatriate allowances would remain.[82] Such strategies were helped by the growth of air travel and the increasing experience of London boards in dealing with Latin America. Both Reckitt & Colman and Glaxo employed senior executives in Britain who had long experience of working in South America and were able to travel, troubleshoot, and reassess strategy in the subsidiaries. International air travel also encouraged more regular visits to Britain by managers in the subsidiaries as well as regional meetings to transfer knowledge.[83]

The staffing of Unilever's successful subsidiary in Argentina is instructive. Lever Hermanos recruited its early management almost entirely from within South America, combining expatriates from other British firms like BAT with Anglo-Argentines. One of the few executives sent from London, a Lintas manager tasked with building up Unilever's advertising, 'did not run straight' and had to be discharged after four years.[84] While visiting directors sometimes expressed concern about the quality and potential of locally recruited staff and frequently recommended bringing them to Britain for further training, a process which would also have helped to socialise them into the firm, a senior executive visiting Buenos Aires in 1942 envisaged that the firm should 'continue to fill many of the senior positions with locally engaged men'.[85] The following year, in fact, Unilever formalised a scheme to develop potential executives in Argentina, aimed at three groups of recruits: Anglo-Argentine volunteers in the forces, who would be selected in London before returning; wartime volunteers who had already returned to Argentina; and promising Argentines. However, in the competitive labour market of late 1940s Argentina, many left for other firms once they had been trained by Levers. There was one significant barrier to the promotion of Argentine executives, noted by a visiting director in 1951:

> It may prove eventually undesirable that so much business at the higher level is conducted in English both in personal contacts and in inter-departmental correspondence. This is discouraging to the Argentines, who consequently believe that their chances of promotion depend more on fluency in English

> than in character and commercial ability. The English community, though still fairly numerous, is diminishing and it will obviously be better to encourage the existing Argentine personnel and to recruit from Argentine schools.[86]

In the same year an Anglo-Argentine recruited by the firm in Buenos Aires in 1928 became chairman of the local board. Helped by the availability of recruits from the British community, the staffing of Lever Hermanos thus preceded Unilever's general adoption of an '–ization' policy in 1956. A major internal conference of senior Anglo-Dutch directors and the managers of the overseas subsidiaries concluded that year that 'provided that we could find and train men of the right quality, there was in fact no job which should not be open to natives, although the question whether we should at all times reserve the position of Finance Director or Chief Accountant to an expatriate had remained undecided'.[87] The main constraint on employing more locally recruited staff was their availability. With only three Argentines at senior level in 1957, when expansion resumed after the fall of Perón, Levers had to use expatriates for position-filling purposes, but in the 1960s it was able to move gradually to 'the promotion of genuine nationals as distinct from Anglo/Argentines'.[88] At the same time its Chilean subsidiary employed only four expatriates in key positions after its reorganisation and expansion in 1962, with the clear expectation that Chileans would subsequently take over these roles.[89]

Other leading industrial firms, especially in Argentina, followed similar strategies, albeit with some variations. In 1951, Reckitt & Colman looked to recruit Anglo-Argentines for junior positions in accounting and chemistry, seeing no reason to bring out more than one English expatriate as a management trainee.[90] Its overseas board in 1954 was explicit about the limited circumstances under which Reckitts would employ expatriates:

> We only send young men abroad if we think that they are good enough to be in the line of succession to a senior post in the Management but the policy has been laid down that we are to maintain the British element in the line of succession by sending out young Englishmen of good quality at intervals . . . At the same time Branch Managers are aware that if there are foreign nationals of the country in which we are trading who prove to be better for the post than the Englishman we have sent out then the local man should in fairness go to the top.[91]

Following a detailed review of overseas staffing needs, the following year the Reckitt & Colman board made it clear that most expatriate assignments would be for position-filling and management development reasons, and that many might become short-term, lasting months rather than years.[92] ICI also had a very limited use for expatriates by the 1950s.

Anglo-Argentines filled many of the trainee posts there and, eventually, under the patronage of one of them, Arthur Edbrooke, several became local directors. When interviewed in 1995, Edbrooke, who had taken charge in 1957 at the beginning of a period of rapid growth, claimed that even then ICI only sent expatriates to Duperial on three-year contracts and expected that they would train local staff to take over.[93] Thereafter Anglo-Argentines and Argentine nationals headed Duperial until ICI sold it in 2001. Even the role of local finance director, which ICI normally reserved for expatriates for ethical reasons, was filled for a long time by an Anglo-Argentine who had studied at Henley Management College and worked in ICI headquarters.[94]

VIII. CONCLUDING REMARKS

British companies in Argentina and Chile followed different strategies with regard to the relative proportions of expatriates, members of the British communities, and locals whom they wished to recruit and develop for senior executive positions. The incoming manufacturing firms often had to use expatriates for position-filling roles in the early stages, but then they were able, like Unilever in Argentina, quickly to adjust to using staff who they recruited locally. By the late 1950s, companies such as ICI or Unilever expected expatriates to train locally recruited successors. However, did this contribute to the overall success of these subsidiaries? Measuring performance, in the absence of consistent and comparable accounting data over the short and the long term is difficult, and the evidence is impressionistic. Nonetheless, it does seem that some of the manufacturing firms proved able to go beyond the 'implementer' role that one might have expected and developed techniques and products that the firm could use elsewhere. In contrast, the older firms, the banks and merchant houses, had to overcome a heritage of dependence on expatriates, a continued preference for them, and, importantly, a hiatus in management recruitment in the 1930s which created a 'generation gap' after the war.

These factors, in part, explain the problems of BOLSA and Gibbs. They were exacerbated by the enormous difficulties of doing business in the volatile and nationalistic economic environments presented by Argentina and Chile from the 1950s to the 1970s, which demanded astute, high-quality and well-networked managers. Staffing issues, therefore, were clearly relevant to the evolution of British business in post-war Argentina and Chile, but only one element in the relative decline of British interests which has concerned successive British governments. It is unknown whether, in their continued preference for expatriates and their failure to recruit and retain high-quality staff, British firms differed from their competitors from North America and Europe, for example, the other foreign banks or trading houses.[95]

What prospects did Anglo-Latin American and locally recruited managers have within the firm, and how did this affect its behaviour and performance? In a seminal article published in 1969, Howard Perlmutter commented that in polycentric firms, meaning a firm where the subsidiaries were semi-autonomous, oriented to local markets, and staffed mainly by locally recruited managers, 'no local manager [could] seriously aspire to a senior position at headquarters'.[96] This verdict fits many of the British manufacturing firms' subsidiaries in Argentina and Chile. A 'glass ceiling' certainly existed in this period: few locally recruited managers moved to the higher levels of the firm in Britain or larger subsidiaries, although expatriates with experience there, such as Michael Perry of Unilever, rose to senior positions. This lack of opportunities may explain the longevity of many chairmen and managing directors in the subsidiaries of companies like Unilever and ICI, as well as the loss of ambitious local recruits to other firms. The MNEs may therefore have not benefited fully from their Argentine and Chilean talent, either because issues like family commitments and heritage held the recruits in their home country, or because recognition of their talent depended on the astuteness of visiting executives with whom they came into contact. However, this also has implications for the control and coordination of the firm. The subsidiaries could become, in effect, local fiefdoms which, at worst, 'went native', and were left untroubled as long as they returned profits and did not run into serious crises. Various interviewees from ICI commented on the distinctly 'Anglo-Argentine' management that developed in ICI/Duperial, which, in the words of one senior executive, 'caricatured an earlier England' and was basically left to its own devices, especially after 1982.[97] Another interviewee, an expatriate sent to run the Argentine subsidiary of J. & P. Coats in 1987, commented that he found the firm had stagnated under Anglo-Argentine managers who lagged behind in accounting techniques, manufacturing processes, and price setting.[98] These subsidiaries were neither contributors nor good 'implementers'; indeed they were probably heading towards becoming small-scale 'black holes' with the potential to damage the firm's long-term interests in emerging markets.

Does the experience of British firms fit with the hypotheses suggested by the international human resource management (HRM) literature about the employment of expatriates? Certainly BOLSA preserved its expatriate character at senior level and showed a reluctance to recruit potential executives locally for much longer than the manufacturing firms, as one would expect in financial services. But others also showed a reluctance to move entirely to local management. Gibbs and other merchants were slow to do so, frequently expressing a desire to maintain a 'British element' at senior level in the subsidiaries, but then so did Reckitts. In following this strategy, Gibbs probably contributed to its own decline: its management problems were deep rooted and change was handicapped by a reluctance to dismiss incompetent British or Anglo-Chilean employees and trust Chileans. The manufacturing firms for which we have evidence did move more quickly towards the use of locally recruited staff in senior executive positions at the 'softer' end of management, in personnel, sales, and marketing, while retaining financial functions under expatriate or Anglo-Latin American control. But all firms differed, and while they compared themselves with each other, especially on salaries and allowances, they also developed their own culture and strategies with regard to staffing in markets like those of South America.

Finally, this analysis has implications for business historians in Latin America at two levels. First, it identifies some serious problems in recruiting technical and managerial talent in markets like Argentina during the rapid industrial expansion of the 1950s and 1960s. While local firms may have gained from the experience of those who left foreign companies, clearly there was enormous competition for talent in boom periods, and these shortages must have affected the management of Argentine industrial companies also. The same was probably true in Chile, although it is noticeable that whereas Unilever executives were unable to find sufficient potential Argentine executives, even by 1969, in Chile the manager was confident in his ability to replace position-filling expatriates with local managers.[99] Second, it demonstrates how the use of international business and management theory can force us to ask different questions about the trajectory of individual firms, taking us beyond the narratives of their development. Their international human resources strategy and means of controlling their subsidiaries to maximise their contribution were essential to their progress or decline. However, this analysis only provides one window on some of the problems of staffing foreign firms in post-war Latin America. Comparisons with firms from other countries would put this particular study into greater relief, and allow us to generalise with more certainty about foreign MNEs in general and British companies in particular.

NOTES

1. Much of the research for this chapter was financed by grants from the Nuffield Foundation (SOC 253[238]) and the Economic and Social Research Council (R000223222). I am grateful for their financial support, and the corporate archivists

who provided access to privately held collections, in particular Jeannette Strickland of Unilever and John Booker and Karen Sampson of Lloyds Banking Group. I am also grateful to seminar audiences at the Facultad de Ciencias Económicas of the Universidad de Buenos Aires and the Association of Business Historians annual conference in 2009, as well as my colleagues (past and present), Stephanie Decker, Heinrich Kramarski, and David Williams, who kindly commented on earlier versions of this chapter. They are not, of course, responsible for the faults in it.

2. For an interim assessment, see Dávila and Miller (1999).
3. Dávila and Barbero (2009).
4. Barbero (2003); Dávila (2003). Special issues of journals focusing on Latin America include (2004) *Enterprise and Society*, **5** (2); (2008) *Business History Review*, **82** (3); and (2009) *Entreprises et Histoire*, **54**.
5. Dávila (2003): 373; Barbero (2003): 333.
6. Jones and Zeitlin (2008).
7. Barbero (2003): 328–31.
8. Marichal (1997): 10, 28.
9. Schneider (2009).
10. Jones and Khanna (2006).
11. Buckley (2009): 307.
12. Stone (1977): 695.
13. On the concept of free-standing companies, see Wilkins (1988) and Wilkins and Schröter (1996). Miller (1988) considers those that operated in Chile and Peru. On investment groups, see Chapman (1985) and Jones (1997).
14. Jones and Greenhill (1977): 111–12; British Chamber of Commerce in Argentina (1928) and (1929); Hausman, Hertner, and Wilkins (2008): 165, 184.
15. Blakemore (1990).
16. Joslin (1963): 176–7, 198–9, 243–5, 267–73.
17. Greenhill and Miller (1998); Jones (2000): 256–8, 282–5, 295–6. Graham Rowe's pioneering initiatives were recognised by other firms as a model: see E.B. Baring to E. Gubbins, 11 December 1929, file 203285, Baring archive; F.L. Dobree to W. Gibbs, 12 September 1931, file 16875/3, Antony Gibbs & Sons archive, Guildhall Library, London (hereafter AGSA).
18. Sir Henry Chilton to Sir John Simon, 18 March 1935, FO371/18628/A2903/111/2, British National Archives.
19. On the high levels of protection in Latin America before the ISI era, see Coatsworth and Williamson (2004).
20. For a review of this literature, see Harzing (2000).
21. Unilever, for example, increased its investment in Chile in 1960 in order to forestall Proctor & Gamble. Minutes of Directors' Conference, 28 October 1960, Unilever Group Archive (hereafter UGA).
22. British Chamber of Commerce in Argentina, *Índice comercial de la Cámara de Comercio Británica en la República Argentina, 1942*, and *'Índice comercial', 1973*.
23. On BOLSA's strategy, especially after 1957, see Jones (1993): 264–8.
24. The relationship between expatriate managers and staff in foreign firms is, of course, also an important issue in international business, but is outside the scope of this chapter. There has been significant literature on the British-owned railroads in Argentina, but other areas have been neglected. The banks and merchant houses faced increasing problems with middle-class unionisation, and serious disputes occurred in the 1960s, but little is known about them. On staff relations on the railroads in Argentina, see especially Horowitz (1985); Tuozzo (1997).
25. Harzing (1999): 14. The section on expatriates was omitted from the subsequent version of this paper published in *Journal of International Business Studies*.
26. Edström and Galbraith (1977). For a survey of the field, see Collings, Dowling, and Scullion (2009).
27. Black and Gregersen (1992).

28. Harzing (2001a), (2001b), and (2001c).
29. Harzing (2001c): 584 and 590.
30. Harzing (2001b): 143 and 149; (2001c): 585 and 591.
31. Harzing (2001c): 591.
32. Harzing (2001b): 146 and 153.
33. Harzing (2001b): 144.
34. Harzing (2001b): 153.
35. Harzing (2001b): 592.
36. Edström and Galbraith's typology was based on just four firms, while Harzing's questionnaire survey achieved a 20 per cent response rate: see Edström and Galbraith (1977): 249; Harzing (2001c): 547. Neither could be called a random or complete sample.
37. Unfortunately the Glaxo archive is no longer available to historians. The research used here was completed in 2001 before it closed.
38. In the case of ICI, BAT, and Pilkington organised archives are known to exist, but they are currently inaccessible to researchers.
39. Jones (2005): 158, 259.
40. Edström and Galbraith (1977): 251.
41. On socialisation and control, see especially Jones (1993): 47–53, and Stang (1983). For an example of such a contract, dating from 1925, see Blakemore (1990): 316–8. The banks also exacted a parental guarantee: 'Report by M.R. Lubbock, 1 April 1952', file #4409, Lloyds Banking Group Archive (hereafter LBGA).
42. Wellcome Foundation Ltd, Minutes of Directors' Meetings, 26 April 1954 and 3 May 1954, Minute Book #5, Glaxo Group Archive, Greenford, London (hereafter GGA).
43. F. Hayward to Dr Wilkes (Greenford), 27 April 1961, file #614/2, GGA.
44. Meeting of Special Committee with Overseas Committee, 21 July 1964, UGA.
45. Minutes of Establishments Committee, 6 November 1951, file #4408, BOLSA papers, LBGA; 'Agenda for Discussion with Mr Gibbons [Managing Director, Santiago]', 12 July 1961, file #16878, AGSA.
46. Buenos Aires Chancery to Foreign Office, 3 September 1935, and V. Cavendish Bentinck to Sir John Simon, 31 May 1935, FO 371/18697/A8245/1536/51, British National Archives.
47. Jakubs (1986): 146–8.
48. Sir Archibald Williamson to Hope Simpson, 21 July 1905, Private Letter-Book 1904–1907, Balfour Williamson archive, University College, London.
49. Williamson to George Guthrie, 1 June 1908, Private Letter-Book 1906–1909, Balfour Williamson archive.
50. The well-known British historian, D.C.M. (Christopher) Platt, was the son of James Westlake Platt, the managing director of Shell's La Diadema subsidiary in Argentina in the 1930s and early 1940s, and educated at St George's before returning to Britain.
51. 'Report by M.R. Lubbock, 1 April 1952', file #4409, LBGA.
52. Interviews with Thomas Hudson (former Chairman of ICI-Duperial), Buenos Aires, 14 August 1995, Derek Foster (ex-Agar Cross and other firms), Buenos Aires, 2 August 2001, David Martin (former Finance Director and Chairman of ICI-Duperial), Buenos Aires, 8 August 2001.
53. G.J. MacGillivray, 'British Status in South America', 8 May 1956, file OV 188/8/16–20, Bank of England archive.
54. Jones (1993): 264.
55. Jones (1993): 460–1.
56. Sir George Bolton to Chancellor of Exchequer, 9 November 1961, file #4412, LBGA.
57. G.M. Furtado, 'Memo on the Compañía Financiera de Londres', 1 October 1964, file #4390, LBGA.
58. BOLSA, 'Report on IDS, BA: Its Past, Present, and Future', 10 April 1968, file #4397, LBGA.
59. Michael Lubbock, 'Staff Policy: Memorandum on Recruitment and Training', 27 September 1949, file #4408, LBGA.

60. BOLSA, Establishments Committee, 5 June 1951, file #4408, LBGA.
61. BOLSA, Establishments Committee, 30 November 1954, file #4409, LBGA.
62. Francis Glyn, 'The Future of the Bank', 6 September 1955, file #4410, LBGA.
63. Weir (2001): 428.
64. Such was the shortage of British expertise on modern Latin America before the late 1960s that the bank employed a historian of the independence period, Professor R.A. Humphreys, to provide briefings to its trainees on the contemporary political and economic situation. Like many British academics of the time, Humphreys had scarcely travelled in South America.
65. BOLSA, Establishments Committee, 5 June 1951, file #4408, LBGA.
66. BOLSA, 'Report by Mr M.R. Lubbock', 1 April 1952, file #4409, LBGA; George F. Bolton, 'Memorandum to the Board', 28 May 1957, file #4410, LBGA. A former executive of Balfour Williamson, which was acquired by BOLSA in 1960, also commented that BOLSA paid its staff badly and did not attract entrepreneurs: interview with Colin Armstrong, London, 22 January 2002.
67. BOLSA, 'Reorganisation and Decentralisation: River Plate Circuit', Executive Committee, 15 November 1966, file #4384, LBGA. All the new initiatives of the 1960s appear to have come from London: collective interview with five former managers of BOLSA, Buenos Aires, 22 August 1995.
68. BOLSA, Establishments Committee, 30 November 1954, file #4409, LBGA.
69. Two of the five BOLSA managers interviewed were Anglo-Argentines recruited locally but later offered expatriate contracts. Only one had ever worked outside Argentina.
70. Blakemore (1990): 279 and 285–6.
71. 'Lord Aldenham's Visit to Chile, December 1949 – January 1950', MS 16898; 'DCC's Agenda for Discussion with Mr Gibbons', 3 October 1961, MS 16878; London to A.N. Beven, 2 February 1965, MS 16876/9, all AGSA.
72. Lord Aldenham, 'Memo, Chile, 1947', MS 16898, AGSA.
73. 'DCC's Agenda for Discussion with Mr Gibbons', 3 October 1961, MS 16878, AGSA.
74. London to A.N. Beven, 19 February 1965, MS 16876/9; T. Gibbon to H. K. Goschen, 9 April 1963, AGSA.
75. A. Gibbs to A.N. Beven, 28 September 1966, MS 16876/9, AGSA.
76. 'Memorandum on Gibbs & Co., Chile, 1961', MS 16878, AGSA.
77. Interview with Colin Armstrong, London, 22 January 2002; interview with Michael Valdes-Scott, London, 2 July 2001.
78. 'Report of Mr C.E. Tatlow on his Visit to the Argentine Republic, November/December 1937', file OSF 1/10; Unilever, Overseas Committee Agendas, 2 April 1940, Book Y; 'Mr J.L. Heyworth's and Mr E. Quin's Report on Visit to Argentine, March 1942', OSF 1/15; 'Report on Mr Arthur Hartog's Visit to SAI Irmaos Lever, Brazil, July 1943', OSF 3/16; 'Notes on Mr H.R. Odling's Visit to Brazil and Argentine, May/June 1955', OSL 6/8, all from UGA.
79. Interview with David Martin, Buenos Aires, 8 August 2001.
80. Interview with David Montgomery, London, 23 January 2002.
81. B. Pleydell-Bouverie and M. Lubbock, 'Report to the Board of Directors: Brazil', 10 February 1954, file #4409, LBGA; B.A. Berthoud, 'Report on Visit to Venezuela to Represent HMG at the Venezuelan National Petroleum Congress (12–18 September 1951)', FO371/91061/AV1532/41, British National Archives.
82. Glaxo Laboratories Ltd, Board Minutes, 10 April 1961, file CA 542, GGA.
83. I.P. Lewis, 'Report on Visit to Central American and South American Markets', Glaxo International Board Minutes, 28 October 1966, file CA 106, GGA.
84. 'Mr J.L. Heyworth's Visit to the Argentine, March-April 1935', file OSF 1/8, UGA. Lintas was Unilever's inhouse advertising agency.
85. 'Mr J.L. Heyworth's and Mr E. Quin's Report on Visit to Argentine, March 1942', OSF 1/15, OGA.
86. 'Visit of Mr J.L. Heyworth to South America, April 1951', file OSF 1/22, UGA.

87. Minutes of Special Committee, Meeting with Overseas Committee and Overseas Managers, 9 March 1956, UGA. On Unilever's'–ization' strategy, see Knox (1976).
88. Minutes of Special Committee Meeting with Overseas Committee and Mr H. Colvill-Jones, 27 March 1957, UGA.
89. Minutes of Special Committee Meeting with Overseas Committee and Mr Bufill, 29 June 1964, UGA.
90. Reckitt & Colman (Overseas) Ltd, Board Minutes, 31 January 1951, Reckitt Heritage Archive (RHA), Hull.
91. Reckitt & Colman (Overseas) Ltd, Board Minutes, 3 March 1954, RHA.
92. Reckitt & Colman (Overseas) Ltd, Board Minutes, 2 March 1955, RHA.
93. Interview with Arthur Edbrooke, Buenos Aires, 22 August 1995. The comments here about ICI/Duperial in Argentina are based on a number of interviews, noted above.
94. Interview with Dr Iain MacFarlane, London, 14 February 2002.
95. Lawrence Clayton's history of W.R. Grace & Co., an obvious comparator, ends in 1930 and does not address the management issues created by the firm's transition and decline thereafter: Clayton (1985).
96. Perlmutter (1969): 12–3.
97. Interview with John Greaves CMG, London, 23 January 2002; Interview with Dr Iain MacFarlane, London, 14 February 2002. The quotation is from the latter.
98. Interview with George Bowen, Oxford, 2 October 2002.
99. Meetings of Special Committee with Overseas Committee, 29 June 1964; R.H. Siddons, 'Chile, Brazil and Argentina: Report to Special Committee', 27 August 1968, Overseas Committee Box 45, UGA.

REFERENCES

Barbero, María Inés (2003), 'Business History in Latin America: Issues and Debates', in Franco Amatori and Geoffrey Jones (eds), *Business History around the World*, Cambridge: Cambridge University Press.

Barbero, María Inés (2003), 'Business history in Latin America: issues and debates', in Franco Amatori and Geoffrey Jones (eds), *Business History around the World,* Cambridge: Cambridge University Press, 317–35.

Black, J. Stewart and Hal B. Gregersen (1992), 'Serving two masters: Managing the dual allegiance of expatriate employees', *Sloan Management Review*, **33** (4), 61–71.

Blakemore, Harold (1990), *From the Pacific to La Paz: The Antofagasta (Chili) and Bolivia Railroad Company, 1888–1988*, London: Lester Crook.

British Chamber of Commerce in Argentina (1928), *Monthly Journal*, **9** (3), 11–2.

British Chamber of Commerce in Argentina (1929), *Monthly Journal*, **9** (5), 25.

Buckley, Peter (2009), 'Business history and international business', *Business History*, **51** (3).

Chapman, Stanley (1985), 'British-based investment groups before 1914', *Economic History Review*, **38** (2), 230–51.

Coatsworth, John and Jeffrey G. Williamson (2004), 'Always protectionist? Latin American tariffs from independence to great depression', *Journal of Latin American Studies*, **36** (2), 205–32.

Collings, Peter, J. Dowling, and Hugh Scullion (2009), 'Global staffing: A review and thematic research agenda', *International Journal of Human Resource Management*, **20** (6), 1253–72.

Dávila, Carlos (2003), 'La historia empresarial en América Latina', in Carmen

Erro (ed.), *Historia empresarial: pasado, presente, y retos del future,* Barcelona: Ariel, 349–81.

Dávila, Carlos and María Inés Barbero (2009), 'Débat: Perspectives sur les Entreprises Latino-Américains et leur Histoire', *Entreprises et Histoire*, **54**, 178–86.

Dávila, Carlos and Rory Miller (eds) (1999), *Business History in Latin America: The Experience of Seven Countries*, Liverpool: Liverpool University Press.

Edström, Anders and Jay R. Galbraith (1977), 'Transfer of managers as a coordination and control strategy in multinational organizations', *Administrative Science Quarterly*, **22** (2), 248–63.

Greenhill, Robert and Rory Miller (1998), 'British trading companies in South America after 1914', in Geoffrey Jones (ed.), *The Multinational Traders*, London: Routledge, 102–27.

Harzing, Anne-Wil (1999), 'An empirical analysis and extension of the Bartlett and Ghoshal typology of Multinational Companies', University of Melbourne Working Paper.

Harzing, Anne-Wil (2000), 'An empirical analysis and extension of the Bartlett and Ghoshal typology of multinational companies', *Journal of International Business Studies*, **31** (1), 101–20.

Harzing, Anne-Wil (2001a), 'Of bears, bumble-bees and spiders: The role of expatriates in controlling foreign subsidiaries', *Journal of World Business*, **36** (4), 366–79.

Harzing, Anne-Wil (2001b), 'Who's in charge? An empirical study of executive staffing practices in foreign subsidiaries', *Human Resource Management*, **40** (2), 139–58.

Harzing, Anne-Wil (2001c), 'An analysis of the functions of international transfer of managers in MNCs', *Employee Relations*, **23** (6), 581–98.

Hausman, William, Peter Hertner, and Mira Wilkins (2008), *Global Electrification: Multinational Enterprise and International Finance in the History of Light and Power, 1878–2007*, Cambridge: Cambridge University Press.

Horowitz, Joel (1985), 'Occupational community and the creation of a self-styled elite: Railroad workers in Argentina', *The Americas*, **42** (1), 55–81.

Jakubs, Deborah Lynn (1986), 'A community of interests: A social history of the British in Buenos Aires, 1860–1914', Ph.D. Dissertation, Stanford University.

Jones, Charles (1997), 'Institutional forms of British direct investment in South America', *Business History*, **39** (2), 21–41.

Jones, Charles and Robert Greenhill (1977), 'Public utility companies', in D.C.M. Platt (ed.), *Business Imperialism, 1840–1930: An Inquiry based on British Experience in Latin America*, Oxford: Clarendon Press.

Jones, Geoffrey (1993), *British Multinational Banking, 1830–1990*, Oxford: Clarendon Press.

Jones, Geoffrey (2000), *Merchants to Multinationals: British Trading Companies in the Nineteenth and Twentieth Centuries*, Oxford: Oxford University Press.

Jones, Geoffrey (2005), *Renewing Unilever: Transformation and Tradition*, Oxford: Oxford University Press.

Jones, Geoffrey and Tarun Khanna (2006), 'Bringing history (back) into international business', *Journal of International Business Studies*, **37** (4), 453–68.

Jones, Geoffrey and Jonathan Zeitlin (eds) (2008), *Oxford Handbook of Business History*, Oxford: Oxford University Press.

Joslin, David (1963), *A Century of Banking in Latin America, to Commemorate the*

Centenary in 1962 of the Bank of London & South America Limited, London: Oxford University Press.
Marichal, Carlos (1997), 'Avances recientes en la historia de las grandes empresas y su importancia para la historia económica de México', in Carlos Marichal and Mario Cerutti (eds), *Historia de las grandes empresas en México, 1850–1930*, México DF: Fondo de Cultura Económica.
Miller, Rory (1996), 'British free-standing companies on the West Coast of South America', in Mira Wilkins and Harm Schröter (eds), *The Free-Standing Company in the World Economy, 1830–1996*, Oxford: Oxford University Press, 218–52.
Perlmutter, Howard (1969), 'The tortuous evolution of the multinational corporation', *Columbia Journal of World Business*, **4** (1).
Schneider, Ben Ross (2009), 'Hierarchical market economies and varieties of capitalism in Latin America', *Journal of Latin American Studies*, **41** (3), 553–75.
Stang, Gudmund (1983), 'Aspectos de la política de personal de las empresas británicas en América Latina, 1880–1930', in Asociación de Historiadores Latinoamericanistas Europeos (AHILA), *Capitales, empresarios y obreros europeos en América Latina*, Stockholm: AHILA, 541–50.
Stone, Irving (1977), 'British direct and portfolio investment in Latin America before 1914', *Journal of Economic History*, **37** (3).
Tuozzo, María Celina (1997), 'As you sow, so shall you reap: Argentine labor and the railroad nationalization', in Jonathan C. Brown (ed.), *Workers' Control in Latin America, 1930–1979*, Chapel Hill: North Carolina University Press, 128–58.
Weir, Ron (2001), 'The day the world fell down and a butterfly flapped its wings', in Pat Hudson (ed.), *Living Economic and Social History: Essays to Mark the 75th Anniversary of the Economic History Society*, Glasgow: Economic History Society.
Wilkins, Mira (1988), 'The free-standing company, 1870–1914: An important type of British foreign direct investment', *Economic History Review*, **41** (2), 259–82.
Wilkins, Mira and Harm Schröter (eds) (1996), *The Free-Standing Company in the World Economy, 1830–1996*, Oxford: Oxford University Press.

7. From a guaranteeing state to an entrepreneurial state: the relationship between Argentina's state and urban utility companies, 1880–1955

Norma Silvana Lanciotti

The role of the state in late-industrializing economies has long been central to debates on Latin American economic development. The critical role of the state was emphasized by the United Nations Commission for Latin America and the Caribbean (ECLAC, or CEPAL in Spanish) after 1948. More recently the neo-institutionalist and corporate governance literatures have revisited state-business relationships as a key component in the economic performance of developing economies. state-business collaboration has been seen in these literatures as an important condition for economic development, provided institutional arrangements could enable the exchange of information via reciprocity and trust-based ties.[1]

In Argentina, development debates have defined the scope of studies focusing on the state policies that shaped the business environment amidst the fluctuating macroeconomic conditions during the second half of the twentieth century. However, the analysis of state intervention forms, procedures and devices, as well as the relationship between the state and companies since the formation of Argentine nation state to the 1950s, has not received similar attention. The historiographical consensus on the existence of a non-interventionist liberal state before 1930 has now started to crumble. The analysis of the policies after the Baring Crisis, the major financial and banking crisis in 1890 when the leading British investment bank Baring Brothers almost went bankrupt because of Argentinean loans, has given way to an alternative view that traces the creation of state-owned companies back to the beginning of the twentieth century, suggesting a much more prominent role for the state much earlier than had been believed.[2]

This chapter looks at the relationship between the state and urban utility companies from the first global economy until the rise of state-owned enterprises. The goal is to identify the historical forms of government involvement (administration, regulation and management) in urban utilities, with a special focus on electricity companies. As historical studies on Argentina's government agencies and state-owned enterprises have omitted a comparative perspective, this chapter sets out to assess the relations between the state and urban utility companies. Comparisons will be made with regulatory regimes in other regions. The chapter employs the notion of the 'relative autonomy of the state' to explore the drivers of state policies in the urban utility sector.[3]

I. UTILITIES, STATE AND COMPANIES

The notion of utilities as currently understood is rather recent. According to early liberal and Old Regime traditions, public services were not associated with state management. Therefore it is necessary to separate the legal principles of utilities in the nineteenth century from the utility practices and organization formats disseminated between the beginning of the twentieth century and 1945, spanning from concession contracts with private companies to the creation of state-owned enterprises.[4]

In Western Europe, the ties between states and public utilities evolved over three stages in this period. The first stage stemmed from public service doctrines encouraging private, decentralized management under municipal supervision. Later, Great Britain and the Scandinavian countries shifted to public, decentralized management, turning water, electricity and gas companies over to county administrations. The utility companies that remained in private hands were subject to state regulation for service fee and quality oversight. After the Great Depression, decentralized management, both public and private, began to overlap with increasingly centralized management schemes run by large national companies. From World War II to the 1973 oil crisis, both nationalization and the development of regional and national networked systems gave way to the supremacy of centralized, state-ownership schemes.[5]

Public utility regulation in the US started off in much the same way as Europe, but then the paths diverged. Conflicts among private companies and municipal officials over concession renewals and network expansion led to the creation of oversight state commissions that set accounting supervision criteria for gas and electricity companies from the early 1900s. The limits of this regime became visible after 1918, but federal intervention did not happen until after the Great Depression. Federal regulatory institutions introduced new control mechanisms to relative success, as most urban utilities continued to be managed by private companies overseen by the central government.[6]

Both in Europe and the US, state policies to regulate urban public utilities increased after World War I and were consolidated in the 1930s, with the creation of regulatory agencies and widespread discretional regulation.[7] In Latin American countries, municipal administrations had outsourced sanitation, tramway, gas and electricity services to private companies, mostly European and American based. This scheme paved the way for the creation of decentralized public utility systems whose economic and financial management was highly centralized under the control of foreign-owned business groups.[8] This model was consolidated around 1900, when the remaining local companies were sold and almost all foreign firms were absorbed by a few multinational holdings and investment trusts. Thus, the initial involvement of foreign and domestic enterprises in tramway, electricity, gas, water and sewage service delivery was replaced by concentrated systems controlled by multinational groups.[9]

These oligopolistic systems operated under contracts granted by local governments, with no intervention from federal or provincial governments until 1930. Changes prompted by the Great Depression, particularly the fall of the gold standard and industrial growth in Latin America, brought the conditions which had enabled the system of local and regional systems managed by multinationals to an end, as nationwide public utility systems supervised by federal governments emerged. This process would conclude with the nationalization of utilities in the decade following World War II.[10]

II. PUBLIC UTILITY COMPANIES AND THE STATE IN THE ERA OF CONCESSIONS, 1880–1919

Historically the role of public utilities was understood in a number of ways. According to classical economics, public utilities were important for the proper working of a market economy. In *The Wealth of Nations*, Smith recommended that the state conducted the public works that would not attract private investors, especially transportation and communication infrastructure and water distribution systems.[11] A political and legal tradition saw public services as provided for, and by the state, to pursue political and military goals, and this was the view taken by early republican regimes in Latin America. At the end of nineteenth century, the concept of public services shifted to 'universal services' which served the 'public interest'. This was influenced by the democratization of Europe and Latin America societies. Both traditions shaped the relations between the state and public utilities from the nineteenth century until 1930.

The engineers employed by municipal agencies for public work projects were the first to set boundaries for state intervention in utilities. Jules Dupuit, Director of Municipal Services of Paris, pointed out that the municipal involvement was crucial for socially-relevant public services to cover the entire population. That was the case of water distribution, as the hefty investments required did not guarantee enough earnings for multiple competing companies. Thus the solution was argued to be municipal management. This view hinged on the state's role to promote a harmonious development of commercial and productive operations, as well as to ensure a healthy urban working class – an issue that became more relevant with the increasing influence of public health movements aimed at improving the hygiene and living standards of workers.[12]

In Argentina, urban infrastructure projects started to rise in municipal agendas during the 1880s. Poor sanitary conditions and high mortality rates resulting from the infectious diseases in fast-growing port cities fueled the state intervention in public health and social hygiene. Contracts were offered to private companies to build waterworks and sewage systems and to pave streets. The insufficiency of gas lighting services also led to the granting of franchises to electric utility firms. Typically, local governments granted concessions to multiple companies.

As previous chapters have shown, this was a boom time for the Argentinean economy. Both local politicians and businessmen agreed that municipal administrations had to guarantee the basic conditions for the supply of services, without any intervention themselves in production or distribution. Liberal, conservative and socialist reformers shared this view. The supply of such services was seen as requiring a local response to swift urbanization. It was only later in the 1930s that the Socialist Party would begin to advocate central government management of public utilities to guarantee an equal supply across counties.

The choice of private management of utilities reflected the spread of economic liberalism, but it was not the only reason. Municipal administrations had scant financial resources as they relied solely on taxes on commercial and industrial activities. Utilities issued stocks and bonds in European markets to finance their businesses. As a result, the system was shaped by foreign investments.

Especially in the second half of the 1880s, British direct and portfolio investments grew substantially in the utility sector. Early tram companies were local – in some cases, managed by British and Argentine boards. When trams started to be powered by electricity, foreign companies became dominant. A similar process followed in the railroad business. Early railroad companies received British funding but were managed by British and Argentine boards in the Pampean region and by national and provincial administrations in non-profitable areas. In 1887, President Miguel Juárez Celman began to promote direct foreign investments in this sector. As a result, by 1896, London-based companies controlled 88 percent of Argentina's railroad system. By 1900, most tramway, sanitation, telephone, electricity and gas companies were British-owned, and even those incorporated in Argentina featured a significant share of British-owned stock and debentures. (see Table 7.1)[13]

These urban utilities had a number of noteworthy characteristics. First, from a production standpoint, electricity, telephone and tram networks required coordinated actions among system components, as service supply in one area became efficient upon joining the network. The system required high initial investments and technology incorporation to enable network effect enhancements and economies of scale in successive stages of expansion. Second, these investments were highly asset-specific and could not be re-used for other operations. The risks associated with fixed asset-specific investments were compensated by lengthy concessions.[14]

While economies of scale promoted the expansion of urban utility systems, asset-specificity and large-scale investment favored concentration, as high barriers to entry and exit prompted the creation of natural monopolies. As companies invested to benefit from economies of scale and economies of network, this business proved to be highly profitable, so long as no exogenous shocks like currency devaluations or import restrictions on equipment and supplies changed the initial conditions.[15] Therefore, from 1900 onwards, the acquisition of the leading British electricity companies facilitated the ownership concentration of electric utility companies in the hands of large foreign groups. Deutsch Uberseeische Elektricitäts-Gesellschaft (DUEG, or CATE in Spanish), created in 1898, began its expansion with the acquisition of British power stations and the construction of new thermo-electric plants in Buenos Aires, Montevideo and Santiago de Chile. A few years later, SOFINA and AEG partnered to consolidate their control over Argentina's electric networks. By 1914, both Belgian and German holding companies owned and controlled the electric and tramway networks in Argentina's most populated districts, while smaller towns remained serviced by British companies.[16]

The use of concession contracts as the main legal device to regulate the relations between the government and companies shows the influence of the modern social contract theory (or contractualism) in the regulation of public utilities. The primary drawback of such concession contracts lay in the risks associated with incomplete contracts. Emerging public service monopolies encouraged opportunistic behavior as a result of contract ambiguities on specific issues. Utility concession contracts were imperfect and incomplete, as agreed terms are affected by technological and economic

Table 7.1 Urban utilities created before World War I in Argentina

Incorporated	Data date	Headquarters	Company name	Equity	(Move to Col 1?)
1855	1899	London	Primitive Gas and Electric Lighting of Buenos Aires Ltd. (Primitiva Gas Co.)	£400,000	Gas and electricity
1869	1899	London	City of Buenos Ayres Tramways Co.	£621,000	Tramways
1876	1899	London	Anglo Argentine Tramways Co.	£1,300,035	Tramways
1880	1899	London	Buenos Aires Gas Co.	£500,000	Gas
1885	1899	London	Buenos Ayres and Belgrano Electric Tramways Co.	£837,500	Tramways
1886	1899	London	United River Plate Telephone Co. Ltd.	£373,000	Telephones
1887	1899	London	The Rosario Waterworks Co./Consolidated Water Works of Rosario	£244,100	Water
1888	1899	London	Rosario City Improvements Company Ltd./Rosario Drainage Co.	£439,555	Sewage
1888	1899	London	South Barracas Buenos Aires Gas & Coke	£37,000	Gas
1888	1899	London	Buenos Ayres New Tramways Co.	£225,000	Tramways
1889	1899	London	River Plate Electricity Co./River Plate Electric Light & Traction Co. Ltd.	£224,000	Electricity
1889	1899	London	Buenos Ayres Grand National Tramways Co.	£362,800	Tramways
1890	1899	London	La Plata and Ensenada Tramways Co.	£105,000	Tramways
1896	1899	Portland	The Córdoba Light & Power Co./Cordoba Light, Power & Traction Co.	£410,947	Electricity and tramways

Table 7.1 (continued)

Incorporated	Data date	Headquarters	Company name	Equity	(Move to Col 1?)
1897	1899	London	River Plate Gas Co. Ltd (inc. Belgrano Gas Co.)	£851,000	Gas
1897	1899	Buenos Aires	Compañía General de Electricidad de Buenos Aires	FF 6,000,000	Electricity
1898	1899	London	Bright's Light & Power Ltd.	£66,667	Electricity
1898	1906	Berlin-Buenos Aires	Cía. Alemana Transatlántica de Electricidad S.A. (DUEG)	DM 72,000,000	Electricity
1902	1910	London	Rosario Electric Company Ltd.	£280,000	Electricity
1902	1910	London	South American Light and Power Co.	£128,500	Electricity
1905	1914	Buenos Aires	Compañía de Electricidad de la Provincia de Buenos Aires	£1,175,000	Electricity
1905	1914	Buenos Aires	Buenos Ayres Lacroze Tramways Co.	£2,187,500	Tramways
1906	1910	Buenos Aires	Anglo Argentina de Electricidad	£887,650	Electricity
1906	1914	London	The Bahía Blanca Waterworks Company	£449,000	Water
1906	1912	Buenos Aires	La Eléctrica del Norte	£1,000,000	Electricity
1906		Brussels	Compañía General de Tramways del Rosario		Tramways
1907	1914	London	Bahía Blanca Gas Company	£220,000	Gas
1908	1908	London	Córdoba Light, Power and Traction Company	£372,547	Electricity and tramways

1908	1910	London	The Province of Buenos Aires Waterworks Co.	£224,000	Water
1908	1914	Buenos Aires	Empresa de Luz y Fuerza de Mendoza	$mn 2,300,000	Electricity
1909	1914	Buenos Aires	General de Electricidad de Córdoba	$mn 2,060,274	Electricity
1909	1914	Buenos Aires	Compañía Argentina de Electricidad	$mn 893,780	Electricity
1910	1914	Brussels	Sociedad de Electricidad de Rosario	$mn 7,561,750	Electricity
1910	1914	Buenos Aires	Compañía Hidroeléctrica de Tucumán	$mn 1,550,000	Electricity
1914	1914	Buenos Aires	Electricidad de Corrientes	$mn 1,000,000	Electricity
1914	1914	Buenos Aires	Alumbrado Eléctrico de Río Gallegos	$mn 76,150	Electricity
1914	1914	Buenos Aires	Compañía Americana de Luz y Tracción	$mn 9000	Electricity
1914	1914	Buenos Aires	Electricidad de Dolores	$mn 500,000	Electricity
1914	1914	Buenos Aires	Andina de Electricidad	$mn 140,000	Electricity
1914	1920	London	Tucumán Tramways, Light and Power Company	£521,527	Electricity and tramways

Sources: 'Monitor de Sociedades Anónimas 1903–1940', *Anuario Pillado, 1899*; *Burdett's Official Intelligence*, London 1895, 1899; *Stock Exchange Official Intelligence,* London, 1906, 1910, 1914, 1920.

changes. This issue was especially severe in the nineteenth century, on account of the asymmetric information between the municipal officials and the technical staffs of foreign companies. In addition, contract clauses became irrelevant in industries undergoing rapid innovation or technology transfer. Thus, municipal administrations were reluctant to switch from direct to alternating electrical current systems, relying on a contract clause that subordinated companies' technological innovations to public officials' approval. Additionally, these imperfect contracts did not include any specific provisions for service operations and extension, nor did they feature quality control devices.[17]

As noted earlier, in Argentina public utilities were outsourced to foreign companies; as a result, external factors concerning access to imported equipment and coal, exchange rates, and incoming capital flows favored higher levels of unpredictability and uncertainty, bringing additional issues to cause potential conflicts.

Initially, contract terms reflected the different interests of local authorities who wanted networks built, and companies who wanted earnings. The terms also reflected local governments' commitment to consumers while the companies' managers sought to protect the interests of stockholders and investors. In general, companies tried to get a state-guaranteed long-term, monopoly concession, while local governments strove to ensure quick construction and network expansion.

Concessions were granted for 50- to 70-year periods.[18] Sanitation companies were awarded exclusive rights and longer concessions, while electricity and tram concessions included preference rather than exclusivity clauses, which brought in more players at the initial phase. According to the contracts, facilities would be transferred to the cities at the end of concessions, with no compensation for sanitation and tram companies, as well as for electric utility companies in Buenos Aires City. In other cities, local governments would pay the electric-utility companies for the replacement cost of the system. Contracts set minimum water volumes and electric power quality for street lighting, establishing sanctions for companies' failure to deliver accordingly. Rosario's sanitation contracts, for instance, foresaw service expansion based on population growth, but failed to provide specific application terms, while in some electric utility concessions, the expansion of electricity networks depended on municipal investments.

Most concessions granted to British companies featured maximum fees set in Argentine gold pesos. Sanitation service fees were based on housing rental prices or the length of buildings, while electricity services featured maximum fees for different user categories: residential, public lighting, commercial and industrial users. Concessions included a technical progress clause that forced companies to lower fees when technical innovations and user growth reduced generation costs. No contract featured any clauses to curtail companies' profitability. All contracts included long-lasting federal and provincial tax exemptions (typically for 20 years) and duty-free input and equipment imports. The only taxation on concessions was municipal, with an annual rate ranging from 1 percent to 6 percent on companies' revenues.

Sanitation contracts established mandatory connections for all residents in network-covered areas. This compulsory connection clause was an administrative procedure intended to broaden the market and maximize the return on costly initial investments. Clauses to prevent opportunistic behaviors were quite imprecise. Municipal oversight rights did not include any details on concession control procedures. Local governments merely inspected construction works and set a maximum fee in gold pesos.[19] The use of gold pesos safeguarded revenues from inflation and exchange rate fluctuations, but it also implied successive fee increases in local currency for users. Water distribution fees were based on housing rental prices, which meant that rent increases in inflationary periods drove water service fees up. Contracts did mention fee reduction prospects, when incomes accommodated them, but there was no maximum earnings limitation, which sparked controversy among parties in the 1930s.

In the early 1900s, the mismatch between corporate investment plans and the growth of cities caused rifts with the sanitation companies. The 1899 contract in Rosario established that sewage systems would expand as per city administrations' requests based on population growth. However, in 1910 the company pressured the city administration to sign a new agreement that made network expansion dependent on gold-peso fee maintenance, preventing any future fee reductions. As former contracts had not specified fee reduction conditions, city demands proved ineffective, as the only provision in this regard actually benefited the company. Sanitation companies were reluctant to expand the sewage system, as it implied supporting underground pipeline installation costs for several years before revenues rose. For telephone and electricity companies, network expansion and cabling were not as costly – immediate connection enabled them to offset increased costs with growing revenues as a result of a larger number of users and rising consumption; in addition, with a higher load factor, the system would be used more intensively and efficiently.

Only rarely did contracts specify the types of investments expected from companies. When Córdoba's provincial government renegotiated its contract with Córdoba Light & Power in 1907, the concession was extended until 1948, provided that the company built four backup power plants. In this case, investment provisions came as a result of a long conflict between public officials and the company for insufficient power supply and recurrent blackouts caused by poor installations.[20]

Service operations and innovations started to cause unpredictable situations that brought frequent tensions to relations among city administrations and private companies. Some of these tensions led to long legal battles, while others were fixed by mutual negotiations. In both cases, complementary mechanisms were used to supplement contracts, including new ordinances, technical and accounting inspections, and the creation of arbitrage courts. These conflicts prompted a shift from the contractual notion of concessions to a view of contracts as a regulatory framework for public services.

Contract breaches by one of the parties also fueled frequent disputes. City administrations' reluctance to force dwellers' mandatory connection to service systems often led to court rulings favoring companies. Non-compliance proved harder to resolve. When faced with this issue, local administrations' only recourse was to terminate the contract. This was an unfeasible option when there were no other companies providing the same service, and cities were unable to manage service supply on their own due to technical and financial constraints. These cases, suitably illustrated by the conflicts among Córdoba's government and electricity companies (Córdoba Light & Power, Córdoba Light, Power & Traction, Compañía General de Electricidad de Córdoba) and Rosario's struggles involving Rosario Drainage Co., River Plate Electricity and River Plate Electric Light & Traction, incurred huge economic and social costs. Services continued to be poor, while rising financial and transaction costs put a strain on companies.

In the case of electricity services, a belated solution came with the transfer of assets to new foreign companies some decades later, when American & Foreign Power Co. acquired the British electric and tram companies that operated in Argentina's hinterlands (Córdoba, Mendoza, Tucumán) in 1928.[21] In turn, with gradual capitalization, the sewage company managed to complete the construction works required over a longer period of time, eventually meeting contract coverage requirements. The reasons leading to corporate non-compliance varied from case to case. Pioneering electricity companies in Córdoba and Rosario failed to make the necessary investments to build an efficient electric utility system as a result of agency issues, a lack of access to required technologies and inadequate management. Instead, the drainage company was unable to meet its contract requirements because the Baring Crisis in 1890 erupted shortly after the company had issued stock to raise the necessary investment funds.

The 1890 crisis largely contributed to the creation of a state agency that would later become a public utility state-owned company. The state's management of water and drainage services in most Argentine cities and towns came as a result of the failure of private concessions in sanitation works in Buenos Aires. In 1887, despite parliamentary opposition, the government sanctioned an exploitation and completion lease to the British Buenos Ayres Water Supply and Drainage Company. Construction works were interrupted in 1890, as the firm funding this venture was Baring Brothers. In 1891, the Buenos Aires' Special Commission for Sanitation Works took over the city's drainage project. A few years later, under the Public Works Ministry's purview, the commission undertook the construction of sanitation systems in capital cities, particularly in Buenos Aires, Mendoza, Salta (along with the local government), and Corrientes, as well as in national territories. At the same time, provincial administrations in Córdoba and Buenos Aires took over the systems in Córdoba and La Plata cities, respectively. Water and drainage services remained under the scope of private British companies only in two heavily populated cities, Rosario and Bahía Blanca, and in smaller cities of Buenos Aires Province.[22]

National Acts numbers 3727 (1896) and 3967 (1900), established that the investment in sanitation works would be funded with National Lottery funds and the federal government's budget allocations. Complementary laws (Act numbers 4158, 4881 and 4312) determined that operating costs be funded by provincial lottery and service revenues. When these funds proved insufficient, special national government budget provisions were used.[23] It should be noted that this legislation set forth a state funding scheme for public works based on taxes – a rather exceptional scheme for the time. However, with renewed external lending in 1903, works were once again funded by issuing medium-term securities.

Network expansion called for a new plan and greater budgets. In 1912, Obras Sanitarias de la Nación became a state-owned company, and shortly thereafter, the government secured a long-term loan in London to fund new investments. After World War I, a new funding scheme was established: debt service and operating expenses would be paid with operating proceeds, with works serving as collateral for bonds issued to fund network construction in new towns. The company maintained low operating cost ratios until World War I; in 1915–25, operating costs rose substantially, but, after a streamlining plan was implemented, costs dropped once again. In the nation's capital, service operations proved profitable, but that was not the case in the provinces, at least until 1925, when revenues started to cover expenses.[24]

Until World War I, the state's intervention in urban utilities sought to encourage economic growth by promoting foreign investment in public utilities in accordance with the ideas of the liberal conservative party who ruled Argentina in those years. From the 1920s onwards, the notion that local administrations could manage public utilities to assure the availability of adequate and reliable utility services to all citizens became widespread. This shift undermined concession contracts and paved the way for the view of utilities as public services that could be controlled or managed by public agencies.

III. THE ROLE OF THE STATE DURING THE FIRST CRISIS OF THE LIBERAL ERA, 1920–43

The drivers that initially prompted a shift towards a new notion of public services and the role of the state, included an investment downturn and a fuel and machinery shortage during World War I. In addition, based on American and European experiences, there was a debate on the legal and economic conditions of utility concessions. Early drafts of legislation drawing from French administrative law, anti-trust American case law, as well as British and Italian turn-of-the-century municipal experiences, were prepared by a group of legal experts, headed by Rafael Bielsa during the 1920s. Strongly influenced by Henry George's doctrines, this group analysed public service theories and elaborated the first studies on concessions' legal and economic issues with a view to arguing for service municipalization.[25] Later, in the early 1930s, municipal commissions were created, engaging these professionals, who kept a close watch on US regulatory developments to oversee utility concessions.[26]

Even before World War I, state regulatory commissions in the US had replaced municipal franchises or concessions for urban utilities. This system's proneness to corruption and regional service network expansion gave way to state regulation. State oversight was initially resisted by large utility corporations. After World War I, accounting method standardization and lower uncertainty resulting from more regulations increased system efficiency and eventually drove companies to come to terms with regulation and its favorable effects.[27] By 1921, all US states, except Delaware, had commissions in place to control service quality and fees, as well as to supervise utilities' accounting and financial practices.

In the late 1920s, state regulation started to prove deficient to oversee accounting and financial issues at utilities controlled by holding companies. State commissions had no control over holding companies as long as they were not utility companies and they kept their headquarters and accounting information in other states. Additionally, criteria for 'reasonable' fee calculations were not standardized, and local conditions affected concessions, with disparities fueling numerous legal claims. As claims were resolved by different courts, amid a general lack of definition for 'reasonability' or 'convenience', commissions were granted different regulatory powers depending on their respective courts' rulings.[28]

The need for federal supervision over holding companies was already included in the debate on public services, but no regulatory agencies had been instituted to that end. At that time, two federal agencies performed tasks that could be redirected with a federal scope: the Interstate Commerce Commission (ICC), created in 1887 to oversee railroad and communications systems, and the Federal Trade Commission (FTC), created in 1914 to fight unfair competition methods.[29] The 1929 financial crash brought about a radical change in sector policies. In 1933, the US Congress sanctioned the Tennessee Valley Authority Act, marking the debut of the state as electricity retailer and distributor. During Franklin Delano Roosevelt's administration, federal intervention was consolidated with the FTC and the Securities and Exchange Commission (SEC), created in 1934 to oversee companies' operations and to recommend stock market legislation changes. Additionally, in 1935, the Public Utility Holding Company Act was passed, mandating all utility holding companies to register at SEC in order to identify those that owned more than one integrated system.[30]

The thrust against utility holding companies focused on excessive charges attributed to overvalued assets and high management and advisory expenses, overcapitalization and undue profits, and, especially, the suspicion of unsubstantiated securities. The criteria applied by state agencies notably differed from the standards set by courts in the previous period. To value assets the FTC opted for historical costs instead of current market valuations, and to assess profits it applied the return on equity ratio (ROE), foregoing the criteria preferred by the Supreme Court. In 1933–38, the US Congress worked hard on these issues and formulated a federal regulatory framework that introduced significant restrictions to large companies with impaired public image as a result of their involvement in the country's financial unraveling.[31]

Unlike its counterparts in other nations, the Argentine state did not introduce any discretionary regulation mechanisms in the 1930s. A few initiatives were launched by municipal or provincial administrations. Municipal utility commissions created in Buenos Aires and Rosario, and provincial commissions in Córdoba and Tucumán, started to look into accounting practices employed by electricity, tram and water companies. At that time, international holding companies dominated electric utilities in Argentina. On the one hand, the US-based American & Foreign Power had reorganized its holdings into five large operating companies, which serviced 156 towns in 15 provinces. On the other hand, the Belgian company, SOFINA, controlled four electricity companies which generated

53 percent of Argentina's electricity, servicing 17 towns in the Pampean region including the city of Buenos Aires.[32]

Commissions' reports revealed asset overvaluation and excessive profits as per FTC earning calculations. As electricity and tram companies were subsidiaries of foreign holding companies such as SOFINA and American & Foreign Power, the reports made the case that foreign monopolies had a negative impact on the provision of reasonably priced and quality services. In contrast, these documents stressed the social gains (public interest ensured by the state), economic advantages (providing non-profit, efficient services), and political benefits (mitigating social and union turmoil), of municipally managed utilities.[33] Similar arguments were used by socialist deputies to submit their bills in the National Congress to regulate electric utilities, to implant control mechanisms for concessionaires, to create an investment promotion fund, and to advocate for the creation of mixed companies.[34]

These efforts yielded no results. As concessions did not feature earning caps or fee adjustment schemes, governments did not follow the course suggested by oversight commissions and congressmen. Companies alleged different contract interpretations and argued that oversight commissions had miscalculated their earnings, avoiding fee reductions. As a result, companies secured concession extensions in Tucumán and Buenos Aires City in 1936. In the nation's capital, the city council, mostly consisting of radical-party representatives, approved municipal ordinance numbers 8028 and 8029, which changed the original concessions for Compañía Hispanoamericana de Electricidad (CHADE) and Compañía Italo Argentina de Electricidad (CIAE).[35] The new contracts established a momentary fee reduction in exchange for the introduction of a number of clauses favoring companies, including a 15-year concession extension, ownership transfer of facilities at replacement cost upon contract termination, the elimination of technical advancement clauses, automatic fee adjustments based on fuel price and salary increases (economic clause) as well as for exchange rate variations (monetary clause), and finally, a repeal of provisions concerning investment oversight.[36]

Provincial governments did not act much differently. The first provincial law on electricity issues (Act 4742) was sanctioned in Buenos Aires in 1939. While this law streamlined several technical issues regarding electricity services in Buenos Aires Province, it did not set any general formulas for fee calculations, and it continued to uphold concessions as a benchmark framework. Its main contribution was to create the Electricity Service Department, to elaborate statistics and industry studies, and the Permanent Electricity Council, to advise city administrations on concessions' technical bases.[37]

These developments revealed an undermining of concessions and the need for state intervention in utilities controlled by foreign companies on the grounds of equity, social welfare and national interest. However, in Argentina, concessions remained unchanged and unquestioned throughout the 1930s. In most Latin American countries, the crisis sparked greater clashes between users and foreign companies, and many concession contracts gave way to the state's discretionary regulation of water and electricity services. The demand for fee reductions urged a review of concessions and the creation of regulatory agencies in Mexico and Brazil. Also, constraints on exchange outflows in Argentina, Brazil, Chile, Colombia, Costa Rica and Ecuador stopped foreign subsidiaries' dividend payments during the crisis.

The Mexican and Brazilian governments introduced fee controls for gas, water and electricity companies. Mexico's revolution brought an earlier rejection of foreign capitals in that country, compounded by greater state intervention as compared to other Latin American nations since the 1920s.[38] In the early 1930s, the Mexican government ordered a 25–33 percent reduction in electricity fees for industrial users. In 1939, a new Electrical Industry Act was passed, setting valuation criteria for investments and establishing fee schemes, investment amortization calculations and mandatory, free asset ownership transfers to the state after 50 years. This law provided a deadline for companies to submit their holding inventories and for state and municipal concessions to adapt to its new provisions. As a result of this law, electricity fees remained frozen until 1943.[39]

In Brazil, Getulio Vargas' administration also embarked on a discretionary regulation path, abolishing exchange rate adjustments for utility concessions in 1933. The next year, the Water Code was sanctioned, establishing that public hydraulic resources under federal jurisdiction would be managed by a Federal Water Commission, which was also empowered to limit concessions' duration, to set the criteria to determine a 'fair return' on investments, and to set fees based on historical cost asset valuations. Brazil's National Water and Energy Council was created in 1939 to oversee electricity distribution, to plan energy source exploitation, and to formulate expansion policies for electric utilities. Two years later, companies were ordered to submit their inventories, valuing their assets at historical costs, in order to calculate a 10 percent maximum return on investments. The government would revise fees every three years and review existing contracts. Fee increases were banned until this process was completed. As a result, fees remained frozen until 1945.[40]

In Panama, a law was approved to authorize the government to regulate fees for all services. The president ordered a 40 percent reduction on electricity, telephone and gas fees, but this markdown was later suspended to jointly agree on new fees. Negotiations between utilities and the governments of Costa Rica and Colombia over concession status brought new fee calculation formulas that included a minimal return rate for investments, adjusted according to exchange rate fluctuations. In turn, the parties agreed on installed capacity and network expansion to other cities. For instance, the agreement forged by Costa Rica's government, supported by Congress, implied a withdrawal of nationalization proposals.[41] Even when state regulatory efforts eventually validated former concession mechanisms, the ability of Latin American governments to intervene in utilities increased, except in Argentina.[42]

In the railroad sector, state intervention took a different turn. Tram companies were vulnerable to international changes, as they failed to secure municipal permission to raise their fees amid their competition with automotive transportation.[43] In the early 1930s, tram companies posted losses in most countries, and their controlling holding companies, including SOFINA and American & Foreign Power, started to transfer them to local governments both in Latin America and Europe. Argentina was no exception. In 1932, Compañía General de Tranvías del Rosario became a public-private company, Empresa Municipal Mixta de Transporte de Rosario, and later a municipal company, although it continued to depend on the electricity provided by the Société d'Electricité de Rosario, a SOFINA subsidiary. Tram companies operating in Buenos Aires were granted a state subsidy that proved insufficient to stop their losses, even in the cases of companies with vast numbers of users, like The Anglo-Argentine Tramways Company and Buenos Ayres Lacroze Tramways.[44]

The municipal commission created to study this situation recommended that the National Congress formulated a transportation streamlining policy. In 1935, Congress sanctioned the creation of Buenos Aires City's Corporación de Transportes, formed by the national government, the city's administration, and the private tram, subway and bus companies operating in the city. The purpose would be to coordinate and monopolize passenger transportation for 56 years. The corporation worked as a mixed company from 1939 to 1944, when the national government seized control. While it never turned a profit, the corporation guaranteed transportation services in a period of vast urban expansion and restricted access to fuel and supplies. In 1951, the company was acquired by the national government for Ar$410 million, and the state-owned company Transportes de Buenos Aires was created the following year. Urban transportation would return to private hands once again during Arturo Frondizi's administration.[45] In the other provincial capitals, private tramway companies continued to work with high operating costs and significant losses in the 1930s. Tram companies that operated separately from electricity networks and in competition with other vendors saw their liabilities grow, and most went bankrupt, like La Plata Electric Tramways.[46]

The state's intervention in the tramway sector was motivated by the same reasons leading to the creation of Obras Sanitarias de la Nación (the state-owned water utility). Faced with a life-threatening crisis that endangered public service continuity, the state took over. By creating the Corporación de Transportes, it not only streamlined the transportation system but also ensured sustained services for both users and tram companies, which were able to recover their assets and to continue operating. Thus, it should be noted that in the 1930s, the state's intervention followed the same pattern as in the former liberal era. On the one hand, concession contracts continued to prevail as the main regulatory strategy, but on the other hand, the state took over utilities when service continuity was threatened. When system collapse was not a risk, the state did not intervene.

IV. DEFICIT, COLLAPSE AND CRISIS: THE STATE TO THE RESCUE OF PUBLIC UTILITIES, 1943–55

In 1943, President Ramón Castillo was overthrown by a nationalist military coup. After that event, state procedures went against concession contract practices. Argentina's Homeland Ministry created two research commissions to review the concessions granted to foreign utility companies in Buenos Aires and other provinces. Additionally, the military regime declared public utility assets subject to expropriation, including urban utility systems. Finally, it created the National Energy Department, the first state agency designed to regulate energy production and distribution as well as to promote the development of non-renewable energy sources.[47]

In order to 'recover all electricity services operated by concessionaires for public ownership' announced by the military regime, the governments of Córdoba, Tucumán and Buenos Aires created agencies to look into provincial electricity systems, anticipating their transfer to the state. Renowned state-owned utility advocates, from Socialist and Radical parties, were appointed to head these agencies. For example, Manuel Varón was appointed head of Tucumán's Provincial Energy Department, while Juan Maggi, a FORJA radical party member, was chosen to serve as Mendoza's Minister of Public Works.[48]

The findings from the research into Buenos Aires' electric utility companies were submitted in the so-called Rodríguez Conde Report. After analysing companies' fees, equity, earnings and expenses, the report concluded that profits drawn by foreign electricity companies were excessive and their assets overrated. It also provided detailed information on the bribes paid by companies to municipal officials and councilmen during negotiations in 1936. As a result, the report recommended revoking CADE's and CIAE's legal status, as well as declaring their concession-related assets subject to public interest and expropriation.[49]

Based on this report and also another report on the concessions held by American & Foreign Power's subsidiaries, President Edelmiro Farrel planned to expropriate foreign electricity companies' 'wrongfully attained assets', but Vice President Juan Perón intervened to suspend the report's publication. Perón's intervention might have been the result of a request by René Brosens, general manager of CADE and member of SOFINA's board who was also a friend of Perón.[50] While it is impossible to corroborate the existence of pressures in favor of this company, the fact remains that this report was never published, and the national government did not seize any of SOFINA's subsidiaries. Instead, the document was sent to provincial governments, so that they would take whatever steps they deemed necessary. Thus, the decision whether to expropriate was left up to the provinces.

The expropriation of American & Foreign Power's subsidiaries began soon afterwards. After federal intervention, provincial governments expropriated American affiliates in Tucumán, Jujuy, Corrientes, Mendoza, Entre Ríos and San Luis. The first seizure in December 1943 took place when Electricidad de Alta Gracia's concession expired, but in subsequent procedures, currently valid contracts were annulled or revoked. In 1944, a federal receiver declared Compañía Eléctrica de Tucumán's concession void, although its contract expired in 1976, and revoked the concessions granted to Compañía de Electricidad del Norte Argentino in Jujuy. Companies' facilities were turned over to the provincial governments. Local governments in Mendoza and Entre Ríos followed similar procedures. Owned by Société Suisse-Américaine d'Electricité, Compañía de Electricidad de Corrientes was also expropriated in 1944, while San Luis revoked Compañía de Electricidad de los Andes' concession the next year.[51]

In response to these seizures, American & Foreign Power filed a number of complaints with the respective provincial courts, claiming that companies had been deprived of their revenues and damage deposits were insufficient. Argentina's Supreme Court rejected its appeal in 1946, on the grounds that concessionaires were part of holding companies.[52]

The rising energy deficit and the creation of Argentina's National Post-War Council, chaired by Perón, brought a significant change into state intervention schemes towards a centralized electricity policy making. The starring role played by energy in the industrial development plan formulated by the National Post-War Council called for a number of decisions made in 1945. Buenos Aires' Compañía Primitiva de Gas was seized by the national government, with its assets transferred to Gas del Estado.[53] Private gas companies operating across the country continued to operate until the end of concessions, and then they were transferred to the state-owned enterprise. In addition, the state-owned Power Plants' General Department was created to plan, build and operate power plants and electricity distribution networks. This agency would undertake energy production and distribution in the districts where networks had been transferred to provincial administrations.[54] Finally, the National Energy Department submitted a hydroelectric program to the National Post-War Council, including plans to build 11 hydroelectric power plants.[55]

The creation of both Gas del Estado and the state-owned Power Plants' General Department to manage energy production and distribution may be viewed as a continuation of the former state intervention scheme in urban utilities. As noted earlier, the state intervened by creating public agencies, state companies or joint ventures whenever service supply was at risk and private companies were unable to invest in their systems. However, these latest initiatives differed from former efforts at least in three aspects. First, for the first time ever, direct management also meant a centralized, streamlined state intervention scheme for the entire nation. Second, the decision to create these agencies and enterprises stemmed from a concern not featured in former intervention scenarios. The state's control over energy production was crucial to support the industrial development policy formulated by military leaders after World War II. State intervention in this sector grew pressing when supply shortages during World War II caused a consumption downturn and forced the substitution of foreign fuels with local replacements. Finally, public utilities started to be funded by taxes. The introduction of taxes on energy use, and the allocation of a share of fuel price hikes to the National Energy Fund created in 1945, marked the beginning of a new state funding scheme for service systems.

By 1946, fuel and equipment supplies for utilities began to normalize, and consumption restrictions as well as the use of emergency fuels were suspended. During Perón's administration, utility policies merged into a government program, with companies' nationalization incorporated into the 1946 Government Plan and the 1949 Constitution. Under the 1949 Constitution, article 40, utilities were to be transferred to the state, either by acquisition or expropriation, valuing assets at their original cost, minus amortization and all returns exceeding a reasonable return-on-investment rate. Perón did not agree with the use of historical costs formulas, rejected by foreign diplomats as being confiscatory, and tried to change this criterion. Nonetheless, article 40 (written by Maggi) was sanctioned as originally drafted.[56]

Argentina's National Electrification Plan (embedded in the 1946 Government Plan) was the cornerstone of the first Peronist administration's energy policy. Perón confirmed Colonel Bartolomé Descalzo as head of the National Energy Department and appointed Juan E. Maggi to lead the state-owned Power Plants' General Department. However, the President's Technical Secretary, José Figuerola, played a key role. Figuerola, who had served in the Spanish dictator Primo de Rivera's administration, moved to Argentina to serve as a CHADE advisor in the 1930s. In 1943, he was appointed chief statistician at Argentina's Labor Department, where he met Perón, who supported his designation as Technical Counsel in 1944. Figuerola was one of the masterminds of the National Post-War Council, whose role was transferred to him when he became the President's Technical Secretary.[57] In this capacity, Figuerola asked provincial governments to submit a report on past seizures and power plant status, as well as compensation paid, demanded by former concessionaires and set by courts.[58]

Based on these reports and on the National Energy Department's 1945 program, the National Electrification Plan proposed taking full advantage of hydraulic potential and expanding the installed capacity, coordinating national, provincial and municipal energy policies, with state intervention whenever necessary. The plan included the construction of 12 thermal plants and 45 hydroelectric plants, with an Ar$2.008 billion investment over a 15-year period.[59] Hydroelectric plants would supply small hinterland towns, while thermoelectric plants would supplement foreign companies' output in heavily populated areas in the Pampas. The electricity companies operating in the Pampean region had built more efficient systems, with more robust operations than American & Foreign Power's subsidiaries, rendering their expropriation unfeasible with the budgetary resources available at the time. Largely as a result of their greater capitalization and less conflicting track record as compared to American & Foreign Power's subsidiaries, the companies owned by SOFINA and the Italian-Swiss group were not seized by the state.[60]

The state's utility management scheme was complemented with the approval of a legal framework for mixed companies in 1946 and the legal provisions for state-owned companies in 1949. In 1947, the General Water and Electrical Energy Department was created to manage waterworks and hydroelectric resources. This agency became the National Energy Enterprise (Empresa Nacional de la Energía) in 1950, taking over the power plants and networks seized by provincial governments. In 1948, after forging an agreement with the national government, British water and sanitation companies sold their assets, which were transferred to Obras Sanitarias de la Nación.[61] Between 1946 and 1948, the national government acquired all the telephone companies operating in Argentina, including the River Plate Telephone Company, a subsidiary of International Telephone and Telegraph, to later create the Empresa Mixta Telefónica Argentina. Managerial and financial problems besieged this short-lived company, and its services were soon transferred to the General Post and Communications Administration.[62]

In late 1946, Córdoba's government seized American & Foreign Power companies, paying no compensation. The last expropriations took place in 1948, conducted by Domingo Mercante in Buenos Aires Province. Unlike the procedures followed during the military regime, this time the national government did not encourage the seizing of electricity companies but merely confirmed provincial initiatives.[63]

While railroad and sanitation companies' nationalization in 1948 unfolded as a result of a negotiation process involving Argentina's government, private companies and the British government, electricity companies were expropriated and transferred to state-owned firms and public agencies, like Agua y Energía Eléctrica, Empresa Provincial de la Energía de Córdoba, and Dirección de Electricidad y Mecánica de Buenos Aires, with no preceding negotiations.[64] As a result, this nationalization was viewed as part of Perón's foreign capital aversion policy. However, the underlying reasons were actually economic in nature, similar to those driving the nationalization of utilities in Western Europe at that time.[65]

First, nationalization was the only viable option in light of the shortcomings that plagued the sector for over a decade, hindering service supply and regional system construction. Foreign companies operating in Argentina's hinterlands had not invested in network expansion since the early 1930s. Except in the Pampas, towns in rural areas did not have electricity; energy continued to be produced by multiple power plants using different technologies; electricity networks were underdeveloped; service was deficient, with frequent outages.[66] The second reason, also economic in nature, was the need to build a nationwide electricity system that would provide the necessary infrastructure for the country's economic and industrial development.

In 1948, the National Congress levied a tax on electricity consumption in the nation's capital, intended to support the National Energy Fund. A part of this fund's resources was used to support electricity companies. Later that year, Argentina's Central Bank allowed Banco Industrial to advance funds to electricity companies to pay for salary increases until a fee rise was approved, as fees had been frozen by the national government. Subsidies and loans granted to foreign electricity companies to pay salaries and to guarantee minimal earnings continued throughout the Peronist administration.[67]

At that time, Latin American countries were revising their views on foreign electric utilities. In 1948, after the agreement signed by Presidents Eurico Gaspar Dutra and Harry Truman (the Abbink Mission), Brazil's government launched a plan for public investments to expand American & Foreign Power's subsidiaries, supported by the Export-Import Bank. Similar agreements were forged with the Mexican and Chilean governments in 1953 and 1955, respectively.[68]

A tense diplomatic relationship with the US curtailed options for Argentina. Perón's successive attempts to reach out to the US and to promote the engagement of American investors in Argentina's oil industry were resisted by nationalist military groups committed to YPF's (Yacimientos Petrolíferos Fiscales) program as well as by his parliamentary opponents, who favored nationalization. Additionally, the expropriation of American companies did not help Perón's amicable approaches.

In 1949, the currency crisis forced Argentina to shift its economic policy, rationalize public works and reduce public spending. As a result, the government tempered its stance before foreign companies. In his congressional address in May 1949, Perón expressed his administration's intent not to seize utilities, pointing out that they would be acquired in friendly terms. Off the record, the president conveyed his desire to settle out of court with British and American companies transferred to the state in order to attract new foreign investments. Thereafter, the compensation complaints filed by Compañía Primitiva de Gas were settled, and negotiations were initiated with American & Foreign Power to agree upon asset valuation criteria, while service fee increases were allowed across the country.[69]

The government's second five-year plan consolidated a more rational approach to public spending and industrial consumption, ending the utility nationalization process. As a result, negotiations for the acquisition of American & Foreign Power's subsidiaries were halted, and an agreement was forged with both CADE and CIAE to undertake joint investments and to grant service subsidies intended to guarantee minimum earnings at 15 percent of revenues. The state intervention scheme based on supplementing private investments to ensure public service supply that had characterized the years before 1943 became the ruling principle once again.[70]

The 1955 military coup brought an end to both Peronist policies and the 1949 Constitution. However, opposition groups supporting the coup did not come to an agreement on the basic guidelines for an alternative policy. Concerning electricity, there were at least two competing projects: one headed by Álvaro Alsogaray that advocated resuming negotiations with foreign companies and driving their turnaround with state assistance, and the other one coming from nationalist army men, who made the case for furthering the expropriation process started in 1943 and halted during

Perón's administration. The latter won in the short term. In 1957, the interim government repealed the 1936 ordinances, effectively reinstating former agreements and terminating CADE's concession that same year. This group's facilities in Buenos Aires Province's northern area were to be transferred to Agua y Energía Eléctrica, a company created in 1957 to replace Argentina's Empresa Nacional de la Energía (National Energy Enterprise).[71]

V. CONCLUDING REMARKS

In Argentina, the relations between the state and urban utility companies were governed by concession contracts before 1943. Contract terms were supported by judicial rulings in a number of legal battles among companies and governments. Regardless of congressional and legal initiatives, no regulatory devices were instituted to oversee electricity, gas and sanitation companies, as had been the case for the production and marketing of other goods, including oil, exportable commodities, and some manufactured products.

As long as companies guaranteed minimal service supply, the state did not engage in discretionary regulation, as other Latin American governments did in the 1930s. Local administrations, whose counterparts in Europe and North America played a key role in utility systems oversight before World War II, also did not regulate utilities. Direct state intervention ensued only when private companies were unable to guarantee minimal system operating conditions, as illustrated by Obras Sanitarias de la Nación and Corporación de Transportes. During the 1930s, the state stepped in to rescue tram companies, under dire economic and financial strain, but this intervention did not stem from the state's responsibility to supply a universal service.

The discretionary regulation schemes used by Latin American countries in the 1930s continued to allow private, foreign management of urban utilities until the 1950s and 1960s. In contrast, the lack of discretionary regulation in Argentina fueled the early nationalization of utilities compared to Mexico, Brazil or Chile. The Argentine military regime that took over in 1943 formulated policies that broke away from the former contract-based scheme, introducing discretionary regulation initiatives, sanctioning decrees that superseded contracts, levying taxes to fund public works, and, more importantly, creating state agencies to seize foreign private companies. In this case, nationalization implied a new view of utilities as universal services provided by the state amid the relatively greater autonomy pursued by this military regime.

Both the military regime and the Peronist government framed their relations with utility companies on the basis of the broader goal of promoting industry-based economic development. However, Perón's policies differed significantly from his predecessors. First, they did not include the creation of mechanisms or institutions to regulate or control urban utilities, setting caps for their earnings or fixing their fees, as other Latin American governments did in the 1930s. The fee freeze established in the administration's early years was driven by macroeconomic policy interests rather than regulatory purposes, as shown by the state subsidies and soft loans granted to electric utility companies, as well as the swift end of the freeze itself. In any case, the companies that were not expropriated were not subject to control or accounting oversight during this period.

Second, utility expropriation did not prove a priority for Peronist policies, as it had been for the military regime. Utility seizures stopped in 1948, and the nationalization of railroad, gas, communications and sanitation companies was undertaken via negotiations with owner groups that included legal agreements on asset valuation criteria, on payment and compensation procedures and terms, signed by the government and each company. The government's disposition to negotiate compensation with foreign companies for seized assets was construed as a requisite for new public-private investment projects that would include foreign funds. Budgetary constraints resulting from the 1949 crisis, the inability of both the ruling party and its parliamentary opposition to agree upon the role played by foreign investments, and Argentina's weakening position in the Southern Cone as a result of US foreign policy immediately after World War II all undermined this proposal, consolidating state-owned companies as the only viable option rather than the pursuit of greater state autonomy.

Thus, increased public investment and state control over urban utilities emerged once again as solutions to mitigate shortcomings of concessions that had brought about deficient, isolated services, especially in the poorly developed provincial economies and amidst an energy deficit. Indeed, the continuity of this state intervention scheme to supplement private management was particularly noteworthy in economically strategic areas, which translated into a number of initiatives to create public agencies, spanning conservative, radical and Peronist administrations: the Administración General de los Ferrocarriles del Estado (1909), Obras Sanitarias de la Nación (1912), YPF (1922), and Dirección General de Agua y Energía Eléctrica (1947).

It comes as no surprise, then, that the final suspension of the 1936 agreements was undertaken by the army's nationalist group that overthrew the Peronist government in 1955, resuming the policies instituted in 1943. The military regime known as *Revolución Libertadora* also rejected the compensation proposals and investment plans elaborated by expropriated foreign companies. At that time, foreign electricity companies gave up their hopes to continue operating in Argentina. However, new economic and financial conditions in the second post-war period, particularly a shift of foreign direct investments to new industrial operations and from Latin America to Europe and the East, gave way to a new utility management scheme, with state-owned companies supported by external funding. Holding companies started to get rid of their utilities in the 1950s, and electricity, gas, communications and transportation companies were nationalized. Argentina, Mexico and Brazil followed this path as well.

In general terms, it may be concluded that until after 1945, Argentina promoted foreign investments and private management for utilities with a non-intervention approach. When this approach proved unfeasible as a result of an economic downturn, financial distress or market flaws, state agencies, public-private and state-owned companies were created to manage services. These agencies and enterprises complemented private companies but failed to coordinate their operations with them. Oddly, Argentina's quick recovery from successive crises strengthened companies' leverage, which, compounded by poor state autonomy, eventually hindered sector policy making. Asymmetrical relations and prevailing foreign capital hampered state-business information transfers and cooperation, opening a gap that grew critical with the 1940s' expropriations.

The developments analysed here do not reveal a gradual growth of state capacities as a result of political decisions. On the contrary, state interventions, driven by economic reasons consistent with liberal state powers, show that the intervention scheme developed by the liberal-conservative state in the nineteenth century continued in place until the end of World War II. This is the most significant difference between Argentina and other Latin American countries, especially Mexico, and most European countries. These policies were primarily intended to mitigate market failures, guarantee the supply of utility services and reorganize the liberal order. Thereafter, the continuity of reform policies depended on the development of the state's institutional capacities, private management alternatives available in each case, and the extent of political autonomy. The technological and financial dependence of Argentina's urban utilities on foreign holding companies and business groups fueled asymmetrical state-business relations that curtailed the development of institutional capacities and mutual information exchanges. In 1943, Argentina's new political military leadership changed state intervention schemes towards a corporate state approach. Thus, the public management of gas, electricity, transportation and communication services became a strategic choice in pursuit of a specific economic goal –promoting a national economic growth based on industrialization.[72]

NOTES

1. Maxwell and Schneider (1997).
2. Lanciotti and Regalsky (2014); Regalsky and Salerno (2008); Salerno (2007) and (2008); Schvarzer (1979); Gadano (2006). A long-term view is echoed in Bussola (2008). For the entrepreneurial state after World War II, see Belini and Rougier (2008).
3. On the problem of the relative autonomy of the state, see Poulantzas (1973). Also see Evans and Rueschemeyer (1985).
4. For a typology of utility regulation options, see Gómez Ibañez (2003).
5. Dard and Margairaz (2005): 5–9; Millward (2000) and (2004).
6. Department on Regulation of Interstate and Municipal Utilities (1913).
7. On the definition and scope of discretional regulation, see Gómez Ibañez (2003): 30–32.
8. The exceptions were Colombia and Venezuela, where foreign utility companies were not dominant. Gómez Ibáñez (2003): 126.
9. For an analysis of investment groups and holding companies controlling electricity services before World War I in Argentina and globally, see Hausman, Hertner and Wilkins (2008).
10. There were only two state-owned public utility companies created in Latin America before 1930: Usinas Eléctricas del Estado (Uruguay) and Obras Sanitarias de la Nación (Argentina). These were both created in 1912 as a result of inadequate private management.
11. Smith (1904).
12. Démier (2005): 39–41.
13. Lewis (1983) and (2008a); López (2007b).
14. Jacobson (2000): 1–17.
15. For the earnings of these companies in Argentina, see Lanciotti (2007); Regalsky and Salerno (2008); Lanciotti (2008a).
16. Hausman, Hertner and Wilkins (2008): 111–24. Also, Lanciotti (2008a).
17. A company's opportunistic behavior is shown by the intention to provide profitable rather than efficient services. In turn, regulatory agencies rely on companies' hefty initial investments in specific assets to leverage contract clause renegotiation opportunities. Jacobson (2000):10–1.
18. The 25-year electric concessions granted by the provincial government of Cordoba were the exception.
19. For the effects of local government inability to manage and control waterworks systems in their early stage of development, see Hassan (1985).
20. Solveira (2006).
21. For the American & Foreign Power, see Hausman, Hertner and Wilkins (2008): 169–89. See also Hausman and Neufeld (1998).
22. República Argentina, Obras Sanitarias de la Nación (1935); Lanciotti and Regalsky (2014).
23. República Argentina, Obras Sanitarias de la Nación, *Obras Sanitarias*.
24. Regalsky and Salerno (2008): 120–9; Lanciotti and Regalsky (2014).
25. Henry George, a social reformer known for his proposal of a single tax on land values, also promoted the regulation of natural monopolies and the municipalization of public utilities.
26. Bielsa (1921) and (1923); Muratti (1928).
27. Blakemore Analytical Reports (1926): vi–vii.
28. Mosher (1929): 32–3.

29. McCraw (1984): 169.
30. McCraw (1984): 170; US Securities and Exchange Commission (1952): 3–5.
31. Edison Electric Institute (1936).
32. American & Foreign Power's subsidiares were Compañía de Electricidad del Norte Argentino, Compañía de Electricidad del Sur Argentino, Compañía de Electricidad del Este Argentino, Compañía Central Argentina de Electricidad and Compañía de Electricidad de los Andes. See Lanciotti and Macchione Saes (2014).
33. Municipalidad de Rosario (1933) and (1935). Córdoba's Commission to study concessions for electricity was created in 1933. See Solveira (2007).
34. Genta (2006): 83–85.
35. Negotiations between SOFINA officials and Radical Party leader Marcelo T. de Alvear included bribes for party councilmen and financial support for Alvear's future campaign.
36. The deal also included the government's approval to reorganize CHADE, whose assets were transferred to the Argentine subsidiary, Compañía Argentina de Electricidad (CADE), as requested by SOFINA, concerned by the Spanish Civil War.
37. Buenos Aires, Ministerio de Gobierno (1939).
38. Lewis (2008b).
39. American & Foreign Power, *Annual Report 1932*, 11; *Annual Report 1933*, 3–4, *Annual Report 1941*, 6–9; de Pina Vara (1964).
40. McDowall (1988): 324–42; American & Foreign Power, *Annual Reports* 1932, 1933 and 1941; de Pina Vara (1964): 568–69.
41. American & Foreign Power, *Annual Reports* 1938, 1940 and 1941; de Pina Vara (1964).
42. In 1939–46, agencies were created to streamline and regulate the electricity industry in Mexico (1939), Brazil (1939), Chile (1943), Argentina (1943), El Salvador (1945) and Colombia (1946). The Chilean state-owned company Empresa Nacional de Electricidad (ENDESA), created in 1943, took over the execution of the National Electricity Distribution Plan. Mexico's Federal Electricity Commission was created in 1939 and reorganized in 1949. See CEPAL (1961): pp. 67 onwards.
43. Lewis (2008b): 42–89.
44. García Heras (1994a): 93–145.
45. García Heras (1994b); UK Foreign Office: Political Departments, *General Correspondence from 1906–1966, Financial interests of UK in tramways in Argentina, The Anglo Tramways Co*., 1956, FO 371/119897.
46. River Mercantile Trust Archive. File on La Plata Electric Tramways: Letter written by RPTLA Secretary in London to Walter Parish, October 1937.
47. 1943 decrees numbers 4910 and 12648.
48. Archivo General de la Nación (AGN), Fondo Documental Secretaría Técnica. Presidencia de la Nación, File 664 *Folder 67* – Cámara de Diputados, *Comunicación sobre concesiones eléctricas, Referencia: Exp. 289 1–1944*. On Maggi, see Gambini (1999): 134–5.
49. Comisión Investigadora de los servicios públicos de electricidad (1974): 643–64.
50. Gambini (1999): 72 and 132–5. Juan Sábato and Juan Pablo Olivier, members of the Commission created to investigate electricity concessions, also blamed Perón for failing to publish the report. See Genta (2006): 83.
51. Lanciotti (2008b): 403–38. AGN, Fondo Documental Secretaría Técnica. Presidencia de la Nación. *File 664, Folder 67* – Cámara de Diputados, *Comunicación sobre concesiones eléctricas*, decree number 1086, dated 3 June 1944, and decree number 1093, dated 7 June 1944, in reference to file number 289 1–1944.
52. American & Foreign Power, *Annual Report 1944*, 5–6; *Annual Report 1945*, 7; *Annual Report 1946*, 7; *Annual Report 1947*, 6.
53. UK, Foreign Office: Political Departments: *General Correspondence from 1906–1966. Claim for compensation for British interests in the Primitiva Gas Company expropriated by Argentina in 1945, 1951*, FO 371/90547.
54. Decree number 22389 (1945); República Argentina. Dirección Nacional de la Energía

(1946), *Memoria de la Dirección General de Centrales Eléctricas del Estado*, Buenos Aires, 1.
55. AGN, Fondo Documental Secretaría Técnica. Presidencia de la Nación, File 664, *Memorándum de la Dirección de Economía y Estadística*, 6 September 1946.
56. Altamirano (2001): 37.
57. Gambini (1999): 35.
58. AGN, Fondo Documental Secretaría Técnica. Presidencia de la Nación, 1946–1955, File 395, Segundo Plan Quinquenal. Plan de Energía Eléctrica. (Exhibits).
59. AGN, Fondo Documental Secretaría Técnica. Presidencia de la Nación, 1946–1955. File 456, Planificación Primer y Segundo Plan Quinquenal Proyectos y Objetivos. File 395, Segundo Plan Quinquenal. Plan de Energía Eléctrica (Exhibits). File 664, 'Memorándum de la Dirección de Economía y Estadística', 6 September 1946.
60. Lanciotti (2008b): 522–6.
61. River Mercantile Trust (ex- River Plate, Trust, Loan & Agency) Archive, Files on The Rosario Drainage Co., Rosario Waterworks Co, legal documents. (UCL, Special collections). Negotiations to acquire water and sewage companies in Rosario had started in 1944.
62. Ugalde (1983): 58.
63. American & Foreign Power, *Annual Report 1946*, 8–9; *Annual Report 1948*, 5–6; *Annual Report 1949*, 7–8.
64. Economic reasons become clear if we consider railroad nationalization as part of Perón's economic policies, as pointed out by Skupch. However, other authors stress his political motives. See Skupch (1972); López (2007a); Escudé (1983).
65. On the economic reasons driving companies' nationalization, see Toninelli (2000): 7–9.
66. Lanciotti (2009).
67. CIAE's *Annual Report 1948* and *Annual Report 1949*; American & Foreign Power, *Annual Report 1947*, 7–8; Rougier (2001): 149, 165–8.
68. The Abbink Mission strengthened the ties forged by the US and Brazil during World War II, as a result of Getulio Vargas administration's support to the Allies. According to US diplomats, Argentina's government was dominated by German-friendly groups in its armed forces, which led to an economic boycott against Argentina that undermined its strategic standing in the Southern Cone. See Di Tella and Watt (1989).
69. UK, Foreign Office: Political Departments: *General Correspondence from 1906–1966*. '*Aide Memoire concerning Primitiva Gas Company of Buenos Aires*', 1951, FO 371/90547. American & Foreign Power, *Annual Report 1949*, 7–8; *Annual Report 1950*, p 7.
70. Consejo Económico Nacional (1952). Fodor has indicated Perón's preference to manage nationalized utilities by public-private partnerships. See Fodor (1989).
71. República Argentina (1957).
72. On the drivers fueling company nationalizations in Europe, see Toninelli (2000): 3–24. See also Foreman-Peck and Millward (1994); Millward (2005); Comín and Díaz Fuentes (2004).

REFERENCES

Altamirano, Carlos (2001), *Bajo el signo de las masas (1943–1973)*, Buenos Aires: Ariel.

Belini, Claudio and Marcelo Rougier (2008), *El Estado empresario en la industria argentina*, Buenos Aires: Manantial.

Bielsa, Rafael (1921), *Derecho Administrativo y Legislación Administrativa*, Buenos Aires: J. Lajouane y Cía.

Bielsa, Rafael (1923), *Relaciones del Código Civil con el Derecho Administrativo*, Buenos Aires: J. Lajounane.

Blakemore Analytical Reports (1926), *The Public Utilities, a Retrospection and Forecast to 1930*, New York: Blakemore Analytical Reports.
Buenos Aires Ministerio de Gobierno (1939), *Antecedentes técnico-legales y debates parlamentarios de la Ley nº 4742 que declara servicio público el suministro de energía eléctrica en la provincia de Buenos Aires*, La Plata.
Bussola, Diego a (2008), 'As empresas de serviços públicos na Argentina (1880–2000)', *Análise Social*, **43** (4), 721–47.
CEPAL (1961), 'Estado actual y evolución reciente de la energía eléctrica en América Latina', in United Nations, *Estudios sobre la electricidad*, vol. 1, New York: United Nations.
Comín, Francisco and Daniel Díaz Fuentes (2004), *La empresa pública en Europa: una perspectiva histórica*, Madrid: Síntesis.
Comisión Investigadora de los servicios públicos de electricidad (1974), *El Informe Rodríguez Conde. Informe de la comisión investigadora de los servicios públicos de electricidad*, Buenos Aires: Eudeba.
Dard, Olivier and Michel Margairaz (2005), 'Le service public, l'économie, la République (1780–1960)', *Revue d'histoire Moderne et Contemporaine*, **52** (3).
Démier, Francis (2005), 'Économistes libéraux et « services publics » dans la France du premier XIXe siècle', *Revue d'histoire Moderne et Contemporaine* **52** (3).
Department on Regulation of Interstate and Municipal Utilities (1913), *Commission Regulation of Public Utilities: A Compilation and Analysis of Laws of Forty-Three States and of the Federal Government for the Regulation by Central Commissions of Railroads and Other Public Utilities*, New York: The National Civic Federation.
de Pina Vara, Rafael (1964), 'El régimen legal e institucional de la industria eléctrica en América Latina', in United Nations, *Estudios sobre la electricidad en América Latina. Documentos del seminario latinoamericano de energía*, New York: United Nations, 537–70.
Di Tella, Guido and D. Cameron Watt (eds) (1989), *Argentina Between the Great Powers, 1939–1946*, London: Macmillan.
Edison Electric Institute (1936), *The Case for Private Ownership of Electric Utilities*, New York: Edison Electric Institute.
Escudé, Carlos (1983), *Gran Bretaña, Estados Unidos y la declinación argentina, 1942–1949*, Buenos Aires: Editorial de Belgrano.
Evans, Peter and Dietrich Rueschemeyer (1985), 'The state and economic transformation: toward an analysis of the conditions underlying effective state intervention', in Peter Evans, Dietrich Rueschemeyer and Theda Skocpol (eds), *Bringing the State Back In*, New York: Cambridge University Press, 44–77.
Fodor, Jorge (1989), 'Argentina's nationalism: myth or reality', in Guido Di Tella and Rudiger Dornbusch, *The Political Economy of Argentina, 1946–1983*, Oxford: MacMillan.
Foreman-Peck, James and Robert Millward (1994), *Public and Private Ownership of British Industry, 1820–1990*, Oxford: Clarendon Press.
Gadano, Nicolás (2006), *Historia del petróleo en la Argentina 1907–1955: desde los inicios hasta la caída de Perón*, Buenos Aires: Edhasa.
Gambini, Hugo (1999), *Historia del Peronismo*, t. I, Buenos Aires: Vergara.
García Heras, Raúl (1994a), *Transporte, negocios y política. La Compañía Anglo Argentina de Tranvías. 1876–1981*, Buenos Aires: Sudamericana.
García Heras, Raúl (1994b), 'State intervention in urban passenger transportation:

the transport corporation of Buenos Aires, 1939–1962', *The Hispanic American Historical Review,* **75** (1), 84–110.

Genta, Guillermo (2006), 'Política y Servicios Públicos. El caso del servicio público de electricidad de la ciudad de Buenos Aires', M.A. in Political Science and Sociology Thesis, FLACSO.

Gómez Ibañez, José (2003), *Regulating Infrastructure: Monopoly, Contracts, and Discretion*, Cambridge, MA: Harvard University Press.

Hassan, John (1985), 'The growth and impact of the British water industry in the nineteenth century', *Economic History Review,* **38** (4), 531–48.

Hausman, William, Peter Hertner and Mira Wilkins (2008), *Global Electrification: Multinational Enterprise and International Finance in the History of Light and Power, 1878–2007,* Cambridge: Cambridge University Press.

Hausman, William and John Neufeld (1988), 'US foreign direct investment in electric utilities in the 1920s', in Mira Wilkins and Harm Schröter (eds), *The Free-Standing Company in the World Economy, 1830–1996*, New York: Oxford University Press.

Jacobson, Charles (2000), *Ties that Bind. Economic and Political Dilemmas of Urban Utility Networks, 1800–1990*, Pittsburg: University of Pittsburg Press.

Lanciotti, Norma (2007), 'Empresas autónomas y grupos de inversión. Las empresas del Grupo Morrison en Rosario, Argentina (1890–1930)', *Investigaciones de Historia Económica*, **3** (8), 109–40.

Lanciotti, Norma (2008a), 'Ciclos de vida en empresas de servicios públicos. Las compañías eléctricas británicas y norteamericanas en Argentina, 1887–1950', *Revista de Historia Económica/Journal of Iberian and Latin American Economic History*, **26** (3).

Lanciotti, Norma (2008b), 'Foreign investments in electric utilities: a comparative analysis of Belgian and American Companies in Argentina, 1890–1959', *Business History Review,* **82** (3), 519–22.

Lanciotti, Norma (2009), 'Patterns of evolution and technological style of urban utilities in three Argentine cities, 1880–1950', in 15th World Economic History Congress, Utrecht, August.

Lanciotti, Norma and Alexandre Macchione Saes (2014), 'American & Foreign Power in Argentina and Brazil (1926–65)', *Australian Economic History Review*, **54** (2), 120–44.

Lanciotti, Norma and Andrés Regalsky (2014), 'Los sistemas de agua potable en Argentina: Gestión pública y gestión privada en dos grandes ciudades, Buenos Aires y Rosario, 1880–1950', *TST Transportes, Servicios y Telecomunicaciones*, **26**, 162–97.

Lewis, Colin (1983), *British Railroads in Argentina, 1857–1914: A Case Study of Foreign Investment,* London: Athlone.

Lewis, Colin (2008a), 'Anglo-criollo rather than British: early investments in Argentinian railroads and utilities', in Jorge Schvarzer, Andrés Regalsky and Teresita Gómez (comps.), *Estudios sobre la historia de los ferrocarriles argentinos (1857–1940),* Buenos Aires: CESPA, 223–70.

Lewis, Colin (2008b), 'Capital, tecnología y nacionalismo; economía política de los tranvías urbanos en América Latina, 1850–1960', *TST Transportes Servicios y Telecomunicaciones,* **14**, 42–89.

López, Mario (2007a), 'Del equilibrio a la crisis de las empresas ferroviarias privadas, 1917–1946', in Mario López and Jorge Waddell (eds), *Nueva historia del ferrocarril en la Argentina,* Buenos Aires: Lumiere, 103–55.

López, Mario (2007b), 'Un sistema ferroviario con empresas privadas extranjeras y control estatal, 1887–1916', in Mario López and Jorge Waddell (eds), *Nueva historia del ferrocarril en la Argentina,* Buenos Aires: Lumiere, 55–101.
Maxwell, Sylvia and Ben Ross Schneider (eds) (1997), *Business and the State in Developing Countries,* Ithaca: Cornell University Press.
McCraw, Thomas (1984), *Prophets of Regulation. Charles Francis Adams, Louis Brandeis, James Landis, Alfred Kahn,* Cambridge, MA: Harvard University Press.
McDowall, Duncan (1988), *The Light: Brazilian Traction, Light and Power Company Limited, 1899–1945,* Toronto: University of Toronto Press.
Millward, Robert (2000), 'State enterprise in Britain in the twentieth century', in Pier Angelo Toninelli (ed.), *The Rise and Fall of State Owned Enterprise in the Western World,* Cambridge: Cambridge University Press, 157–184.
Millward, Robert (2004), 'European governments and the infrastructure industries', *European Review of Economic History*, **8**, 3–28.
Millward, Robert (2005), *Private and Public Enterprise in Europe: Energy, Telecommunications and Transport, 1830–1990,* Cambridge: Cambridge University Press.
Mosher, William (ed.) (1929), *Electrical Utilities: The Crisis in Public Control,* New York and London: Harper & Brothers.
Municipalidad de Rosario (1933), *Informe de la Comisión Municipal Fiscalizadora de las Compañías Consolidadas de Aguas Corrientes del Rosario y Obras de Salubridad de Rosario,* Rosario: Municipalidad de Rosario.
Municipalidad de Rosario (1935), *Informe de la Comisión Fiscalizadora e Investigadora de la SER,* Rosario: Municipalidad de Rosario.
Muratti, Natalio (1928), *Municipalización de los servicios públicos. Estudio económico financiero, político, jurídico y social,* Buenos Aires: Librería Jurídica.
Poulantzas, Nicos (1973), *Political Power and Social Classes,* London: New Left Books.
Regalsky, Andrés and Elena Salerno (2008), 'En los comienzos de la empresa pública argentina: la administración de los ferrocarriles del Estado y las Obras Sanitarias de la Nación antes de 1930', *Investigaciones de Historia Económica,* **4** (11), 107–36.
República Argentina (1957), *Informe y Decreto del gobierno provisional sobre nulidad de las concesiones eléctricas de la CADE y la CIADE,* Buenos Aires: Secretaría de Prensa de la Nación.
República Argentina, Obras Sanitarias de la Nación (1935), *Obras Sanitarias de la Nación reseña general histórica descriptiva y estadística,* Buenos Aires: Kraft.
Rougier, Marcelo (2001), *La política crediticia del Banco Industrial durante el primer peronismo (1944–1955),* Buenos Aires: CEEED-FCE-UBA, Working Paper No. 5.
Salerno, Elena (2007), 'La evolución y los problemas de los ferrocarriles del Estado durante la primera mitad del siglo XX', in Mario López and Jorge Waddell (eds), *Nueva historia del ferrocarril en la Argentina,* Buenos Aires: Lumiere, 395–437.
Salerno, Elena (2008), 'La inversión pública en los Ferrocarriles del Estado (1930–1940)', *TST Transportes, Servicios y telecomunicaciones,* **15**, 146–67.
Schvarzer, Jorge (1979), 'Empresas públicas y desarrollo industrial en Argentina', *Economía de América Latina,* **3**, 45–68.
Skupch, Pedro (1972), 'Nacionalización, libras bloqueadas y sustitución de importaciones', *Desarrollo Económico,* **12** (47), 477–93.

Smith, Adam (1904), *An Inquiry into the Nature and Causes of the Wealth of the Nations,* Book V, Part III, London: Methuen & Co.
Solveira, Beatriz (2006), 'Objetivos y estrategias de producción de las principales empresas eléctricas de la provincia de Córdoba, 1893–1946)', in *XX Jornadas de Historia Económica*, **2**, AAHE, Mar del Plata.
Solveira, Beatriz (2007), 'Relación Estado-Empresas de electricidad en la provincia de Córdoba durante la primera mitad del siglo XX', in Jorge Schvarzer, Teresita Gómez and Marcelo Rougier, *La empresa ayer y hoy. Nuevas investigaciones y debates*, Buenos Aires: CESPA-FCE-Universidad de Buenos Aires, 55–92.
Toninelli, Pier Angelo (ed.) (2000), *The Rise and Fall of State Owned Enterprise in the Western World,* Cambridge: Cambridge University Press.
Ugalde, Alberto (1983), *Empresas públicas en la Argentina; su magnitud y origen,* Buenos Aires: CEPAL, Working Paper No. 3.
US Securities and Exchange Commission (1952), 'The Public Utility Holding Company Act of 1935', Washington: US Government Print.

8. Public-private relationships in Chile after 1990

Oscar Muñoz[1]

I. INTRODUCTION

Over the past two decades, theoretical and empirical studies on economic development have highlighted the benefits of collaborative relationships between the state and the private sector. Indeed, it is now widely accepted that markets require institutions to set the rules of the game.[2] Neo-institutionalism theories underscore the need to build quality institutions that contribute to streamlining the activities of economic agents, while promoting long-term visions, credibility, trust, learning, and technological innovation.[3] The discussion on new development strategies that meet both equity and competitiveness requirements also highlight the need for adequate cross-sector public-private cooperation mechanisms. For instance, the Nobel Prize laureate Joseph Stiglitz has argued 'a new development strategy . . . should not only include coordination among several agencies within government but also between public and private sectors as well as among private sector segments'.[4]

From another standpoint, the Harvard economist Dani Rodrik has stressed that numerous market flaws and state shortcomings require that competitiveness policies be viewed as a 'process' driving collective learning and a 'discovery' of new opportunities to enhance competitiveness and growth. 'What is needed instead', he argued, is a more flexible form of strategic collaboration between public and private sectors, designed to elicit information about objectives, distribute responsibilities for solutions, and evaluate outcomes as they appear.'[5] In turn, a review by CEPAL (Comisión Económica para América Latina y el Caribe) in 2008 of equity-based productive transformation strategies over a 20-year period indicated that 'the public-private alliance is paramount to formulate and execute strategies at a time of globalization and increasing international competition'.[6] This report describes several levels of public-private partnerships, ranging from governments' unilateral imposition of public policies to an intermediate stage characterized by informal consultations, and finally, the creation of consensual agreements based on formal dialogue. From the viewpoint of social agents, these relationships may be forged bilaterally by government and business; in a three-way fashion, incorporating organized labor, or with a broader scope, engaging civil society sectors, such as academic, scientific, environmental and other agents. In terms of issues, cross-sector relations may be divided into those revolving around a specific policy-making field, like labor, natural monopoly regulation, or education, and broader fields that encompass long-term strategic issues.

This need to approach development strategies by means of public-private alliances has also been brought up in Chile, as proven by a document published by its National Council for Innovation and Competitiveness, which reads:

> Successfully adding knowledge to production requires a systemic approach and a new alliance that merges private entrepreneurial efforts with a public involvement geared to . . . ensuring the supply of public goods supporting innovation . . . physical and technological infrastructure networks, scientific research, and . . . a framework of incentives and rules of the game.[7]

These arguments as well as empirical and historical evidence suggest that the old debate confronting the role of the state and the market, the public versus the private sectors is giving way to an approach that views state, private sector and citizenry cooperation and complementariness as indispensable for the accomplishment of dynamic development goals. Chile's experience over the past 20 years provides an interesting case in point, as in contrast with past antagonistic excluding relations, Chile has tried a number of social dialogue schemes to build consensus since 1990. At the same time, its updated institutions have stood out in Latin America, proving instrumental for successful economic and social outcomes. However, at times conflicting and clashing interests have surfaced, interrupting this search for agreements. In fact, local literature works sketch a number of hypotheses – some signaling a primarily confrontational private sector response to governments' consensus-building efforts,[8] and others suggesting that those governments have prioritized economic growth over democratization, focusing as a result nearly solely on business agents.[9] A more positive look at the events in Chile reveals that government-business relations have been fluent and fruitful, contributing to proper political system operations and governability.[10]

This chapter draws from the hypothesis that public-private relations build a fabric of formal and informal practices and institutions, and that they are becoming highly relevant for the economic development strategies of emerging markets. Additionally, it will argue that, over the course of a history of a nation such as Chile, development is characterized by, among other traits, a transformation of public-private relations, turning them from predominantly informal to more formal, which influences greatly the effectiveness of economic policies and the quality of other institutions. This may be attributed to the fact that greater formality leads to more transparent, credible, and equitable economic policies, particularly when they bear an impact on long-term economic development.

Another component of the hypothesis underlying this chapter is that structural transformations in the Chilean economy have driven a greater private sector involvement in public policy-making and management, primarily due to three reasons. First, as the open, competitive market economy system consolidates, the private sector plays a more decisive role as economic growth driver than the state. In turn, this implies greater business commitment to conditions favoring economic growth, investments and technological advancement. These conditions are significantly determined by the nature and quality of economic policies.

Second, a growing gap separating economics and politics, as opposed to what happened during the post-war period, paved the way for the emergence of an economic technocracy with remarkable autonomy to shape economic policies. The same happened in the private sector, as business associations have grown more technical, and while they have preserved their political dimension and continued to represent their interests, they have been induced to strengthen their technical and professional operations. Thus, public and private technocracies increasingly share communication and cultural similarities that have facilitated more formal interactions.

This development is also linked to a third factor that has influenced a change in the nature of public-private relations in Chile. Starting in the 1990s, a new generation of business leaders has followed those who were at the helm from the late 1960s through to the 1970s who became the promoters of a 'new neo-liberal order' in the 1980s and 1990s. These new business leaders, who are less bound to ideology and more committed to a productive development embracing globalization and social change, have come to adopt a more technocratic role based on differentiated public policy agendas. In this respect, they have become interlocutors with the government and are more willing to be part of the many channels of participation now available for contributing to economic development.[11]

This does not mean that public-private relations do not ultimately involve a confrontation component – or at least diverging interests, as public concerns focus on the common good, while private interests largely refer to specific, individual concerns. Thus, when public-private relations are analysed, there will always be a suspicion that these two types of interests oppose each other, and that after apparently conciliatory speeches, they will continue to fight for supremacy endlessly. Therefore, the state's amicable attitude towards the private sector might just conceal its co-option by the latter through the 'capture' of public agents. This might occur either by the political system, when private and public interests merge into a single government (for example, in the case of public officials recruited from the business world),[12] or by means of a 'common belief system'. This is a 'cultural capital' of sorts shared by business and financial elites and governments' economic officials, since financial power can be extremely appealing in rising, bubble-creating cycles, as noted some years ago by Simon Johnson,[13] or through more rudimentary methods such as the corruption and bribery that characterize the infamous dictatorships that have existed and continue to exist in Latin America.

It would be naïve to disregard this dimension. All in all, the real problem is not that there are distinctive, eventually clashing interests, but that public decisions and institutions follow common good interests by means of the democratic mechanisms established and that the rules of the game are transparent, so that citizens can watch and monitor public and private agents' behavior. Moreover, it comes as no surprise that, in a globalized world where nations compete with each other, that a country's interest supersedes the interests of some groups. International competition and technological changes create uncertainties that affect nations as a whole, bringing possibilities for public-private interest similarities that serve as the basis for cooperation strategies. This is what many Asian countries, like the so-called 'tigers', understood several decades ago, paving the way for their 'economic miracles'.

A particularly significant dimension refers to the role played by organized labor, as unions are relevant counterparts for both the business sector and the state. Historically, capital-labor relations in business have been conflicting, as they involve diverging interests with very dissimilar leverages. This is particularly true in slow-growing economies, where zero-sum games tend to prevail. As ideological biases have tended to permeate negotiation platforms, this has grown national. However, in a setting characterized by strong economic dynamism and technological innovation, as today in the second global economy, the possibilities for collaborative capital-labor relations become more relevant, while their individual sector interests do not vanish entirely.

Thus, a more complete overview of public-private relations cannot neglect their tripartite dimension,[14] which grows even more relevant because the development strategies pursued by governments have been explicitly committed to merging economic growth and equity – in addition to democratic governability. A successful development strategy does not only require policy efficiency, but also a general consensus on goals that also includes workers and citizens at large. Thus, a public-private relationship that only factored in business – especially, large business – interests would risk a loss of legitimacy, and could fuel mistrust in massive society sectors, which would in turn jeopardize political governability.

To explore these issues, this chapter is organized as follows. The following section addresses key methodological challenges. The third section briefly reviews Chile's historical background, with its informal, markedly oligarchic public-private relations in the early twentieth century, which later turned more formal but highly antagonistic, serving as a backdrop for the democratic collapse in 1973. The fourth section will discuss, from a political macroeconomic perspective, how Chile managed to build non-antagonistic and eventually friendly formal cross-sector relationships that included organized labor – a process that unfolded since the early years of Chile's transition to democracy and consolidated in the 1990s. Next, the topic of tripartite social dialogue is introduced in the fifth section as a recurrent effort that has failed to consolidate thus far. The final section presents major conclusions and proposals.

II. METHODOLOGICAL CHALLENGES

The relations between the state and the private sector are one of the cornerstones supporting economic governability and public policy-making in a market economy. With the private sector playing a leading role in creating wealth, governments are not oblivious to its support or opposition. Ultimately, successful economic policies depend on growing output, investments, and employment – all very susceptible to business decisions. Nonetheless, the private sector's return on investments, depend largely on public policies, institutions, incentive schemes and overall business environment. Thus, there is a mutual interest in a good relationship between governments and businesses, which provides the foundation for a system of more or less institutionalized ties and ongoing negotiations.

The private sector notion itself conceals a major ambiguity. While this term is normally used to refer to the business community in general, it is widely known that this is an extremely diverse sector that includes large local and foreign-owned companies with considerable economic power as well as small enterprises and micro-ventures. There are also business associations, which supposedly represent business owners and leaders, but this representation is also known to vary greatly, depending on engagement and affiliation, as well as on business groups' ability to lead their peers. Chile boasts a huge range of business associations in many industries, regions and operations, but they do not necessarily share the same interests. For instance, associations representing small businesses typically resent large companies' management practices, deemed as abusive in their trade relations. Traditionally, the most powerful associations have been those of farmers (SNA, National Farming Society), manufacturers (SFF, Manufacturing Promotion Society), and miners (SNM, National Mining Society). These and other more recent associations joined forces in the 1930s, creating Chile's Production and Trade Confederation (CPC).[15] This organization has served as the most recognized representative of the so-called private sector, although, at times, specific sector unions, particularly the SFF, have exercised greater leadership as a result of their more consistent interests. Yet, it would be naïve to ignore that large financial groups are influential on their own, especially when it comes to safeguarding their specific interests if they think they are threatened.

At the same time, the state also displays great diversity, both in terms of public policy formulation and public agencies' operations. Economic policies include macro-economic policies, largely formulated by the economy or Finance Ministry, and to a lesser extent, by the Central Bank in its monetary policy manager capacity; sector policies, managed by each specific ministry, and cross-sector policies, encompassing a vast range of interests, including foreign trade, science and technology, fair competition, labor relations, environmental issues, and the like, which may be designed by one or more public agencies.

Organized labor features several segments with specific interests too. In Chile, unions from high productivity export industries, like copper, paper and cellulose, often elaborate labor demands that are not represented by larger trade union associations like CUT (Unitary Workers Central). Public sector workers also hold their own interests, which have only recently been upheld by CUT. Ideological views create rifts as well. In Chile, this has led to the creation of other union confederations aside from CUT, which have a strong socialist-communist influence, such as CAT (Autonomous Workers Central) and UNT (Chilean Workers Union).

Finally, it should be noted that the very notion of public-private relations also encompasses different meanings. The most traditional one involves negotiations about public policy-making, but these relations may also be built for technical cooperation when public policies need to address new fields in which there is little knowledge and information available, such as technological innovation or environmental issues, or relations based on private sector collaboration for the supply of public goods or services, as in the case of public work concessions, workers' training programs, or social institutions providing social security, education, healthcare, housing construction, among other services.

The next section will explore the classical theses that have interpreted

Chile's public-private relations in contemporary times, as well as their evolution in terms of formality/informality and interest convergence/divergence.

III. PUBLIC-PRIVATE RELATIONSHIPS IN CHILE DURING THE NEO-LIBERAL PERIOD

Chile's extreme neo-liberalism in the 1970s and 1980s, compounded by its violent repression of organized labor, brought extreme freedom for private companies to operate without much accountability.[16] Businessmen largely welcomed the military coup in 1973 that did away with nationalization and growing union demands threats. However, very soon, as the military regime's team of civilian economists imposed its technocratic, autonomous views and initiated a number of recessionary adjustments and neo-liberal reforms, the private sector felt economically vulnerable, with limited leverage to become a social agent and uphold its interests, except for a number of individual business leaders who held high-ranking jobs in the administration (for example, Fernando Léniz was appointed Economy Minister by General Augusto Pinochet).[17] Indeed, Chile's economy began to shed its state controls, regulations and interventions of the past, as the new regime hoped that markets would start to self-regulate by means of prices. This included the consumer, capital and labor markets, while the foreign exchange market was excluded as the exchange rate was pegged to holding Chile's monetary system attached to the international financial system, albeit with enough leeway for capital flows. These were the new rules of the game for Chilean business.[18]

During the 1970s, the regime's market liberalization alienated some business support, both from small- and medium-sized business owners and industrial companies, which started to feel the pressure of the increased competition and rising financial costs. However, companies which exported much of their output and financial groups profited greatly, as the former benefited from the real exchange rate devaluation and tariff reductions, while the latter seized opportunities to acquire banks and privatized companies on beneficial terms. Chile's financial deregulation and new and considerable access to foreign lending fueled the creation of strong business networks that managed these resources freely and in a discretionary manner.

A financial and expenditure bubble, supported by foreign borrowing and the stimulation of growing consumption by banks, especially through imported goods, propelled a huge balance-of-payment deficit that came to a head in 1981. The government argued that as debts remained private, the system was not at risk, since it would be banks rather than the state which would need to address any crisis. Still, booming imports drove companies that were unable to adjust and compete in the new environment out of business. The government regarded this outcome as part of a resource reallocation scheme that would enhance economic efficiency and long-term growth.

The Chilean administration failed to anticipate that, as a result of the United States' persistent high inflation rates, the Chairman of the Federal Reserve, Paul Volcker, would establish a stringent high interest rate policy that drove international rates up, restricting loans to over-indebted Latin American countries and leading to a severe balance-of-payment deficit. This brought about an exchange and financial crisis that started in 1982, drastically changing Chile's outlook. The crisis caused a political earthquake in the government, forced large private business groups to file for bankruptcy, and clearly revealed the issue of 'moral hazard'. Several banks collapsed and the state needed to come to their rescue. Despite its natural authoritarianism, the regime resented losing businessmen's support. The private sector grew wary of the economic disarray, and some businessmen publicly announced that the economic crisis was causing worse losses than the previous administration of president and its expropriations. Cattle breeders expressed their concern for a dropping meat demand, and a government spokesman suggested that 'they should eat the cows'.

The government was forced to revise its overall economic policy goals, while middle- and lower-income segments banged their pots on the streets at night to show their discontent. The belief that this could mark the end of Pinochet's dictatorship spread quickly, based on similar developments that occurred in 1931, when as a result of the Great Depression, General Ibáñez's regime was overthrown and the ousted dictator had to flee the country. After a series of currency devaluations that started in 1982, the government pursued a more pragmatic approach, first increasing protectionism and nationalizing private external debts with state guarantees in 1983–84, and later granting large subsidies and loans to banks (creating the so-called 'subordinated debt') and dollar-denominated debtors as well as resorting to indirect interest and exchange rate regulation.

A new team of economists was brought into the government to find realistic solutions that drew away from the extreme ideologies of the 1970s. This team focused on renegotiating Chile's foreign debt and privatizing the banks under state intervention. It also set out to create the financial conditions that would encourage a secondary market for foreign debt bonds. The country's solvent public finances strengthened in the late 1970s, and rising copper prices contributed to a swift economic recovery, with increased foreign investments, dropping unemployment and steady economic growth in the second half of the 1980s. This process peaked when old state companies were privatized in the late 1980s, with better terms for the state but little transparency in the use of inside information, which helped private groups to secure huge capital gains. Astonished, civil society witnessed this transfer of public resource to a handful of private groups, while prevailing political conditions prevented it from exercising its democratic rights.

The success of the post-1985 adjustment plan and recovery shows the differences separating both economic teams' styles. While the initial team (1975–82) remained oblivious to its policies' economic effects and social consequences, including those affecting businessmen, the team that took over after 1982 paid a lot more attention to political side effects, taking into account the need to have business support, as the business community was the only ally for the regime.[19]

A new type of public-private relations ensued, characterized by the government's special consideration for business interests. Chile's administration started to listen to the business community more explicitly, and public-private relations became more institutionalized. The CPC elaborated a document entitled, *Economic Recovery – Analysis and Propositions*, published in July 1983.[20] Its demands included: (1) a low exchange rate, (2) increased tariff protection, (3) an expansive monetary policy, (4) low interest rates, (5) cancellation of debts, and (6) industry promotion policies. The document also requested the institutionalization of decision-making relations between the government and business associations.[21] After some hesitation, the administration finally decided to ask business leaders to join in in the formulation of some economic policies. This invitation softened some of the critiques.[22] Chile's Construction Chamber, the association gathering large local construction companies, submitted a three-year recovery plan.

Business associations reorganized and made professional their study departments to elaborate their own information and to update their policy proposals. The institutionalization of business-government relations materialized with the creation of an Economic and Social Council (CES), the National Trade Commission, and the National Industry Commission – all advisory bodies.[23] The spirit underlying these efforts sought to build consensus between the government and business leaders rather than to deepen conflicts. Small- and medium-sized enterprises (SMEs) did not participate in this process.

Oddly enough, during this period, while government technocracy became more pragmatic, albeit furthering its market economy advocacy, business associations adopted an ideological stance that, regardless of their specific public policy proposals, leaned towards a neo-liberal social order project, as opposed to their earlier defensive tactics.[24] This may be partly attributed to the fact that a number of former public officials and technocrats who left the government after the external debt crisis joined the private sector around this time, bringing their ideas from the earlier military regime years with them. Also influential was the growing so-called 'Gremialista' movement, who were young intellectuals who emerged from a student movement which opposed reforms at the Catholic University of Chile, which later turned into a conservative political party. This ideological current translated into a neo-liberal society model, with business playing a starring role as the source of social advancement. Chile's swift economic recovery after the crisis, partly accomplished with the nationalization of private debts and the massive transfer of financial resources to banks, restored businessmen's standing as social leaders, which they had lost during the crisis.[25]

IV. TRANSITIONING TO DEMOCRACY AFTER 1990

As the center-left Coalition of Parties for Democracy (or Concertación de Partidos por la Democracia in Spanish) intended to both regulate and further market economy policies while advancing towards an equity-based competitive transformation, public-private relations acquired a strategic nature that prevailed across all Coalition administrations between 1990 and 2009. No Coalition government has shied away from open communications and coordination with the private sector. At first, even before taking office, this Coalition built by several political parties was committed to forging fluent relations with the private sector, for this was viewed as instrumental to ensuring continued economic and employment growth. Political parties needed to dispel what Genaro Arriagada has called businessmen's 'great fear', proving that the new government would not threaten their legitimate rights but only encourage them to operate according to the rules of the democratic game.[26] Agreements had to be politically negotiated to build a new social and economic order, and the business sector had to be recruited for development efforts.

Thus, since Chile's transition to democracy began in 1989, public-private relations have developed at several levels simultaneously, some of them evolving with difficulty, characterized by divergent ideas on the development process – such as the changes in labour market institutions – while others evolved more smoothly. These relationships have been pursued in several formats, from tripartite negotiation tables and social dialogues, to the formal, steady engagement of business leaders in public agencies' boards or in public-private councils devoted to the study and formulation of public policy proposals. From another perspective, the fact that Chile's president and his or her finance ministers have attended the annual business meetings held by ICARE (Chilean Institute of Rational Business Management), a summit that gathers leading politicians and businessmen for an entire day, has also contributed to the exchange of public speeches intended to convey sector assessments on the state of the nation.[27] Other communication channels have included the ongoing involvement of outstanding business leaders in presidential trips abroad, public-private commissions built to address specific public policy issues, like SME challenges, environmental norms, technological innovation, labor laws, and trade agreements with other countries. In late 2001, the SFF submitted an agenda for growth that tackled a number of micro-economic issues. This combination of joint forums has driven business trust in Chile's economy and public officials, albeit with some resentment and suspicion by groups that have felt excluded from these fluent, frequent interactions with top government officials.

Nonetheless, this has not been an easy road, especially for early Coalition governments, and its outcomes were not assured or permanent. This process required constant renewal, with periods of closeness followed by tension, although both sides implicitly acknowledged that they needed each other. In light of this historical overview, public-private relations since 1990 can be divided into three development phases.

A. First Phase: Rough Initial Relations between 1988 and March 1990

Before the 1989 presidential election, business leaders, neo-liberal economists and top military regime officials made the gloomiest forecasts about the aftermath of an opposition electoral win (indicating that it would surely lead to chaos, inflation, and capital flight, among other horrors). It should be noted that the Political Party Alliance Against Pinochet's Re-election, which preceded the Coalition, included the Socialist Party of President Allende. Despite the guarantees provided by the 'protected democracy' institutionalized and authoritarian provisions established in Chile's 1980 Constitution (for example, a clause for 'appointed senators', which made it difficult for transition governments to secure a Senate majority, and the Subsidiary State Act sanctioned at the end of the military regime, constitutionally banning the state from creating public enterprises), Chile's business community viewed this transition to democracy as a two-fold threat.

On the one hand, business leaders feared that social turmoil would come hand in hand with excessive politicization (a massive outbreak of citizen engagement and union conflicts). On the other hand, a sharp fiscal imbalance would follow if the new government gave in to social demands and chose to adopt populist measures (sky-rocketing public spending). In this scenario, a reversal of privatization and Chile's return to a corporate state also seemed possible if the Coalition government rallied enough electoral support to repeal that law.

As noted earlier, leading businessmen, as a social group, had felt fully vindicated by Pinochet's authoritarian regime, whose ideology and reforms granted businesses and markets a star role in Chile's economy. However, as the regime's end neared after Pinochet's defeat in the 1988 plebiscite, their old fears for state intervention rekindled.[28] Their concern grew stronger as right-wing political parties were weakened by the 1988 plebiscite defeat and internal rifts caused by unresolved leadership struggles. Chile's right wing primarily faced a choice between a modern, renewed approach to politics, suiting the country's transition to democracy, and a return to authoritarian, conservative ways, more reliant on personal leadership and charisma than on consistent policy programs. Against this political backdrop, business leaders chose to draw away from both Pinochet's regime and right-wing politicians to focus on defending the market economy model, a strategy eventually pursued by a vast majority of leading Chilean businessmen.[29]

In turn, the Political Party Alliance Against Pinochet's Re-election also faced a complex scenario, featuring businesses' hard-line stance and stalwart defense of the current model versus a highly expectant organized labor sector that wished to restore unions' leverage before 1973. Anticipating its victory in the 1989 presidential elections and committed to initiating a transition to democracy, after long deliberations among its member parties, the Coalition formulated a political strategy to pursue five basic goals: (1) accomplishing a successful transition, which meant neutralizing potential threats from both military groups (Pinochet would stay on as the army's commander-in-chief) and escalating social demands; (2) ensuring macro-economic stability in order to guarantee investments and growth, curbing a rather high inflation rate; (3) legitimizing Chile's market economy, private property and free enterprise scheme; (4) validating workers' right to unionize and organize themselves to negotiate a labor reform agenda; (5) assuring fiscal solvency as the basis for a social security program for poverty-stricken sectors. Every one of these primary strategic goals set for the fledgling democratic order would require delicate negotiations with all leading social agents, opposing political parties, and the outgoing administration's leadership, consisting of a group of strong civilian and military Pinochet supporters.

As regards this chapter's central topic, Coalition leaders decided to conduct these negotiations by means of a progressive social dialogue process that already engaged union heads and could now incorporate business representatives. This process was helped along by Coalition leaders' support for market economy, private property and business as development drivers. The emergent government was also strategically interested in maintaining Chile's fast-paced growth, which neared 10 percent a year right before the Coalition took office,[30] and controlling inflation. These signals conveyed a significant political message: they showed that the Coalition was willing to support a dynamic, stable economy and that its government program steered away from populist temptations. This was a need for economic legitimacy. Secondly, fast growth was also required to support the ambitious program intended to remedy the so-called 'social debt' – in other words, a program to substantially reduce poverty. This embodied the social legitimacy needed by the new administration.

However, the successful pursuit of these goals called for a trusting business community in order for investments to perform their driving role. In fact, at a press conference shortly after taking office, the Finance Minister appointed by the new government in 1990, Alejandro Foxley stated:

> . . . We are betting on an open economy, wagering on economic modernization and Chile's full integration to world markets. We are betting on productivity gains to drive this modernization process significantly supported by Chilean business leaders' ability to successfully rise to this challenge . . . We expect our business community to be able to venture into much more sophisticated processes and phases in order to become competitive.'[31]

It should be noted that both Foxley and Boeninger, Christian Democrat economists, had opposed Allende; as a result, their appointments as Finance Minister and Secretary of the Presidency, respectively by President Patricio Aylwin (1990–94), was also a sign meant to convey to the private sector that the new government's economic policy would stay away from the populist temptations feared by many.

The CPC, Chile's largest business association, started to participate in working commissions with Coalition economists, political and union leaders in order to discuss the basic principles of the new political and social order. This dialogue between the Coalition's political and technical leadership with business leaders and organized labor heads – to build consensus around government programs and a shared commitment to continue on the economic approach already consolidated in the country, complemented with basic labor reforms – proved instrumental to securing a modicum of business trust, prompting business leaders to give the government the benefit of the doubt, at least in the short term.[32]

Thus a new period started, with both the business and organized labor elites expectantly regarding the Coalition government and frequently interacting with each other. This process mitigated their mutual distrust and created a more relaxed atmosphere that paved the way for the development of cooperation ties among the new administration, businessmen and workers.[33] In fact, private investments continued as scheduled, and economic operations suffered no major disturbances, except for the effects of an international crisis caused by the Gulf War.

B. Second Phase: Trust under Bounded Dissent in the 1990s

The new government that took over in 1990 decided to embark on a major initiative to consolidate the trust-based framework that supported the new economic and social order established in Chile. This initiative hinged on engaging business and union leaders to agree upon the key guidelines for this new order, and particularly the new tenets for labor relations. In a nutshell, the idea was to get the leaders of both sectors to mutually acknowledge businesses' right to free enterprise and private property as well as workers' rights to unionize, organize federations and labor contracts with collective bargaining. On the one hand, business associations feared that long-repressed labor demands would jeopardize companies' management autonomy, which would in their view impair their property rights. On the other hand, workers' unions resented the repression they had suffered during the military regime, and more importantly the denial of rights they believed to be essential to organized labor.

Indeed, two dissimilar views of business-labor relations, with their respective traditional approaches, came into play. While harmonious labor relations prevailed in the business approach, which would fit in perfectly with the order inherited from the military regime, both government officials and union leaders had different views. Chile's current labor institutions failed to guarantee workers' basic rights, including the right to termination of contracts with an established cause, or to organize federations and confederations, which could lead to abuses that would be unacceptable in the new national political framework. Labor unions also harbored mixed feelings, as while some groups aspired to restore the Labor Code in force before the 1973 military coup, others realized conditions had changed drastically, calling for new labor rules that factored in the new international economic setting.[34]

The policy dialogue organized on the eve of the new government's taking office, which included the systematic participation of union and business leaders, and technical and political directors of the Coalition, formed the basis for the formal agreement among these sectors established by the government. The objective was to define the broad guidelines for the new labor market institutions. As a result, the so-called Framework Agreements were built by businessmen, workers and the government. Their purpose was to set the groundwork for peaceful, democratic co-existence, based on social dialogue and the mutual recognition of these social agents' legitimacy, notwithstanding their individual right to uphold their own interests in future legislation projects.[35]

This consensus-building process proved strategically crucial, as it boosted system legitimacy, especially for organized labor, which had suffered the most severe exclusion over the dictatorship years. Chilean sociologist Gonzalo Falabella has described this predicament as a result of unions' 'symbolic power', even if organized labor is a weak movement with little leverage, it still holds a symbolic power on account of its demands, and its involvement in labor decisions are relevant for other participating agents.[36] The latter sought to legitimize the new system, and this would not have been accomplished without the engagement of unions. Furthermore, this agreement proved strategically significant for the preservation of peaceful labor relations at companies, also supported by the government's social policies and complementary reforms geared to consolidate the change in Chile's current economic model.

Indeed, once the Framework Agreements had been forged, the government turned its attention to two other issues that were sensitive for business leaders and crucial to reconcile the country's macro-economic stability with public social expenditures. Two reforms were set in motion: introducing changes to the Labor Code inherited from the military regime, and tax changes to raise public revenues equivalent to 2 percent of Chile's gross domestic product (GDP). These additional revenues would be used to fund new social programs. These reforms were meant to contribute to improving living conditions for the poorest population segments and to safeguarding the country's social and political stability, enhancing the economic system's legitimacy among these groups and workers at large. In the long run, social stability would also benefit businesses, as it would lay the groundwork for new investment opportunities.

These two reforms were met with defensive reactions by the business community, as they were considered a threat to what business leaders viewed as accomplishments achieved during the military regime – a low income tax rate and labor laws that greatly favored companies. Increasing businesses' tax burden, raising income tax from 10 percent to 15 percent, to support greater social spending was viewed as a sign of a return to statism. It was impossible to rally social consensus on these reforms, and the government was forced to negotiate the terms with opposition parties in Congress, finally securing its approval, amidst divided opinions in the right wing opposition bloc. Labor reforms encompassed several issues, including labor contract terms, union federations, collective bargaining, individual labor contracts, and associations for public officials. These projects were discussed with social agents who were not entirely satisfied because they considered the changes to be either insufficient (union leaders) or excessive (business leaders), and were ultimately debated in Congress where they were sanctioned as laws in 1990 and 1991.[37]

For organized labor leaders, these reforms had to be followed by further measures, including greater protection for unions, workers' right to have information on their companies, and more important, an expansion of collective bargaining to include inter-company unions, seasonal or temporary workers, as well as a ban to replace workers on strike.[38] The second Coalition government, presided over by Eduardo Frei Ruiz-Tagle (1994–2000), vowed to legislate on these issues and submitted a new labor reform bill to Congress in early 1995.[39]

The history of this reform project shows a series of confrontations that, nonetheless, managed not to escalate into a wider purview of public-private relations. The bill submitted by President Frei was approved by the House of Representatives but rejected by the Senate, where opposition parties held a majority with some 'designated' senators. For business leaders, this new project was unacceptable, and to justify their views they elaborated a number of arguments, ranging from the threat it posed to their autonomy to manage their businesses to rebuttals based on orthodox economic theories. According to their interpretation, this reform would set rigid labor market norms that would benefit employed workers but harm unemployed workers and employment opportunities in small and medium-sized companies. The reforms approved in 1990–91 should be final, and labor issues should not be revisited, lest they would lead to constraints and uncertainties that could deter investment. Amid strong discrepancies among business and union leaders that threatened to frustrate this initiative once again, Senator William Thayer proposed an agreement that was approved by the Labor Minister at the time, Jorge Arrate. However, the Senate rejected the bill in 1999.[40]

Nevertheless, a new government, inaugurated in 2000 and headed by President Ricardo Lagos, resumed this initiative. The president submitted a new bill, omitting inter-company negotiations but introducing a number of norms intended to raise unlawful firing costs, to facilitate unionization, to increase penalties for anti-union practices, and to reduce working hours as of 2005.[41] This bill's approval in 2001 caused new frictions between the government and business leaders that threatened to polarize their positions. Then, the government decided for a six-month gradual enactment. 'It is a long . . . complex reform, as it deals with issues or contents of substantial nature and others of a more instrumental nature', María Ester Feres, Director of Labor at the time, noted.

> Some norms are easy to read and understand, and will not require special interpretation, for they will prove easy to apply . . . However, there are other reforms . . . that, while not difficult to understand, will prove difficult to apply . . . We are going to establish – and these will be nationwide instructions – rallies, primarily educational oversights, complimentary reports, when only the norms associated with this reform are compromised . . . The idea is to move forward gradually, because we are interested in a real change – first, making the law known to all, and, then, progressing towards compliance – not just the sanction of a law.[42]

Regardless of its specific contents, this reform revealed clearly the underlying arguments supported by the two major views on labor institutionality. One views social security as a 'gravel' that has been accumulated in the investment incentive system as a result of new regulations (for instance, environmental or, now, labor norms). From this standpoint, this labor reform contributed to build up this 'gravel'. At a time marked by high unemployment due to the Asian crisis effects (nearing 10 percent of the labor force), this reform went against the trend of making the labor market more flexible. For business leaders, a more 'rigid' labor market impaired growth potential and raise unemployment. As Andrés Concha, SFF Secretary General at the time,[43] pointed out when the bill was discussed in Congress, 'The measures we are positing . . . are intended precisely to encourage more hiring and, clearly, more investments to create more jobs. Thus, this often leads to antagonistic positions in some cases'.[44] Later that same year, the spokesman stated that 'we find nothing good in this project. On the contrary, I believe it has disturbed companies' labor stability, because people in many sectors are concerned about what the Parliament may approve next'.[45] Indeed, the debate grew more aggressive in tone, threatening to bring back the confrontational atmosphere of the past.[46]

For union leaders, the more 'flexible' labor market demanded by the business community became tantamount to a social setback that would render workers subject to the 'laws of the market'. This sector was not pleased with the reform either, and announced that its agenda would continue to feature their rejected demands. Business arguments were viewed as exaggerated as the reform had introduced rather timid changes into labor laws, as compared to those in force today in developed nations.[47] Since Chile was negotiating several free trade agreements, including one with the United States and the European Union, if it did not adjust its labor laws to international standards, and particularly to International Labour Organization (ILO) recommendations, 'social dumping' accusations might hamper the successful completion of these negotiations.

Organized labor sectors also argued that strengthening social cohesion should be a priority goal for a market economy like Chile's, where income distribution had suffered a sharp downturn with the financial adjustments made in the 1970s and 1980s and had yet to return to its historical standards. Moreover, employment quality – construed in terms of labor contract existence and compliance, social security contribution payments, workers' turnover, employer overtime demands – was severely impaired, turning jobs more unstable.[48] Under this rationale, Chile's economic growth came at the expense of social equity and workers' rights. These and other considerations on living conditions might have fueled some discontent with the outcomes of economic growth, especially among low- and middle-income population segments.[49]

This rather complex topic bears a substantial impact on the core issue of the relationship between equity and development. It has been widely acknowledged that in the 1990s economic growth proved more effective than distributive equity. The initiative for a labor reform was launched halfway through that decade when Chile boasted high growth rates, making efforts to improve labor negotiation terms and practices perfectly legitimate and necessary. Unfortunately, the debate took too long, as both parties refused to compromise in order to forge consensual agreements. This debate eventually led to a reform that the government viewed as minimal but failed to please either business or union leaders. In addition, this law was finally sanctioned amidst an economic downturn marked by international uncertainty – very bad timing for a reform that made labor more costly.[50]

The business community's insistent assertion that this reform would have a negative impact on employment, as it focused on safeguarding employed workers' rights to the detriment of unemployed workers, heated up the debate and led the CUT chairman to claim that business leaders were planning massive layoffs before the 2001 parliamentary election in order to spark animosity against the government, damaging Coalition candidates' winning chances. This claim brought an end to business leaders' dialogue with organized labor and their withdrawal from the fledgling Social Dialogue Council that President Lagos planned to create.

The 2001 labor reform shows, once again, the permanent tension between economic efficiency criteria, stemming from a choice in favor of growth and globalization, and social equity and justice criteria that consistently besieged the Coalition. A renowned editorialist artfully described this as 'the tension between the two Coalition souls'.[51] This tension was unavoidable, for the Coalition program simultaneously sought growth and equity. The labor reform project addressed a social aspiration that was long overdue and was finally tackled at a time of consolidated economic growth, with fast-increasing incomes – especially for high-income groups. It was meant to adjust Chile's labor institutions to the international standards the government had embraced. Unfortunately, the prolonged debate and lack of political agreement meant that the bill, with all the modifications it had undergone along the way, was finally approved just when conditions for growth were severely weakened and the unemployment rate was soaring.

C. Third Phase: Cooperation after 2000

The 2001 labor reform did not satisfy either business or union leaders. These agents and the government blamed each other, and public-private relations seemed to navigate troubled waters.[52] However, the situation soon changed significantly. As a result of the Asian financial crisis, economic growth had tumbled down and failed to regain its pace from the former decade. Macroeconomic policies were widely regarded as appropriate but proved unable to prevent sluggish growth, largely caused by the international shock that affected Chile's economy in 1998–2001 but also due to the so-called microeconomic 'bumps' (bureaucratic rigidities). Indeed, Chile's GDP annual growth rate dropped from 7.7 percent during President Aylwin's administration to 5.4 percent in the following term, with President Frei at the helm – this drop was influenced by the Asian crisis (1998–2000), even with a slight absolute fall in 1999.[53]

Many agreed that Chile's economy was suffering from a number of shortcomings that combined into a systemic problem. One diagnosis outlined by government officials in the Finance Ministry and the Corporación de Fomento de la Producción de Chile (Corfo), stressed that a major weakness stemmed from poor technological innovation efforts.[54] The private sector believed several economic system rigidities called for reforms and changes. As a result, complementary criteria surfaced around the key issues to be raised immediately in the public-private agenda. This consensus was largely made possible by the leadership exercised by both the nation's president and the new SFF chairman, Juan Claro. The latter represented a new generation of business leaders who had been joining business leadership over recent years. With an approach that drifted away from neo-liberal fundamentalism to rise to the new challenges that Chile faced on account of globalization – free-trade treaties, and the swift technological changes brought about by the digital era – in late 2001 SFF introduced an Agenda for Growth that was welcomed by the government and marked the beginning of a new collaboration scheme for both sectors. This agenda conveyed the explicit and public decision made by one of Chile's leading business associations to cooperate with the government on shared-interest issues. SFF's Agenda for Growth primarily posited that Chile needed to decisively promote a number of institutional, micro-economic changes.

Private sector diagnoses zeroed in on inadequate regulations (for instance, in the fishing industry), rigidities caused by labor laws that discouraged hiring, outdated capital market regulations, excessive bureaucracy (slow environmental impact assessments for investment projects), shortcomings in technological and human resources policies, and insufficient educational reform (for example, lacking an incentive system for educational institutions' managers).[55]

In his 2001 end-of-the-year address at SFF, President Lagos expressed his commitment to building a common, broad agenda for the government to work with the private sector in order to foster new micro-economic reforms. However, he underscored the progress made thus far, including a new and modern domestic tax system, hailed as one of the most efficient in the world as a result of the introduction of new information technologies; faster environmental approval procedures, whose delay had been reduced by a third; and the expansion of public work concessions to new areas, such as jail and hospital construction. President Lagos also mentioned a US$ 4.6 billion investment portfolio that the government was willing to drive through concessions to private agents, especially promoted for foreign investors.

As arranged by the government and SFF, the Agenda for Growth was discussed at 28 working commissions that gathered public, private and academic experts, and worked for over 60 days in 2001. At the end of their meetings, the commissions formulated a number of proposals for bills that the government would submit to Congress or execute via administrative orders. Primary focal areas included a regulatory system overhaul, especially for the energy and telecom industries, technological policies, tax scheme, capital market updating, and improving public spending efficiency.[56]

In the technological realm, a significant step was taken when the government approached Silicon Valley corporations, luring high-tech companies to invest in Chile. To this end, the Digital Country Foundation was created, involving the private sector to maintain and promote public-private ties for the development of a digital economy. This goal was incorporated in the Program to Attract Foreign High-Tech Investments, driven jointly by Chile's Economy Ministry, Corfo and Foreign Investments Committee. Three other programs underway in this area were the Internet Development Strategy, the Technological Innovation Program, and the Venture Capital Industry Promotion.[57]

How should this Agenda for Growth be politically assessed? One way or another, its contents had pervaded the debate on growth institutionality for some time.[58] Nonetheless, Chile's political scenario in late 2001 was particularly suitable for a relaunch of these issues. First, a persistently slow growth rate averaging 3 percent yearly in 1998–2001 had sparked general concern, especially as Chile was also having a hard time returning to its historical unemployment rate – around 6 percent. Second, this growth pace would also prevent the country from effectively reducing extreme poverty. Third, the government believed that for the first time since 1989, it looked as though the right could actually challenge the political supremacy held by the Coalition since 1990s. Fourth, the frictions caused by labor reform discussions in past years drove the government to revamp its public-private agenda to raise the issues that were likely to lead to consensual agreements.

At first glance, a likely electoral win for the right might have been expected to encourage the private sector's reluctance to cooperate with the government in order to further tilt the scales against it. Upon closer examination however, the business sector should be separated from right-wing politicians. Business leaders' primary goal is economic growth and market system betterment, as both lay the groundwork for profit maximization. From a political standpoint, economic and social institutionalization served their core requirements, as it guaranteed macro-economic stability, international trade, market and competition rules, as well as entrepreneurship. Furthermore, the government was committed to update the capital market, as long requested by the private sector, in order to allow for investment, funding and risk diversification. These conditions satisfied the most ambitious business demands.

Even viewing business behavior from a political perspective, it seems perfectly reasonable that business leaders would bet on the Agenda for Growth.[59] Empirical evidence shows that high growth is a necessary – albeit insufficient – condition to meeting the most urgent social needs. A reduction of extreme poverty rates to nearly half over the ten first Coalition government years (from 38.6 percent in 1990 to 20.6 percent in 2000) was possible because Chile's economy grew at an average 8 percent annual rate until 1997. It has been widely acknowledged that a slower growth pace would not have sufficed to accomplish further poverty mitigation goals. In this scenario, business leaders would not have only seen their earnings lag but would have also been forced to face stronger social demands or new tax reforms – that is, more distributive demands. In fact, this has been happening in recent years, as slow growth has consolidated and 'economic model' critiques have grown stronger.[60]

The Agenda for Growth also helped curb the rising tensions among agents, as a result of the labor reform approved in 2001. Harsher, more distant relations between both social agents certainly undermined the likelihood of joint efforts and agreements to overcome the economic crisis. Thus, SFF's initiative proved particularly important, as it brought a proposal for collaborative work that probably surprised national officials. A quick, positive response by President Lagos, befitting his charismatic personality, put an end to a period of animosity and marked the beginning of new phase characterized by close working ties among the technicians and advisors involved in the commissions that elaborated the First Agenda for Growth, followed by the Second Agenda for Growth. Improved government-business relations were not of minor importance after 2002. President Lagos finished his term in office with the highest popularity score among Coalition presidents thus far, even among business leaders.

V. TRIPARTITE SOCIAL DIALOGUE DURING PRESIDENT FREI'S ADMINISTRATION[61]

The need to build a path for social dialogue that created institutions to represent existing social interests and to forge negotiated agreements had been voiced since 1990. The best way to prevent public-private relations from merging into an oligarchic, excluding scheme (regardless of the specific oligarchy in question) – a pervasive temptation – is to build those relations in an institutional framework, so that agendas are formulated and addressed openly before society in a transparent, accountable manner. This statement is supported by a game theory corollary positing that more frequent games or interactions make the replacement of distrust games by trust-based games more likely. Agreements require trust. Sporadic or random interactions among parties are dominated by non-cooperative strategies, as shown by the prisoner's dilemma, and outcomes are poor for all parties. On the contrary, when interactions are more frequent and regular, trust-based strategies prevail.[62] Social dialogue institutionalization contributes to increasing the frequency of interactions among social agents, with clear, pre-established, transparent and equitable rules, revealing parties' expectations and decisions agents are willing to make in a cooperative setting.

In comparison to how some European countries have built public-private relations, Chile's institutionalization is still lagging. Despite the progress described earlier, private-sector engagement is still accomplished on an ad-hoc basis, either through government invitation or the initiative of business associations.[63] There are still rare interactions involving other social agents, including workers' unions, consumer and environmental groups, and other stakeholders. Negotiations are more regarded as equations to be sorted out than as processes affording society a chance to participate and to voice its interests or concerns.

In contrast, European nations have built broadly-based social participation platforms, known as Economic and Social Committees, since World War II. These bodies have enabled the formal involvement of business, labor and other social organizations in the quest for agreements and consensus that may guide public policies. These committees helped to strengthen European democracies, extremely weakened at the time, and, instead of shying away from conflicts, they provided a means to deal with them in order to forge agreements that were acceptable for all parties. These consultations are certainly not binding, but, as a result of the committees' formality, their proposals are largely and seriously taken into account by public powers. This is a key ingredient of modern, participative democracies, as it enables citizens not only to vote in government elections but also to express their more permanent, substantial concerns.

As noted earlier, the first social dialogue experience in Chile unfolded in the early years of President Aylwin's administration, leading to the Framework Agreements and the labor reform that, under René Cortázar's leadership, when he served as Labor Minister, paved the way for new labor relations.[64] Nonetheless, this process grew somewhat impaired nearing the end of that administration (1990–94). Union leaders felt that their key demands, notably extending collective bargaining beyond full-time workers and industry negotiations, were largely neglected by government officials.

Later, President Frei launched a new initiative to move forward on tripartite dialogue efforts, inviting major social agents involved in development issues – that is, business and labor leaders – to join the government in building a National Forum for Productive Development – and its respective regional forums. The goal was to create a platform for social interaction in order to elaborate development guidelines, reconciling equity and competitiveness with a long-term outlook for national development. Reinstating a tripartite social dialogue, the objective was now to view labor issues from the broader stance of competitive, equity-based development. The plan was to remove the discussion from the confrontational setting historically associated with labor issues and to approach it from a positive-sum game approach – with a view to forging strategic alliances among companies and workers in order to drive technological advancement – whose benefits could be distributed equitably between business and labor. This approach required an assorted agenda, with issues merging on the notion of economic growth with income redistribution.[65] These alliances should stem from mutual commitments made by business leaders and workers, based on the understanding that companies' success – crucial for employment and compensation – requires productivity growth, training, quality and output efficiency enhancements, with their implications for labor organization. However, workers' commitment to these goals implies that companies adopt labor and compensations policies in keeping with their greater productivity. In turn, the government undertook the promotion of productive development policies at national and regional levels, allocating resources to training, technical support and infrastructure.

This experience was carried out between 1994 and 1999, with meetings addressing such diverse issues as requirements to achieve international systemic competitiveness based on job training, quality improvements, environmental care, and technological innovation, as well as formulas to enhance distributive equity and fairer labor contracts. This initiative failed to continue after 2000, despite President Lagos' intention to organize a Social Dialogue Council, as a result of a rift that drove union and business leaders apart due to the tone of the labor debate in those years, as mentioned before. However, a number of more profound, underlying reasons, discussed below, suggested that the initiative was premature in light of labor organizations' lack of modernization – particularly in the case of workers affiliated to CUT.

By means of a working methodology consisting of annual meetings of high-ranking leaders from business, labor and the government, and ad-hoc national and regional working committees, the forum became a platform for direct dialogue among these social agents, intended to create trust and to prompt shared reflections on the greater challenges posed by national development, especially in areas plagued by opposing views and conflicting interests. However, expectations were only fulfilled partially. In 1994–99, four national meetings and over 20 regional, provincial and district meetings were held, while several formal working groups were created to deal with specific topics. In retrospect, the forum amounted to an attempt to turn social dialogue into an ongoing process as well as a novel means to encourage social involvement in decisions associated with economic development. Nonetheless, the forum faced a number of hurdles that curtailed its possibilities and contributed to its disappointment.

The forum's insufficient political and legal strength proved initially and institutionally challenging, as its agreements lacked political weight. The fact that its executive secretariat was housed at the Economy Ministry conferred a sectorial nature on it, concealing its intended cross-sector scope and discouraging the engagement of other ministerial officials (except for the Labor Minister), which weakened the forum's institutional grounds.

A second hurdle, associated with the nature of participating labor organizations, was their fear to forge tripartite agreements without enough internal support, which led to delays and absenteeism. This weakness primarily affected the labor sector, represented by CUT, whose leadership has been characterized by a precarious political and ideological balance among various degrees of radical anti-market views.

Third, a significant disagreement among participants on the importance to be awarded to specific issues also undermined leaders' commitments. While business leaders promoted a vast agenda with a broad variety of topics, organized labor preferred to focus on the labor reform project that the government had submitted to Congress at the time, which was not approved, as noted earlier. Probably the root of the difficulties that prevented the forum from becoming a more successful initiative lay in its undefined specific purpose. Political authorities viewed it as a pathway to build a national project for Chile, hinging on competitive, equity-based development and encompassing all social agents – a goal strongly demanded by several political sectors. Business leaders accepted this offer, albeit reluctantly when it came to dealing with more conflicting issues with workers unions – such as labor reforms geared to expand collective bargaining. For organized labor heads, the latter were the focal points, to the exclusion of all other issues, which they viewed as not as relevant to their sector.

Fourth but just as important, mutual distrust among business and labor leaders endured as a result of unions' frequent complaints of companies' anti-union practices and businessmen's fear of workers' demands for a labor reform that, in their opinion, would impair labor market flexibility.[66]

Finally, it should be noted that Chile's marked political centralism has given rise to a culture of concentrated decision-making in the hands of government and political parties. Despite rhetoric that favors social involvement, social organizations can participate effectively and influence decisions in very few initiatives.[67] Political parties and Parliament are reluctant to share their decision-making power with other sectors, arguing that the political constitution grants legislative power solely to Congress. Nonetheless, this does not prevent Parliament members from receiving social sectors' suggestions or opinions on the issues at hand, but this input is not binding. In Europe, parliaments are legally bound to take into account economic-social committees' non-binding rulings. The executive branch is in charge of government and policy-making and may legitimately resort to citizen consultations to perform its duties. This does not undermine parliament's legislative power in the least, as it is in parliament where bills are debated and sanctioned.

Still, business and labor leaders both validated the National Forum, stressing the need to maintain and perfect it. A review of its operations reveals that its decisions and recommendations led to the creation of Chile's National Productivity and Quality Center in 1995. This tripartite body disseminates quality and productivity improvement techniques and methodologies that also enhance salaries and working conditions at companies. This program effectively drove Chile to embrace quality issues, as it worked with large, small and medium-sized companies. Other Forum recommendations included: a gradual reform for export subsidy policies to adjust them to World Trade Organization's standards while allocating resources to technical training and support; a SENCE (National Training

Service) reform to expand its benefits to small business owners; the formulation of consumer rights and their incorporation to corresponding laws; the Clean Production Program, intended to formalize voluntary agreements with companies to introduce environmentally-friendly technologies; a bill for unemployment insurance or suspended workers' protection; easier procedures to organize SMEs; a supplier program for SMEs, meant to coordinate large companies' input demands to create market opportunities for SMEs; a regional productive development policy intended to decentralize and streamline public investments, among others. Indeed, most of these policies derived from public sector initiatives, but the forums discussed their goals, execution roadmaps, and elicited agreements among government, business and labor around them.

In its association agreement with the European Union, Chile pledged to institutionalize social dialogue, but this decision was delayed, and both government officials and sector leaders have opted for bilateral, ad-hoc meetings. This shows that the Coalition's model has suffered from a social involvement deficit; however, despite that, its political programs have explicitly referred to the state's responsibility in this regard and the need to institutionalize and encourage social involvement. This shortcoming does not affect organized sectors as much, for they have the ability to voice their demands, but it does wreak havoc for other social sectors that find it harder to organize themselves, such as consumers – a vast, heterogeneous sector that has been unable so far to build an effective participation network. Some existing initiatives have failed to prosper beyond the National Consumer Service, a public agency primarily intended to provide information on consumer rights.

However, the desire to keep communication channels open persists. Nearing the end of President Lagos' administration, CUT and CPC rekindled their intention to build a bilateral forum that did not include the government, but they did not make much progress. With a more favorable spirit, President Bachelet's first administration (2006–10) pledged to promote it on employment, training and employment quality topics.[68] While some meetings did take place to deal with specific issues, like the 2009 Agenda for Employment, efforts to institutionalize a more steady and formal social dialogue proved fruitless, indicating that Chilean social agents still harbor distrust for each other.

VI. CONCLUDING REMARKS

A number of important conclusions emerge from this chapter. First, major social agents involved in economic development in Chile, including the government, explicitly recognize the need to maintain open, fluent communications among themselves. Since the late 1980s, they have agreed on the uncertainties, threats and risks faced by the country in this new global economic order and as a result of new technologies. Changes are quick and bear significant consequences, driving both businessmen and workers away from positions they historically held. Both sectors view governments as responsible for adjusting public policies and institutions to new scenarios in order to minimize adjustments costs and to provide opportunities for new ways to integrate countries into the global economy. Governments are also aware of their political vulnerability amidst major changes, knowing that they do not have enough information to anticipate the future and assess strategic choices. Thus, they are interested in forging commitments and agreements with social agents to jointly determine the best possible options. All the center-left Coalition (Concertación) governments (1990–2010) included social dialogue in their political programs.

Second, in increasingly deliberative democracies, with social agents having much more and better information than ever before and with growing demands for government transparency and accountability, the need to streamline cross-sector dialogue and communications through more formal institutions is paramount. This makes agreements broader and more legitimate, enhancing their potential to turn into effective public policies. Chile has made significant progress in this direction, but strong asymmetries persist in the relative engagement of business and labor leaders, favoring the former, partly as a result of their unequal resources to invest in information and analysis as well as to impose their terms.

Third, despite this aforementioned 'national interest', differing concerns and ideological views persist, giving rise to rifts and disputes, as is typically the case in every democracy. Conflicts should be resolved through well-established political and judicial institutions, but dialogue mechanisms used to forge agreements may significantly contribute to avoid artificial clashes derived from false perceptions or insufficient information. Social agents may even harbor these differences inside their internal forums, as both business and labor groups display differing views on the nature of challenges and how to overcome them. In the business community, there are sectors that, based on traditional and conservative views, value their autonomy to manage their companies, while others have been embracing more modern views that recognize companies' social responsibility and understand that their surroundings are just as relevant for business results as internal process management. Something similar happens in organized labor, with contrasts among groups still upholding notions like class struggles, while other segments incorporate views on the complementariness of business and labor, without neglecting the advocacy of internationally recognized labor rights.

A way to lessen the role of ideologies in social dialogue is to innovate in dialogue procedures and controversy management – participants often attend debates with previously defined proposals and solutions, and this hinders agreements greatly. Solutions emerge as a result of open negotiations based on shared, objective diagnoses – rather than through arguments on closed proposals that normally lead to zero-sum games.[69] In other words, solutions are negotiation outcomes rather than premises.

Fourth, Chilean efforts to institutionalize social dialogue since the 1990s have not been fully successful in terms of continuity and consolidation. Several reasons discussed in this chapter may explain this fact, but it is clear that moving forward, Chile needs to strengthen these efforts and to look for institutional formulas that make social dialogue viable and sustainable, with incentives and resources to prompt engagement. A significant hurdle that hampers social dialogue institutionalization lies in Chile's centralized, insufficiently transparent, political culture. Despite their announced intentions, governments so far have failed to take meaningful steps in this direction, but this social demand is clear, and it is starting to translate into the electoral rejection of the prevailing options offered by the political system – and, fortunately rarely, into violence. The institutionalization of social dialogue will require considerable attention to making the range of participating agents highly representative, enabling processes to be seen as legitimate, and securing the right mix of local, regional and national agendas.

Finally, it has to be noted that the institutionalization of social dialogue awakens fears for many reasons, including the possible interference with state powers, especially the executive and legislative branches, or with political parties. It needs to be understood that to promote social dialogue, an institution does not compete with the decision-making powers of governments and parliaments. Representative democracies require these bodies, which should preserve their independence and power. However, these powers cannot rule without regard for social interests, and without the information social agents can contribute.

This chapter has explored how Chile's private sector has become more relevant in public policy-making on account of its specific and practical knowledge, and as a result of its financial capability to allocate resources to those ends. Similarly, it is possible that other social agents will make valuable contributions if they have the resources to do so. None of this relieves governments of their responsibility to rule, or parliaments from their duty to establish legal order. Their jobs become more complex when broader and more diverse interests are taken into account. Ultimately, a better and more effective democracy comes at a price. Since 2011, events in Chile, including massive student demonstrations and nationwide strikes demanding a formal voice for better quality education, public education strengthening, and a substantial increase of public resources for the sector, have clearly proven the urgent need to improve social participation in general and to create formal institutions for social dialogue in particular.

NOTES

1. This chapter forms part of a research project undertaken with support from CIEPLAN (Latin American Economic Research Corporation).
2. For example, see the World Economic Forum's *Global Competitiveness Report (2008–2009)*.
3. North (1990).
4. Stiglitz (1998).
5. Rodrik (2004): 18.
6. CEPAL (2008): 261.
7. Consejo de Innovación (2007): 91.
8. Arriagada (2004).
9. Garretón (2003): 52–4.
10. Boeninger (2007): 97.
11. This hypothesis was formulated in an interesting article by Campero (2003).
12. President Jorge Alessandri's administration (1958–64) has been dubbed 'the managers' government', as the president came from a large private company.
13. This author recalls some people consider that the United States believed that 'what was good for General Motors was good for the country' for a long time. Later, this belief was changed for a time into 'what is good for Wall Street is good for the country'. See Johnson (2009): 2.
14. Other social agents are also making a strong entrance, like consumer groups, environmental advocates, academics and students, who also demand to join in development strategy formulation processes.
15. In 1999 several associations for small and medium-sized companies came together to create the National Small and Medium-Sized Company Council (CONAPYME) to discuss sector issues with the government.
16. For a historical background of Chilean public-private relations, see Pinto (1985).
17. Rehren (1995).
18. Unless otherwise referenced, the following paragraphs draw heavily on Ffrench-Davis (2003); Silva (1996); and Montero (1997).
19. From 1982 until early 1985, a number of economic officials tried to overcome the crisis to no avail, with a variety of approaches that even drew away from the orthodox schools of thought prevailing until then, as was the case of Economy Minister Luis Escobar Cerda. Minister Hermán Büchi, appointed in 1985, restored neo-liberal goals, albeit with a more pragmatic approach and amidst improving conditions.
20. Silva (2003).
21. Dingemans (2008).
22. Silva (1996): 155 onwards.
23. Schneider (2004).
24. Campero (2003): 165.
25. Campero emphasized that this process granted business leaders a strong cultural identity that hinged on an ethos based on creativity, economic and social success. Campero (2003).
26. Arriagada (2004): 166. Arriagada served as Minister Secretary General of the presidency

from 1994 to 1996, was the Chilean Ambassador to the United States from 1998–99, head of the presidential campaign for Ricardo Lagos in 1999 and a board member of the State Bank of Chile from 2000–06.

27. The Public Studies Center (CEP), a think-tank created by some large companies to disseminate liberal public policy views, provides another highly influential political forum that gathers top business leaders and State officials.
28. Rehren (1995).
29. Montero (2000); Rehren (1995).
30. It should be noted that these years were a period of recovery after the severe external debt crisis.
31. Foxley (1990).
32. See Boeninger (2007): 460 onwards.
33. See Rehren (1995).
34. Campero (2007).
35. April 1990 Agreements. See Cortázar (1993) and Campero (2007). These Framework Agreements did not specifically deal with labor reforms, but they did establish a new minimum wage adjustment policy that came into force in 1992.
36. Falabella (2006).
37. Campero (2007).
38. Joignant et al. (2000): 42.
39. At the same time, President Frei deemed it convenient to reinitiate the formal practice of tripartite social dialogue. To that end, he designed the Productive Development Forum and invited business and union leaders to build a common agenda for Chile's long-term development (see Section V.).
40. Joignant et al. (2000): 47–54.
41. *El Diario* (2001a): 30.
42. Feres (2001).
43. Elected SFF chairman in 2009.
44. Concha (2001).
45. According to a press release issued by SFF's Labor Department on 30 May 2001.
46. Eduardo Silva characterized this process as a near-rift between Lagos' administration and business leaders that was eventually mended. See Silva (2002).
47. *El Diario* (2001b): 33.
48. Infante (2005).
49. In the late 1990s, a debate also began inside the Coalition, with the so-called 'self-indulging' faction confronting the 'self-punishing' group. These names clearly portrayed the feelings that have permeated the Coalition's body of ideas.
50. A similar situation unfolded in 2009.
51. Flisfisch (2001): 9.
52. Silva (2002).
53. Small and medium-sized enterprises (SMEs) were among the hardest hit sectors, leading several associations to create the National Council for SMEs (CONAPYME), which joined the Economy Ministry and a sympathetic group of Congressmen to create a special forum known as the Public-Private Committee for SMEs. This forum was asked to formulate SME by-laws. Other early forum initiatives included a rescheduling of SME bank debts, laws on micro-ventures, changes for family business laws, and a state purchase law.
54. The next section discusses the Productive Development Forum – organized by Frei's administration – and its extensive discussion of these systemic issues.
55. Claro (2001): 34.
56. See SFF (2002).
57. Muñoz (2009).
58. For example, a Presidential Commission organized by President Frei to elaborate an information technology development plan incorporated several of these issues.
59. During Lagos' administration, many of the authoritarian provisions bequeathed by

the military regime and embedded in the political constitution were abolished, like the inclusion of designated and life-long senators. However, this did not cause concern for the business elite, probably because the public opinion largely believed that it was necessary to update political institutions. Also, Pinochet was no longer a threat after his arrest in London. In poor health, the former dictator had withdrawn from public life.

60. However, oddly enough, during President Bachelet's administration, economic growth rates have been the lowest in Coalition governments, partly due to the world financial crisis beginning in 2007. Yet this administration has also embarked on an unprecedentedly intense social policy and income distribution program that has brought unparalleled popularity for President Bachelet. This may be partly attributed to the massive fiscal resources yielded by the highest copper prices in decades. Nevertheless, CUT's attempts to raise once again the issue of collective negotiations in Parliament's agenda, despite government support, proved fruitless yet again as a result of the rising unemployment caused by the world crisis.
61. This section draws extensively from Muñoz (2007): Chapter 2.
62. Axelrod (1984).
63. An illustrative example was the above-mentioned Agenda for Growth. Early on in her administration, President Bachelet built several working commissions to address some institutional reforms. These commissions are primarily technical in nature, although they do seem to remain open to new, plural social and political views.
64. See Boeninger (1997); Cortázar (1993); Campero (2007).
65. Muñoz (2000).
66. Montero (2000).
67. After President Bachelet summoned a working commission to reform Chile's electoral system in March 2006, Independent Democratic Union's (UDI) Senator Longueira argued against his party joining the commission, stating that bills and institutional reform projects should be discussed and decided by Congress. Later, however, Senator Frei Ruiz-Tagle moved to create an Economic-Social Council, and the Senate required government support for the project. While supported by some sectors, the motion met with skepticism from political parties, some government spokesmen and the media.
68. According to statements made by Osvaldo Andrade, Labor Minister, in an interview with *El Mercurio*, on 14 April 2006, B24. Still, there were no formal initiatives in this regard until 2009, when on account of the international financial crisis, an Agenda for Employment was agreed upon by the government, businessmen and workers, represented by their respective organizations (*La Nación*, 7 May 2009).
69. Devlin and Moguillansky (2009).

REFERENCES

Arriagada, Genaro (2004), *Los empresarios y la política*, Santiago de Chile: LOM.

Boeninger, Edgardo (1997), *Democracia en Chile. Lecciones para la gobernabilidad*, Santiago de Chile: Andrés Bello.

Boeninger, Edgardo (2007), *Políticas públicas en democracia. Institucionalidad y experiencia chilena 1990–2006*, Santiago de Chile: UQBAR Editores.

Campero, Guillermo (2003), 'La relación entre el gobierno y los grupos de presión: el proceso de la acción de bloques a la acción segmentada', *Revista de Ciencia Política*, **23**, 159–76.

Campero, Guillermo (2007), 'La economía política de las relaciones laborales 1990–2006', *Serie Estudios Socio/Económicos*, **37**.

CEPAL (2008), *La transformación productiva 20 años después*, Chapter VI, Santiago de Chile: CEPAL/United Nations.

Claro, Juan (2001), 'La economía política del país está ante una encrucijada', *El Diario*, 31 October.
Concha, Andrés (2001), comments made at the Industry Building on Friday 12 January, as he attended the lecture delivered by SFF's labor advisor, Huberto Berg. See http://www.sofofa.cl/opinion/2001/laboral/1-4-2001/Informe_Laboral_H_berg.pdf, accessed 15 December 2014.
Consejo de Innovación (2007), *Hacia una estrategia nacional de innovación para la competitividad,* Vol. I, Santiago de Chile: Consejo Nacional de Innovación para la Competitividad.
Cortázar, René (1993), *Política laboral en el Chile democrático: avances y desafíos en los noventa*, Santiago de Chile: DOLMEN.
Devlin, Robert and Graciela Moguillansky (2009), 'Alianzas público-privadas como estrategias nacionales de desarrollo a largo plazo', *Revista de la CEPAL*, **97**, 97–116.
Dingemans, Alfonso (2008), 'Una historia económica sin fin. Chile y Argentina en la formación de una economía de mercado (1973–2001)', Thesis for a Doctoral Degree in American Studies with a History Major, Universidad de Santiago de Chile, Departamento de Historia.
El Diario (2001a), 30 November.
El Diario (2001b), Interview with labor law specialists, Attorneys Diego Corvera and Juan Gumucio, 19 October.
Falabella, Gonzalo (2006), *Tripartism in Chile: A Case of Union Symbolic Power,* Chile: Sociology Department, Universidad de Chile.
Feres, María Ester (2001), Speech at SFF's seminar on 'Labor Reform and its Effects for Business', 24 October, accessed 8 November 2009 at www.sofofa.cl/sofofa/index.aspx?channel=3562.
Ffrench-Davis, Ricardo (2003), *Entre el neo-liberalismo y el crecimiento con equidad. Tres décadas de política económica en Chile*, Santiago de Chile: J.C. Sáez Editor.
Flisfisch, Ángel (2001), 'Sobre el presente y futuro de la Concertación', *La Segunda*, 5 September.
Foxley, Alejandro (1990), 'La política económica para la transición', in Oscar Muñoz (comp.), *Transición a la democracia. Marco político y económico*, Santiago de Chile: CIEPLAN, pp. 101–20.
Garretón, Manuel Antonio (2003), 'La (in)conducción política del Segundo Gobierno Democrático', in Oscar Muñoz and Carolina Stefoni (eds), *El período del presidente Frei Ruiz-Tagle*, Santiago de Chile: FLACSO-Editorial Universitaria.
Infante, Ricardo (2005), 'Nuevos sectores sociales: empleo y calidad de vida', in *Aportes para el debate*, Santiago de Chile: Eds. Chile 21.
Johnson, Simon (2009), 'The quiet coup', *The Atlantic*, May, accessed 15 December 2014 at http://www.theatlantic.com/magazine/archive/2009/05/the-quiet-coup/307364/.
Joignant, Alfredo et al. (2000), *Negociación de la reforma laboral: evaluación de actores y estrategias mediante diferentes modelos analíticos*, Santiago de Chile: Public Policy Study Fund, Industrial Engineering Department, Universidad de Chile.
Montero, Cecilia (1997), *La revolución empresarial chilena*, Santiago de Chile: Dolmen-Cieplan.
Montero, Cecilia (2000), 'Las relaciones laborales: ¿un asunto público?', in Oscar

Muñoz et al., *El Estado y el sector privado. Construyendo una nueva economía en los años 90*, Santiago de Chile: DOLMEN/FLACSO.
Muñoz, Oscar (2007), *El modelo económico de la Concertación 1990–2005. ¿Reformas o cambio?*, Santiago de Chile: FLACSO-Catalonia.
Muñoz, Oscar (2009), 'El desarrollo institucional de Corfo y sus estrategias desde 1990', in Oscar Muñoz (ed.), *Desarrollo productivo en Chile. La experiencia de Corfo entre 1990 y 2009*, Santiago de Chile: CORFO/FLACSO/Catalonia.
North, Douglass (1990), *Institutions, Institutional Change and Economic Performance*, Cambridge: Cambridge University Press.
Pinto, Aníbal (1985), 'Estado y gran empresa: de la pre-crisis hasta el gobierno de Jorge Alessandri', *Colección Estudios CIEPLAN*, **16**, 5–40.
Rehren, Alfredo (1995), 'Empresarios, transición y consolidación democrática en Chile', *Revista de Ciencia Política,* **XVII** (1–2), 5–61.
Rodrik, Dani (2004), 'Industrial policy for the twenty-first century', Harvard University, John F. Kennedy School of Government, accessed 15 December 2014 at http://www.hks.harvard.edu/fs/drodrik/Research%20papers/UNIDOSep.pdf.
Schneider, Ben Ross (2004), *Business Politics and the State in Twentieth Century Latin America*, New York: Cambridge University Press, p. 166.
SFF (2002), 'Ministros de Estado informan resultados del trabajo en conjunto con la SOFOFA', 31 January, accessed 21 April 2015 at http://www.sofofa.cl/opinion/2002/del%20presidente/ene-abril/agenda31.1.pdf.
Silva, Eduardo (1996), *The State and Capital in Chile: Business Elites, Technocrats and Market Economics*, Boulder, Colorado: Westview Press.
Silva, Eduardo (2002), 'Capital and the Lagos presidency : business as usual?', *Bulletin of Latin American Research,* **21**, 339–57.
Silva, Eduardo (2003), 'Capitalist regime loyalties and redemocratization in Chile', *Journal of Interamerican Studies and World Affairs*, **34**, 77–117.
Stiglitz, Joseph (1998), 'Towards a new paradigm for development: strategies, policies and processes', Prebisch Lecture at UNCTAD, accessed 15 December 2014 at http://web.worldbank.org/WBSITE/EXTERNAL/TOPICS/TRADE/0,,contentMDK:20025537~menuPK:167371~pagePK:64020865~piPK:149114~theSitePK:239071,00.html, 9.

9. Argentine and Chilean business in the second global economy

Geoffrey Jones and Andrea Lluch

I. A REVERSAL OF FORTUNES

Business in Argentina and Chile has faced sharply contrasting macroeconomic environments during the second global economy, and the response of firms and entrepreneurs has also differed. As earlier chapters have shown, traditionally Argentina was wealthier than Chile. By 1913, the per capita gross domestic product (GDP) of Argentina was 50 percent higher than that of Chile. Argentina's GDP per capita was also 75 percent of that of the United States, and higher than that of Germany or France.

Table 9.1 gives comparative per capita GDP data for benchmark years after 1820.

After the onset of the Great Depression, Argentina never returned to its glory days as one of the world's most vibrant economies, but the economy

Table 9.1 Per capita GDP of Argentina, Chile and select countries 1820–2013[1]

	1820	1870	1913	1950	1970	1980	1992	2000	2013
Argentina	NA	1578	4570	6003	9593	10,089	9167	10,292	18,600
Brazil	NA	NA	235	1059	3466	7573	7025	7921	12,100
Chile	1113	1229	1394	2779	6500	5369	7703	10,475	21,911
Mexico	604	1039	2082	2326	7145	10,402	10,513	12,071	15,600
Great Britain	2588	4808	7415	10,090	17,671	18,482	23,191	29,172	37,300
United States	1914	3654	7892	14,236	24,696	25,506	32,058	39,108	52,800

Note: 1. 1820–2005 in constant 2005 US international dollars. Source: UN, World Development Indicators; Angus Maddison, *Monitoring the World Economy, 1820–1992*, OECD Development Centre, 1995. The 2013 number is current GDP per capita at purchasing power parity.

Source: CIA World Factbook. https://www.cia.gov/library/publications/the-world-factbook/geos/ar.html.

Table 9.2 Annual GDP growth in Argentina and Chile in constant US$ 1961–2013 (percent)

	Argentina	Chile		Argentina	Chile
1961	5	4	1987	3	7
1962	−1	5	1988	−3	7
1963	−5	6	1989	−7	11
1964	10	3	1990	−2	4
1965	11	0	1991	13	8
1966	−1	10	1992	12	12
1967	3	4	1993	6	7
1968	5	4	1994	6	6
1969	10	3	1995	−3	11
1970	3	2	1996	6	7
1971	6	9	1997	8	7
1972	2	−1	1998	4	3
1973	3	−5	1999	−3	−1
1974	6	2	2000	−1	4
1975	−0	−11	2001	−4	3
1976	−2	3	2002	−11	2
1977	7	9	2003	9	4
1978	−5	7	2004	9	6
1979	10	9	2005	9	6
1980	4	8	2006	8	4
1981	−6	5	2007	8	5
1982	−5	−10	2008	3	3
1983	4	−4	2009	0.1	−1
1984	2	8	2010	9	6
1985	−8	7	2011	9	6
1986	8	6	2012	1	5
			2013	3	4

Source: World Data Bank, World Development Indicators.

was not hit as hard as some in the southern hemisphere, especially Chile, and there were still spurts of growth. Even in 1980, Argentina's GDP per capita was second highest in Latin America after Mexico.

However, from 1984 the Chilean economy began to consistently outperform Argentina. Table 9.2 compares GDP growth in the two countries.

In 2000, Chilean GDP per capita passed that of Argentina. By 2013, using a different measure of GDP per capita at purchasing power parity, Chilean per capita had reached US$ 21 000, the highest in Latin America. In contrast Argentina passed through major economic crises during the second global economy. Although the official economic data were no longer considered reliable, one estimate of the country's GDP per capita at purchasing power parity was US$ 18 600 in 2013.

Argentina's economic history over the last century has puzzled Argentinean citizens and economic historians alike. How did such a rich country lose its way? Before 1914, the country was one of the most dynamic nations in the first global economy, attracting a record amount of foreign investment and massive inflows of immigrants. In 1914, half of Buenos Aires's population was foreign-born, and it could be regarded as one of the world's greatest global cities. The country suffered a significant setback during World War I, but later recovered.[1] Unlike Chile, it managed to weather the Great Depression and to avoid severe difficulties during World War II.

In the second half of the century, Argentina's economic performance became weaker, and prone to volatility and inflation. Growth spurts were always interrupted by a crisis, which drove GDP down, followed by slow recovery, only to regain, years later, previous levels. There was economic growth in the 1960s, but starting in 1975, Argentinean growth rates dropped, and other Latin American countries matched or overtook its per capita GDP. The decade of the 1980s was disastrous. It ended in hyperinflation. During the early 1990s, as market oriented reforms were implemented, the economy grew, recording about 4.8 percent per capita growth for the period 1989–94. However, the economy fell into a recession in 1995, with unemployment reaching record levels of close to 20 percent.[2] A longer recession started in 1998, after the Asian financial crisis. In 2001, a severe economic downturn, growing indebtedness, and an unprecedented banking collapse resulted in a government default and economic collapse. By 2002, the country's real GDP was nearly one-fifth smaller than in 1998. The Argentinean economy started to recover in 2003, with GDP growth rates of 8 to 9 percent per year in the period 2003–07.

A noteworthy feature of the country was inflation.[3] Argentina suffered several cycles of hyperinflation, which were followed by attempts at stabilization before a new inflationary cycle took over. Table 9.3 shows the annual inflation rates in Argentina and Chile after 1961.

In 1976, Argentina's annual inflation rate reached 438 percent, and achieved an all-time high in 1989 at 3058 percent (Table 9.3). Inflation had fallen back to only 12 percent in 1992, and price levels stabilized during the second half of the 1990s. By 2002, inflation was back up to 31 percent, before halving by 2007. It is not clear what has happened since. In 2007, the government made changes in the personnel of INDEC, the statistical institute, and in the methods used in gathering and processing statistical data.

Table 9.3 Inflation in Argentina and Chile by GDP deflator, 1961–2013

	Argentina	Chile		Argentina	Chile
1961	20	7	1987	127	26
1962	29	12	1988	388	23
1963	26	44	1989	3058	14
1964	29	46	1990	2077	22
1965	21	41	1991	133	22
1966	26	28	1992	12	13
1967	29	25	1993	−1	12
1968	10	34	1994	3	14
1969	8	40	1995	3	10
1970	6	41	1996	−0	3
1971	31	18	1997	−0	4
1972	64	86	1998	−2	2
1973	66	414	1999	−2	2
1974	31	665	2000	1	10
1975	198	335	2001	−1	4
1976	438	251	2002	31	4
1977	159	106	2003	10	6
1978	161	58	2004	8	7
1979	147	46	2005	11	8
1980	91	29	2006	15	13
1981	106	13	2007	17	5
1982	208	9	2008	21	0.5
1983	382	31	2009	10	4
1984	607	13	2010	17	9
1985	626	31	2011	17	3
1986	74	22	2012	18	1
			2013	18	2

Source: World Data Bank, World Development Indicators. The data for Argentina for 2008 onwards is based on official data which is believed to underestimate inflation.

Official inflation data became so distorted that even estimating it became difficult. In 2013, Argentina became the first country ever to be censured by the International Monetary Fund (IMF) for not supplying accurate economic data. In 2014, *The Economist* believed it may have reached over 50 percent per annum.[4]

Chile's historical experience was different. During most of the twentieth century Chile's overall performance was poor.[5] The country's heavy dependence on exports of natural nitrates became a source of weakness in the 1920s, in part because of the discovery of synthetic nitrates, and this turned into a catastrophe with the onset of the Great Depression.[6] Per capita GDP fell by 47 percent and exports by 79 percent during the Great Depression.[7]Average per capita growth was just 1.4 percent per annum between 1938 and 1973.[8] During 1970–73, the instability associated with the democratic government of President Salvador Allende led to the real GDP contracting by 5.6 percent.

The 1973 coup by General Augusto Pinochet became one of the most notorious events in twentieth century Latin American political history, given both its suppression of opponents and the covert support of the United States. The new regime implemented deep structural reforms in many areas (see Section II), but as a result of domestic policy mistakes and two major world recessions, average growth was modest between 1974 and the mid-1980s, and volatility was high. At the beginning of the 1980s, another profound economic crisis hit the Chilean economy.[9] In 1985, a new plan was launched to promote output and employment recovery. Chilean exports grew at unprecedented rates and the Chilean economy performed better than Argentina. From 1990–98, GDP in Chile grew at an average rate of 7.4 percent. Subsequent performance was less outstanding, with average annual GDP growth averaging only 3.5 percent between 1998 and 2005, but it was back up to 6 percent as the economy recovered from the 2008 global financial crisis.[10]

Chile shared with Argentina periods of high and volatile inflation. After 1930, average annual inflation reached 45 percent.[11] Hyperinflation threatened the economy in the early and mid-1970s (reaching 505 percent in 1974). Although the rate fell, inflation averaged around 20 percent per annum until 1990. Since then, inflation in Chile has declined to less than 10 percent in 1995–98, and less than 4 percent from 1999 to 2007. In marked contrast to Argentina, it was 3 percent in 2013.

If Argentina faced obstacles to economic growth particularly in the most recent decades, then the opposite occurred in Chile. Recent decades have been called the 'golden age of growth', which has been the subject of multiple studies and interpretations. For some scholars, the economic success of this era was a result of successful market-oriented structural reforms,[12] while others believed that Chile was able to experience faster and more sustained growth than other Latin American countries mainly due to its better institutions.[13] As for Argentina's frustrating historical experience, several studies have suggested that institutional instability has been a major determinant.[14]

II. INSTITUTIONAL CONTEXT AND BUSINESS PERFORMANCE

The work of Douglass North identified the role of institutions in providing the incentive structure of economies, and consequently in business performance.[15] Although economists continue to disagree on the nature of this institutional foundation, most studies have characterized many of Latin America's problems as resting on weak institutions.

There are several interpretations of how these weak institutions arose. Engerman and Sokoloff highlighted the impact of European colonization in altering the composition of the populations. In Latin America and the Caribbean, they argued, soils and climates gave them a comparative advantage in growing crops for which they used slaves or natives. The resulting extreme inequality in distribution of wealth, they suggested, gave them institutions which contributed to the persistence of substantial inequality.[16] Acemoglu, Johnson and Robinson, distinguishing between institutions of 'private property' and 'extractive institutions', also pointed to the impact of European colonialism. In prosperous and densely settled areas, like parts of Latin America, Europeans introduced or maintained extractive institutions to force people to work in mines and plantations. In sparsely settled areas, like North America, Europeans settled and created institutions of private property.[17]

A different institutional perspective has come from law and finance literature. These authors have argued that the legal tradition countries inherited or adopted in the distant past has a long-term effect on financial development. Countries that had a common law system inherited from Britain had on average better investor protection that most civil law countries inherited from France or Spain. This literature points to a major effect on financial development, which in turn can be assumed to have impacted the nature and speed of economic development.[18]

It is evident that such broad generalizations from institutional theory are unhelpful in explaining differences between Argentina and Chile, given that both countries were the result of Spanish colonization, and had legal systems rooted in civil law systems. Yet the impact of institutions cannot be entirely ignored because there were long-term differences in institutional arrangements between the two countries even though they shared broad institutional similarities. In particular, a significant institutional difference was that Argentina was a federal system, while Chile was more centralized. Argentina had a presidential form of government with a bicameral legislature and considerable provincial autonomy. Federalism affected policy-making through the role that sub-national authorities (governors) played in the design and implementation of public policies, and through their interaction with national level actors such as the president and legislators. Chile also had a presidential system and bicameral congress, but the president had almost sole control of the issues handled by congress, as he/she could submit and veto bills, virtually deciding on matters dealt with by the legislature.[19]

These institutional differences may help to explain observed differences in policy-making. Contemporary Argentina has been characterized recently as displaying 'volatile and non-cooperative policymaking'.[20] According to one study, the Argentine Congress is a weak policy-making arena that lacks professionalization.[21] Argentine federalism has conferred a high degree of political and institutional power to the provinces, especially as veto players in the national arena.[22] Within this context, attempts at reform need to have the support of the regional structures of power in the periphery.[23] Among other institutional factors, fiscal federalism is a key factor in almost every policy issued, adding rigidities to policy-making.[24] The federal fiscal game, as it has been called, meant that provinces undertake a large fraction of the total spending, yet collect only a small fraction of taxes.

On the contrary, public policy in Chile has shown a remarkable level of stability in recent decades. Chile is a unitary state with no fiscal decentralization. According to some analysts, the main effects of the bicameral system on the workings of the policy-making process are that it reduces the number of relevant actors to few parties organized into two broad-based stable coalitions.[25] As noted by Oscar Muñoz in Chapter 8, Chile's marked political centralism has given way to a culture characterized by highly concentrated government and political party initiatives and decisions. However, this has failed to turn the Chilean Congress into a more instrumental arena for public policy processes.[26] Indeed, Chile's public policies have proven remarkably stable since 1980s.

There have been significant differences as well as major similarities in policy regimes. During the twentieth century, both countries saw major economic and political instability and experienced fluctuating policy regimes. However, the timing and nature of the instability and policy shifts differed. Chile pioneered the import substitution policies that spread in Latin America during the interwar years. Later, in the 1970s, Chile was also the pioneer in abandoning import substitution in favor of free-market policies.

In contrast, after 1945 and under Peronist rule, Argentina fully embraced import substitution strategies, and its subsequent governments continued on that path. In the 1970s, the country switched to free-market policies, but later and less-comprehensively than Chile. These differences and their consequences will be discussed at greater length in the following sections.

III. BUSINESS IN THE SECOND GLOBAL ECONOMY

The institutional environment and macro-economic context had an evident impact on business, but until recently a lack of sources has hindered attempts to explore more precisely this impact. The availability of new primary materials created by the Creating Emerging Markets (CEM) project at the Harvard Business School permits a more nuanced examination of the issues. The following sections draw extensively on interviews with leading business figures in Argentina and Chile undertaken by this project. Parallel interviews with business leaders in Africa, Brazil, Mexico, Peru, South Asia and Turkey enable international comparisons to be made. The interviews and other materials are publically available.[27]

A. Chile

After leading Latin American's turn towards import substitution policies in the 1930s, Chile also spearheaded the region's move towards neo-liberal economic reforms from the 1970s. During the 1970s, the Chilean state increased its involvement in the local economy, with dozens of state-owned companies and firms controlled by CORPO (National Development Corporation). Indeed, Chilean businesses, and especially large business groups, benefited from protectionist policies and relied on state intervention, which made business associations highly influential on policy-making, much more so than in Argentina.[28]

General Pinochet's government brought about a radical change in Chile's economic strategy, as well as in state-business relations, by adopting pro-market policies, including large-scale privatization, financial liberalization, and market deregulation.[29] Privatization was one of the more visible reforms. In 1973, state-owned companies held a 39 percent share of the nation's overall gross output – up from 14 percent in 1965. The state controlled over 500 public companies that accounted for 40 percent of Chile's gross production value. By 1975, as Bucheli notes in Chapter 3, the state had a controlling stake in eight of Chile's ten largest companies. The new government turned to privatization to reduce its deficit and to remedy the legal status of a number of companies that Allende's administration had confiscated.

Between 1974 and 1978, the assets and stock of 197 of those companies were sold, disregarding laws that forbade private citizens or business groups to acquire more than 5 percent of banks' shares. As a result, large business groups emerged, particularly around banks, exploiting their advantages to purchase privatized companies, as Islas discusses in his chapter. By 1979,

Chile's ten largest business groups had taken control of 135 of the nation's leading 250 companies, and nearly 70 percent of corporate stock was listed on Santiago's stock exchange.[30] The two fastest-growing groups from 1973 to 1980 were Vial and Cruzat-Larraín, holding companies that controlled approximately half the equity of all companies listed on Santiago and Valparaíso's stock exchanges.[31]

This initial reform stage also featured trade liberalization measures – particularly, a standard 10 percent tariff that was imposed on nearly all imports.[32] The previous import substitution industrialization (ISI) regime had caused most companies to focus on the domestic market. Now, they were forced to adapt to a more open economy.[33] This shift brought uncertainty to the business community, as many feared companies would be unable to survive foreign competition. Even in the public sector, the steel magnate Roberto de Andraca observed, 'many people simply walked out, because they did not agree with official measures. In their opinion, eliminating advantages and protection was highly irresponsible'.[34] In a similar vein, Eliodoro Matte, a prominent business leader in the pulp and paper industry, described this situation for CMPC, one of the most emblematic and historical Chilean companies: 'CMPC had been a protectionist company, and its old administration posed objections'.[35] To adapt to this new setting, companies needed to radically revise their strategies and managerial systems. Not all Chilean businesses were ready to meet this new challenge, or to overcome it successfully.

Matte described how CMPC was forced to undertake a number of changes, including the development of 'marketing policies . . . productive processes, invested in renovation, updated infrastructure and organization, introduced new technologies – everything you have to do when you have to deal with competition, especially when it comes from all over the world, because here, in Chile, since 1979, the tariff rate stood at a mere 10%'.[36] Chilean companies had to rationalize operations and apply new management techniques to brace themselves to confront Chile's market opening. CMPC had to change its structure, Matte noted, 'from being a hierarchical company to becoming a more open company, able to face both domestic and foreign competition'.[37]

Adding to the shock of market opening and liberalization reforms on Chilean companies, a number of policy mistakes were made. This resulted in two severe international recessions. In 1982, the country experienced the worst economic downturn since the Great Depression, which proved devastating for many businesses. 'With the crisis in the early 1980s', Matte noted, 'both the company's and the country's survival were at stake'.[38] Business conditions had started to deteriorate in the late 1970s, but the difficulties escalated to unprecedented levels in 1981 and 1982. 'The dollar traded at Chilean $39, and imports were flooding into the country', Matte remembered. 'On account of the fixed exchange rate and a highly under-valued local currency, companies competing with imports faced enormous problems'.[39] This globalization shock resulted in widespread bankruptcies.

By 1982, it became clear that companies' indebtedness was stifling Chile's economy. Many companies were forced to sell assets to pay their debts. Heavily indebted companies went bankrupt or were taken over, and the large business groups collapsed.[40] Finally, the state stepped in to save Chile's financial sector, shutting down 14 financial institutions and undoing many of the privatizations carried out a decade earlier. Surviving companies associated their resilience to their ability to adjust to former reforms and, primarily, to their lower debt levels. As the banker Andrónico Luksic noted, 'Our low debt enabled us to navigate and survive the crisis'.[41]

To overcome the crisis, the government launched a new plan to promote production and bolster employment.[42] Export-oriented operations were promoted (highlighting other products in addition to copper), and a currency devaluation helped restore export competitiveness.[43] This measure proved particularly beneficial for business groups that had managed to survive the crisis, mostly because they focused on exports and had low debt levels. The government made further adjustments after 1982, reinstating some tariffs, enforcing stringent regulations on the financial system, implicitly nationalizing private debt, renegotiating Chile's sovereign debt with banks, and providing massive financial support to private firms via subsidies.[44] In 1985, a second privatization wave began.[45] Pinochet's government chose to complete the nation's transition to an open economy, based on private sector development, foreign debt conversion into national assets, and increased contributions to pension funds. Chile's financial system had grown more diversified since the crisis, and the private capital market played a key role in funding Chilean companies.[46]

Chile's second privatization round was not limited to transferring companies seized by Allende's administration; instead, it also encompassed firms formerly belonging to large business groups which had been nationalized during the Pinochet era, and later, utilities – some created after CORPO's inception.[47] Saltpeter and steel production operations were also privatized. The government kept a few significant companies, including CODELCO (copper) and ENAP (oil).[48]

A hallmark privatization involved CAP (Pacific Steel Company). Roberto de Andraca oversaw the privatization. 'The government charged us' he noted, 'with the task of determining how to go about the ownership transfer'.[49] New privatization methodologies were used, including approaches such as 'popular capitalism', 'indirect popular capitalism', and 'workers' capitalism'.[50] 'At the time', De Andraca described, 'since nobody would buy the company, we persuaded workers to take stock options as part of their eventual compensation, so that by the time they retired, they would receive both stock and compensation. We negotiated several agreements in order to ensure that workers would neither lose nor win with this compensation package, but rather assume a reasonable risk. Thus, workers took 40 percent ownership of the company'.[51] These policies were complemented by auctions, debt equity swaps, stock sales, and sales to pension fund management companies (Administradora de Fondos de Pensiones, or AFPs) with the intention of avoiding the concentration of economic power seen when the business groups emerged in the 1970s.[52]

As a result of these reforms, the state's role in Chile's economy was substantially reduced.[53] There were major changes in the corporate sector as well. The second business and bank privatization round triggered the consolidation of some 'old' groups, dating back to the 1960s, and the creation of new ones.[54] The business groups that had survived the crisis benefited from Chile's currency devaluation. In 1982, Luksic observed, 'I set out to detect opportunities in large economic groups that had split up, or had otherwise suffered state liquidation or intervention. . . . As a group, we were able to tap into opportunities arising from this asset reshuffling'.[55]

Both Chilean privatization rounds implied the transfer of a considerable amount of assets and resources from the public to the private sector.[56] While some business groups vanished, others grew stronger, seizing control of re-privatized or bankrupt companies. Sven Von Appen, a leading shipping entrepreneur, noted, 'After the banking crisis, which was the result of widespread, unbacked indebtedness in many Chilean companies, and which forced the government to intervene the banking system and assume its liabilities, we took advantage of opportunities to buy low-priced stock that later recovered'.[57]

By the late 1980s, the Chilean economy was in better shape. As in earlier times in Chile's history, several years of rising copper prices (especially in 1988 and 1989) greatly influenced economic policy. The transition from Pinochet's regime to a democratic government was a remarkable event that had significant repercussions for Chilean companies. While Chile made a political turn, the Coalition government chose to avoid radical economic policy changes, seeking 'change with continuity', which translated into maintaining many of the previous policies,[58] despite the private sector's initial mistrust of the new government.[59]

Indeed, the democratically elected governments that ruled Chile after 1990 stayed on a free-market path, preserving the focus on exports instituted by the military regime, although with greater emphasis on social programs, particularly those geared towards mitigating poverty and social inequity.[60] Another goal was sustained fiscal responsibility, and the design of other measures to reduce inflows of hot money. The 1990s, as noted earlier, was a successful decade for the Chilean economy.

During these years, stock ownership became increasingly concentrated in Chilean companies. Also noteworthy was the dominant role business groups have played in the nation's economy.[61] With regard to business groups' stability and continuity, it has been noted that 11 of Chile's leading 12 groups in 2007 were already in operation in 1988.[62] This does not mean that no new economic firms have emerged, because the number of groups registered with Chile's SVS (Securities and Insurance Commission) has simultaneously boomed. According to this study, in 1998 the SVS reported the existence of 71 groups, and this number had climbed to 137 ten years later. As a result, most Chilean business groups are relatively young, and only three have operated continuously since the 1960s – Matte, Angelini and Luksic. All three have extensive unrelated diversification. These long-lasting Chilean groups have demonstrated a considerable ability to adjust swiftly to macroeconomic changes and international shifts.[63]

Indeed, large, both old and new, conglomerates' globalization reveals a noteworthy feature. Starting in the late 1980s, this process intensified during the 1990s, when large Chilean companies made direct investments abroad, taking advantage of their management progress and the opportunities provided by regional conditions. 'In the first place', Jorge Marín Correa, the president of the electricity and gas utility CGE noted, 'market conditions were favorable. Second, financial resources and mechanisms were available. Third, our people were ready and motivated to face new challenges'.[64]

Sizable investments were made in electricity generation and distribution, but other sectors, like manufacturing and retailing, also rallied interest.[65] Exploring new opportunities abroad was systematically linked with domestic market challenges. 'We are forced to venture abroad, and that again is a significant advantage', Horst Paulmann, president of the retailer Cencosud, noted. 'In the past, we were fortunate enough that foreign players would not come here due to the lack of a market. Today, we are forced to venture abroad'.[66] Therefore, this was a response to both regional economic openings and available funding to cross national boundaries. Chilean business leaders are aware and articulate about their ability to 'appreciate what was happening in Latin America, before Spanish, American and European businessmen in general realized it was coming'.[67]

The existence of business groups, and their globalization processes, should not disguise the fact that foreign business has increased its role in Chile. Foreign investors exploited government incentives in the mid-1980s. Through transnational affiliates or partnerships with local firms, these investors bid for companies. They focused particularly on dynamic sectors for investment like agribusiness, paper, cellulose, and fishing.[68] This phase concluded in the late 1990s. According to Islas, in 2005 foreign investors controlled – either directly or indirectly – over 50 percent of voting shares in 36 of the 100 largest public companies.[69] In 2012, Chile's stock of inward foreign direct investment (FDI) was US$ 206 504 million, or almost twice the level in Argentina. Chile was the third largest host economy in Latin America for multinationals after Brazil and Mexico. It was also the third largest outward investor in Latin America after Brazil and Mexico. The country's stock of outward FDI reached US$ 97 141 in 2012, or three times the level of Argentina. During that year alone, Chilean companies made massive acquisitions, including the US$ 3.4 billion acquisition of the Brazilian airlines TAM by LAN Chile and acquisitions by Cencosud in Colombia and Brazil for more than US$ 3 billion.[70]

Finally, Chilean economic success had a marked impact on the ideology of business leaders themselves. They began to see themselves as innovative, dynamic agents who could perform successfully in any world market and whose leadership shaped their nation's and their companies' future. This was the 'ideological revolution', as described by Cecilia Montero, that reframed Chile's business community.[71] As Muñoz notes in Chapter 8, economic reforms in Chile fueled the development of a new corporate culture that broke away from past notions characterizing former business leaders. A new business mindset, with a competitive and international focus, became widespread, with a new enthusiasm to build professional management capabilities and invest in technological innovation.[72]

B. Argentina

After World War II Argentina adopted an extreme import substitution policy. High tariffs contributed to Argentina's industrial development, but its exports failed to increase substantially.[73] As time went by, this policy brought about economic stagnation, leading eventually to policy reversal, as elsewhere in Latin America. The dynamics of so-called stop-and-go cycles – inherent to the very substitution scheme rationale, revealed that severe problems faced the country. In Chapter 4, López assessed Argentina's performance during the import-substitution phase, characterizing it as rather poor, due to marked institutional volatility, frequent policy changes, strong redistributive pressures, and a closed economy. These factors handicapped Argentina from seizing the benefits of international trade during a time of significant expansion.

Starting in 1969, political instability and violence increased in Argentina. The rules of the game changed often as a result of high political and social unrest, which translated into a quick succession of civilian and military governments. Companies operated in a volatile setting that became increasingly violent over the 1970s. It was a difficult time for business. 'Argentina was almost paralyzed', noted Guillermo Murchinson.[74]

In 1976, a new dictatorship tried to implement a market-oriented program with financial and trade liberalization. The ostensible intention was to reduce the role of the state, and to open the economy to external competition, but its implementation was flawed. In practice, both inflation and the prevalence of fiscal deficits made the exchange rate system unsustainable. From 1979 to 1981, capital flight accounted for 20 percent of the nation's GDP, leaving the government with significant foreign debt (partly belonging to the private sector and absorbed by the state) that jeopardized Argentina's future economic performance.

During the period of chaotic economic policies developed between 1976 and 1983, a group of industrial companies grew stronger, owing to reforms which in practice failed to reduce the power of the state, which, in turn, favored these business formats.[75] Business groups, diversified into several industries, boasted some export capacity, though some depended largely on the profits they drew from their role as state suppliers. As discussed in earlier chapters, policies intended to support domestic companies, launched in 1970 and continued by the Peronist administration in 1973–76, remained in place. Additionally, the departure of foreign companies' affiliates in the 1970s during an international crisis further contributed to the strengthening of some existing business groups and to the creation of new, diversified groups, as Barbero and López explain in their chapters (Chapters 1 and 4). In the early 1980s, company rankings showed the emergence and rise of these groups, while also revealing others' demise or setback. New groups displayed diversified interests, which can be attributed to a risk mitigation strategy when operating in a context of high inflation and instability.[76]

Macroeconomic conditions grew even more unfavorable in the early 1980s. The 1981–82 crisis also affected Argentina, driving the military government to forgo its reform attempts and reinstating exchange and interest rate controls. The democratic government that took over in 1983 inherited a significant external and fiscal imbalance as a result of the military regime's failed economic liberalization reforms and unruly adjustments.[77] The Radical Party administration (1983–89) made several attempts to bring stability to Argentina's macroeconomic setting, but its plans failed due to the country's persistent macroeconomic imbalances, compounded by strong distributive pressures and some policy-making issues.

Indeed, the steps taken in the 1980s may be construed as short-term efforts to manage a volatile, conflict-ridden economy that eventually led to hyperinflation in early 1989.[78] This crisis highlighted companies' shortsighted strategies. 'In the 1970s and 1980s', the banker Manuel Sacerdote commented, 'I positioned the bank so that it could be run like a speedboat – I mean, so that we could turn it around at any moment; so that, if it was going one way, we could head the opposite way the very next day'.[79] Adapting to changing environments seems to have been the key for business survival in Argentina 'My career', Sacerdote added, 'was based on watching reality very closely at all times and adjusting very quickly to each setting, changing radically'.[80] Economic predictions were founded on uncertainty, and business leaders expressed their frustration with high inflation rates: 'There, all of sudden, the annual budget and three-year forecast routines were maintained', Tomas Hudson, who led the Argentinean affiliate of the British chemical company ICI, remarked. 'But the notion of strategy was put away, right? In the most critical times, it was just next month'.[81]

In this unstable setting, long-term planning often seemed futile. Inflation management and short-term policies characterized businessmen's experiences at this time: 'I started working in 1962, and, for 30 years, until 1992, my entire experience revolved around a high-inflation setting', Rodolfo Viegener, president of the plumbing manufacturer Ferrum remembered. 'I focused strictly on the short term, adjusting to short-term conditions. I just thought, "I just have to get through today; tomorrow we'll see"'.[82] 'The local currency had lost considerable value and price fixing was an almost impossible task', Luis Pagani, a food manufacturer, remembered of his experiences during the 1989 hyperinflation. 'Credit was cut off'.[83]

In 1989, Argentina's economy was spiraling out of control with hyperinflation, major recession and high unemployment. The business leaders interviewed for the CEM project remembered their universal conviction that state intervention had to be reduced, and the economy opened.[84] In accordance with these ideas, Carlos Menem's government in the 1990s launched a number of pro-market reforms geared towards stabilizing macroeconomic conditions, deregulating Argentina's financial system, and privatizing state-owned companies.[85] However, at first, the new Peronist government lacked credibility. Menem appointed a Bunge y Born Group representative as Minister of the Economy in his first cabinet. Early stabilization attempts failed, and new bouts of inflation in 1990 led to the resignation of two Economy Ministry heads.

A second phase began in 1991, when the Convertibility Plan was launched, featuring a monetary reform that pegged Argentina's peso to the US dollar on a one-to-one basis. The plan also included measures to liberalize markets and boost privatizations, which unfolded at remarkable speed: 80 percent of privatizations were carried out in 1990–93.[86] This process encompassed most state-owned companies, as well as other public assets that had not been managed like stand-alone enterprises before this time.[87] Companies and assets were transferred to private hands under a number of schemes, including open international auctions; concessions; initial public offerings (IPOs); licenses; leasing, rental, and management contracts, and exploration permits. Parallel with these events the Mercosur customs union was launched in 1991. Argentina, Brazil, Paraguay, Uruguay, and Venezuela were the initial members.

During the 1990s, inward FDI flows reached unprecedented heights.[88] As described by López in Chapter 4, FDI flowed in large amounts changing Argentina's business landscape. While in the early 1990s, nearly all large private domestic companies continued to be family-owned businesses, this investment boom substantially increased multinational companies' operations in Argentina, seizing over 80 percent of top firms' value added and exports by 2000. As a result, state-owned companies nearly disappeared from top business rankings, and some business groups shrank. Among the new trends seen in the 1990s was, as in Chile, the sudden arrival of Spanish-based multinationals, as well as investments by 'multi-Latina' firms based in Brazil and Chile in particular.[89] As in Chile a decade earlier, Argentine privatizations also influenced local firms, as some companies diversified by building alliances with foreign partners.

As a result of these measures, the government withdrew from the production of goods and services, as had happened in Chile during the previous decade. With inflation under control, Argentina enjoyed sudden macroeconomic stability and economic growth between 1991 and 1994, and the opportunities of globalization beckoned. 'I anticipated a changing scenario in Argentina; players had changed', Luis Pagani observed. 'MERCOSUR [in Spanish, Mercado Común del Sur] was a larger market, so to speak, and Brazil offered major opportunities – it still does. We said to ourselves, "this is the new map; we have to adapt ourselves to it". Globalization was a fact'.[90]

Argentina's economic recovery brought increased investment. Companies actively sought new opportunities in the context of price stability and greater availability of supplies and capital goods. The changed environment was also a test of corporate capabilities. 'Companies that were not prepared in terms of logistics IT and management, especially family-owned businesses', Federico Braun of the supermarket chain La Anónima noted 'were forced to sell or failed'.[91] The opening of capital markets and access to foreign loans enabled other Argentine companies to grow in size and to expand internationally, especially into MERCOSUR countries. 'In 1993, 1997 and 1998, many long-standing and traditional local competitors decided to sell out', Pagani noted. 'That was a distinguishing feature of the 1990s. However, we opted to double our bet, both in Argentina and abroad, and to focus on international expansion in Latin America. Between 1993 and 1999, we opened several industrial plants, with considerable investment efforts.'[92]

During the second half of the 1990s, Argentina's economic growth slowed down again.[93] Menem was re-elected president in 1995, after successfully championing constitutional reform, but his government failed to make further progress. There continued to be protectionism in some sectors, and weak governance and regulation in the provinces over some privatized sectors.[94] Starting in 1998, Argentina descended towards an economic and political meltdown.[95] In 2001, Argentina's convertibility experiment reached breaking point as a result of a severe economic, social and political crisis that resulted in further social exclusion and vulnerability.[96]

The business community felt enormous frustration as the country encountered yet another economic crisis.[97] Amalia Fortabat, the president of a large cement manufacturer, remembered feeling the crisis was 'the most difficult one – there seemed to be no future, no way out'.[98] Argentine business leaders constantly stress how their country's instability shaped decision-making, though for some there were lessons to be learned. 'Ours is a very dynamic company', Acevedo noted. 'I am persuaded that its greatest past, current and future strength lies in its ability to adapt to changing scenarios'.[99]

Policy instability provided the context for corporate leaders to concentrate on making incremental adjustments to adapt to environmental changes, or in some cases, on making highly profitable financial investments. 'I think Argentina's business sector has been greatly affected by all these recurring crises we have endured over the past 40 years', Sacerdote noted. 'But, after facing crisis after crisis, after so much government intervention, we ended up having a business sector that tried to adjust more to government policies.'[100] The contrast with Chile was striking. 'Chile is different', Jorge Marín Correa observed. 'Its stability allows you to plan into the future with reasonable certainty.'[101]

The structure of big business in Argentina changed significantly in these decades. In 1990, three-fifths of the 500 largest firms by revenues were locally-owned. Between 1990 and 2004, this share declined to 26 percent as locally-owned firms were bought up by foreign businesses during the 1990s and again after the crisis of 2001. The process of foreign takeovers of the large businesses continued in the phase of post-convertibility. The number of the largest companies by production value with more than 50 percent of foreign capital rose from 161 to 282 between 1993 and 2009.[102]

IV. CONCLUDING REMARKS

The second global economy saw a reversal of fortunes between Argentina and Chile. In Chile, policy continuities and institutional stability encouraged business to invest and grow. In Argentina, fluctuations in policy, macro-economic instability and high inflation had a less productive impact. Argentinean businesses usually followed strategies that attempted to maximize short-term benefits. 'Volatility', Federico Braun concluded, 'is the reason why Argentina lacks a business sector'.[103]

While Chilean business leaders secured legitimacy for their role in Chilean economic success, in Argentina their role remained more contested. The result was a fragmented business community. 'Many problems in Argentina stem from a lack of coherence among Argentine businessmen', Acevedo observed. 'The reason we are like that may be explained in many ways, but our business community is not cohesive or united.'[104]

It is sometimes argued that Argentina's inability to formulate and maintain consistent, stable policies and sound institutions partly derived from the massive economic hurdles the country has had to overcome. This argument ignores the historical fact that both Chile and Argentina experienced throughout the twentieth century severe political and institutional instability, incurring steep social and political costs. The difference between the countries may not be found in the type of economic policies they followed, but, rather in their respective policy-making processes.[105] This chapter suggests that this predicament has also greatly influenced the decision-making processes of business leaders.

Argentina under the presidency of Cristina Fernández entered yet another era of uncertainty. The economy recovered from the world financial crisis and recession of 2008 and 2009, but by 2011 there were already signs of difficulties, even as the government pursued expansionary fiscal and monetary policies which kept inflation in double digits. The government's role in the economy again expanded. In 2012, 51 percent of the oil company, YPF, was expropriated from Spain's Repsol. The government imposed new restrictions on imports. During 2013, Central Bank foreign reserves fell sharply. Inflation reached at least 25 percent according to private estimates, which were needed as the official data was so unreliable. The peso was devalued by 20 percent in 2014 and in July of that year the country technically defaulted on its foreign debt for the second time in 13 years after an unseemly dispute with a group of US-based hedge funds.[106]

Chile continued to receive accolades. The country was named the best country in Latin America to do business by the World Bank in 2013.[107] In the same year Transparency International ranked Chile as number 22 in its Corruption Perceptions Index. This was the second highest ranking in

Latin America, just behind Uruguay. The United States itself was ranked number 19. The same index ranked Argentina as number 106, one of the world's most corrupt countries, ranking even lower by this measure than such notorious cases as India and Thailand.[108]

Yet Chile, too, had emergent problems. There was growing public uproar about the social inequality which had accompanied economic success. In 2014, four-fifths of Chilean workers earned less than US$ 12000 a year. Schools, universities, healthcare and pensions had to be largely paid for privately, and the quality was not good.[109] During the second presidency of Michelle Bachelet, which began in March 2014, taxes were sharply raised and laws passed to remove market incentives from schools and other public institutions.[110] Over the last decade much of Chile's economic growth was driven by Chinese demand for copper. In 2015, Chile and the still state-owned Codelco produced one-tenth of the world's copper. As Chinese economic growth slowed, Chile caught a cold.[111] In the second global economy, economies were interlinked by trade and investment flows. This offered new potential for economic growth, but it also meant that small, peripheral economies were vulnerable to shocks and economic shifts far from their borders and out of their control.

NOTES

1. Maddison (2006); della Paolera and Taylor (2003); Cortés Conde (2008); Gerchunoff and Llach (1998).
2. Hofman (2000): 139.
3. Fanelli and Frenkel (1990).
4. *The Economist* (2014a). In February 2014, the government introduced a new consumer price index (IPCNU) which was developed with the assistance of the IMF. This recorded inflation at 23.9 percent for 2014, a figure which was below most non-official estimates, which were as high as 40 percent. See *Buenos Aires Herald* (2015).
5. Lüders (1998).
6. Schmidt-Hebbel (2006); Monteón (1998).
7. Lüders (1998).
8. Schmidt-Hebbel (2006): 3.
9. Hofman (2000): 31.
10. Schmidt-Hebbel (2006).
11. Morandé and Vergara (1997).
12. See, for example, Gallego and Loayza (2002).
13. Corbo, Hernández and Parro (2005); Wiesner Durán (2008).
14. Prados de la Escosura and Sanz-Villarroya (2004).
15. North (1990) and (2005).
16. Engerman and Sokoloff (2012).
17. Acemoglu, Johnson and Robinson (2002).
18. La Porta, Lopez-de-Silanes, Shleifer and Vishny (1998).
19. Scartascini (2007): 58.
20. Spiller and Tommasi (2007a): 70.
21. For an in-depth analysis on these topics, see Spiller and Tommasi (2007b).

22. Acuña, Galiani and Tommasi (2006).
23. Acuña, Galiani and Tommasi (2007).
24. Jones, Sanguinetti and Tommas (2000).
25. Aninat, Londregan, Navia and Vial (2008): 176.
26. Tommasi (2008): 24.
27. The interviews of business practitioners in Argentina and Chile were conducted by Andrea Lluch. The transcripts can either be downloaded from the CEM website or requested electronically. See http://www.hbs.edu/businesshistory/emerging-markets/Pages/default.aspx.
28. Schneider (2004).
29. Wisecarver (1992).
30. Maloney (1994).
31. See Chapter 2 in this volume.
32. Ffrench-Davis (2002).
33. Meller (1996): 182.
34. Roberto de Andraca, interview by Andrea Lluch, CEM, May 27 2008, http://www.hbs.edu/businesshistory/emerging-markets.
35. Interview with Eliodoro Matte, interview by Andrea Lluch, CEM, May 28 2008, http://www.hbs.edu/businesshistory/emerging-markets.
36. Ibid.
37. Ibid.
38. Ibid.
39. Ibid.
40. Ricardo Claro, interview by Andrea Lluch, CEM, May 28 2008, http://www.hbs.edu/businesshistory/emerging-markets.
41. Andrónico Luksic Craig, interview by Andrea Lluch, CEM, September 3 2008, http://www.hbs.edu/businesshistory/emerging-markets.
42. Arellano and Marfán (1987); Arellano (1988).
43. Meller (1996): 275.
44. Ffrench-Davis (2002): 13.
45. Hachette and Lüders (1994).
46. Schmidt-Hebbel (2000).
47. Ffrench-Davis (2002): 32.
48. Critics point to a lack of transparency in several such deals. See Meller (1996): 270.
49. Roberto de Andraca, interview by Andrea Lluch, CEM, May 27 2008, http://www.hbs.edu/businesshistory/emerging-markets.
50. Maloney (1994).
51. Interview with Roberto de Andraca, 27 May 2008, Santiago, Chile, CEM.
52. See Chapter 2 in this volume.
53. Larroulet (1994).
54. Abarca, Arturo Fuentes, Majluf and Rodríguez (1998); Lefort and Walker (2000).
55. Andrónico Luksic Craig, interview by Andrea Lluch, CEM, September 3 2008, http://www.hbs.edu/businesshistory/emerging-markets.
56. Lefort (2005).
57. Sven Von Appen, interview by Andrea Lluch, CEM, May 28 2008, http://www.hbs.edu/businesshistory/emerging-markets.
58. Muñoź (2007).
59. Silva (1995).
60. Corbo and Fischer (1994).
61. Lefort (2010).
62. Lefort and Urzúa (2008).
63. Lefort and Walker (2000).
64. Jorge Correa, interview by Andrea Lluch, CEM, January 16 2008, http://www.hbs.edu/businesshistory/emerging-markets.
65. Calderón Hoffmann and Griffith-Jones (1995).

66. Horst Paulmann, interview by Andrea Lluch, May 29 2008, http://www.hbs.edu/businesshistory/emerging-markets.
67. Statement by Eliodoro Matte, quoted in Fazio (2000).
68. Moguillansky (1999): 183.
69. See Chapter 2 in this volume.
70. United Nations (2013).
71. Montero (1990) and (1997).
72. Muñoz (1995); Silva (1995).
73. Kosacoff, Lucángeli and Sourrouille (1985); Katz and Kosacoff (1989).
74. Guillermo Murchinson, interview by Andrea Lluch, CEM, February 29 2008, http://www.hbs.edu/businesshistory/emerging-markets.
75. Schvarzer (1983).
76. See Chapter 1 in this volume.
77. Damill and Frenkel (1996).
78. Heymann and Kosacoff (2000).
79. Manuel Sacerdote, interview by Andrea Lluch, CEM, December 21 2008, http://www.hbs.edu/businesshistory/emerging-markets.
80. Ibid.
81. Tomas Hudson, interview by Andrea Lluch, CEM, December 17 2008, http://www.hbs.edu/businesshistory/emerging-markets.
82. Rodolfo Viegener, interview with Andrea Lluch, CEM, May 23 2008, , http://www.hbs.edu/businesshistory/emerging-markets.
83. Luis Pagani, interview by Andrea Lluch, CEM, November 18 2008, http://www.hbs.edu/businesshistory/emerging-markets.
84. See, for example, the interviews with Manuel Sacerdote, Guillermo Murchison and Rodolfo Viegener, CEM. http://www.hbs.edu/businesshistory/emerging-markets.
85. Galiani, Heymann and Tomassi (2002); Bambaci, Saront and Tommasi (2002).
86. Azpiazu and Schorr (2002).
87. Galiani and Petrecolla (2000).
88. Chudnovsky and López (2008).
89. Bianco, Moldovan and Porta (2008).
90. Luis Pagani, interview with Andrea Lluch, CEM, November 18 2008, http://www.hbs.edu/businesshistory/emerging-markets.
91. Federico Braun, interview by Andrea Lluch, CEM February 6 2008, http://www.hbs.edu/businesshistory/emerging-markets.
92. Luis Pagani, interview by Andrea Lluch, CEM November 18 2008, http://www.hbs.edu/businesshistory/emerging-markets.
93. Heymann and Kosacoff (2000).
94. Acuña, Galiani and Tommasi (2006).
95. Durán (2008): 96; Galiani, Heymann and Tomassi (2002).
96. Acuña, Galiani and Tommasi (2006).
97. Heymann (2007).
98. Amalia Fortabat, interview by Andrea Lluch, CEM, May 12 2008, Roberto de Andraca, interview by Andrea Lluch, CEM, May 27 2008, http://www.hbs.edu/businesshistory/emerging-markets.
99. Arturo Acevedo, interview by Andrea Lluch, CEM, August 29 2008, http://www.hbs.edu/businesshistory/emerging-markets.
100. Manuel Sacerdote, interview by Andrea Lluch, CEM, December 21 2008, http://www.hbs.edu/businesshistory/emerging-markets.
101. Jorge Marín Correa, interview by Andrea Lluch, January 16 2008, http://www.hbs.edu/businesshistory/emerging-markets.
102. Encuesta Nacional a Grandes Empresas (ENGE), Instituto Nacional de Estadística y Censos (INDEC), Buenos Aires, Argentina. Years 1993–2009 available at http://www.indec.mecon.ar/nivel4_default.asp?id_tema_1=3&id_tema_2=4&id_tema_3=50, accessed 21 April 2015. See also Santarcángelo (2012).

103. Federico Braun, interview by Andrea Lluch, CEM, February 6 2008, http://www.hbs.edu/businesshistory/emerging-markets.
104. Arturo Acevedo, interview with Andrea Lluch, August 29 2008, http://www.hbs.edu/businesshistory/emerging-markets.
105. Stein and Tommasi (2007).
106. Mander (2015).
107. Accessed 8 November 2014 at http://data.worldbank.org/indicator/IC.BUS.EASE.XQ.
108. Accessed 10 November 2014 at http://www.transparency.org/cpi2013/results.
109. *The Economist* (2014b).
110. Rathbone (2014).
111. Mander and Rathbone (2014).

REFERENCES

Abarca, Nureya, Luis Arturo Fuentes, Nicolás Majluf and Darío Rodríguez (1998), 'Governance and ownership in Chilean economic groups', *ABANTE*, **1**, 111–39.

Acemoglu, Daron, Simon Johnson and James A. Robinson (2002), 'Reversal of fortune: Geography and institutions in the making of the modern world income distribution', *The Quarterly Journal of Economics* **117** (4), 1231–94.

Acuña, Carlos, Sebastián Galiani and Mariano Tommasi (2006), 'Understanding the political economy of structural reform: The case of Argentina' (co-authored by Sebastián Galiani and Mariano Tommasi), Working Paper 91, Economics and Liberal Arts Departments, Universidad de San Andrés.

Acuña, Carlos, Sebastián Galiani and Mariano Tommasi (2007), 'Understanding the political economy of structural reform: The case of Argentina', in José M. Fanelli and Gary McMahon (comps), *Understanding Reform in Latin America,* Palgrave: McMillan, 31–72.

Aninat, Cristóbal, John Londregan, Patricio Navia and Joaquín Vial (2008), 'Political institutions, policymaking processes, and policy outcomes', in Ernesto Stein, Mariano Tommasi, Carlos G. Scartascini, Pablo T. Spiller, Inter-American Development Bank, *Policymaking in Latin America: How Politics Shapes Policies*, Cambridge: David Rockefeller Center for Latin American Studies, Harvard University.

Arellano, José Pablo (1988), *Políticas Sociales y Desarrollo: Chile 1924–1984*, Santiago de Chile: CIEPLAN.

Arellano, José Pablo and Manuel Marfán (1987), '25 años de Política Fiscal en Chile', *Colección de Estudios CIEPLAN*, **21**, 129–62.

Azpiazu, Daniel and Martín Schorr (2002), *Privatizaciones, rentas de privilegio, subordinación estatal y acumulación del capital en la Argentina contemporánea*, Buenos Aires: Facultad Latinoamericana de Ciencias Sociales (FLACSO).

Bambaci, Juliana, Tamara Saront and Mariano Tommasi (2002), 'The political economy of economic reforms in Argentina', *Journal of Policy Reform*, **5** (2), 75–88.

Bianco, Carlos, Pablo Moldovan and Fernando Porta (2008), 'La internacionalización de las empresas brasileñas en Argentina', *Documento de Proyecto*, Santiago de Chile: CEPAL.

Buenos Aires Herald (2015), 'INDEC: 23.9 percent inflation in 2014', 17 January.

Calderón Hoffmann, Álvaro and Stefany Griffith-Jones (1995), 'Los flujos de capital extranjero en la economía chilena. Acceso renovado y nuevos usos', *CEPAL, Serie Desarrollo Productivo*, **24**.

Chudnovsky, Daniel and Andrés López (2008), 'Foreign investment and sustainable development in Argentina', Working Group Discussion Paper DP12, April 2008, Working Group on Development and Environment in the Americas.

Corbo, Vittorio and Stanley Fischer (1994), 'Lessons from the Chilean stabilization and recovery', in Barry Bosworth, Rudiger Dornbusch and Raúl Laban (eds), *The Chilean Economy: Policy Lessons and Challenges*, Washington DC: The Brookings Institution.

Corbo, Vittorio, Leandro Hernández and Fernando Parro (2005), 'Institutions, economic policies and growth: Lessons from the Chilean experience', Working Paper No. 317, Banco Central de Chile.

Cortés Conde, Roberto (2008), *The Political Economy of Argentina in the Twentieth Century*, Cambridge: Cambridge University Press.

Damill, Mario and Roberto Frenkel (1996), 'Democratic restoration and economic policy: Argentina 1984–91', in Juan Antonio Morales and Gary McMahon (eds), *Economic Policy and the Transition to Democracy: the Latin American Experience*, New York: IDRC-MacMillan Press, 49–111.

della Paolera, Gerado and Alan Taylor (eds) (2003), *A New Economic History of Argentina*, Cambridge: Cambridge University Press.

Díaz, José B., Rolf Lüders, and Gert Wagner (2007), 'Economía Chilena 1810–2000. Producto Total y Sectorial. Una Nueva Mirada', Working Paper No. 315, Pontificia Universidad Católica de Chile.

Engerman, Stanley L. and Kenneth L. Sokoloff (2012), *Economic Development in the Americas since 1500*, New York: Cambridge University Press.

Fanelli, José María and Roberto Frenkel (1990), 'Desequilibrios, políticas de estabilización e hiperinflación en la Argentina', in José María Fanelli and Roberto Frenkel, *Políticas de estabilización e hiperinflación en la Argentina*, Buenos Aires: Tesis.

Ffrench-Davis, Ricardo (2002), *Economic Reforms in Chile: From Dictatorship to Democracy*, Ann Arbor: University of Michigan Press.

Galiani, Sebastián, Daniel Heymann and Mariano Tomassi (2002), *Missed Expectations: The Argentine Convertibility*, Ann Arbor: Davidson Institute.

Galiani, Sebastián and Diego Petrecolla (2000), 'An ex post view of the privatization process in Argentina', *The Quarterly Journal of Economics and Finance*, **36** (2), 131–52.

Gallego, Francisco and Norman Loayza (2002), 'La época dorada del crecimiento en Chile: explicaciones y proyecciones', *Economía Chilena*, **5** (1), 37–67.

Gerchunoff, Pablo and Lucas Llach (1998), *El ciclo de la ilusión y el desencanto. Un siglo de políticas económicas argentinas*, Buenos Aires: Ariel.

Hachette, Dominique and Rolf Lüders (1994), *La privatización en Chile*, Santiago de Chile: CINDE.

Heymann, Daniel (2007), 'Macroeconomics of broken promises', Project documents LC/W.105, Buenos Aires: CEPAL.

Heymann, Daniel and Bernardo Kosacoff (eds) (2000), *La Argentina de los noventa: Desempeño económico en un contexto de reformas*, Buenos Aires: CEPAL-Eudeba.

Hofman, André (2000), *The Economic Development of Latin America in the Twentieth Century*, Cheltenham, UK: Edward Elgar.

Jones, Mark, Pablo Sanguinetti and Mariano Tommas (2000), 'Politics, institutions, and fiscal performance in a federal system: An analysis of the Argentine provinces', *Journal of Development Economics*, **61**, 305–33.
Katz, Jorge and Bernardo Kosacoff (1989), *El proceso de industrialización en la Argentina: evolución, retroceso y prospectiva*, Buenos Aires: CEPAL-CEA.
Kosacoff, Bernardo, Jorge Lucángeli and Juan V. Sourrouille (1985), *Transnacionalización y política económica en la Argentina*, Buenos Aires: CEAL.
La Porta, Rafael, Florencio Lopez-de-Silanes, Andrei Shleifer and Robert W. Vishny (1998), 'Law and finance', *Journal of Political Economy*, **106** (6), 1113–55.
Larroulet, Cristián (1994), 'Efectos de un programa de privatizaciones: El caso de Chile (1985–1989)', *Estudios Públicos*, **54**, 175–222.
Lefort, Fernado (2005), 'Ownership structure and corporate governance in Latin America', *ABANTE*, **8** (1), 55–84.
Lefort, Fernando (2010), 'Business groups in Chile', in Asli M. Colpan, Takashi Hikino, and James R. Lincoln (eds), *The Oxford Handbook of Business Groups*, Oxford: Oxford University Press.
Lefort, Fernando and Francisco Urzúa (2008), 'Board independence, firm performance and ownership concentration: evidence from Chile', *Journal of Business Research*, **61**, 615–22.
Lefort, Fernando and Eduardo Walker (2000), 'Ownership and capital structure of Chilean conglomerates: Facts and hypotheses of governance', *ABANTE*, **3** (1), 3–27.
Lüders, Rolf (1998), 'The comparative economic performance of Chile: 1810–1995', *Estudios de Economía*, **25** (2), 217–49.
Maddison, Angus (2006), *The World Economy: Volume 1: A Millennial Perspective and Volume 2: Historical Statistics*, Development Centre Studies, Paris: OECD Publishing.
Maloney, William (1994), 'Privatization with share diffusion: Popular capitalism in Chile, 1985–1988', in Werner Baer and Melissa Birch (eds), *Privatization in Latin America: New Roles for the Public and the Private Sectors*, London: Praeger, 136.
Mander, Benedict (2015), 'Argentina shortages underline default woes', *Financial Times*, 20 January.
Mander, Benedict and John Paul Rathbone (2014), 'Limits to growth', *Financial Times*, 2 July.
Matte, Eliodoro (2000), Statement by Eliodoro Matte, quoted in Hugo Fazio, *Transnacionalización de la economía chilena. Mapa actual de la extrema riqueza al año 2000*, Santiago de Chile: LOM-ARCIS.
Meller, Patricio (1996), *Un siglo de economía política chilena (1890–1990)*, Santiago de Chile: Andrés Bello.
Moguillansky, Graciela (1999), *La inversión en Chile: ¿El fin de un ciclo en expansión?*, Santiago de Chile: CEPAL/Fondo de Cultura Económica.
Monteón, Michael (1998), *Chile and the Great Depression: The Politics of Underdevelopment, 1927–1948*, Tempe: Center for Latin American Studies Press, Arizona State University.
Montero, Cecilia (1990), 'La evolución del empresariado chileno: ¿Surge un nuevo actor?', *Colección Estudios CIEPLAN*, **30**, 91–120.
Montero, Cecilia (1997), *La revolución empresarial chilena*, Santiago de Chile: Dolmen.
Morandé, Felipe and Rodrigo Vergara (eds) (1997), *Análisis empírico del crecimiento*

en Chile, Santiago de Chile: Centro de Estudios Públicos-ILA-DES/Georgetown University.

Muñoz, Oscar (1995), *Los inesperados caminos de la modernización económica*. Santiago de Chile: Universidad de Santiago, Instituto de Estudios Avanzados.

Muñoz, Oscar (2007), *El modelo económico de la Concertación. ¿Reformas o cambio?*, Santiago de Chile: Catalonia/FLACSO.

North, Douglass (1990), *Institutions, Institutional Change, and Economic Performance*, Cambridge: Cambridge University Press.

North, Douglass (2005), *Understanding the Process of Economic Change*, Princeton: Princeton University Press.

Prados de la Escosura, Leandro and Isabel Sanz-Villarroya (2004), 'Institutional instability and growth in Argentina: a long-run view', Working Paper 04–67, Economic History and Institutions Department, Universidad Carlos III de Madrid.

Rathbone, John Paul (2014), 'Chile rethinks its free market experiment', *Financial Times*, 7 December.

Santarcángelo, Juan Eduardo (2012), 'Concentración, rentabilidad y extranjerización en Argentina. Una mirada desde la cúpula empresaria', *Ensayos de Economía*, **40**, 39–59.

Scartascini, Carlos (2007), 'Determinantes institucionales de transacciones políticas', RES Working Paper 4484, Inter-American Development Bank, Research Department.

Schmidt-Hebbel, Klaus (2000), 'La contribución de la Reforma de Pensiones al Desarrollo Económico', in *Conferencia Internacional AFP 18 años: Logros y Desafíos*, AFP Chile, Logros y Desafios: CIEDESS.

Schmidt-Hebbel, Klaus (2006), 'El crecimiento económico de Chile', Working Paper No. 365, Banco Central de Chile.

Schneider, Ben Ross (2004), *Business Politics and the State in 20th Century Latin America*, New York: Cambridge University Press.

Schvarzer, Jorge (1983), 'Cambios en el liderazgo industrial argentino en el período de Martinez de Hoz', *Desarrollo Económico*, **23** (91), 395–422.

Silva, Patricio (1995), 'Empresarios, neoliberalismo y transición democrática en Chile', *Revista Mexicana de Sociología*, **57** (4), 3–25.

Spiller, Pablo and Mariano Tommasi (2007a), 'Political institutions, policymaking processes and policy outcomes in Argentina', in Ernesto Stein and Mariano Tommasi (eds), *Policymaking in Latin America: How Politics Shapes Policies*, Washington: Inter-American Development Bank/David Rockefeller Center for Latin American Studies, Harvard University.

Spiller, Pablo and Mariano Tommasi (2007b), *The Institutional Foundations of Public Policy in Argentina*, Cambridge: Cambridge University Press.

Stein, Ernesto and Mariano Tommasi (eds) (2007), 'Policymaking in Latin America: How politics shapes policies', Washington, DC: Inter-American Development Bank/David Rockefeller Center for Latin American Studies, Harvard University.

The Economist (2014a), 'Inflation in Argentina. New data, old qualms', 14 February, accessed 8 December 2014 at http://www.economist.com/blogs/americasview/2014/02/inflation-argentina.

The Economist (2014b), 'The moderates fight back', 19 July.

Tommasi, Mariano (2008), *Un país sin rumbo. Política, políticas públicas y desarrollo en la Argentina,* unpublished manuscript, Universidad de San Andrés.

United Nations (2013), *World Investment Report 2013: Global Value Chains: Investment and Trade for Development*, United Nations Conference on Trade and Development, Geneva: United Nations.

Wiesner Durán, Eduardo (2008), *The Political Economy of Macroeconomic Policy Reform in Latin America: The Distributive and Institutional Context*, Cheltenham, UK: Edward Elgar.

Wisecarver, Daniel (1992), *El modelo económico chileno*, Santiago de Chile: CINDE, Economics Institute, Pontificia Universidad Católica de Chile.

Select bibliography

This select bibliography lists major works on the business and economic history of Argentina, Chile and Latin American more generally. Individual chapters of this book contain a large number of references on specific topics.

Barbero, María Inés and Carlos Dávila (2009), 'Introduction: A view from Latin America', *Entreprises et Histoire*, **54**, 6–15.

Barbero, María Inés (2008), 'Business history in Latin America: A historiographical perspective', *Business History Review,* **82,** 555–75.

Barbero, María Inés and Raul Jacob (eds.) (2008), *La nueva historia de empresas en América Latina y España,* Buenos Aires: Editorial Temas.

Bertola, Luis and José Antonio Ocampo (2012), *The Economic Development of Latin America since Independence*, New York: Oxford University Press.

Bulmer Thomas, Victor, John Coatsworth, and Roberto Cortés Conde (eds.) (2006), *The Cambridge Economic History of Latin America*, Cambridge: Cambridge University Press.

Cerutti, Mario (ed.) (2006), *Empresas y grupos empresariales en América Latina, España y Portugal*, Monterrey, Mexico: Universidad Autónoma de Nuevo León.

Coatsworth, John and William Summerhill (2012), 'The new economic history of Latin America: Evolution and recent contributions', in José Moya (ed.) *The Oxford Handbook of Latin American History*, Oxford University Press: New York, pp. 407–23.

Dávila, Carlos and Rory Miller (eds.) (1999), *Business History in Latin America: The Experience of Seven Countries*, Liverpool: Liverpool University Press.

Davila, Carlos (2013), 'The current state of business history in Latin America', *Australian Economic History Review*, **53**, 109–20.

Della Paolera, Gerardo and Alan Taylor (eds.) (2003), *A New Economic History of Argentina*, Cambridge: Cambridge University Press.

Fernández Pérez, Paloma and Andrea Lluch (eds.) (2015), *Familias empresarias y grandes empresas familiares en América Latina y España. Una visión de largo plazo*, Bilbao: Fundación BVVA.

Ffrench-Davis, Ricardo (2002), *Economic Reforms in Chile: From Dictatorship to Democracy*, Ann Arbor, MI: University of Michigan Press.

Fracchia Eduardo, Luiz Mesquita and Juan Quiroga (2010), 'Business groups in Argentina', in Asli M. Colpan, Takashi Hikino, and James R. Lincoln (eds.), *The Oxford Handbook of Business Groups,* Oxford: Oxford University Press, pp. 325–52.

Hachette, Dominique and Rolf Luders (1992), *La privatización en Chile,* Santiago: Centro Internacional para el Desarrollo Económico.

Harvard Business School (2008–2015), *Creating Emerging Markets*, http://www.hbs.edu/businesshistory/emerging-markets/Pages/default.aspx

Heymann, Daniel and Bernardo Kosacoff (eds.) (2000), *La Argentina de los noventa: Desempeño económico en un contexto de reformas*, Buenos Aires: CEPAL-Eudeba.

Hofman, André (2000), *The Economic Development of Latin America in the Twentieth Century*, Northampton, MA, USA and Cheltenham, UK: Edward Elgar.

Kosacoff, Bernardo (ed.) (2007), *Crisis, recuperación y nuevos dilemas: la economía argentina 2002-2007*, Buenos Aires: CEPAL. Lefort, Fernando (2010), 'Business groups in Chile', in Asli M. Colpan, Takashi Hikino, and James R. Lincoln (eds), *The Oxford Handbook of Business Groups,* Oxford: Oxford University Press, pp. 387–423.

López, Andrés (2006)*, Empresarios, instituciones y desarrollo económico: el caso argentino*, Buenos Aires: CEPAL.

Meller, Patricio (1996), *Un siglo de economía política chilena (1890-1990)*, Santiago de Chile: Andrés Bello.

Miller, Rory (2010), 'Foreign firms and business history in Latin America', *Cátedra Corona*, no. 18, Universidad de los Andes, Colombia.

Montero, Cecilia (1997), *La revolución empresarial chilena*, Santiago de Chile: Dolmen.

Muñoz, Oscar (2007), *El modelo económico de la Concertación. ¿Reformas o cambio?*, Santiago de Chile: Catalonia/FLACSO.

Ocampo, José Antonio and Jaime Ros (2011), *The Oxford Handbook of Latin American Economics*, New York: Oxford University Press.

Schneider, Ben Ross (2004), *Business Politics and the State in Twentieth-century Latin America*, Cambridge: Cambridge University Press.

Silva, Eduardo (1996), *The State and Capital in Chile: Business Elites, Technocrats, and Market Economics*, Boulder, CO: Westview Press.

Williamson, Jeffrey G. (2010), 'Five centuries of Latin American income inequality'*, Revista de Historia Económica / Journal of Iberian and Latin American Economic History* (second series), **28** (02), 227–52.

Index